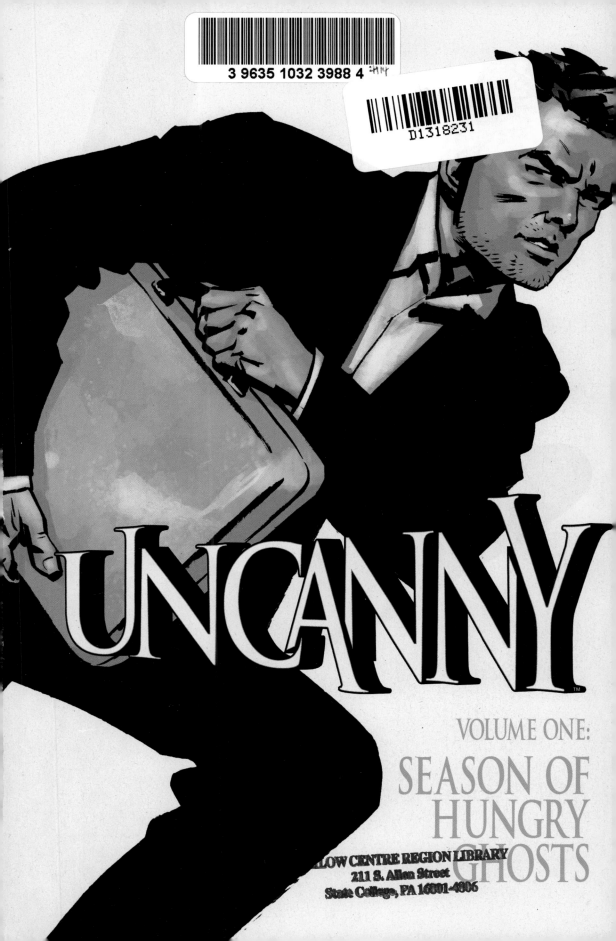

UNCANNY

VOLUME ONE:

SEASON OF HUNGRY GHOSTS

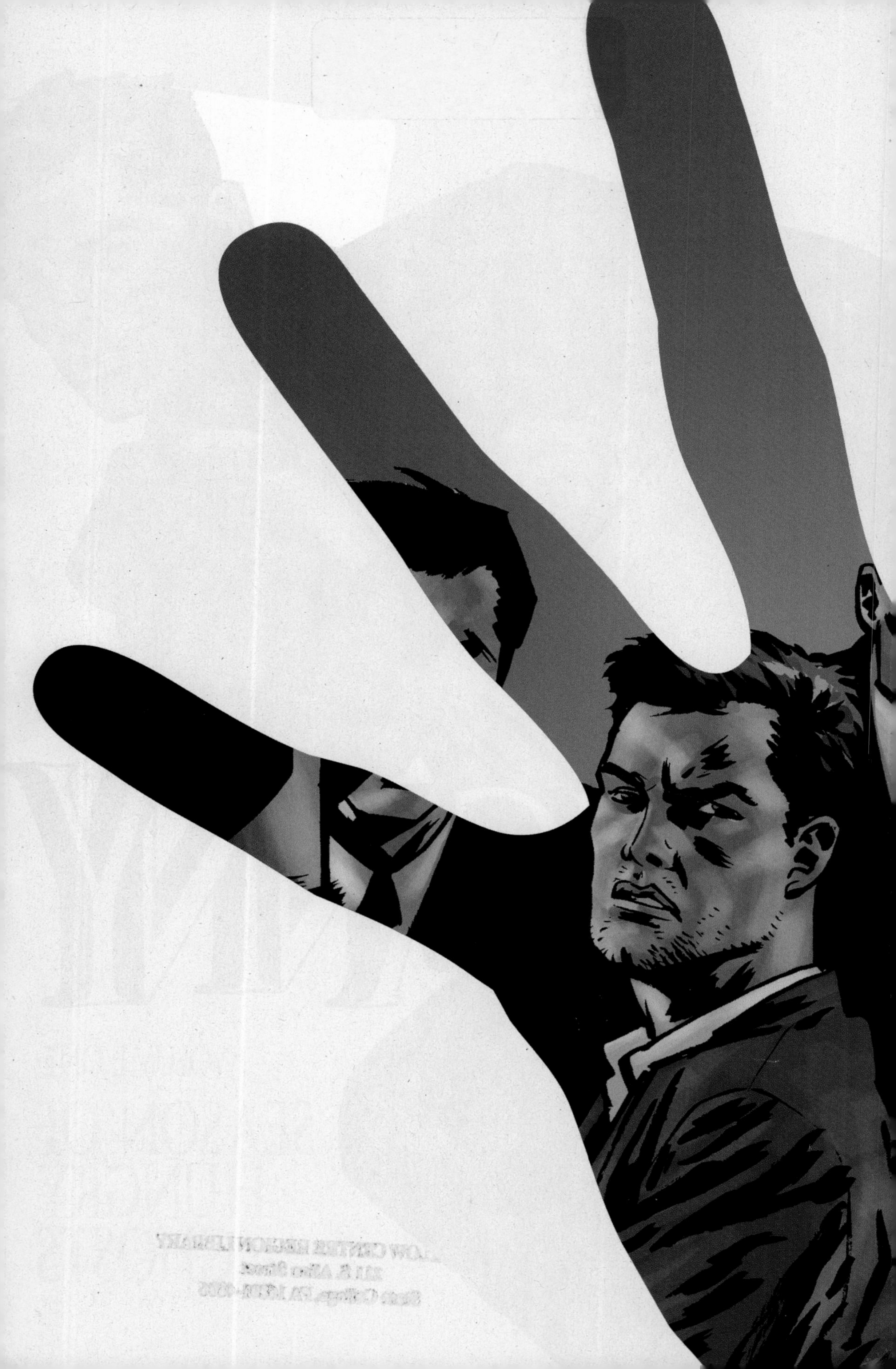

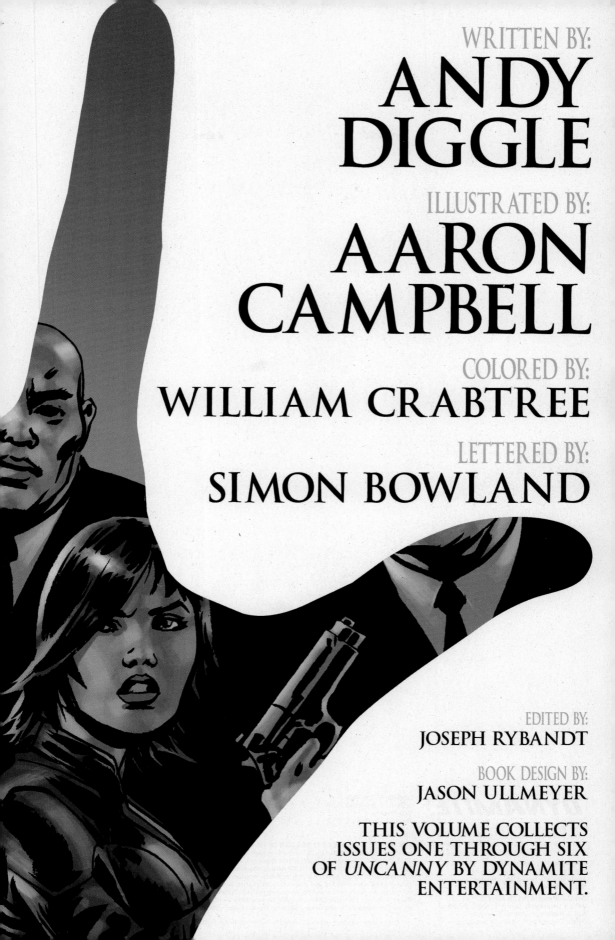

WRITTEN BY:

ANDY DIGGLE

ILLUSTRATED BY:

AARON CAMPBELL

COLORED BY:

WILLIAM CRABTREE

LETTERED BY:

SIMON BOWLAND

EDITED BY:
JOSEPH RYBANDT

BOOK DESIGN BY:
JASON ULLMEYER

THIS VOLUME COLLECTS
ISSUES ONE THROUGH SIX
OF *UNCANNY* BY DYNAMITE
ENTERTAINMENT.

Nick Barrucci, CEO / Publisher
Juan Collado, President / COO
Rich Young, Director Business Development
Keith Davidsen, Marketing Manager

Joe Rybandt, Senior Editor
Hannah Gorfinkel, Associate Editor
Josh Green, Traffic Coordinator
Molly Mahan, Assistant Editor

Josh Johnson, Art Director
Jason Ullmeyer, Senior Graphic Designer
Katie Hidalgo, Graphic Designer
Chris Caniano, Production Assistant

ISBN-10: 1-60690-462-0
ISBN-13: 978-1-60690-462-6
First Printing
10 9 8 7 6 5 4 3 2 1

Visit us online at **www.DYNAMITE.com**
Follow us on Twitter **@dynamitecomics**
Like us on Facebook **/Dynamitecomics**
Watch us on YouTube **/Dynamitecomics**

ISSUE ONE

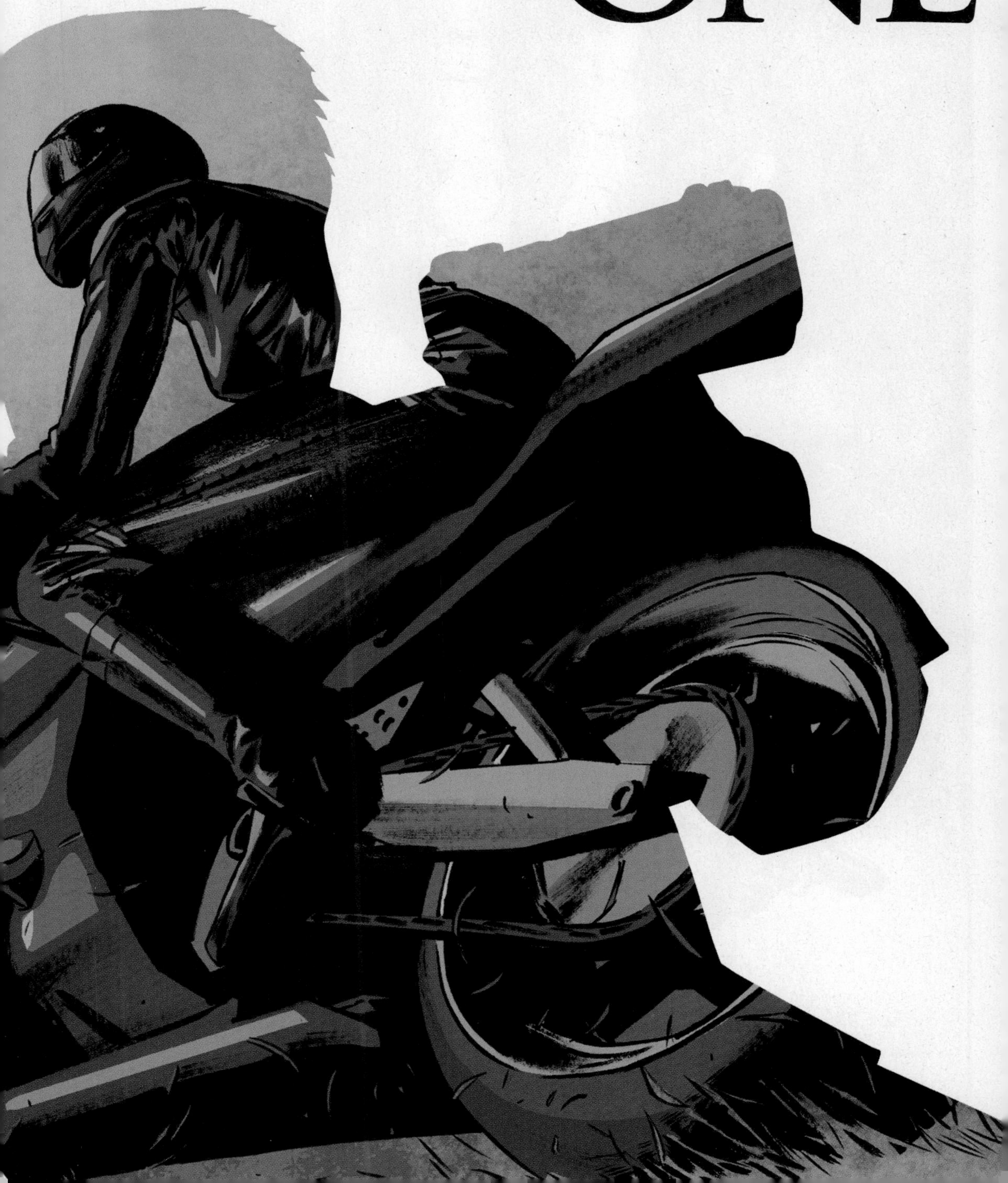

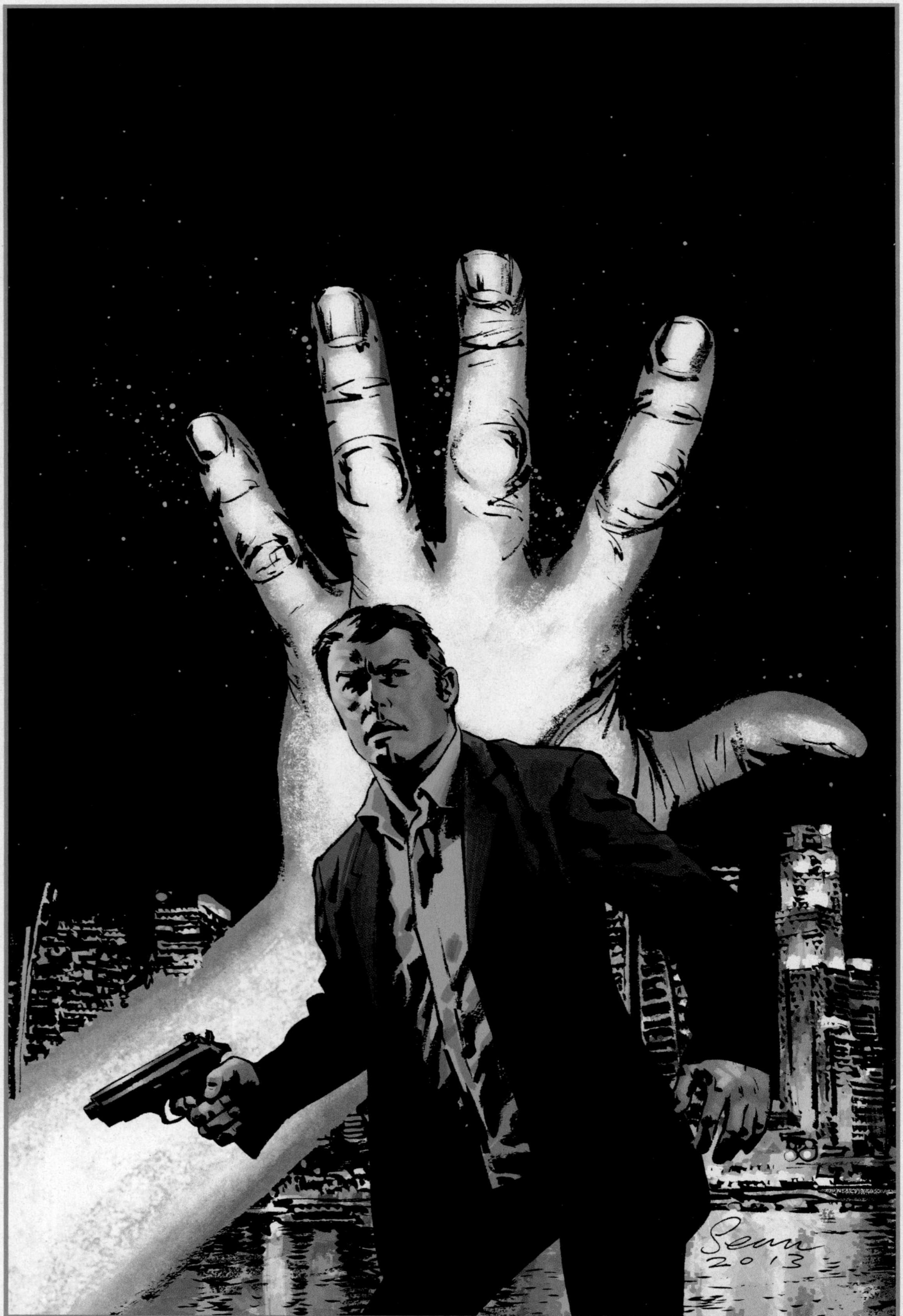
Sean
2013
ISSUE ONE COVER BY SEAN PHILLIPS

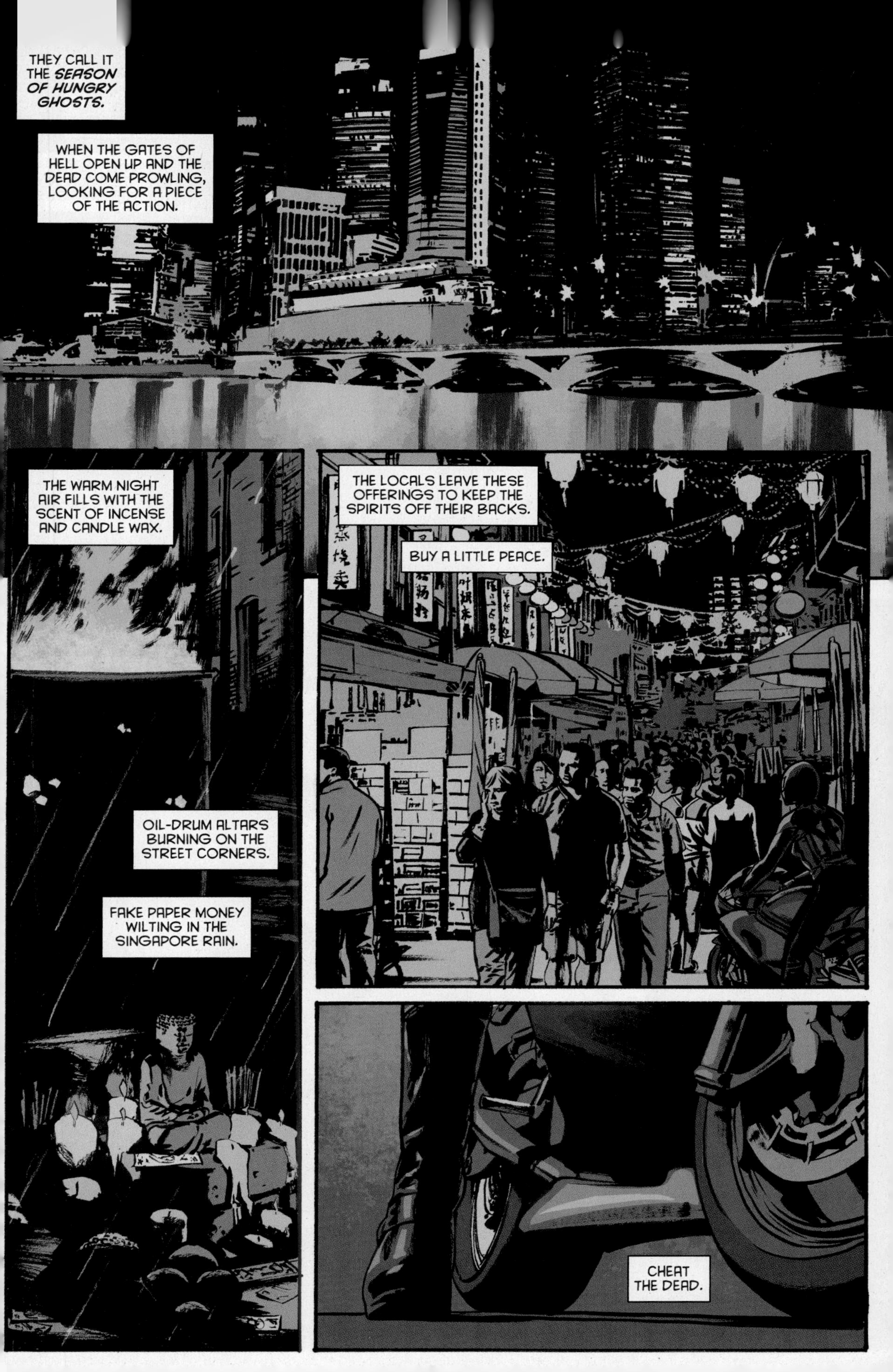
THEY CALL IT THE SEASON OF HUNGRY GHOSTS.
WHEN THE GATES OF HELL OPEN UP AND THE DEAD COME PROWLING, LOOKING FOR A PIECE OF THE ACTION.
THE WARM NIGHT AIR FILLS WITH THE SCENT OF INCENSE AND CANDLE WAX.
OIL-DRUM ALTARS BURNING ON THE STREET CORNERS.
FAKE PAPER MONEY WILTING IN THE SINGAPORE RAIN.
THE LOCALS LEAVE THESE OFFERINGS TO KEEP THE SPIRITS OFF THEIR BACKS.
BUY A LITTLE PEACE.
CHEAT THE DEAD.

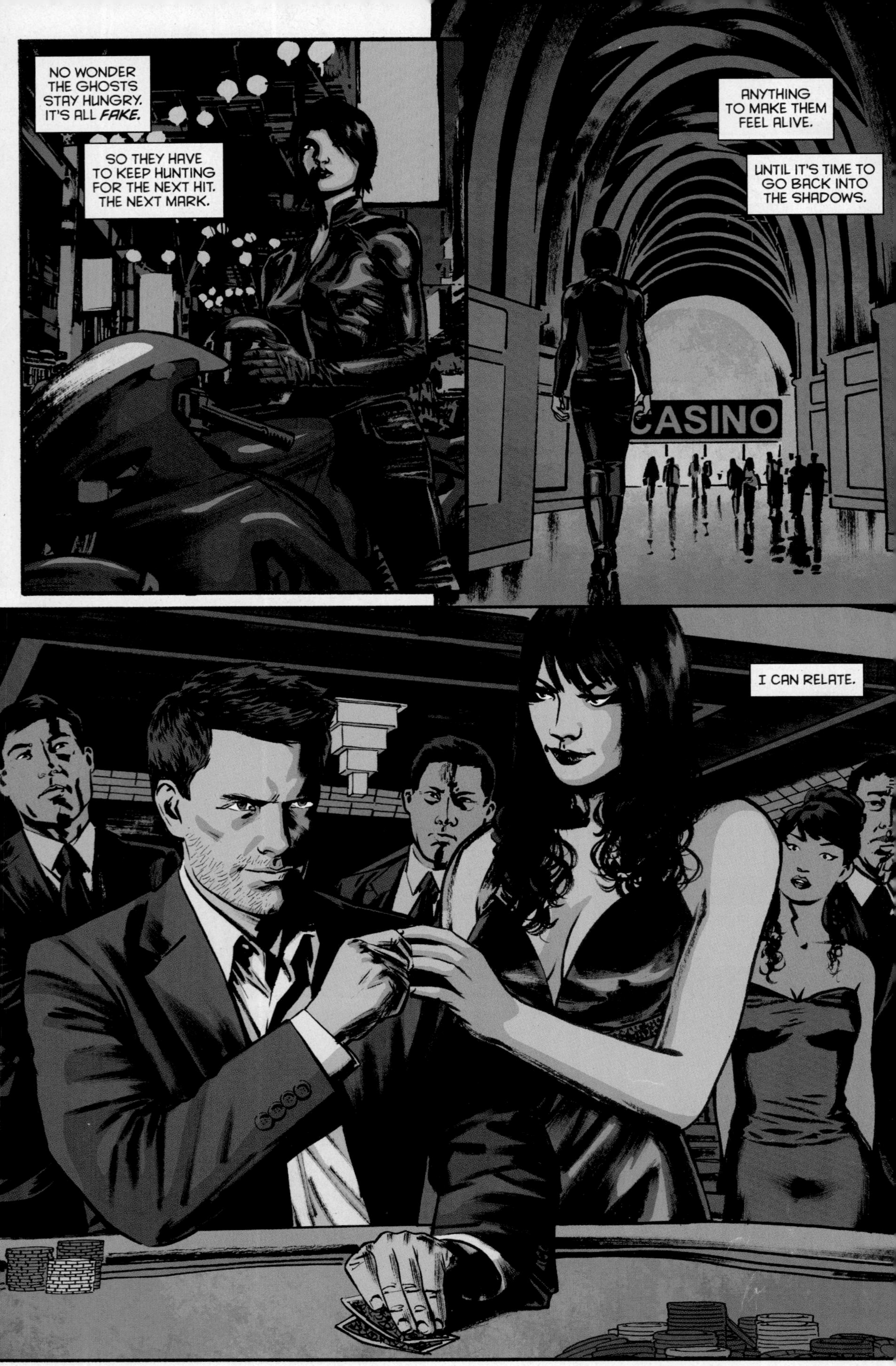
NO WONDER THE GHOSTS STAY HUNGRY. IT'S ALL *FAKE.*
SO THEY HAVE TO KEEP HUNTING FOR THE NEXT HIT. THE NEXT MARK.
ANYTHING TO MAKE THEM FEEL ALIVE.
UNTIL IT'S TIME TO GO BACK INTO THE SHADOWS.
CASINO
I CAN RELATE.

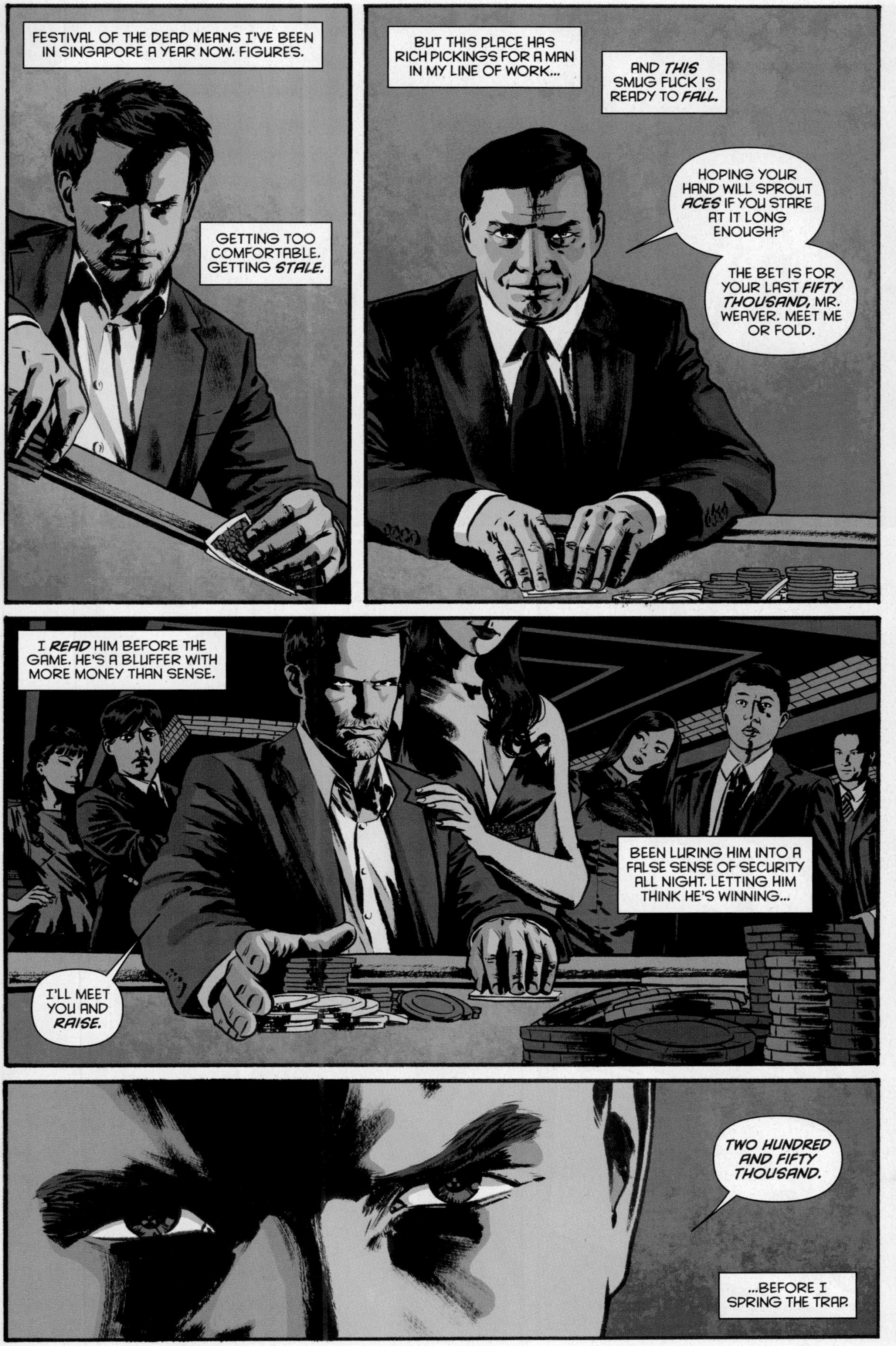
FESTIVAL OF THE DEAD MEANS I'VE BEEN IN SINGAPORE A YEAR NOW. FIGURES.
GETTING TOO COMFORTABLE. GETTING *STALE.*
BUT THIS PLACE HAS RICH PICKINGS FOR A MAN IN MY LINE OF WORK...
AND *THIS* SMUG FUCK IS READY TO *FALL.*
HOPING YOUR HAND WILL SPROUT *ACES* IF YOU STARE AT IT LONG ENOUGH?
THE BET IS FOR YOUR LAST *FIFTY THOUSAND,* MR. WEAVER. MEET ME OR FOLD.
I *READ* HIM BEFORE THE GAME. HE'S A BLUFFER WITH MORE MONEY THAN SENSE.
BEEN LURING HIM INTO A FALSE SENSE OF SECURITY ALL NIGHT. LETTING HIM THINK HE'S WINNING...
I'LL MEET YOU AND *RAISE.*
TWO HUNDRED AND FIFTY THOUSAND.
...BEFORE I SPRING THE TRAP.

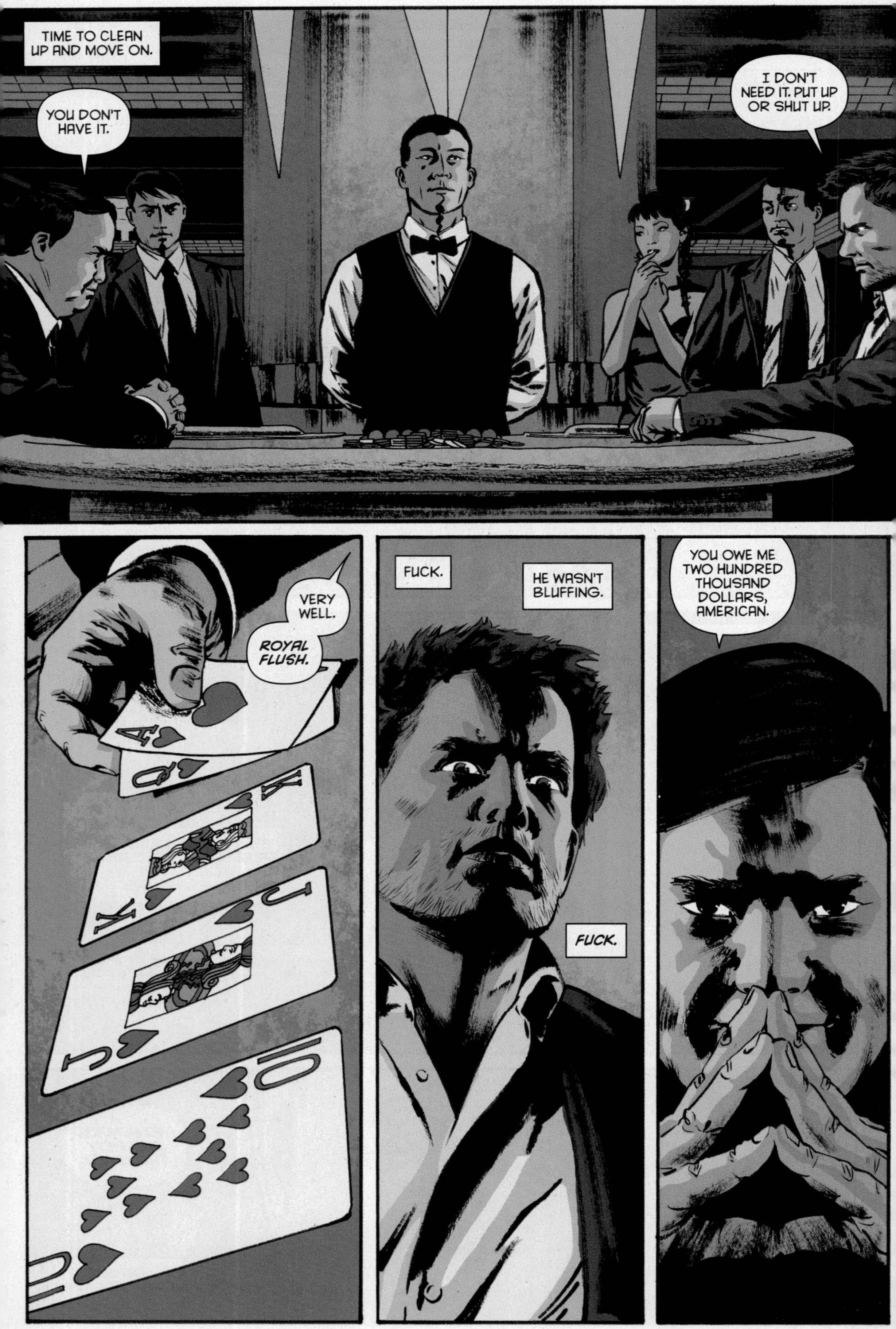

TIME TO CLEAN UP AND MOVE ON.
YOU DON'T HAVE IT.
I DON'T NEED IT. PUT UP OR SHUT UP.
VERY WELL.
ROYAL FLUSH.
FUCK.
HE WASN'T BLUFFING.
FUCK.
YOU OWE ME TWO HUNDRED THOUSAND DOLLARS, AMERICAN.

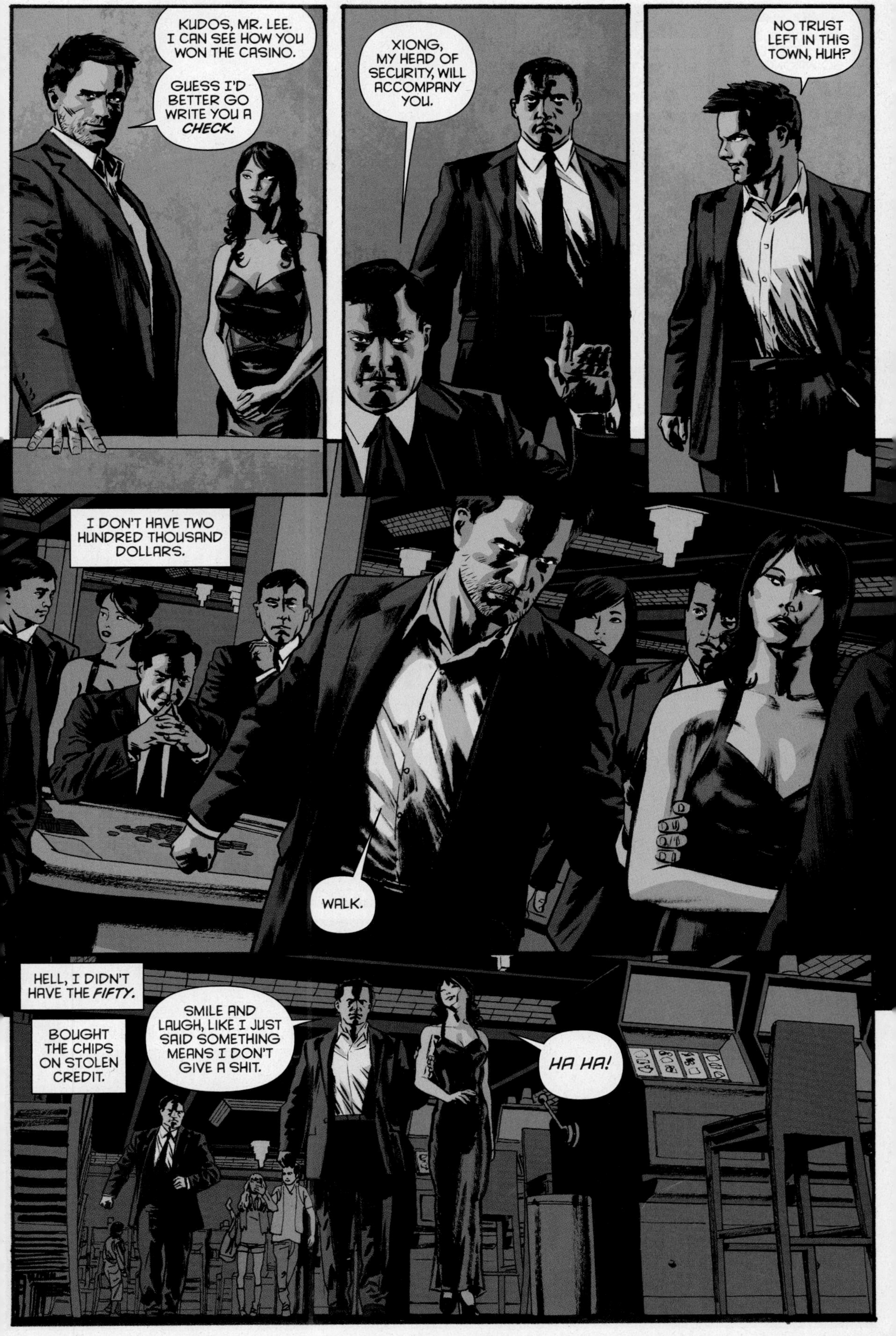
KUDOS, MR. LEE. I CAN SEE HOW YOU WON THE CASINO.
GUESS I'D BETTER GO WRITE YOU A *CHECK.*
XIONG, MY HEAD OF SECURITY, WILL ACCOMPANY YOU.
NO TRUST LEFT IN THIS TOWN, HUH?
I DON'T HAVE TWO HUNDRED THOUSAND DOLLARS.
WALK.
HELL, I DIDN'T HAVE THE *FIFTY.*
BOUGHT THE CHIPS ON STOLEN CREDIT.
SMILE AND LAUGH, LIKE I JUST SAID SOMETHING MEANS I DON'T GIVE A SHIT.
HA HA!

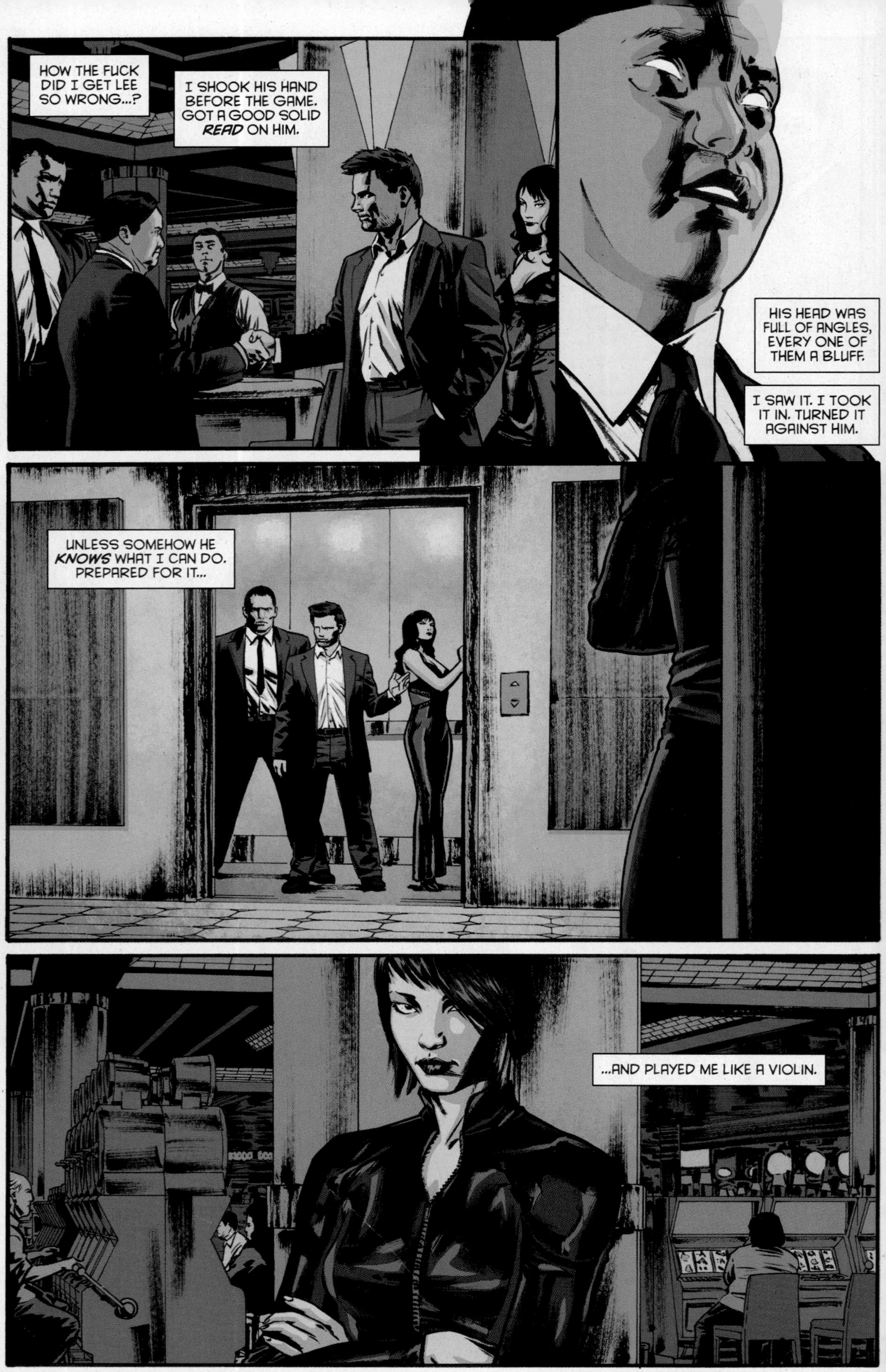
HOW THE FUCK DID I GET LEE SO WRONG...?
I SHOOK HIS HAND BEFORE THE GAME. GOT A GOOD SOLID *READ* ON HIM.
HIS HEAD WAS FULL OF ANGLES, EVERY ONE OF THEM A BLUFF.
I SAW IT. I TOOK IT IN. TURNED IT AGAINST HIM.
UNLESS SOMEHOW HE *KNOWS* WHAT I CAN DO. PREPARED FOR IT...
...AND PLAYED ME LIKE A VIOLIN.

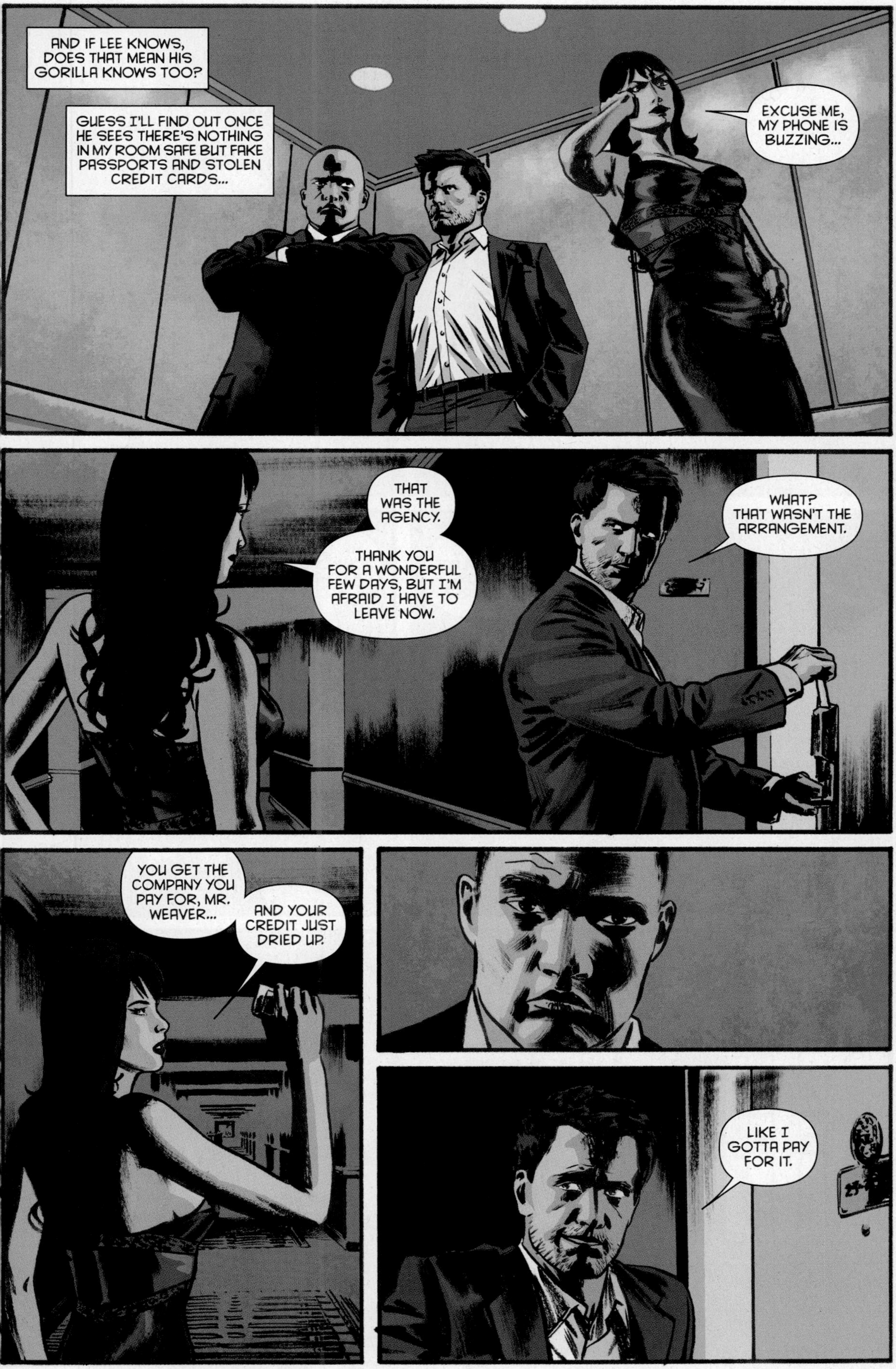
AND IF LEE KNOWS, DOES THAT MEAN HIS GORILLA KNOWS TOO?
GUESS I'LL FIND OUT ONCE HE SEES THERE'S NOTHING IN MY ROOM SAFE BUT FAKE PASSPORTS AND STOLEN CREDIT CARDS...
EXCUSE ME, MY PHONE IS BUZZING...
THAT WAS THE AGENCY.
THANK YOU FOR A WONDERFUL FEW DAYS, BUT I'M AFRAID I HAVE TO LEAVE NOW.
WHAT? THAT WASN'T THE ARRANGEMENT.
YOU GET THE COMPANY YOU PAY FOR, MR. WEAVER...
AND YOUR CREDIT JUST DRIED UP.
LIKE I GOTTA PAY FOR IT.

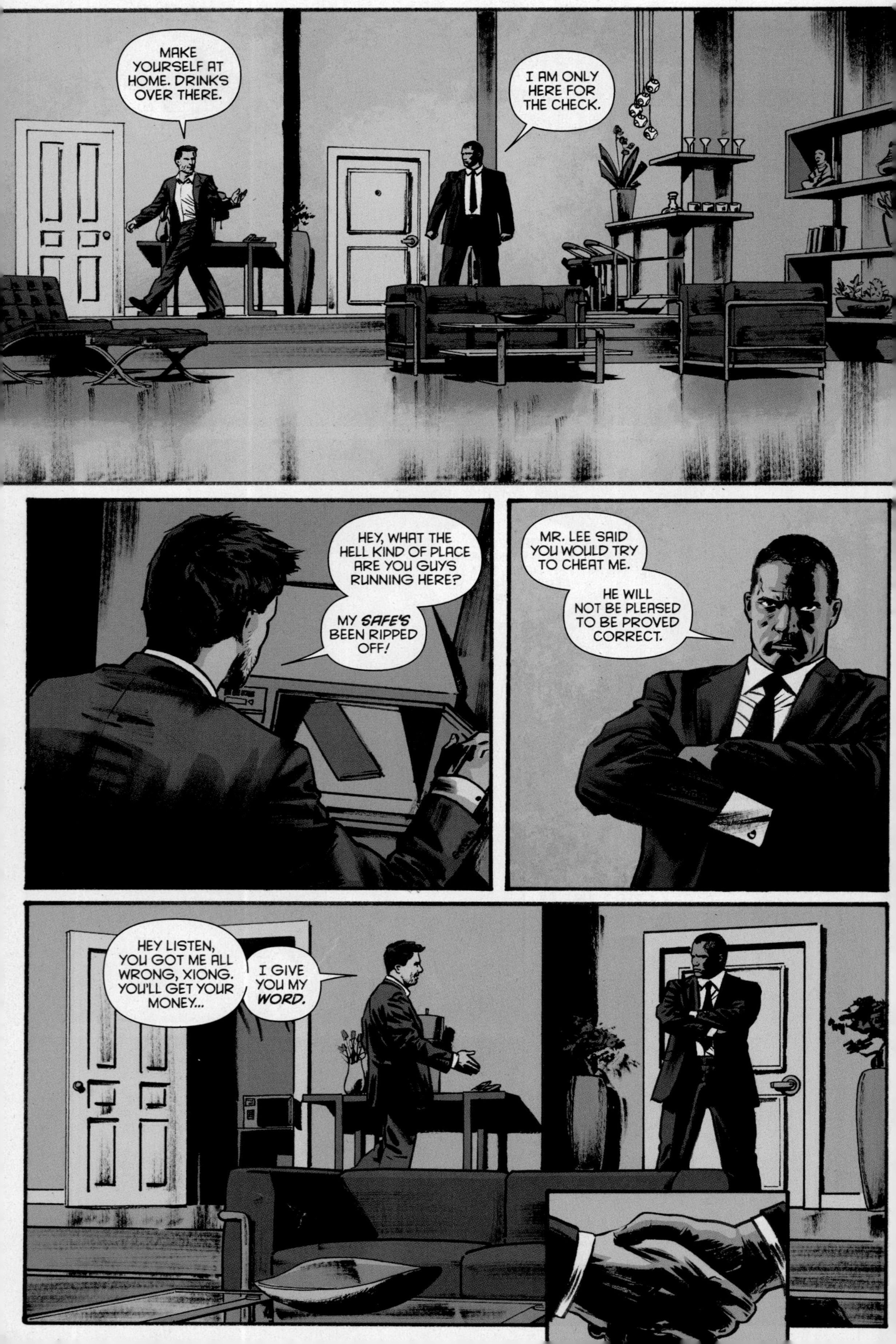
MAKE YOURSELF AT HOME. DRINKS OVER THERE.
I AM ONLY HERE FOR THE CHECK.
HEY, WHAT THE HELL KIND OF PLACE ARE YOU GUYS RUNNING HERE?
MY *SAFE'S* BEEN RIPPED OFF!
MR. LEE SAID YOU WOULD TRY TO CHEAT ME.
HE WILL NOT BE PLEASED TO BE PROVED CORRECT.
HEY LISTEN, YOU GOT ME ALL WRONG, XIONG. YOU'LL GET YOUR MONEY...
I GIVE YOU MY ***WORD.***

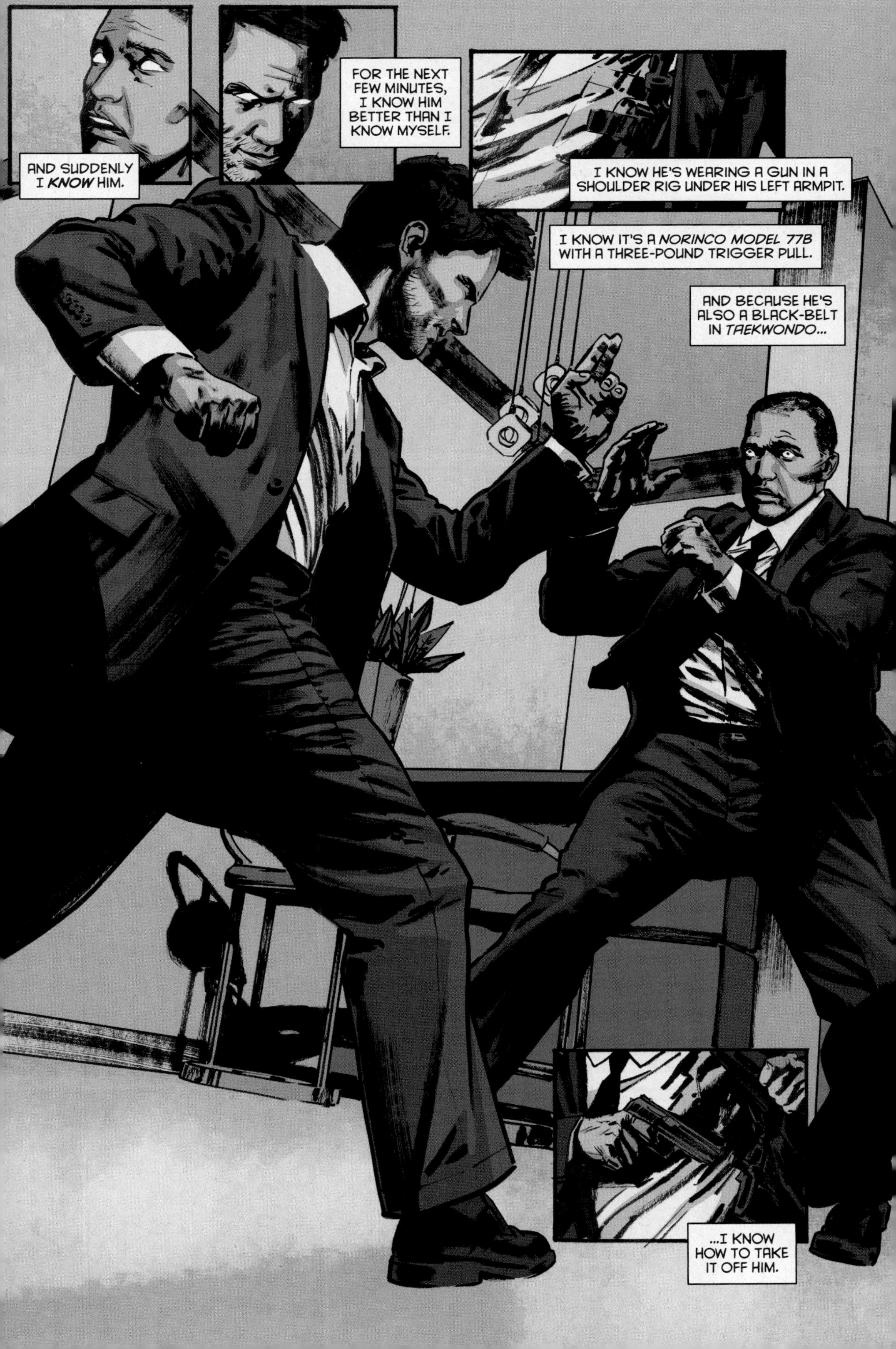
AND SUDDENLY I *KNOW* HIM.
FOR THE NEXT FEW MINUTES, I KNOW HIM BETTER THAN I KNOW MYSELF.
I KNOW HE'S WEARING A GUN IN A SHOULDER RIG UNDER HIS LEFT ARMPIT.
I KNOW IT'S A *NORINCO MODEL 77B* WITH A THREE-POUND TRIGGER PULL.
AND BECAUSE HE'S ALSO A BLACK-BELT IN *TAEKWONDO*...
...I KNOW HOW TO TAKE IT OFF HIM.

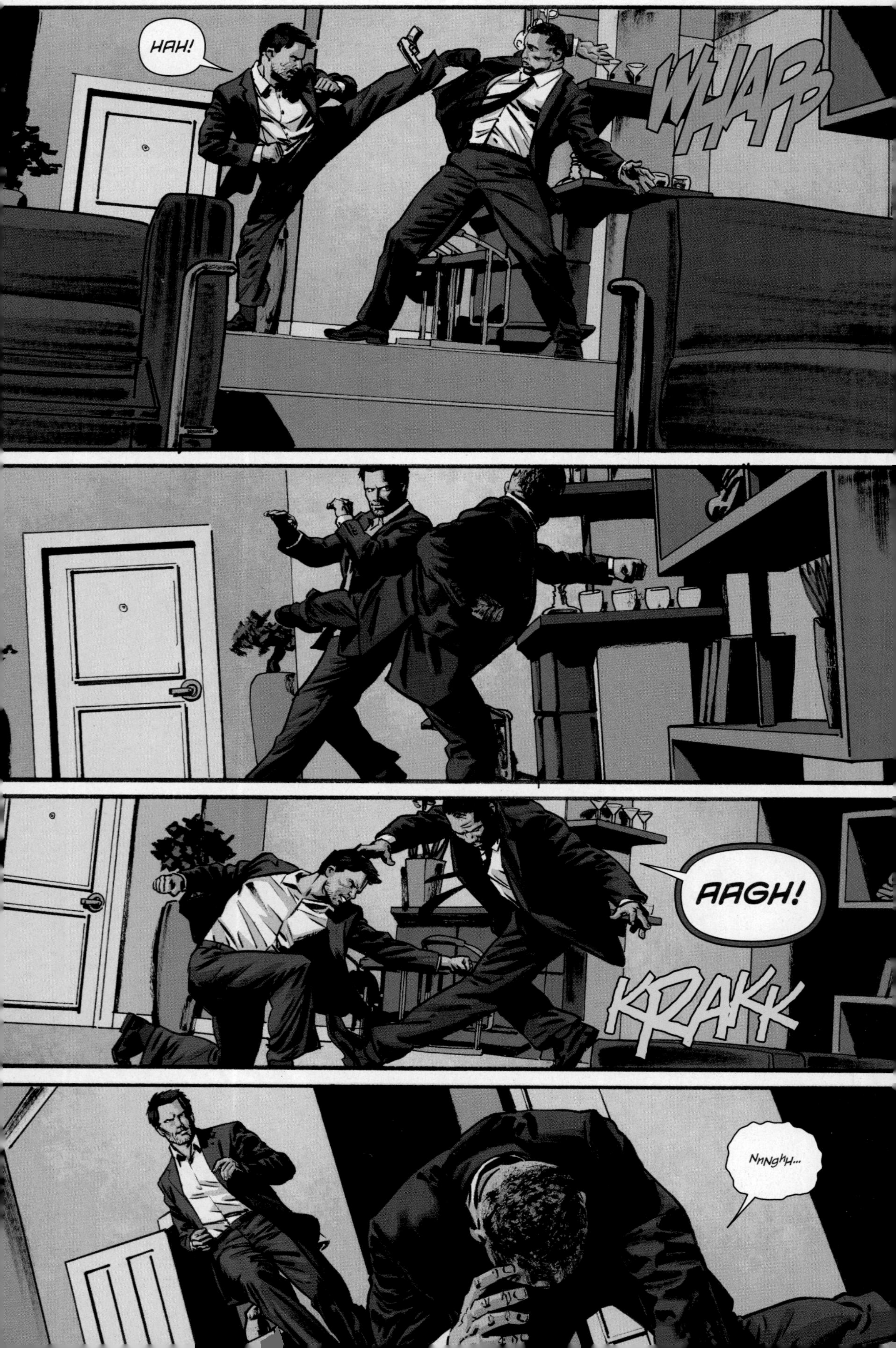

HAH!
WHAP
AAGH!
KRAKK
Nnngh...

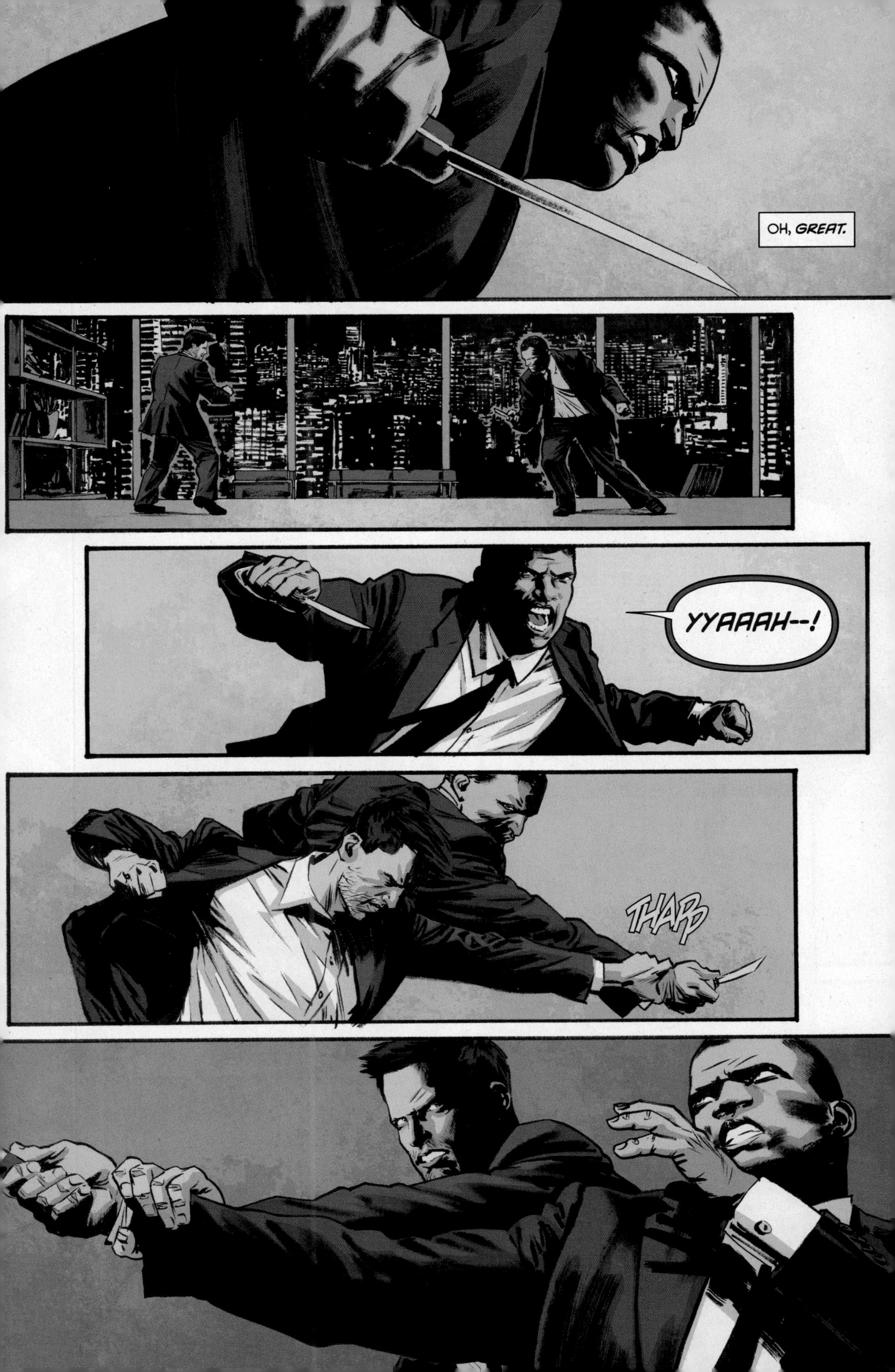
OH, GREAT.
YYAAAH--!
THAP

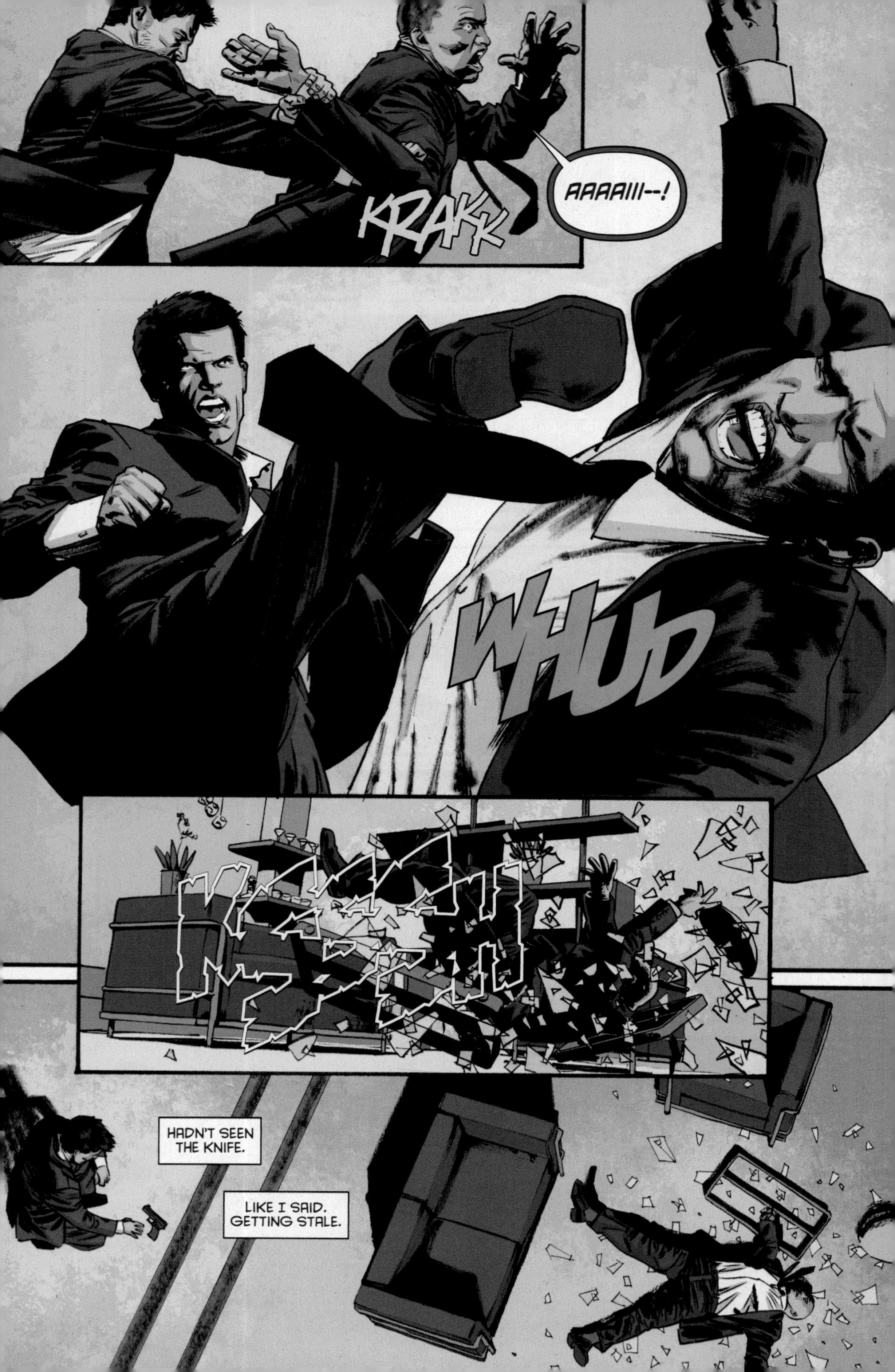
KRAKK
AAAAIII--!
WHUD
KRASH
HADN'T SEEN THE KNIFE.
LIKE I SAID. GETTING STALE.

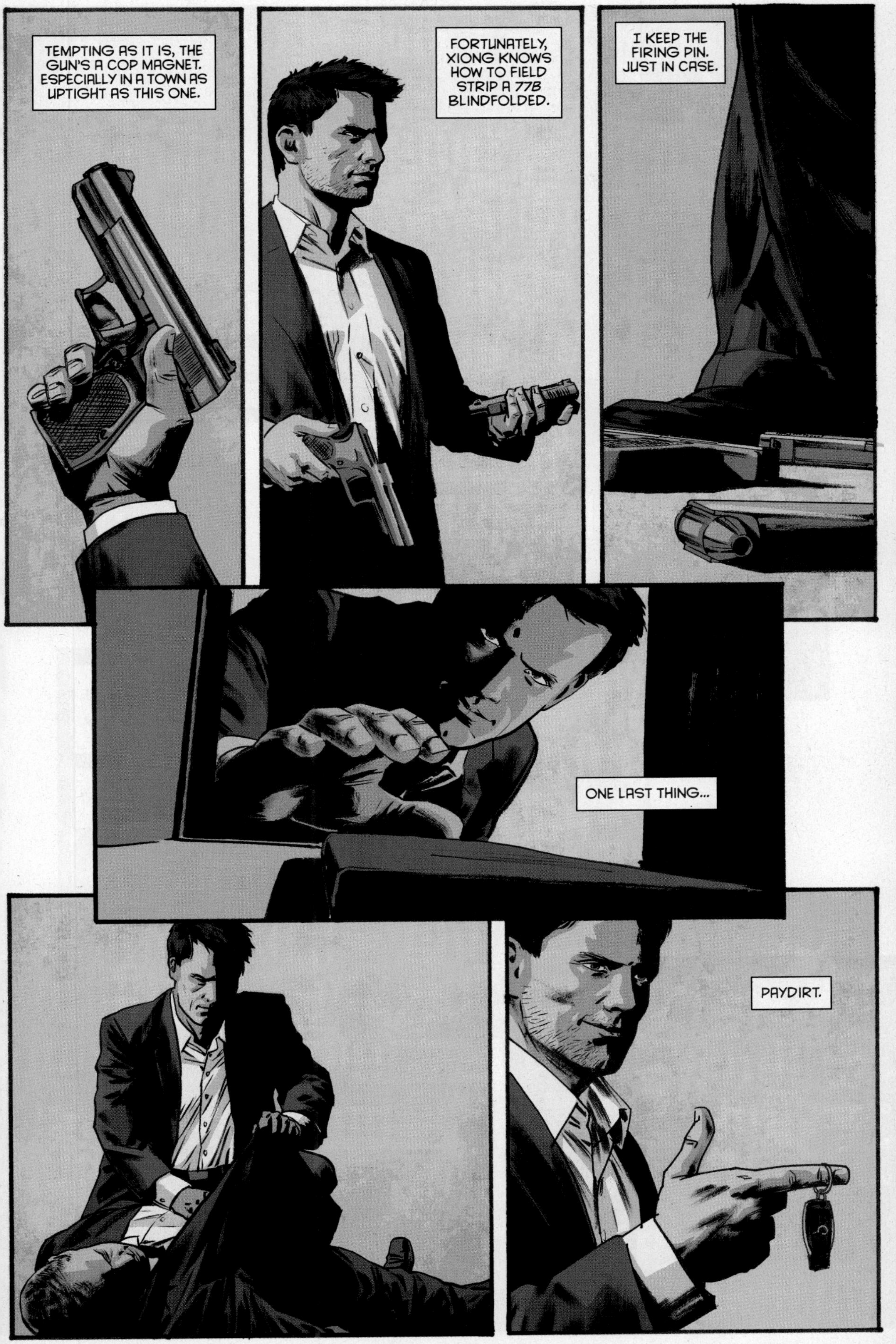
TEMPTING AS IT IS, THE GUN'S A COP MAGNET. ESPECIALLY IN A TOWN AS UPTIGHT AS THIS ONE.
FORTUNATELY, XIONG KNOWS HOW TO FIELD STRIP A *77B* BLINDFOLDED.
I KEEP THE FIRING PIN. JUST IN CASE.
ONE LAST THING...
PAYDIRT.

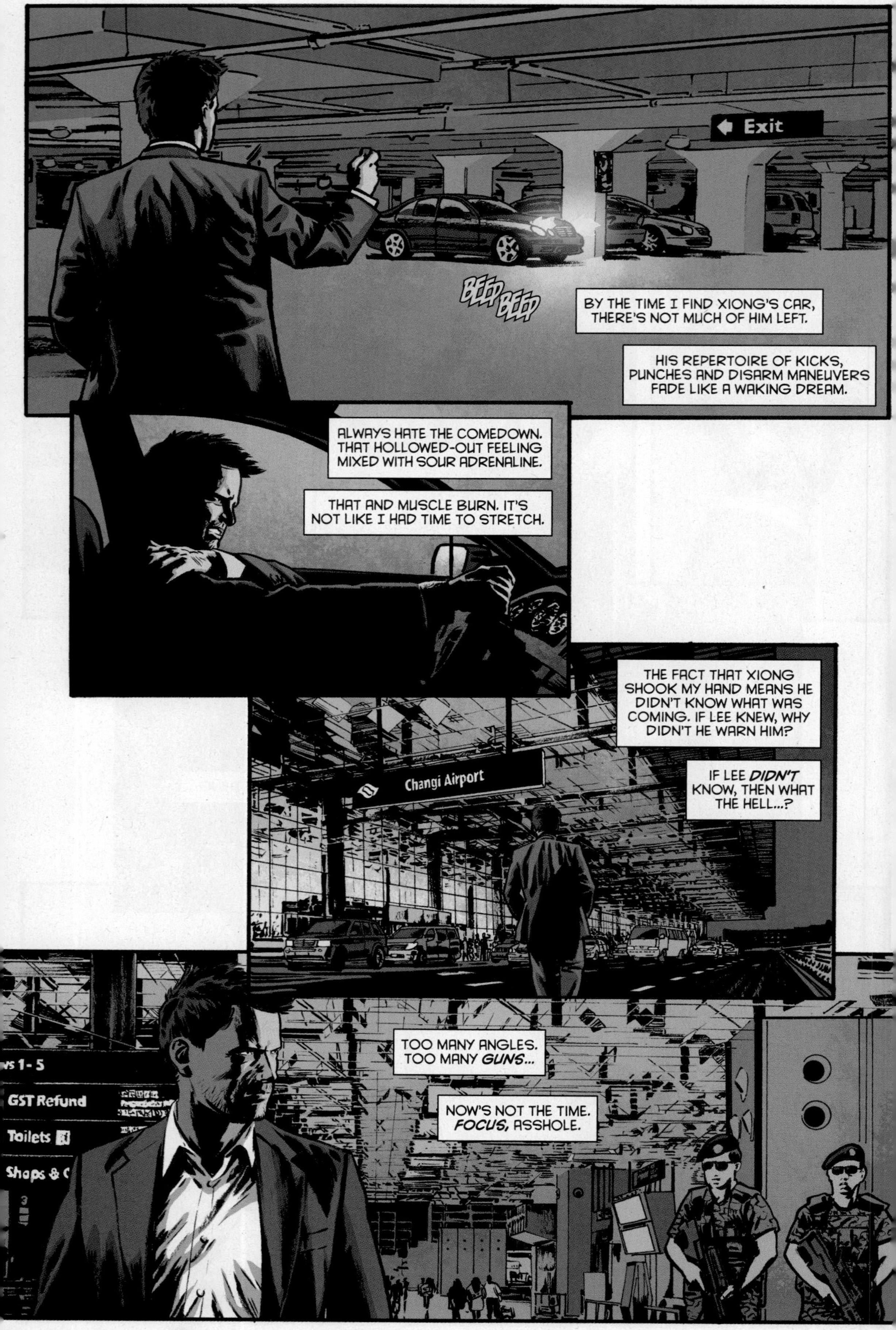
Exit
BEEP BEEP
BY THE TIME I FIND XIONG'S CAR, THERE'S NOT MUCH OF HIM LEFT.
HIS REPERTOIRE OF KICKS, PUNCHES AND DISARM MANEUVERS FADE LIKE A WAKING DREAM.
ALWAYS HATE THE COMEDOWN. THAT HOLLOWED-OUT FEELING MIXED WITH SOUR ADRENALINE.
THAT AND MUSCLE BURN. IT'S NOT LIKE I HAD TIME TO STRETCH.
THE FACT THAT XIONG SHOOK MY HAND MEANS HE DIDN'T KNOW WHAT WAS COMING. IF LEE KNEW, WHY DIDN'T HE WARN HIM?
IF LEE *DIDN'T* KNOW, THEN WHAT THE HELL...?
Changi Airport
TOO MANY ANGLES. TOO MANY *GUNS*...
NOW'S NOT THE TIME. ***FOCUS,*** ASSHOLE.
GST Refund
Toilets

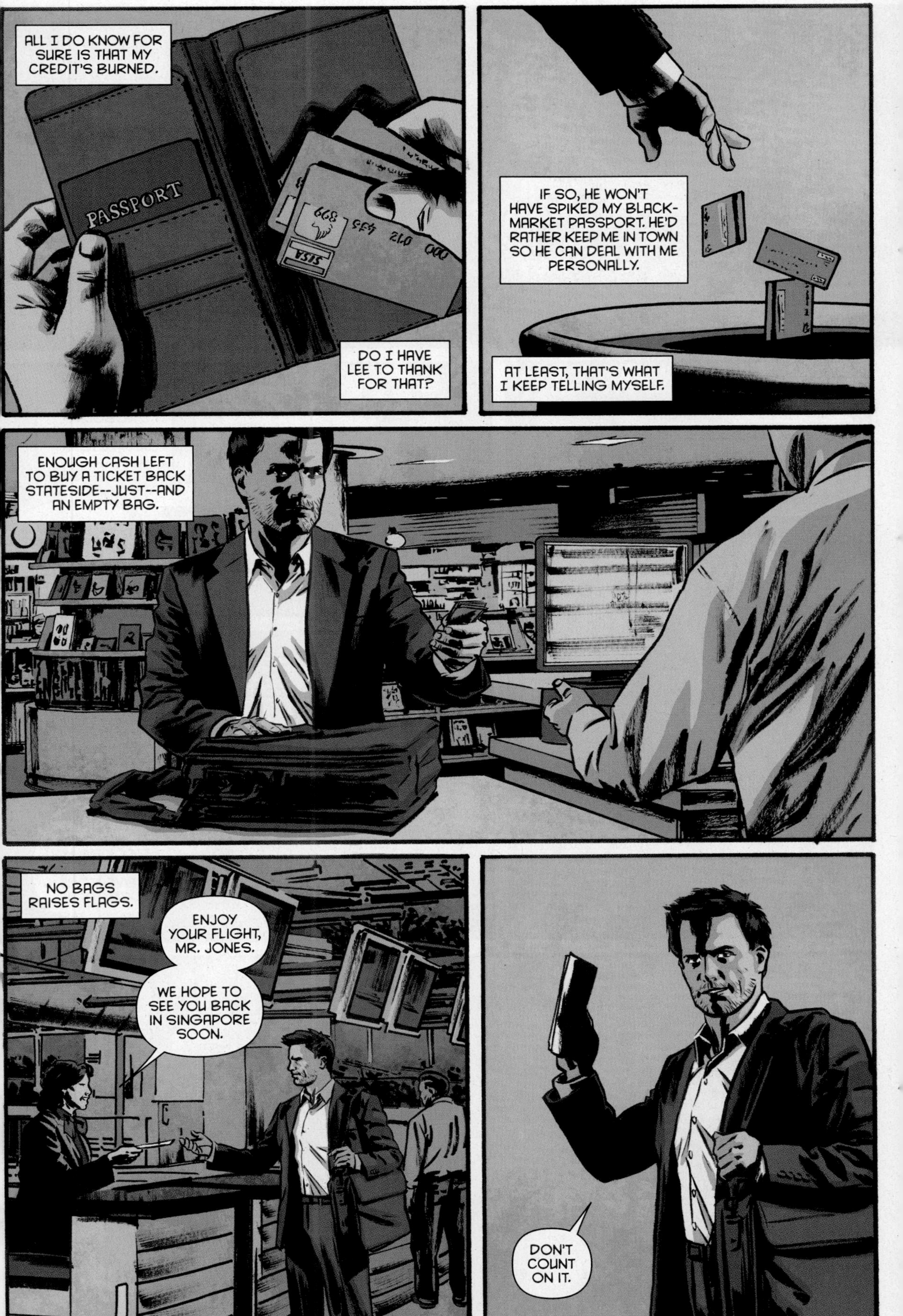
ALL I DO KNOW FOR SURE IS THAT MY CREDIT'S BURNED.
PASSPORT
DO I HAVE LEE TO THANK FOR THAT?
IF SO, HE WON'T HAVE SPIKED MY BLACK-MARKET PASSPORT. HE'D RATHER KEEP ME IN TOWN SO HE CAN DEAL WITH ME PERSONALLY.
AT LEAST, THAT'S WHAT I KEEP TELLING MYSELF.
ENOUGH CASH LEFT TO BUY A TICKET BACK STATESIDE--JUST--AND AN EMPTY BAG.
NO BAGS RAISES FLAGS.
ENJOY YOUR FLIGHT, MR. JONES.
WE HOPE TO SEE YOU BACK IN SINGAPORE SOON.
DON'T COUNT ON IT.

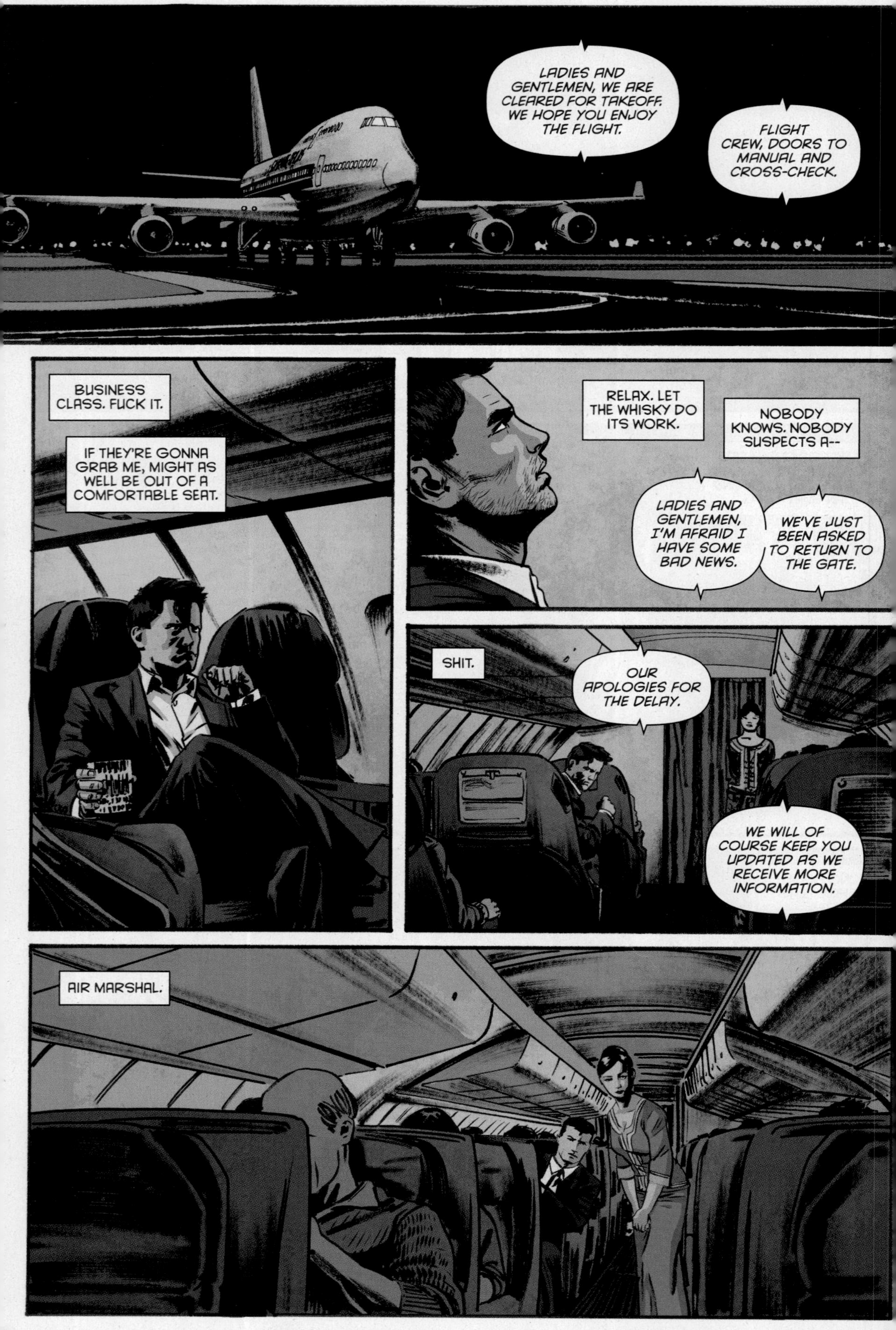

LADIES AND GENTLEMEN, WE ARE CLEARED FOR TAKEOFF. WE HOPE YOU ENJOY THE FLIGHT.
FLIGHT CREW, DOORS TO MANUAL AND CROSS-CHECK.
BUSINESS CLASS. FUCK IT.
IF THEY'RE GONNA GRAB ME, MIGHT AS WELL BE OUT OF A COMFORTABLE SEAT.
RELAX. LET THE WHISKY DO ITS WORK.
NOBODY KNOWS. NOBODY SUSPECTS A--
LADIES AND GENTLEMEN, I'M AFRAID I HAVE SOME BAD NEWS.
WE'VE JUST BEEN ASKED TO RETURN TO THE GATE.
SHIT.
OUR APOLOGIES FOR THE DELAY.
WE WILL OF COURSE KEEP YOU UPDATED AS WE RECEIVE MORE INFORMATION.
AIR MARSHAL.

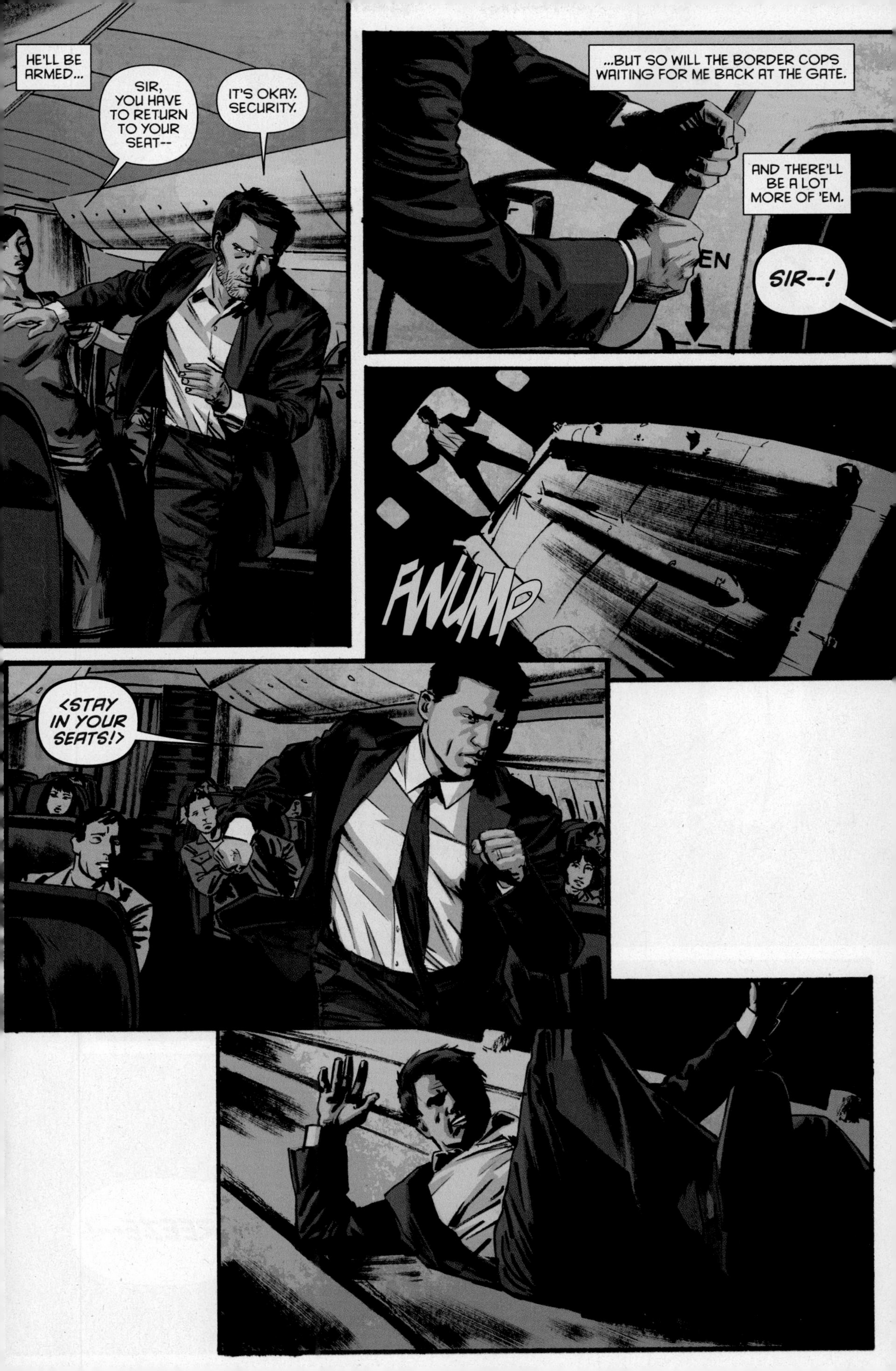
HE'LL BE ARMED...
SIR, YOU HAVE TO RETURN TO YOUR SEAT--
IT'S OKAY. SECURITY.
...BUT SO WILL THE BORDER COPS WAITING FOR ME BACK AT THE GATE.
AND THERE'LL BE A LOT MORE OF 'EM.
EN
SIR--!
FWUMP
<STAY IN YOUR SEATS!>

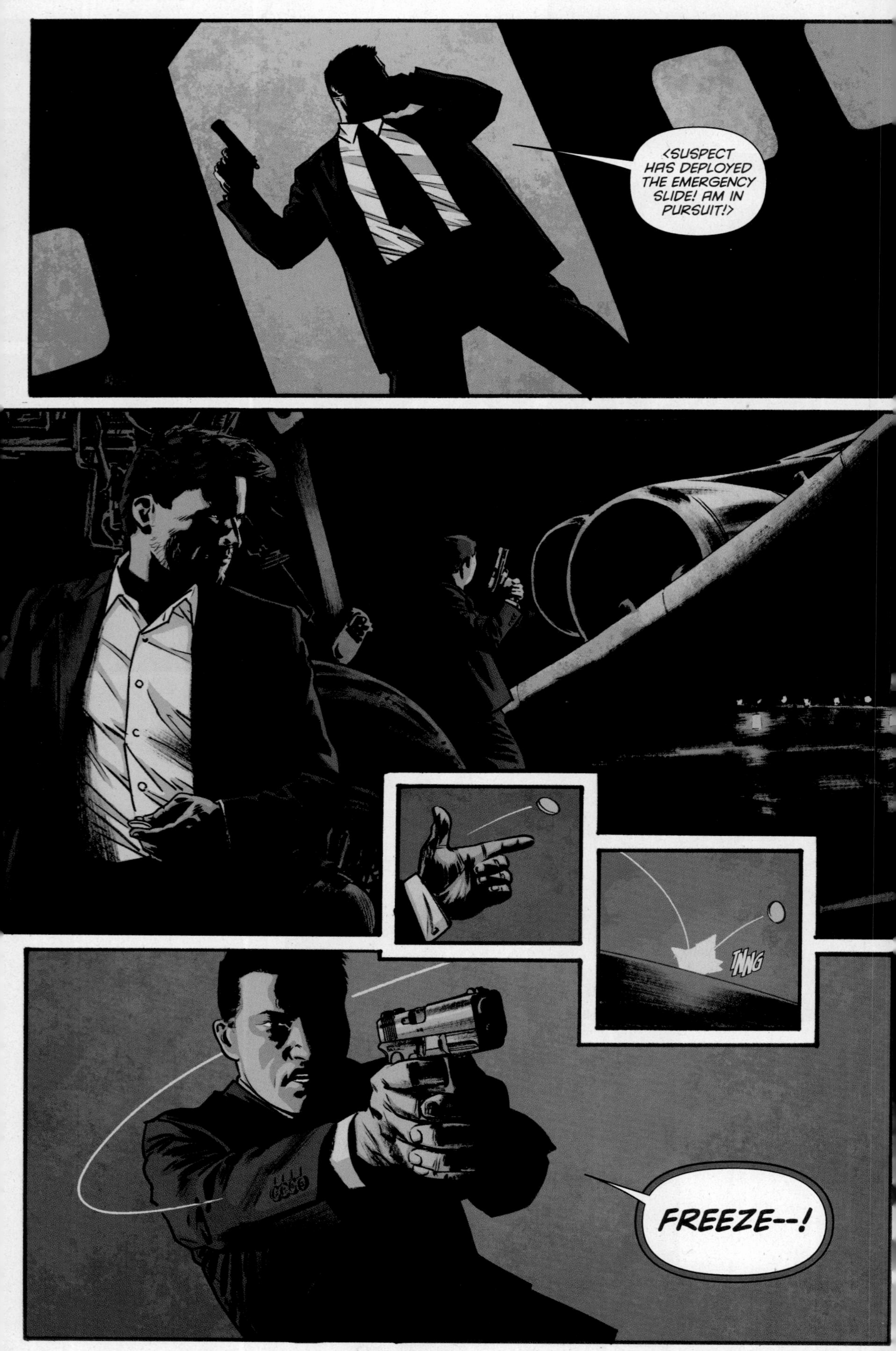
<SUSPECT HAS DEPLOYED THE EMERGENCY SLIDE! AM IN PURSUIT!>
TNNG
FREEZE--!

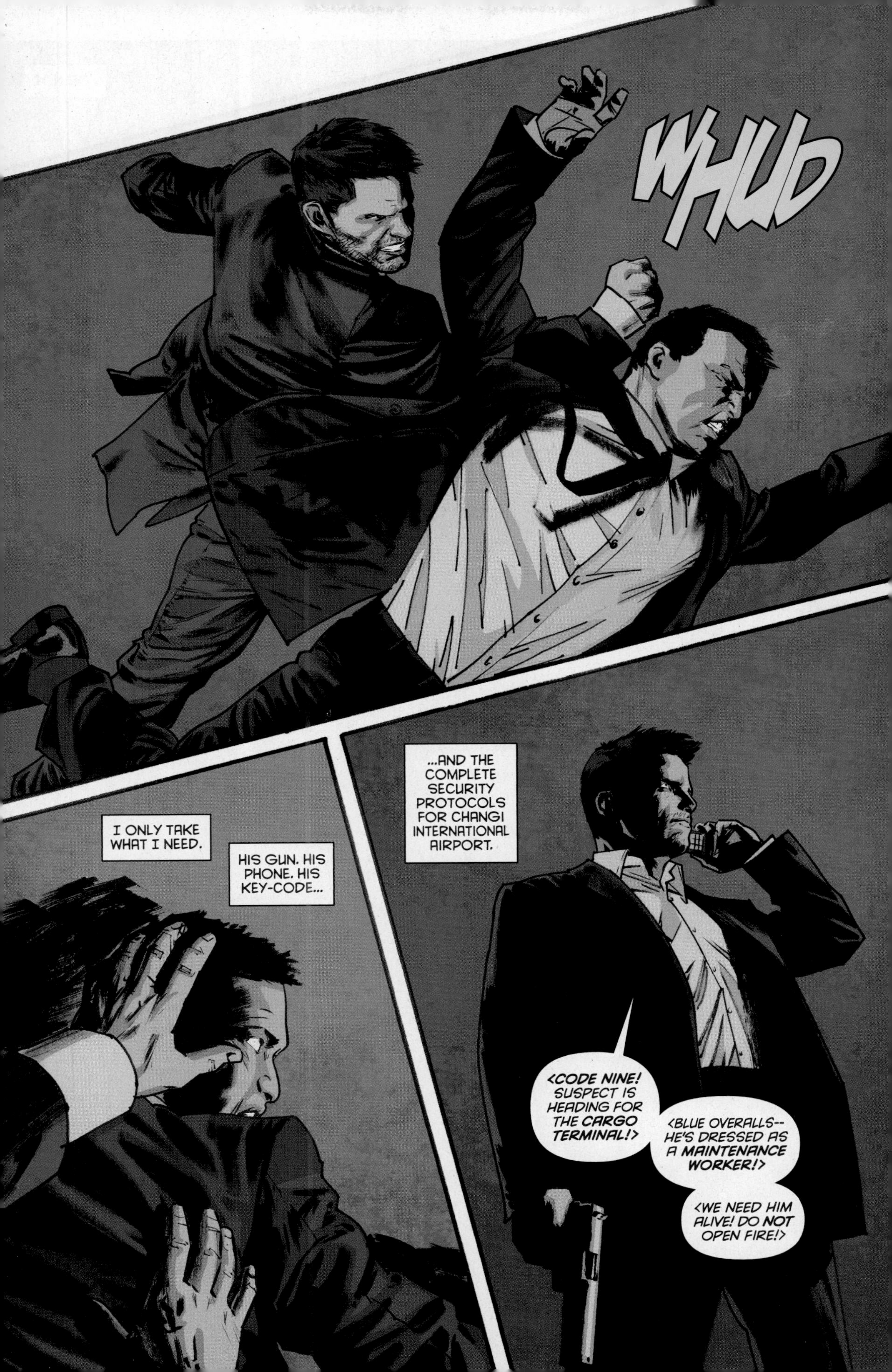
WHUD
I ONLY TAKE WHAT I NEED.
HIS GUN. HIS PHONE. HIS KEY-CODE...
...AND THE COMPLETE SECURITY PROTOCOLS FOR CHANGI INTERNATIONAL AIRPORT.
<CODE NINE! SUSPECT IS HEADING FOR THE CARGO TERMINAL!>
<BLUE OVERALLS-- HE'S DRESSED AS A MAINTENANCE WORKER!>
<WE NEED HIM ALIVE! DO NOT OPEN FIRE!>

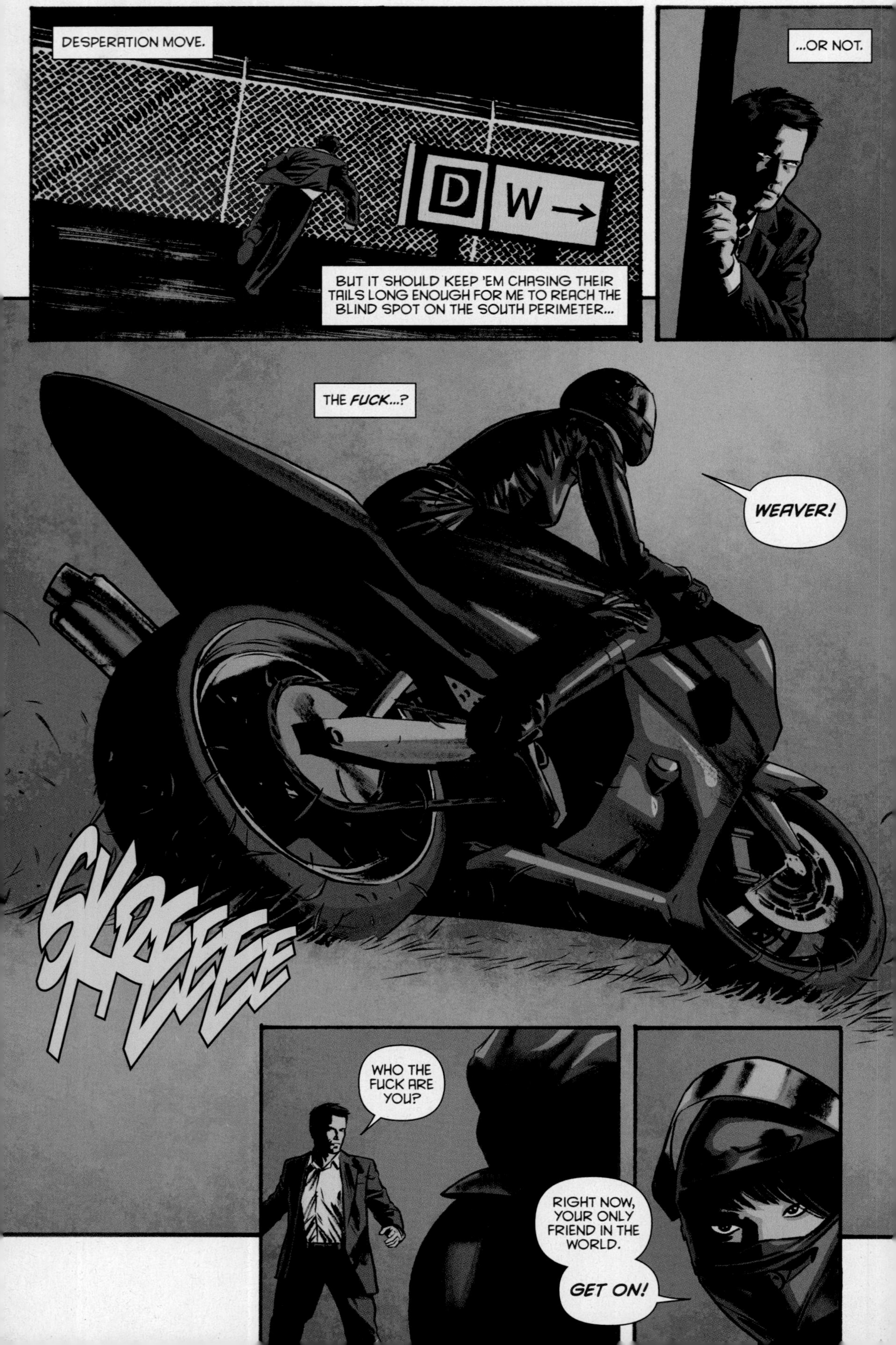

DESPERATION MOVE.
D W →
BUT IT SHOULD KEEP 'EM CHASING THEIR TAILS LONG ENOUGH FOR ME TO REACH THE BLIND SPOT ON THE SOUTH PERIMETER...
...OR NOT.
THE *FUCK*...?
WEAVER!
SKREEEE
WHO THE FUCK ARE YOU?
RIGHT NOW, YOUR ONLY FRIEND IN THE WORLD.
GET ON!

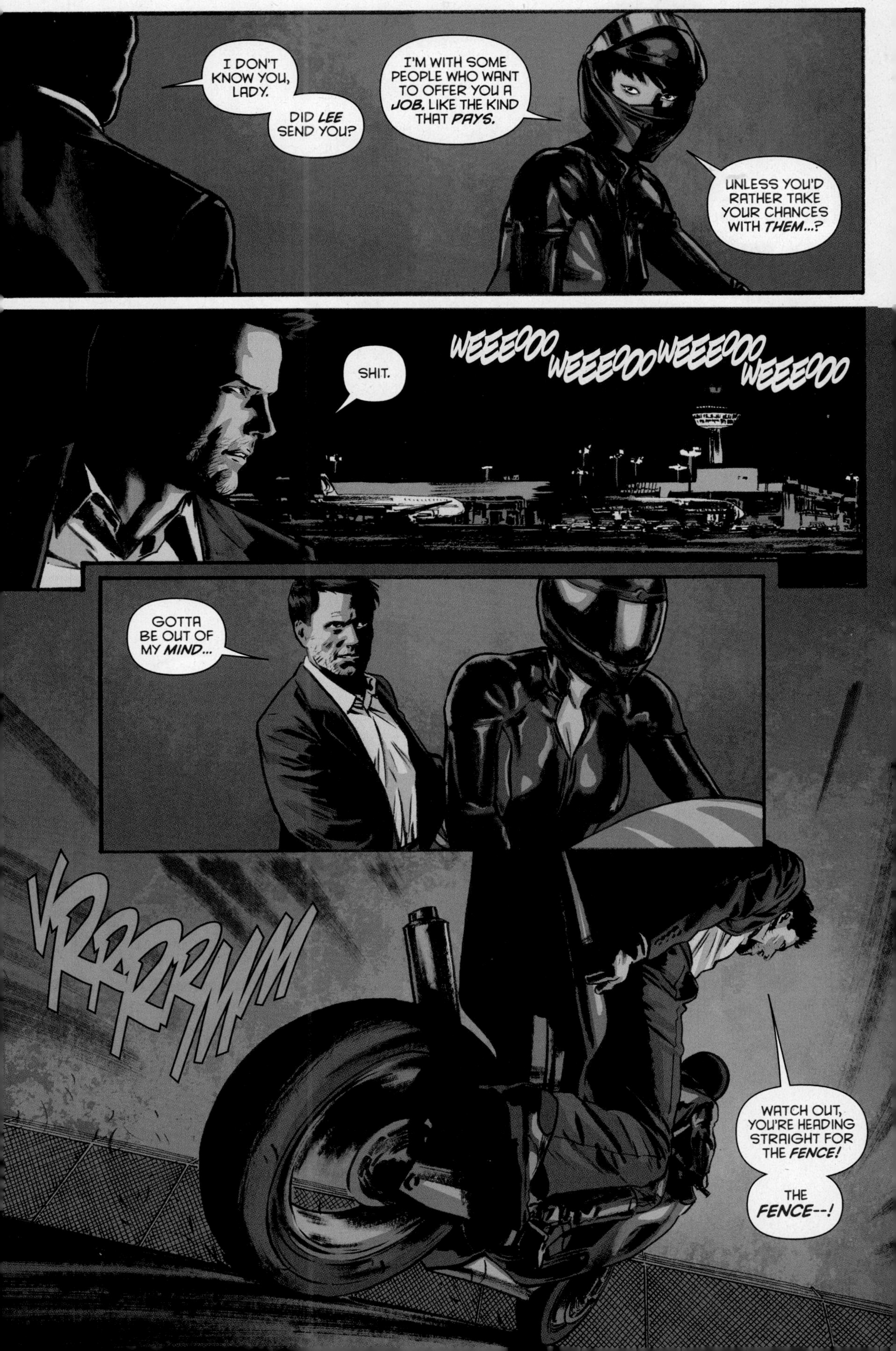

I DON'T KNOW YOU, LADY.
DID *LEE* SEND YOU?
I'M WITH SOME PEOPLE WHO WANT TO OFFER YOU A *JOB.* LIKE THE KIND THAT *PAYS.*
UNLESS YOU'D RATHER TAKE YOUR CHANCES WITH *THEM*...?
SHIT.
WEEEOOO WEEEOOO WEEEOOO WEEEOOO
GOTTA BE OUT OF MY *MIND*...
VRRRRMM
WATCH OUT, YOU'RE HEADING STRAIGHT FOR THE *FENCE!*
THE *FENCE*--!

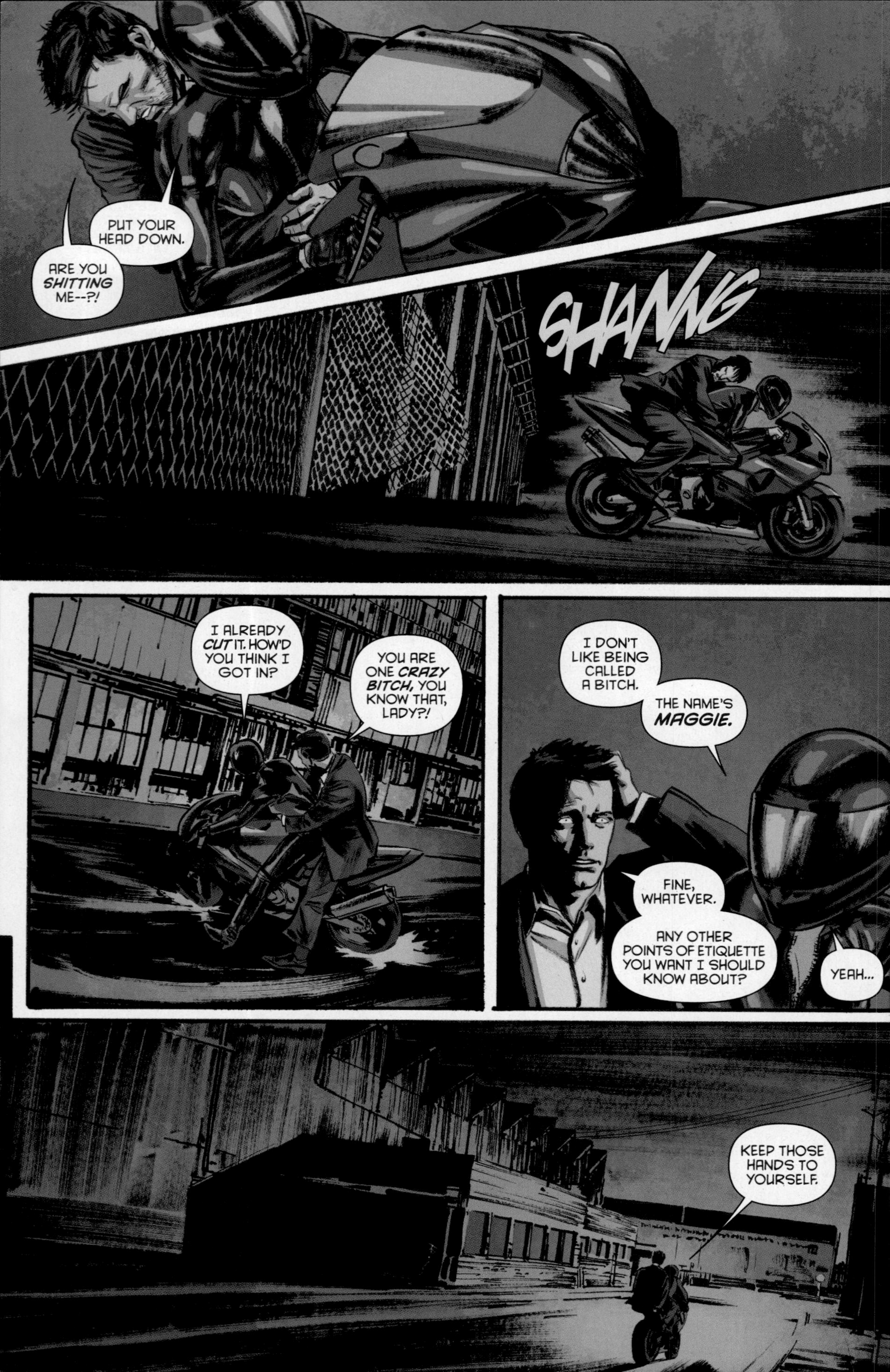
PUT YOUR HEAD DOWN.
ARE YOU SHITTING ME--?!
SHANNG
I ALREADY CUT IT. HOW'D YOU THINK I GOT IN?
YOU ARE ONE CRAZY BITCH, YOU KNOW THAT, LADY?!
I DON'T LIKE BEING CALLED A BITCH.
THE NAME'S MAGGIE.
FINE, WHATEVER.
ANY OTHER POINTS OF ETIQUETTE YOU WANT I SHOULD KNOW ABOUT?
YEAH...
KEEP THOSE HANDS TO YOURSELF.

ISSUE TWO

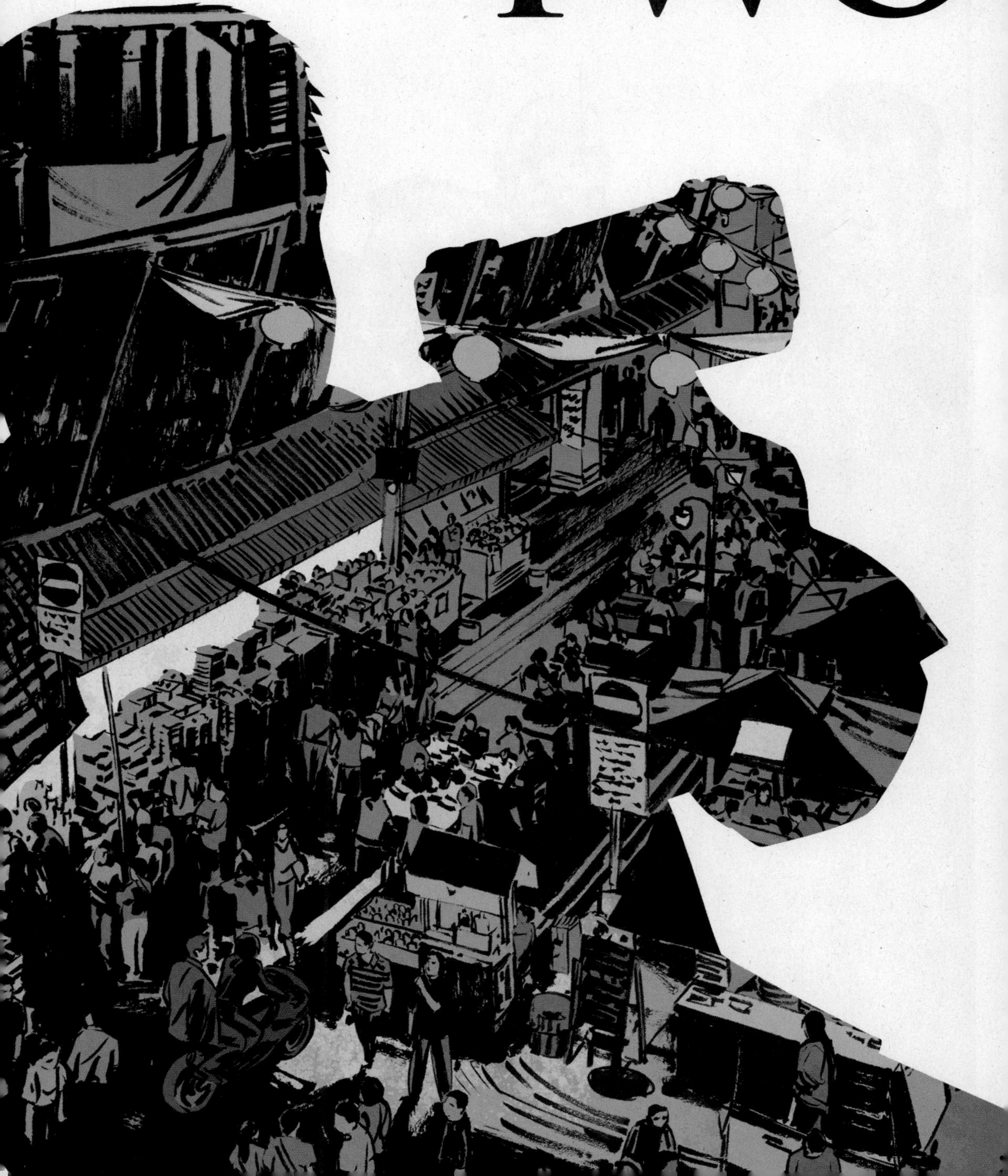

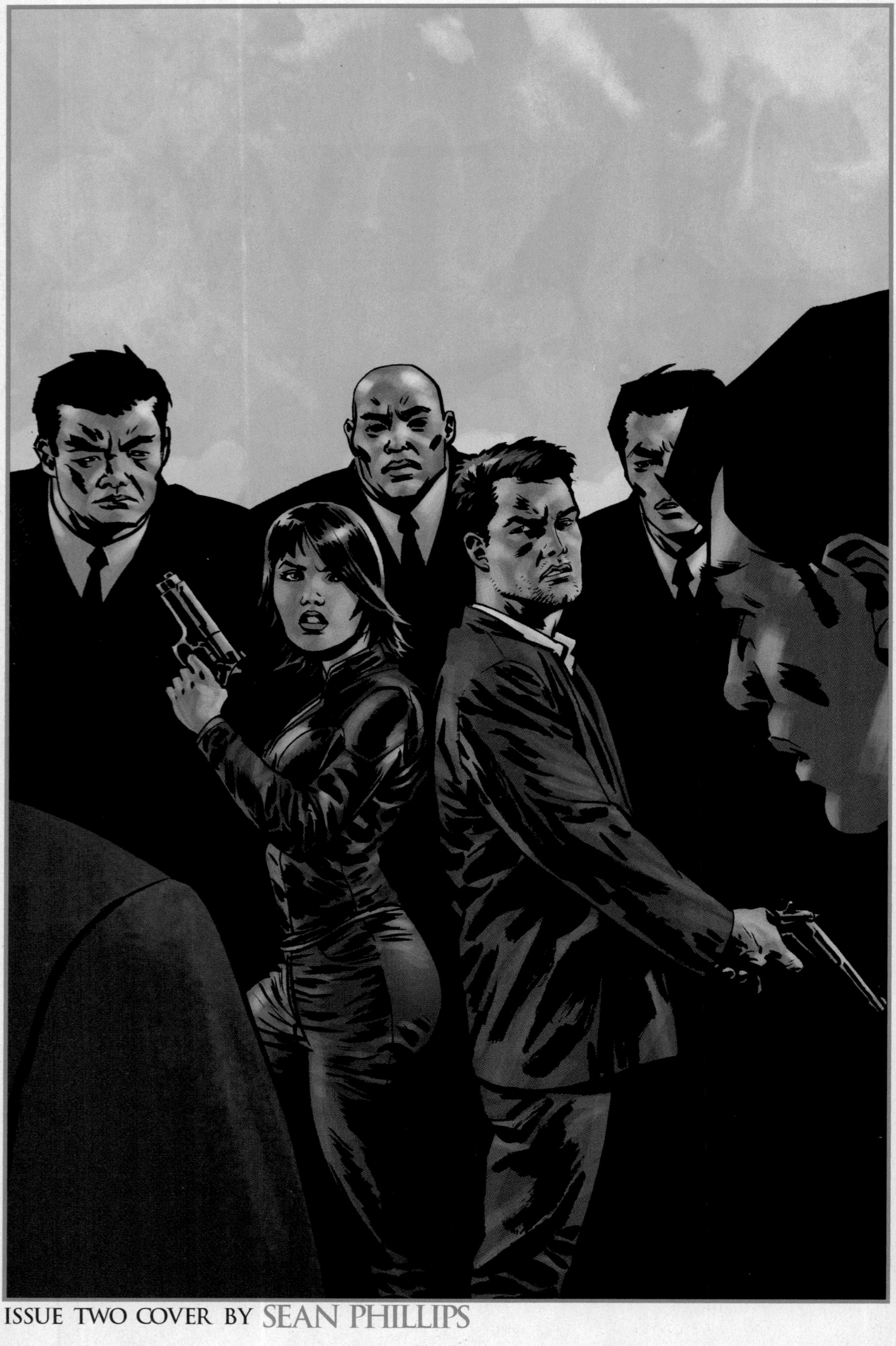

ISSUE TWO COVER BY SEAN PHILLIPS

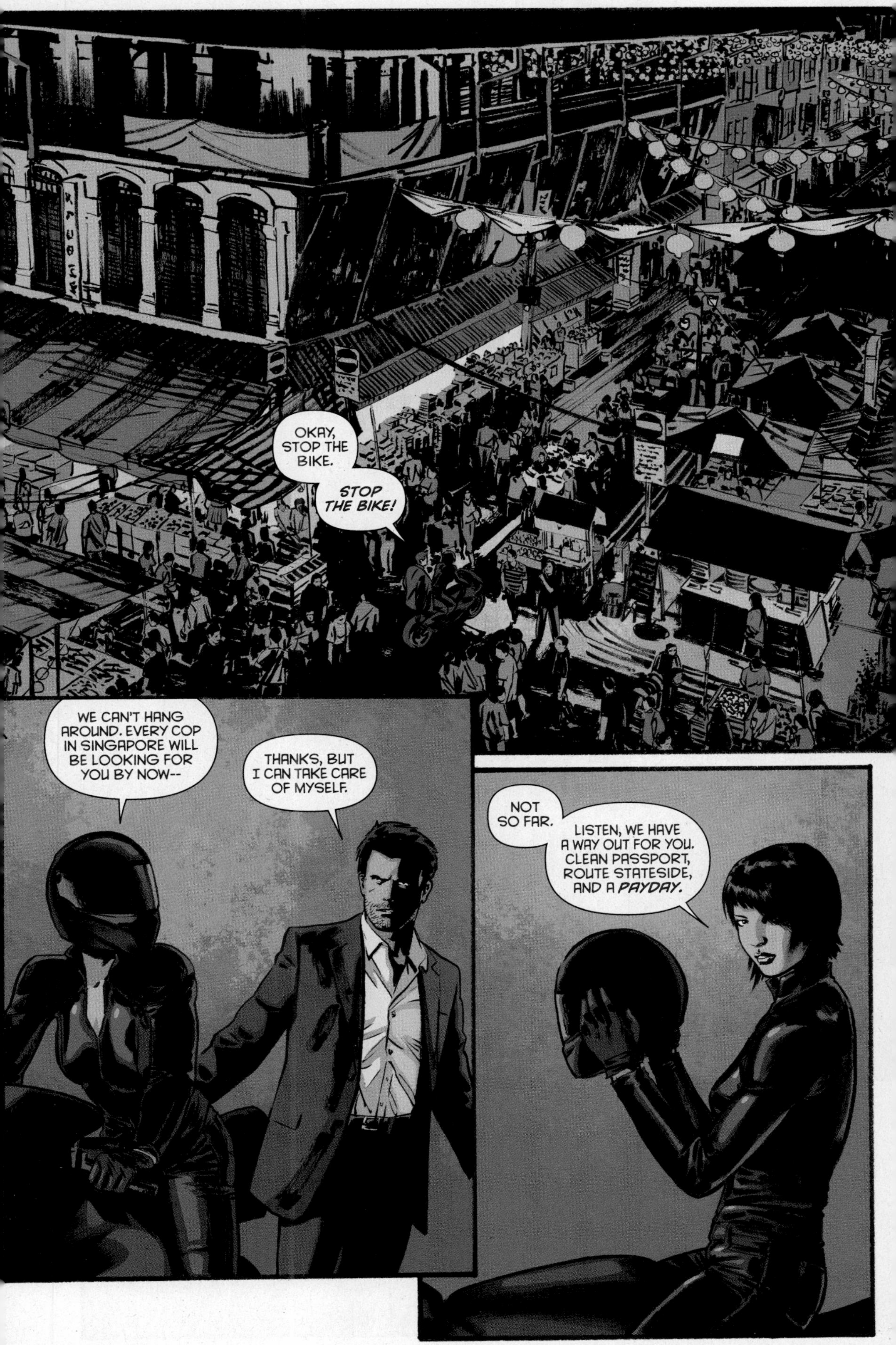
OKAY, STOP THE BIKE.
STOP THE BIKE!
WE CAN'T HANG AROUND. EVERY COP IN SINGAPORE WILL BE LOOKING FOR YOU BY NOW--
THANKS, BUT I CAN TAKE CARE OF MYSELF.
NOT SO FAR.
LISTEN, WE HAVE A WAY OUT FOR YOU. CLEAN PASSPORT, ROUTE STATESIDE, AND A *PAYDAY.*

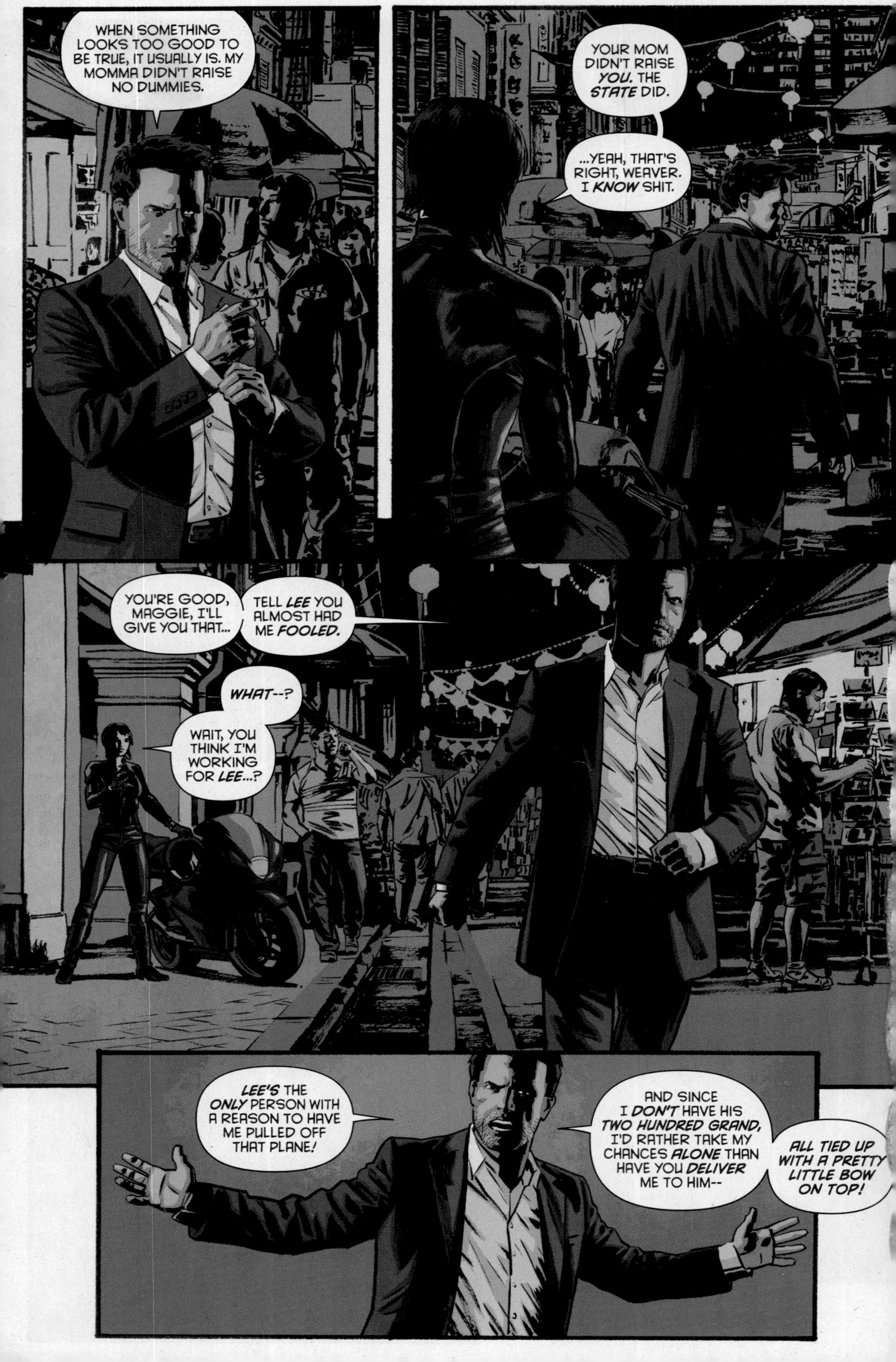
WHEN SOMETHING LOOKS TOO GOOD TO BE TRUE, IT USUALLY IS. MY MOMMA DIDN'T RAISE NO DUMMIES.
YOUR MOM DIDN'T RAISE *YOU.* THE *STATE* DID.
...YEAH, THAT'S RIGHT, WEAVER. I *KNOW* SHIT.
YOU'RE GOOD, MAGGIE, I'LL GIVE YOU THAT...
TELL *LEE* YOU ALMOST HAD ME *FOOLED.*
WHAT--?
WAIT, YOU THINK I'M WORKING FOR *LEE*...?
LEE'S THE *ONLY* PERSON WITH A REASON TO HAVE ME PULLED OFF THAT PLANE!
AND SINCE I *DON'T* HAVE HIS *TWO HUNDRED GRAND,* I'D RATHER TAKE MY CHANCES *ALONE* THAN HAVE YOU *DELIVER* ME TO HIM--
ALL TIED UP WITH A PRETTY LITTLE BOW ON TOP!

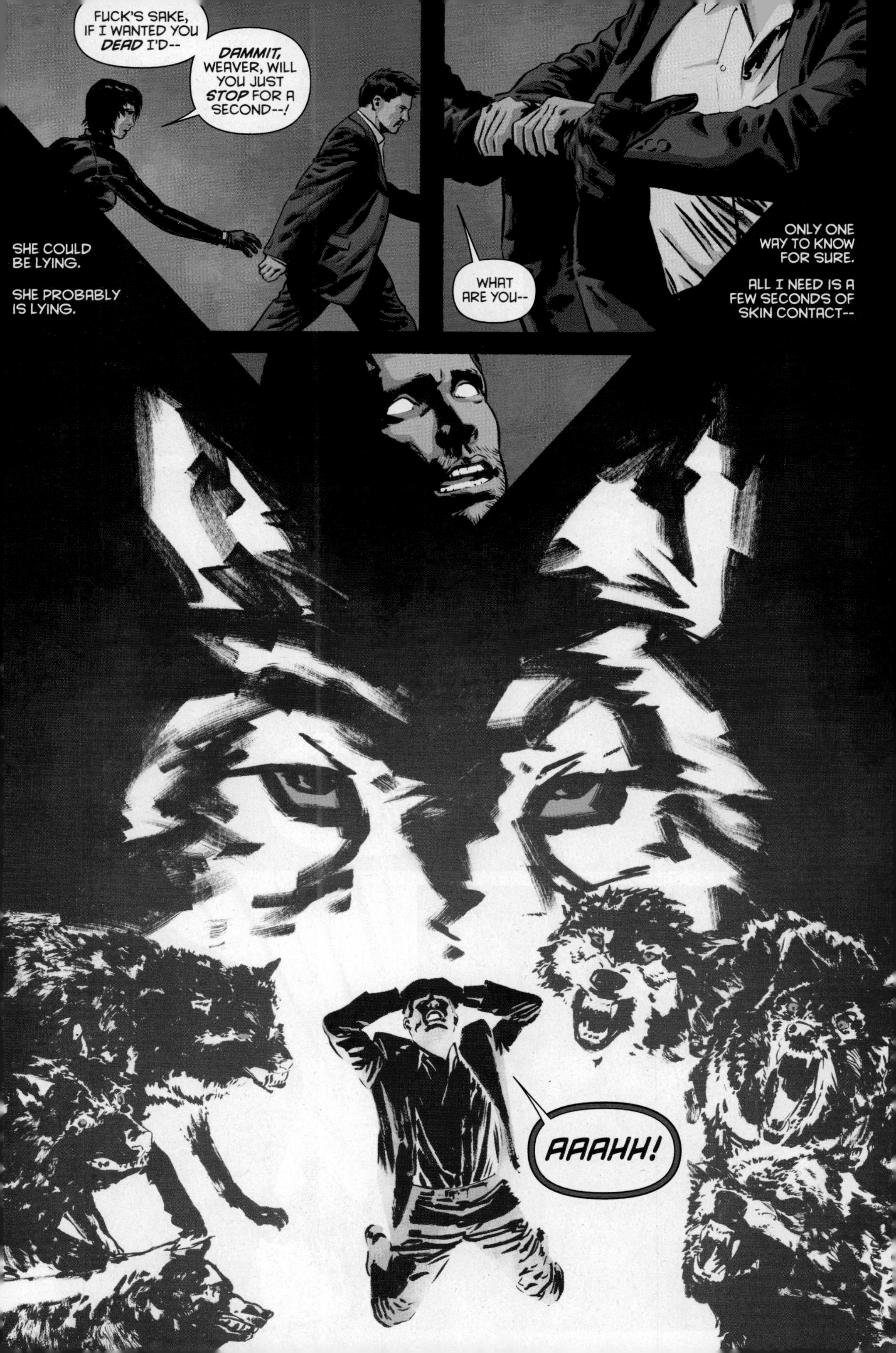
FUCK'S SAKE, IF I WANTED YOU DEAD I'D--
DAMMIT, WEAVER, WILL YOU JUST STOP FOR A SECOND--!
SHE COULD BE LYING.
SHE PROBABLY IS LYING.
WHAT ARE YOU--
ONLY ONE WAY TO KNOW FOR SURE.
ALL I NEED IS A FEW SECONDS OF SKIN CONTACT--
AAAHH!

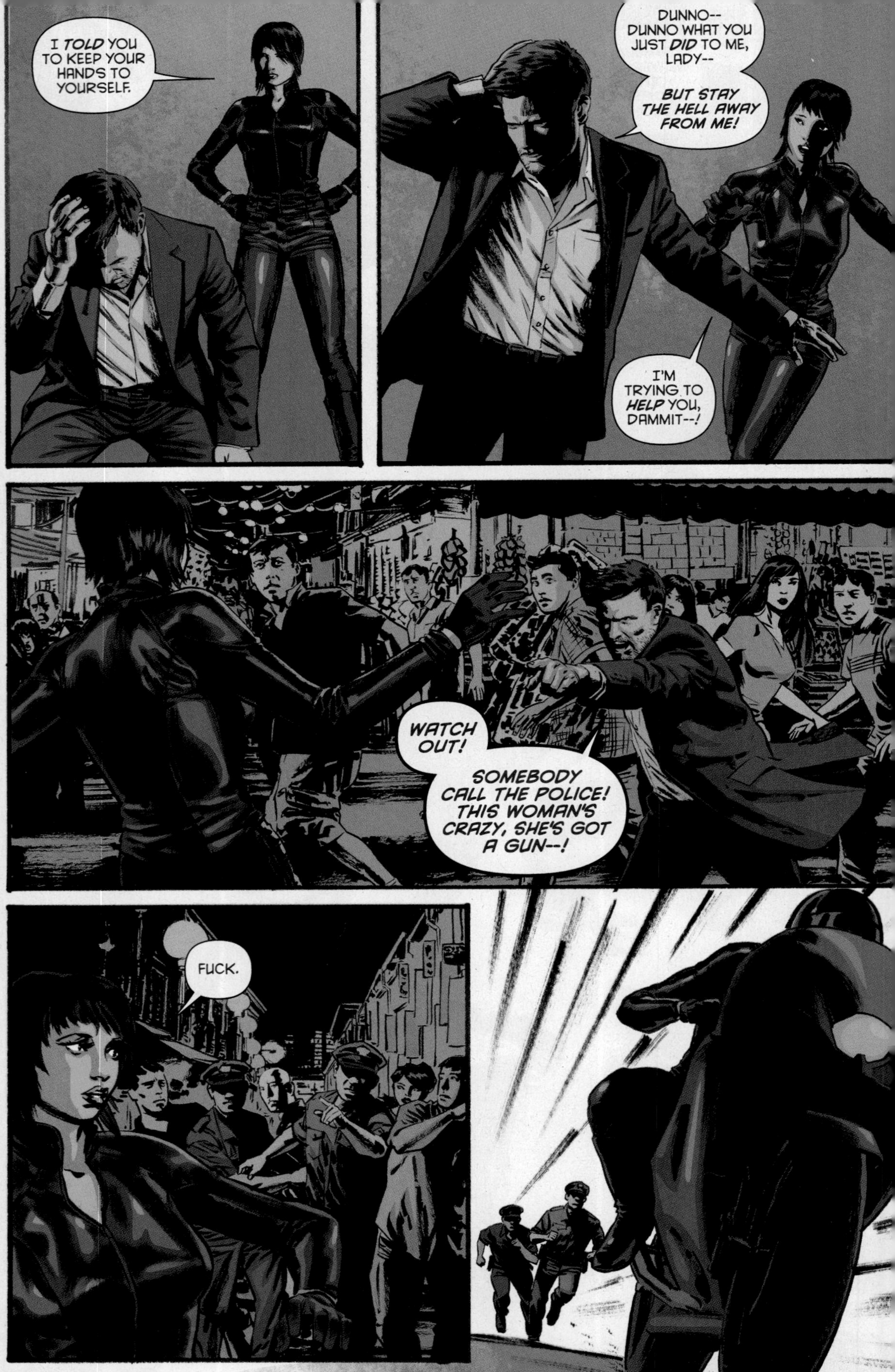
I TOLD YOU TO KEEP YOUR HANDS TO YOURSELF.
DUNNO-- DUNNO WHAT YOU JUST DID TO ME, LADY--
BUT STAY THE HELL AWAY FROM ME!
I'M TRYING TO HELP YOU, DAMMIT--!
WATCH OUT!
SOMEBODY CALL THE POLICE! THIS WOMAN'S CRAZY, SHE'S GOT A GUN--!
FUCK.

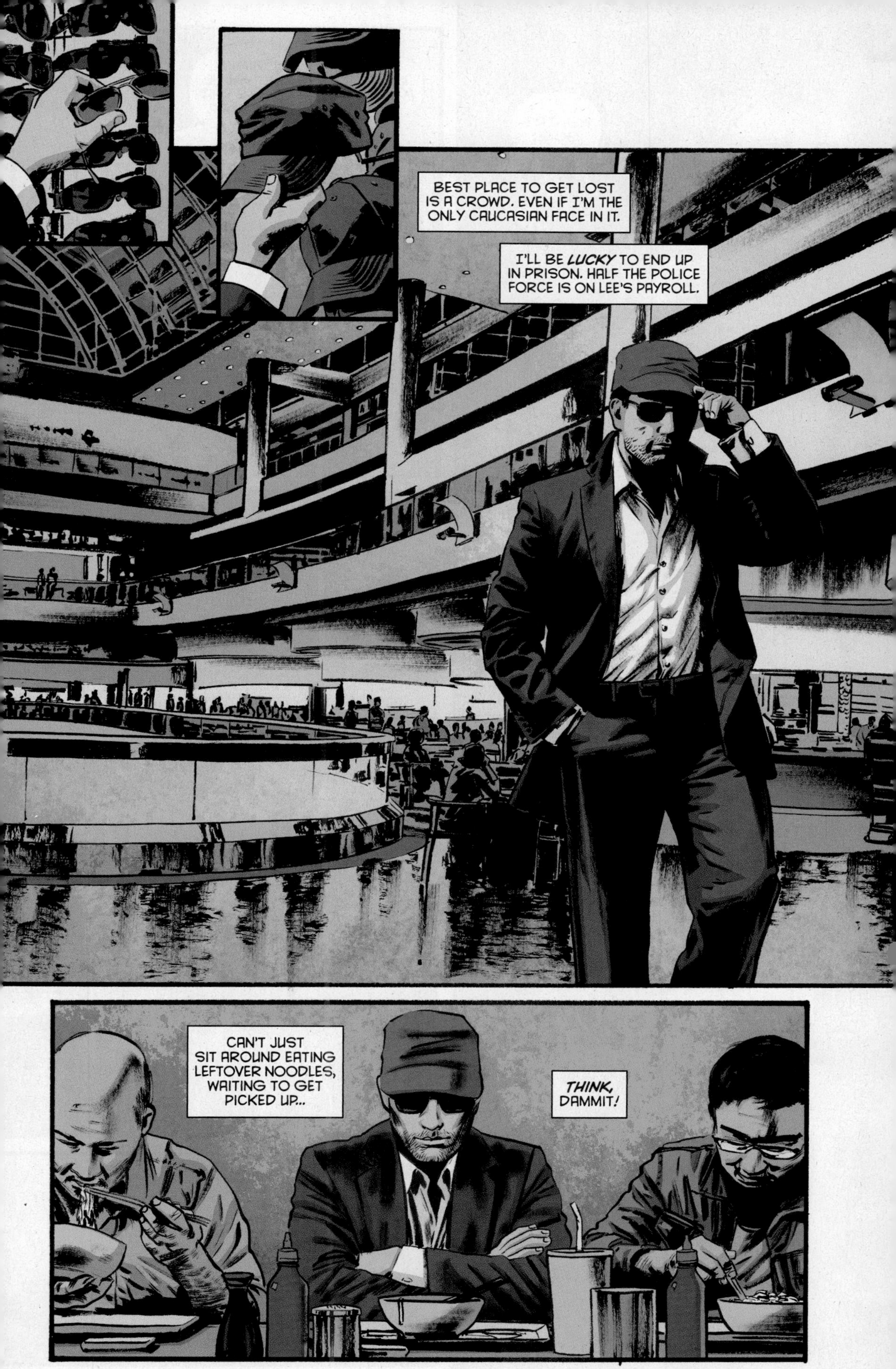
BEST PLACE TO GET LOST IS A CROWD. EVEN IF I'M THE ONLY CAUCASIAN FACE IN IT.
I'LL BE LUCKY TO END UP IN PRISON. HALF THE POLICE FORCE IS ON LEE'S PAYROLL.
CAN'T JUST SIT AROUND EATING LEFTOVER NOODLES, WAITING TO GET PICKED UP...
THINK, DAMMIT!

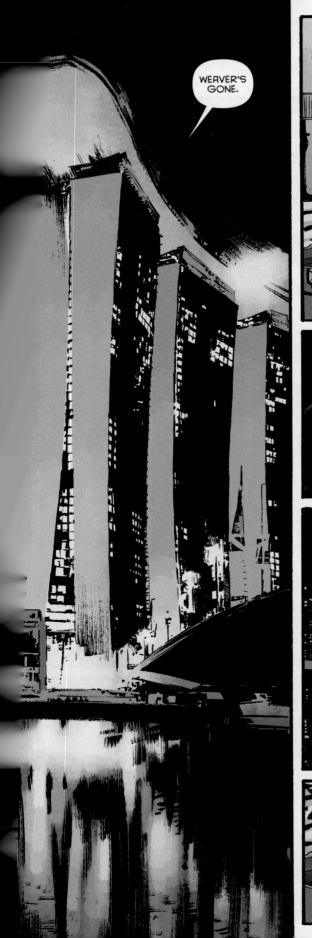

WEAVER'S GONE.

YOU LOST HIM?

I DIDN'T *LOSE* HIM. HE LOST HIS SHIT AND *BAILED.*

FUCK WAS I SUPPOSED TO DO, *SHOOT* HIM?

JUST DO YOUR JOB, MAGGIE. FIND HIM.

HOW? HE BURNED HIS I.D., HE'S A GHOST.

DID HE *READ* YOU?

TRIED TO. DIDN'T WORK.

SOMETHING HAPPENED, IT WAS WEIRD...

THEN WE CAN *TRACK* HIM.

STAND BY.

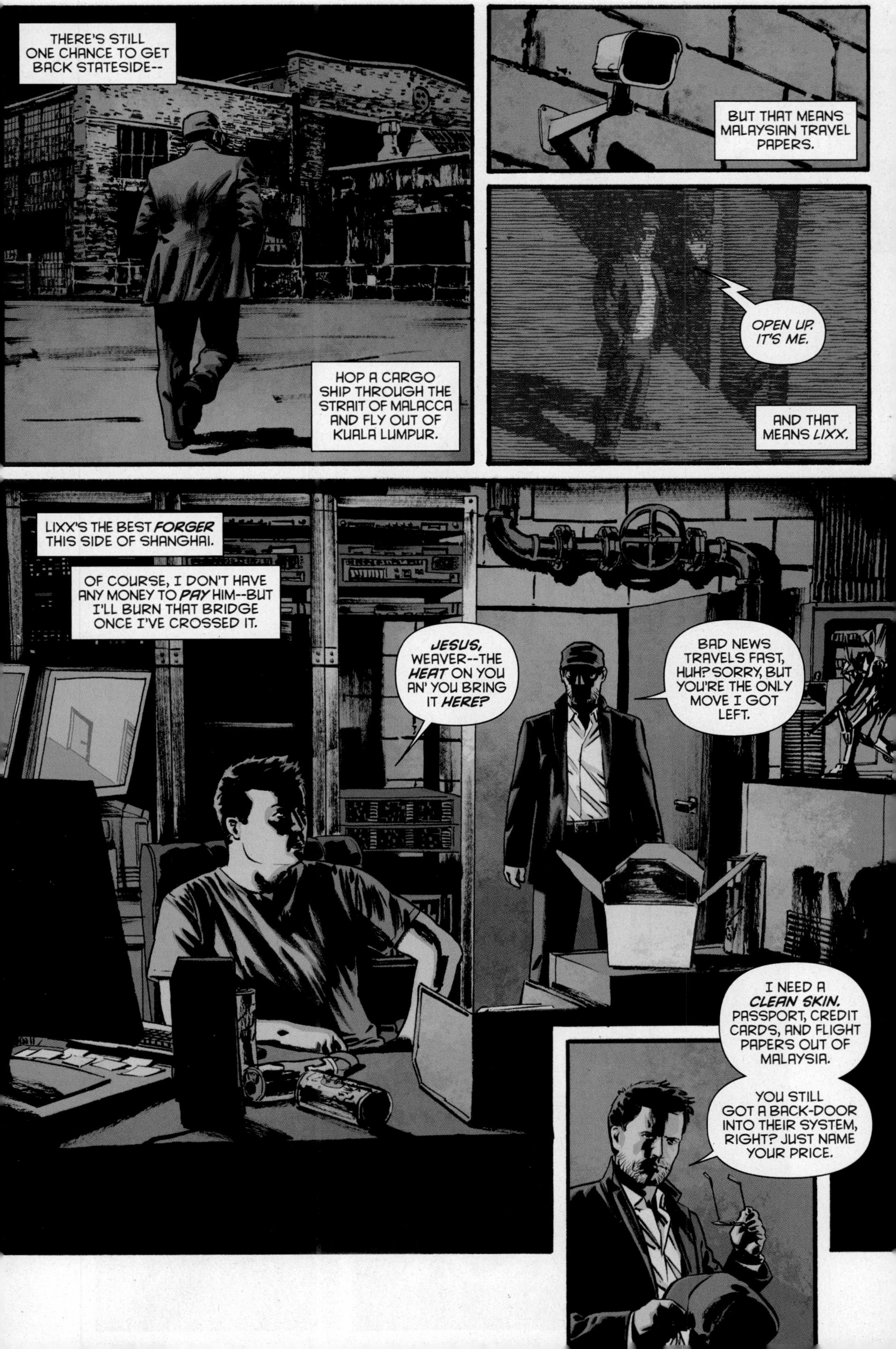
THERE'S STILL ONE CHANCE TO GET BACK STATESIDE--
HOP A CARGO SHIP THROUGH THE STRAIT OF MALACCA AND FLY OUT OF KUALA LUMPUR.
BUT THAT MEANS MALAYSIAN TRAVEL PAPERS.
OPEN UP. IT'S ME.
AND THAT MEANS LIXX.
LIXX'S THE BEST FORGER THIS SIDE OF SHANGHAI.
OF COURSE, I DON'T HAVE ANY MONEY TO PAY HIM--BUT I'LL BURN THAT BRIDGE ONCE I'VE CROSSED IT.
JESUS, WEAVER--THE HEAT ON YOU AN' YOU BRING IT HERE?
BAD NEWS TRAVELS FAST, HUH? SORRY, BUT YOU'RE THE ONLY MOVE I GOT LEFT.
I NEED A CLEAN SKIN. PASSPORT, CREDIT CARDS, AND FLIGHT PAPERS OUT OF MALAYSIA.
YOU STILL GOT A BACK-DOOR INTO THEIR SYSTEM, RIGHT? JUST NAME YOUR PRICE.

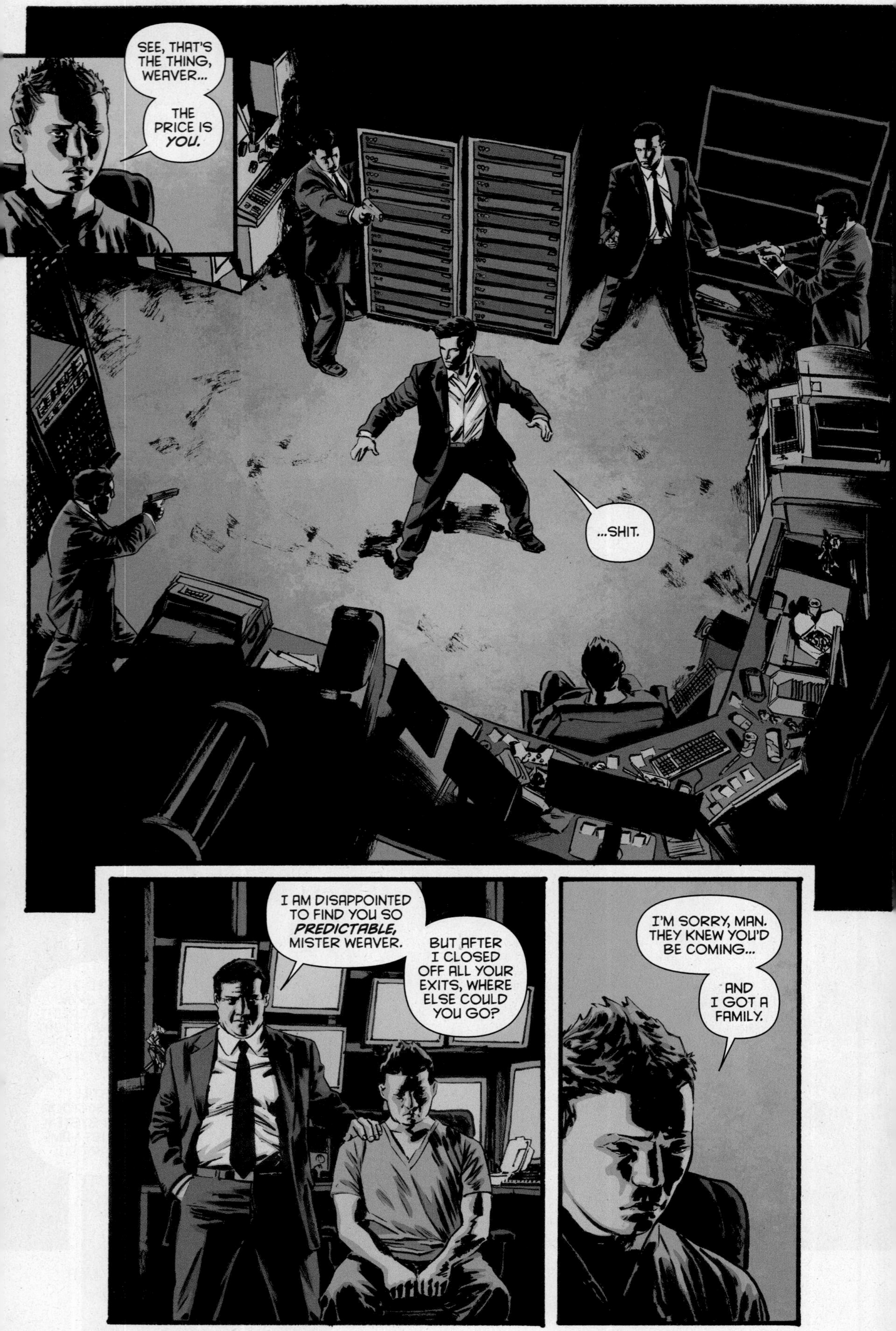
SEE, THAT'S THE THING, WEAVER...
THE PRICE IS *YOU.*
...SHIT.
I AM DISAPPOINTED TO FIND YOU SO *PREDICTABLE,* MISTER WEAVER.
BUT AFTER I CLOSED OFF ALL YOUR EXITS, WHERE ELSE COULD YOU GO?
I'M SORRY, MAN. THEY KNEW YOU'D BE COMING...
AND I GOT A FAMILY.

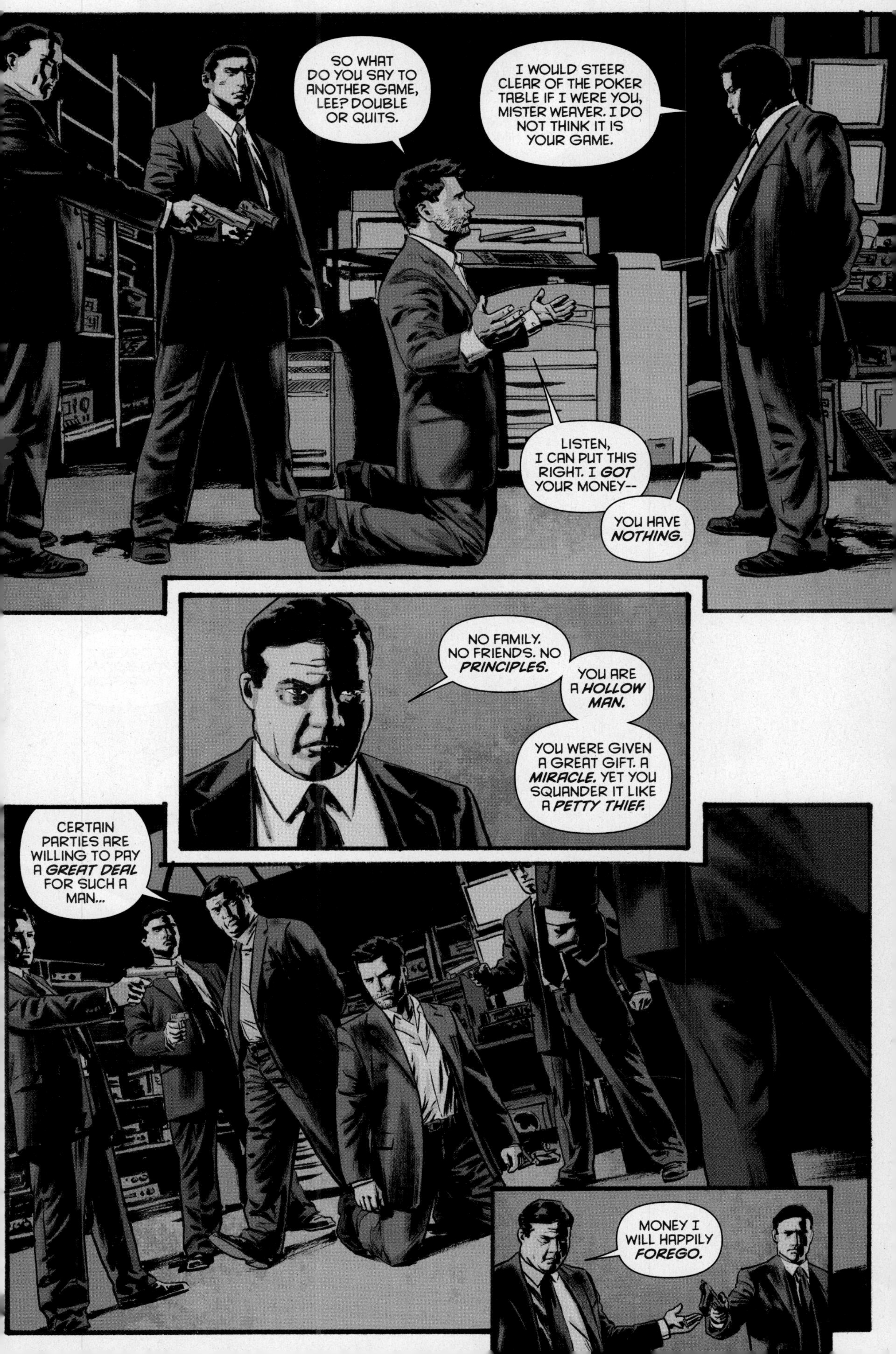
SO WHAT DO YOU SAY TO ANOTHER GAME, LEE? DOUBLE OR QUITS.
I WOULD STEER CLEAR OF THE POKER TABLE IF I WERE YOU, MISTER WEAVER. I DO NOT THINK IT IS YOUR GAME.
LISTEN, I CAN PUT THIS RIGHT. I *GOT* YOUR MONEY--
YOU HAVE *NOTHING.*
NO FAMILY. NO FRIENDS. NO *PRINCIPLES.*
YOU ARE A *HOLLOW MAN.*
YOU WERE GIVEN A GREAT GIFT. A *MIRACLE.* YET YOU SQUANDER IT LIKE A *PETTY THIEF.*
CERTAIN PARTIES ARE WILLING TO PAY A *GREAT DEAL* FOR SUCH A MAN...
MONEY I WILL HAPPILY *FOREGO.*

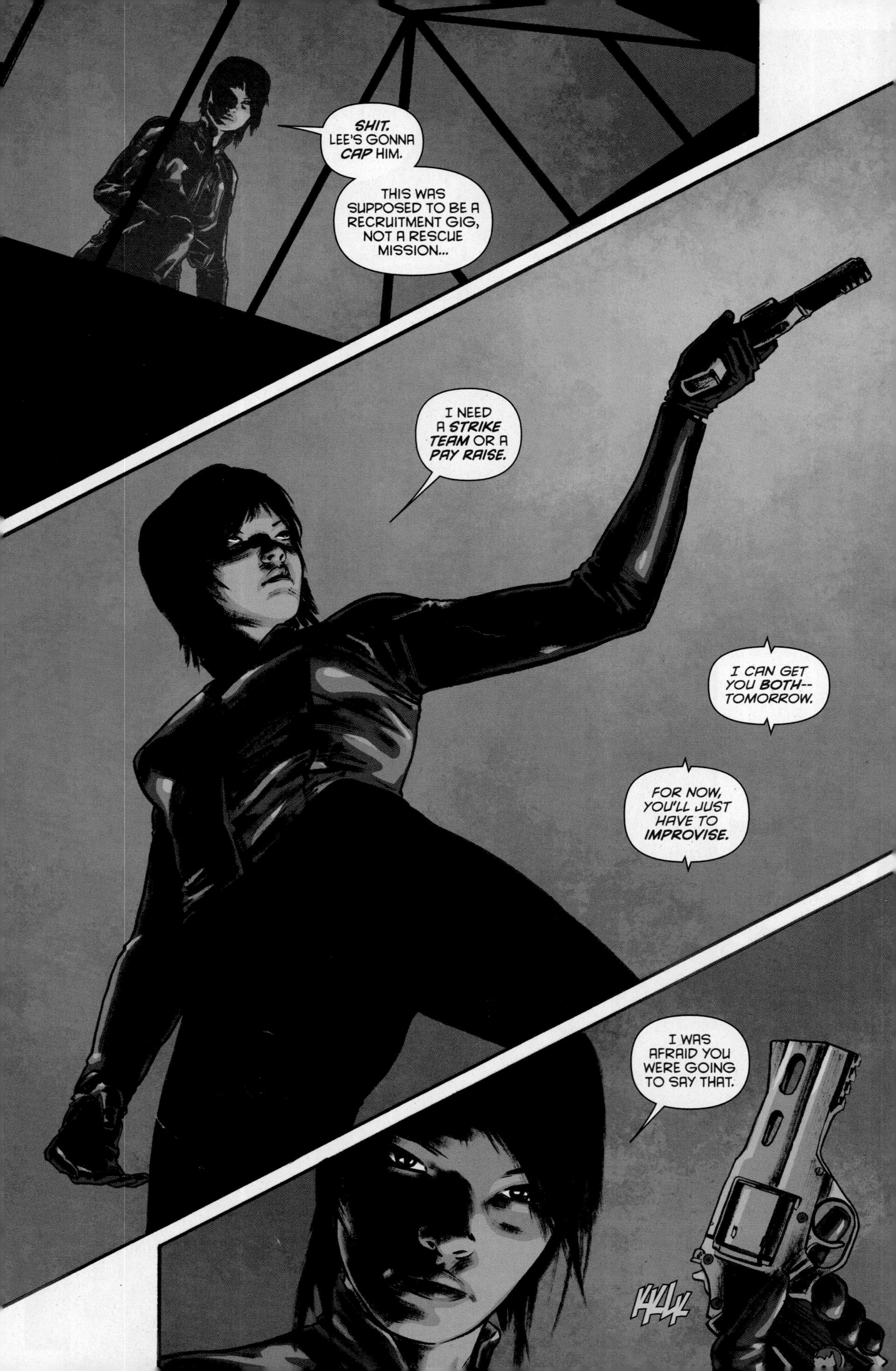
SHIT. LEE'S GONNA CAP HIM.
THIS WAS SUPPOSED TO BE A RECRUITMENT GIG, NOT A RESCUE MISSION...
I NEED A STRIKE TEAM OR A PAY RAISE.
I CAN GET YOU BOTH--TOMORROW.
FOR NOW, YOU'LL JUST HAVE TO IMPROVISE.
I WAS AFRAID YOU WERE GOING TO SAY THAT.
KLIK

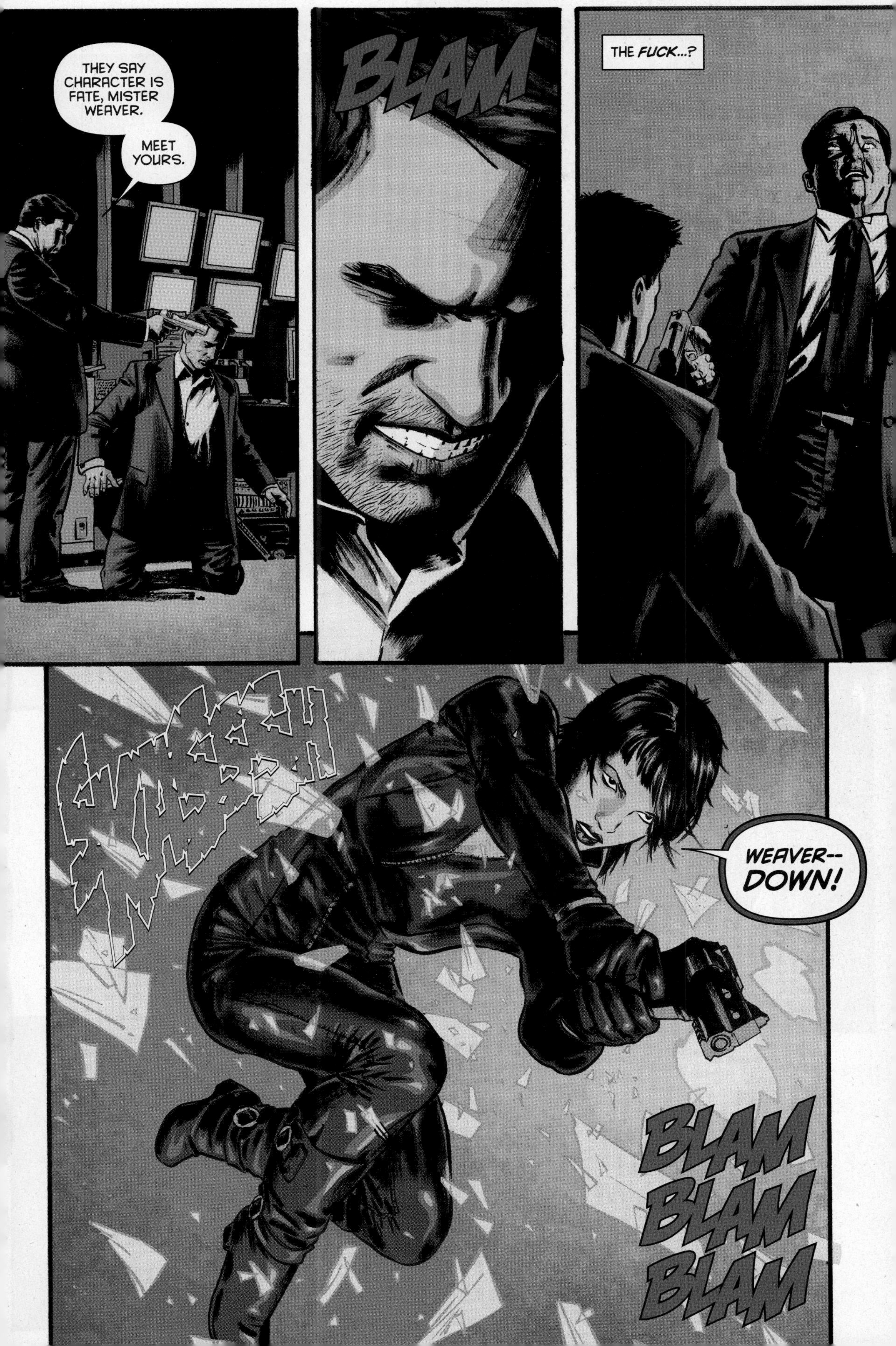
THEY SAY CHARACTER IS FATE, MISTER WEAVER.
MEET YOURS.
BLAM
THE *FUCK*...?
WEAVER-- DOWN!
BLAM
BLAM
BLAM

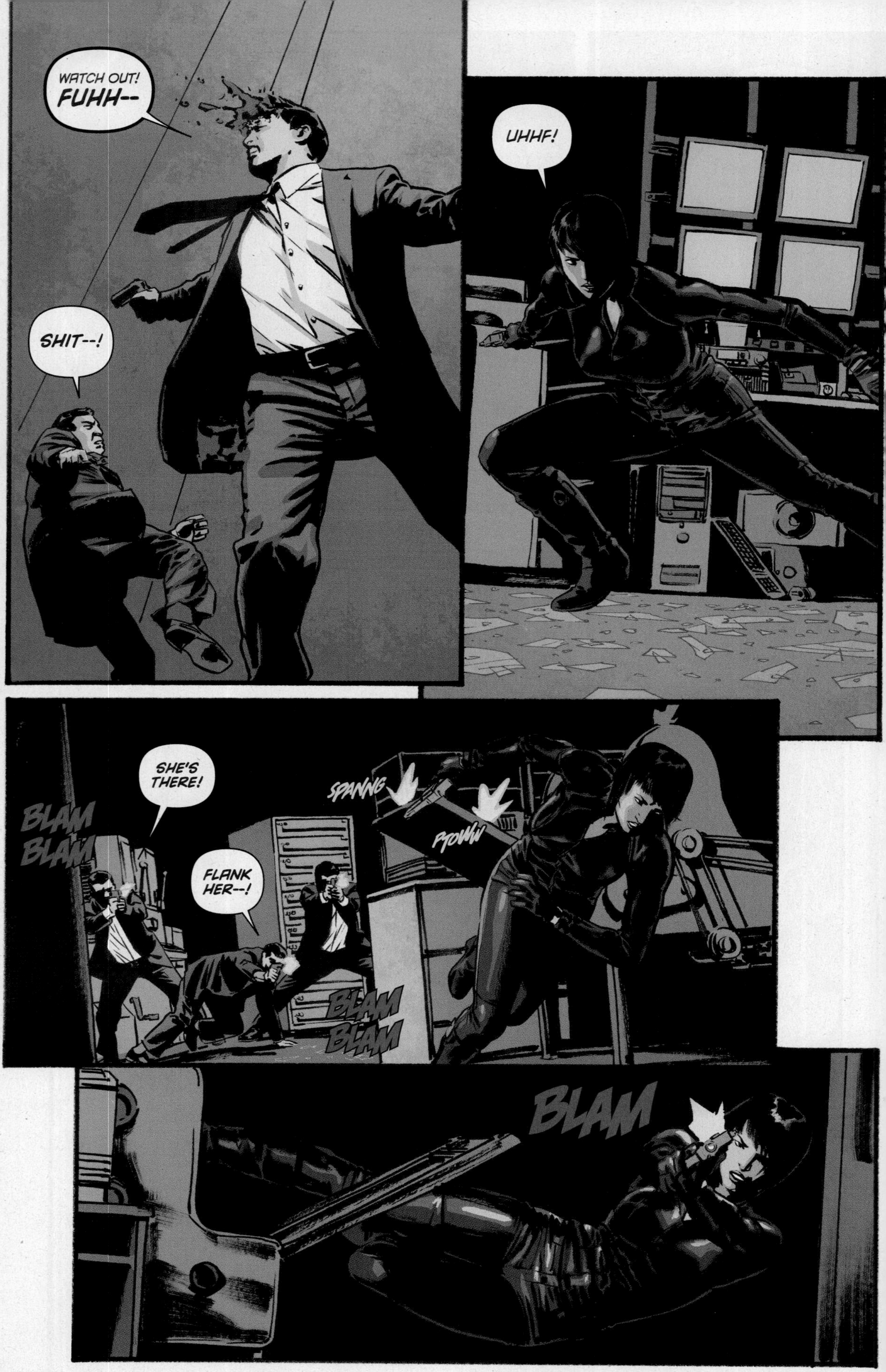
WATCH OUT! FUHH--
SHIT--!
UHHF!
BLAM BLAM
SHE'S THERE!
FLANK HER--!
SPANNG
PTOWW
BLAM BLAM
BLAM

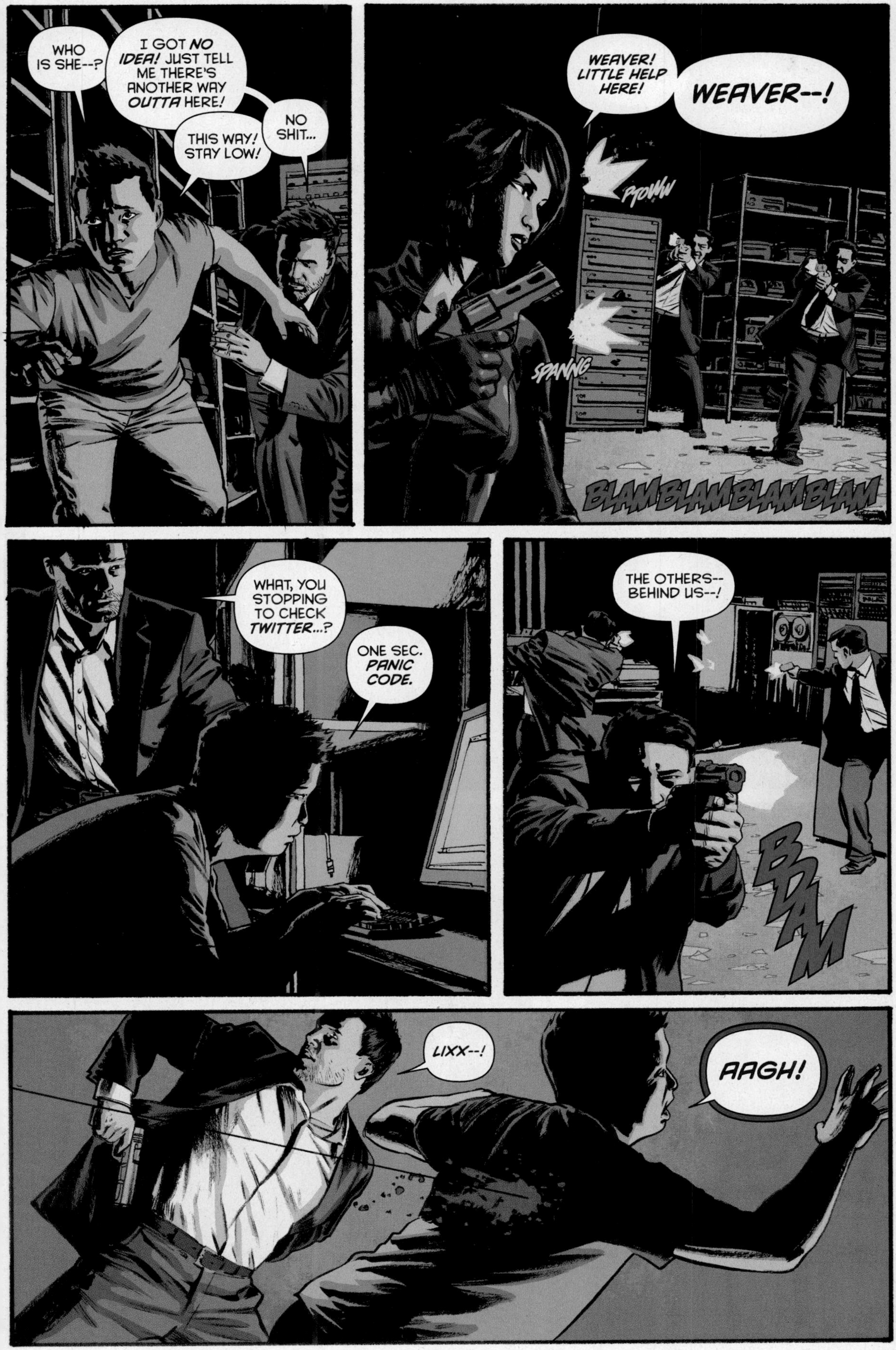
WHO IS SHE--?
I GOT NO IDEA! JUST TELL ME THERE'S ANOTHER WAY OUTTA HERE!
NO SHIT...
THIS WAY! STAY LOW!
WEAVER! LITTLE HELP HERE!
WEAVER--!
PTOWW
SPANNG
BLAMBLAMBLAMBLAM
WHAT, YOU STOPPING TO CHECK TWITTER...?
ONE SEC. PANIC CODE.
THE OTHERS-- BEHIND US--!
BDAM
LIXX--!
AAGH!

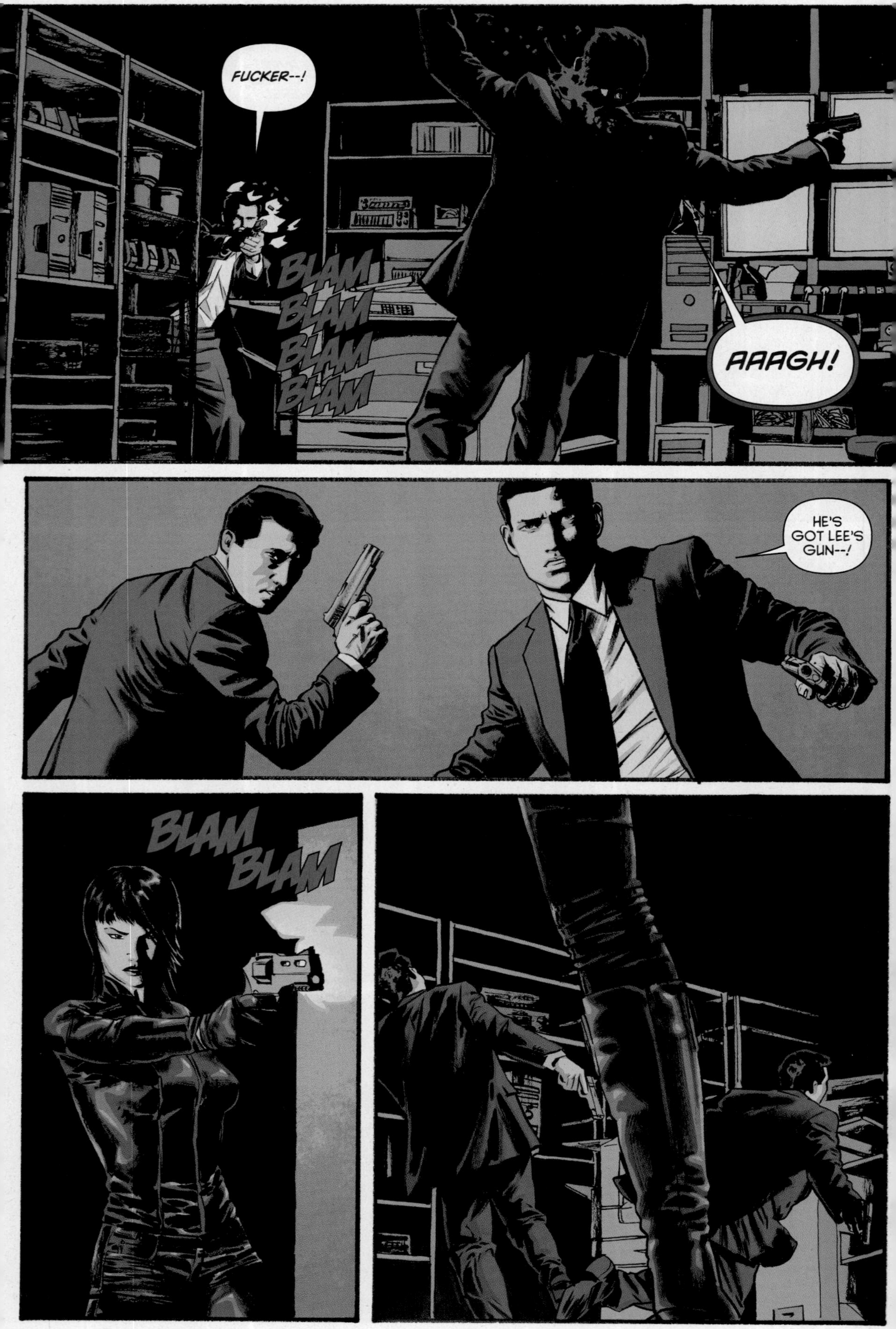
FUCKER--!
BLAM BLAM BLAM BLAM
AAAGH!
HE'S GOT LEE'S GUN--!
BLAM BLAM

Oh JESUS...IT HURTS--!

HANG IN THERE, MAN. WE GOTTA GET OUT OF HERE.

HE'S FUCKED.

C-CAN'T MOVE...MY LEGS--

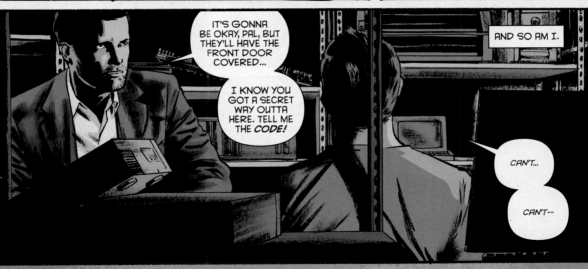

IT'S GONNA BE OKAY, PAL, BUT THEY'LL HAVE THE FRONT DOOR COVERED...

I KNOW YOU GOT A SECRET WAY OUTTA HERE. TELL ME THE CODE!

AND SO AM I.

CAN'T...

CAN'T--

UNLESS...

HERE. TAKE MY HAND.

I CAN HELP.

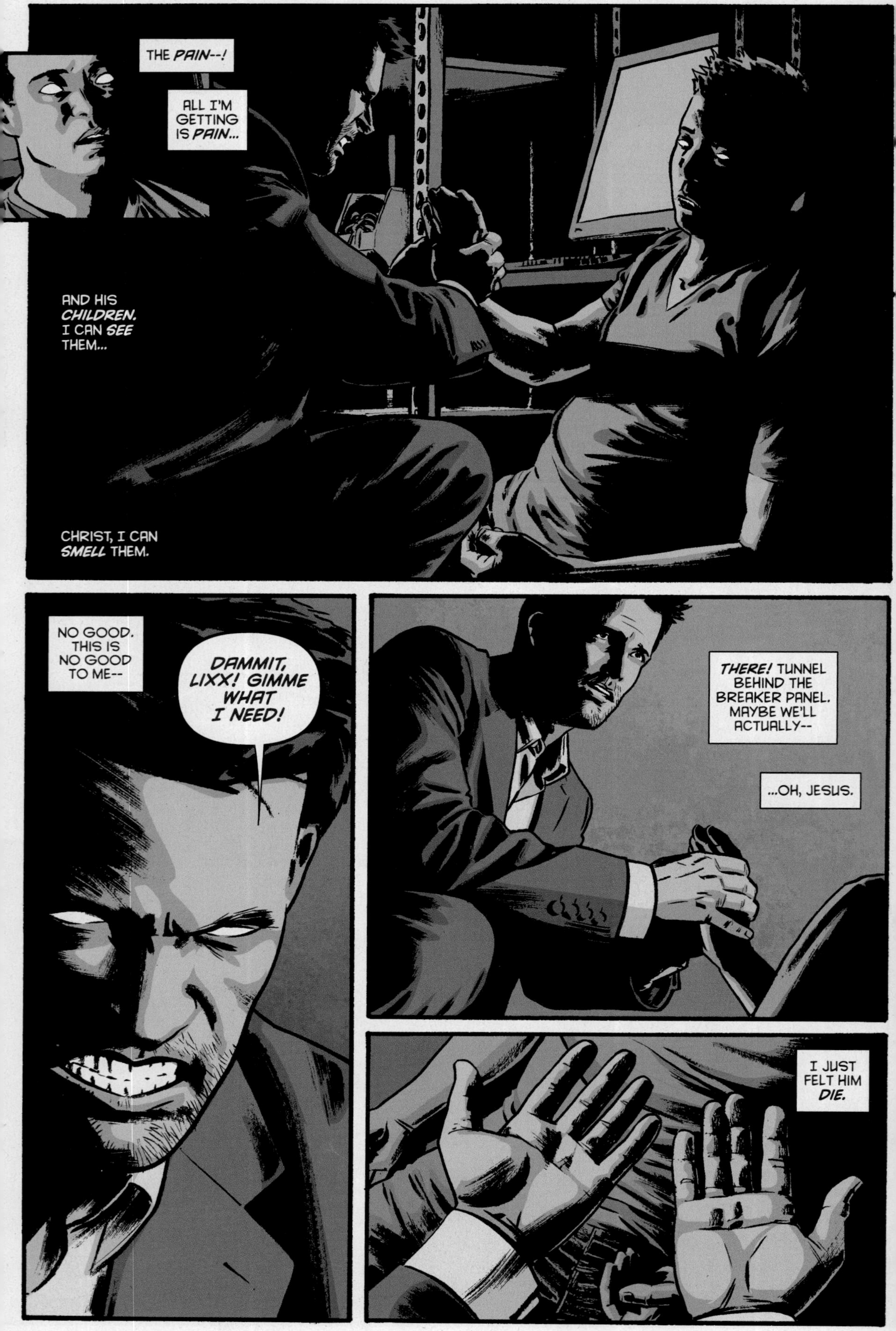

THE PAIN--!
ALL I'M GETTING IS PAIN...
AND HIS CHILDREN. I CAN SEE THEM...
CHRIST, I CAN SMELL THEM.
NO GOOD. THIS IS NO GOOD TO ME--
DAMMIT, LIXX! GIMME WHAT I NEED!
THERE! TUNNEL BEHIND THE BREAKER PANEL. MAYBE WE'LL ACTUALLY--
...OH, JESUS.
I JUST FELT HIM DIE.

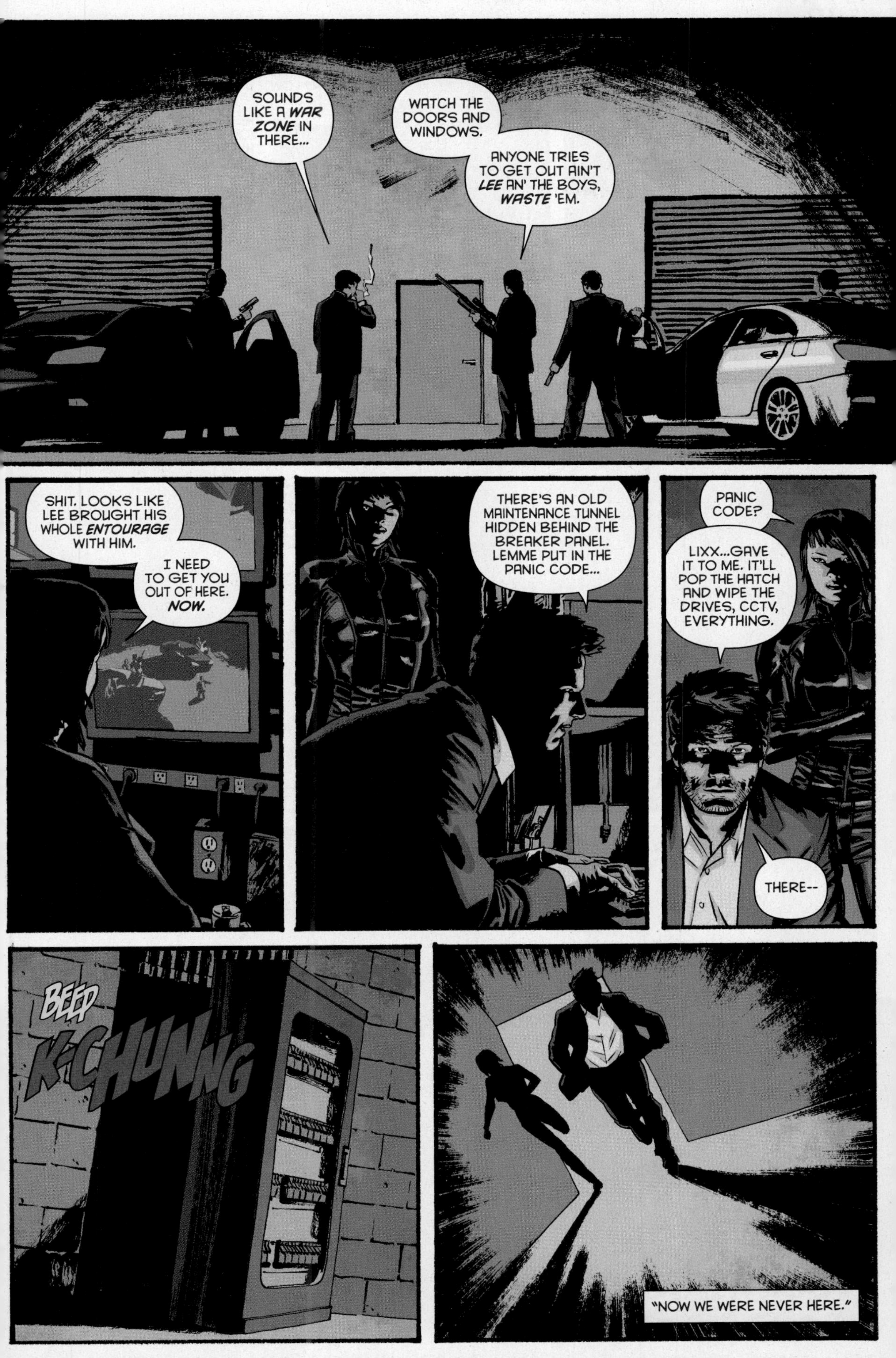
SOUNDS LIKE A *WAR ZONE* IN THERE...
WATCH THE DOORS AND WINDOWS.
ANYONE TRIES TO GET OUT AIN'T *LEE* AN' THE BOYS, *WASTE* 'EM.
SHIT. LOOKS LIKE LEE BROUGHT HIS WHOLE *ENTOURAGE* WITH HIM.
I NEED TO GET YOU OUT OF HERE. *NOW.*
THERE'S AN OLD MAINTENANCE TUNNEL HIDDEN BEHIND THE BREAKER PANEL. LEMME PUT IN THE PANIC CODE...
PANIC CODE?
LIXX...GAVE IT TO ME. IT'LL POP THE HATCH AND WIPE THE DRIVES, CCTV, EVERYTHING.
THERE--
BEEP
K-CHUNNG
"NOW WE WERE NEVER HERE."

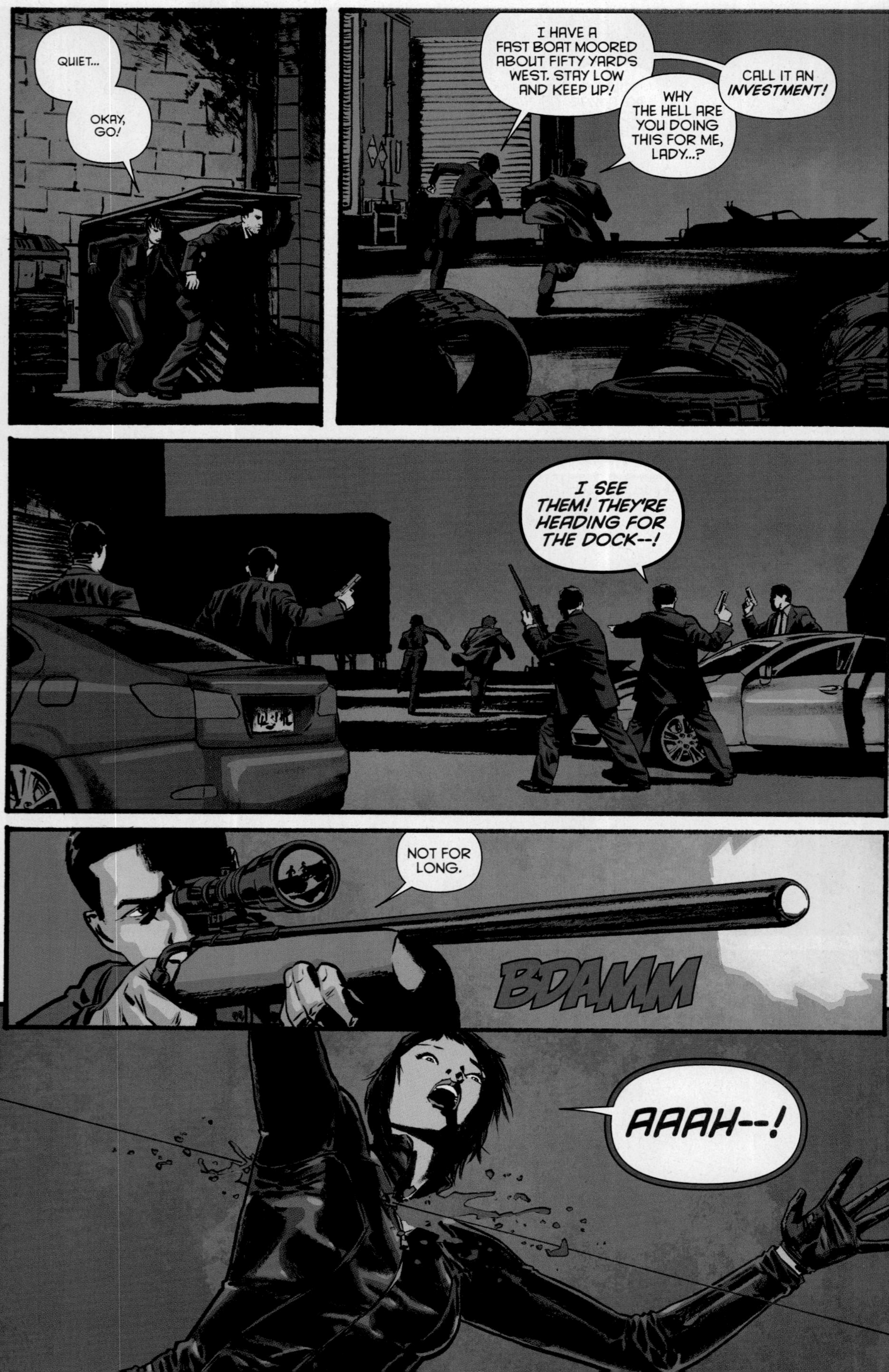
QUIET...
OKAY, GO!
I HAVE A FAST BOAT MOORED ABOUT FIFTY YARDS WEST. STAY LOW AND KEEP UP!
WHY THE HELL ARE YOU DOING THIS FOR ME, LADY...?
CALL IT AN INVESTMENT!
I SEE THEM! THEY'RE HEADING FOR THE DOCK--!
NOT FOR LONG.
BDAMM
AAAH--!

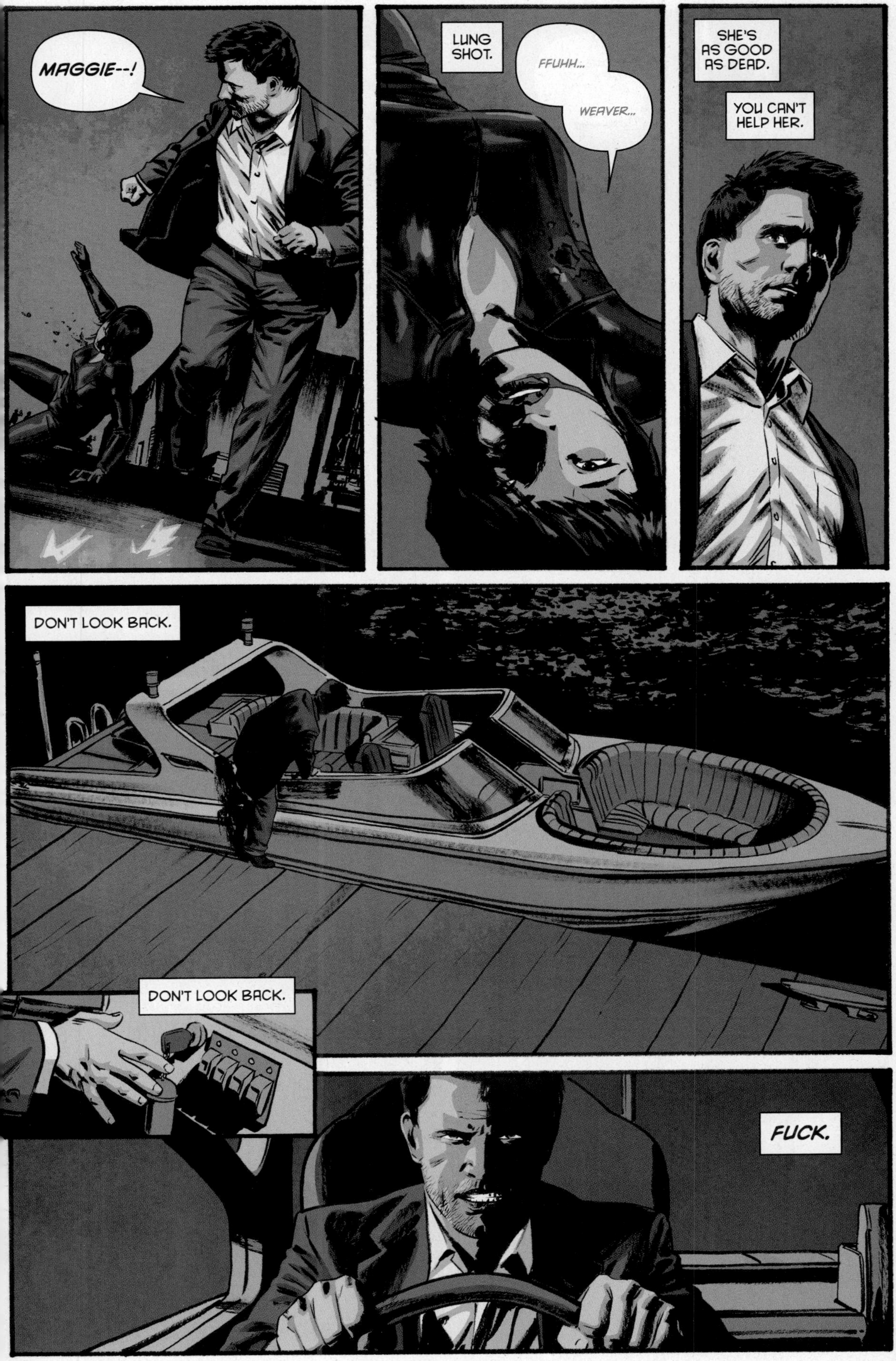
MAGGIE--!
LUNG SHOT.
FFUHH...
WEAVER...
SHE'S AS GOOD AS DEAD.
YOU CAN'T HELP HER.
DON'T LOOK BACK.
DON'T LOOK BACK.
FUCK.

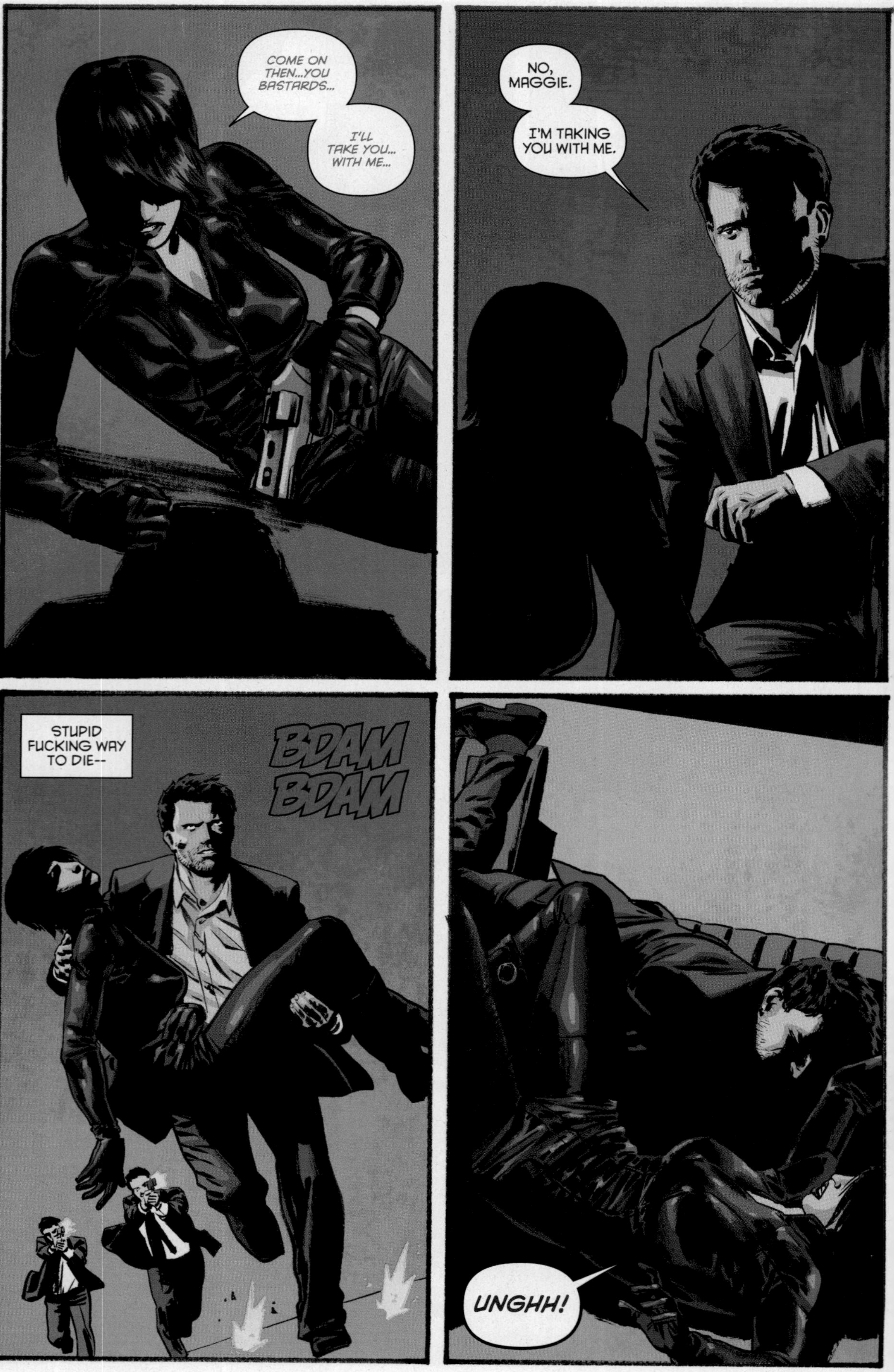
COME ON THEN...YOU BASTARDS...
I'LL TAKE YOU... WITH ME...
NO, MAGGIE.
I'M TAKING YOU WITH ME.
STUPID FUCKING WAY TO DIE--
BDAM BDAM
UNGHH!

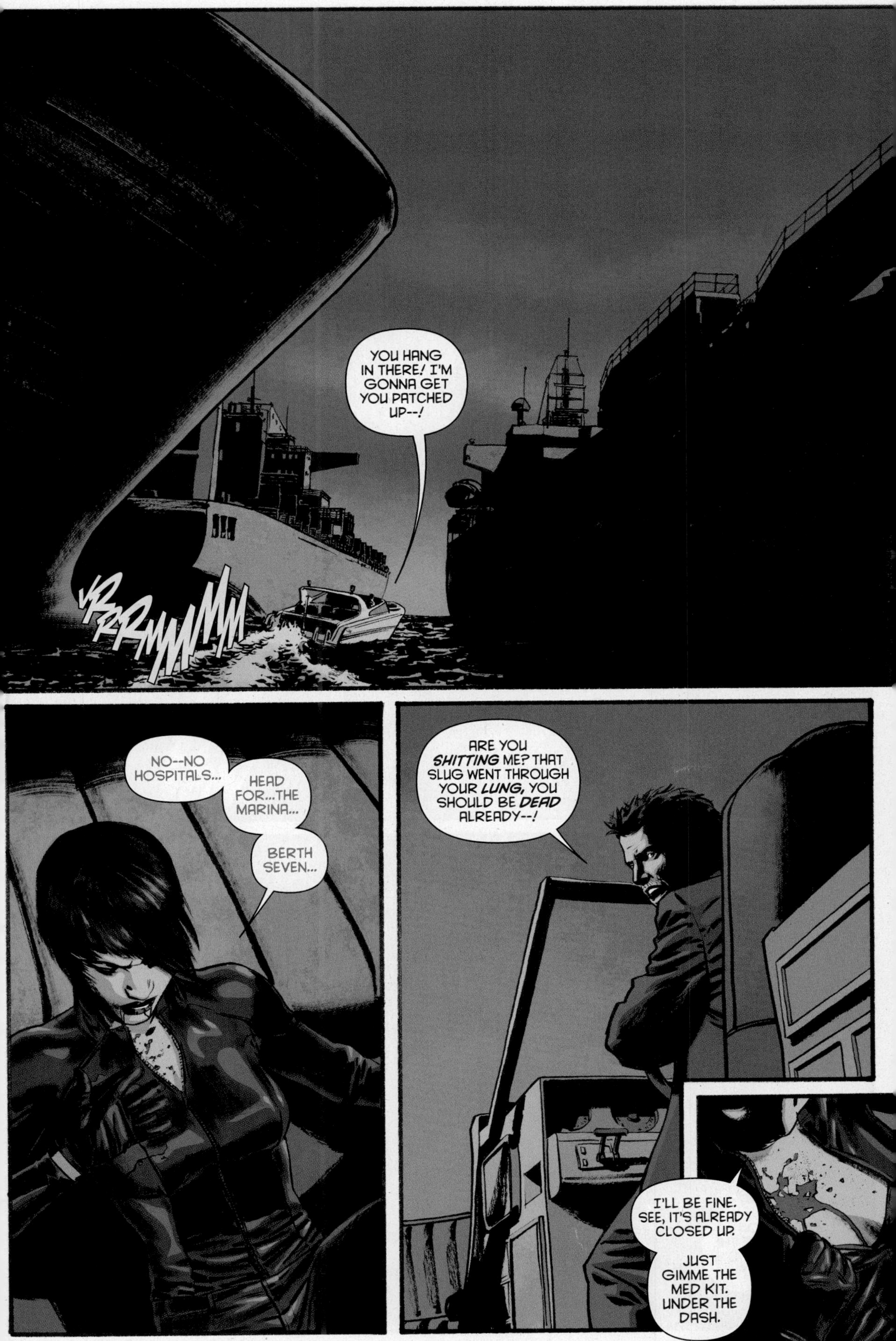
YOU HANG IN THERE! I'M GONNA GET YOU PATCHED UP--!
VRRRMMMMM
NO--NO HOSPITALS...
HEAD FOR...THE MARINA...
BERTH SEVEN...
ARE YOU SHITTING ME? THAT SLUG WENT THROUGH YOUR LUNG, YOU SHOULD BE DEAD ALREADY--!
I'LL BE FINE. SEE, IT'S ALREADY CLOSED UP.
JUST GIMME THE MED KIT. UNDER THE DASH.

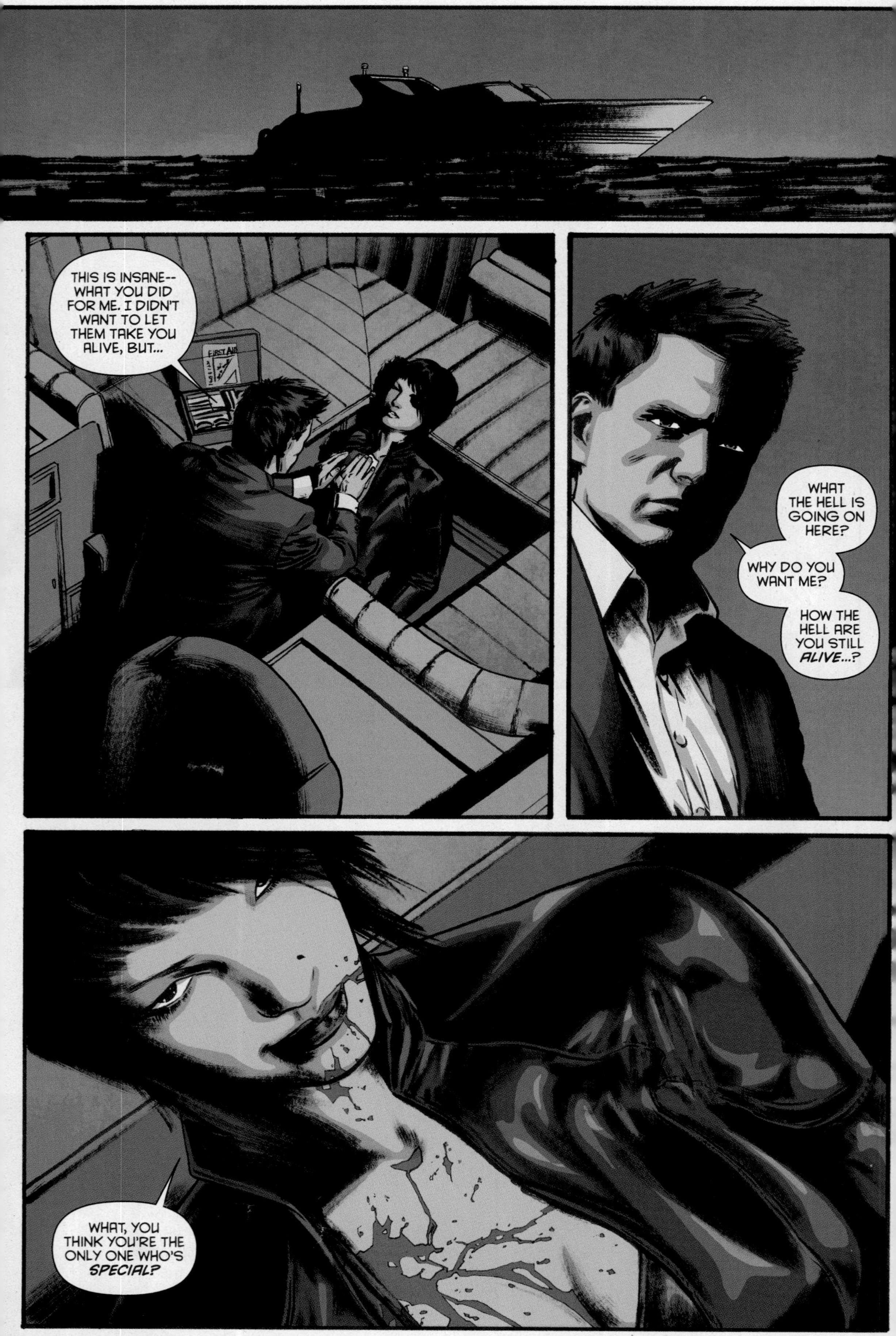
THIS IS INSANE-- WHAT YOU DID FOR ME. I DIDN'T WANT TO LET THEM TAKE YOU ALIVE, BUT...
FIRST AID
WHAT THE HELL IS GOING ON HERE?
WHY DO YOU WANT ME?
HOW THE HELL ARE YOU STILL *ALIVE*...?
WHAT, YOU THINK YOU'RE THE ONLY ONE WHO'S *SPECIAL?*

ISSUE THREE

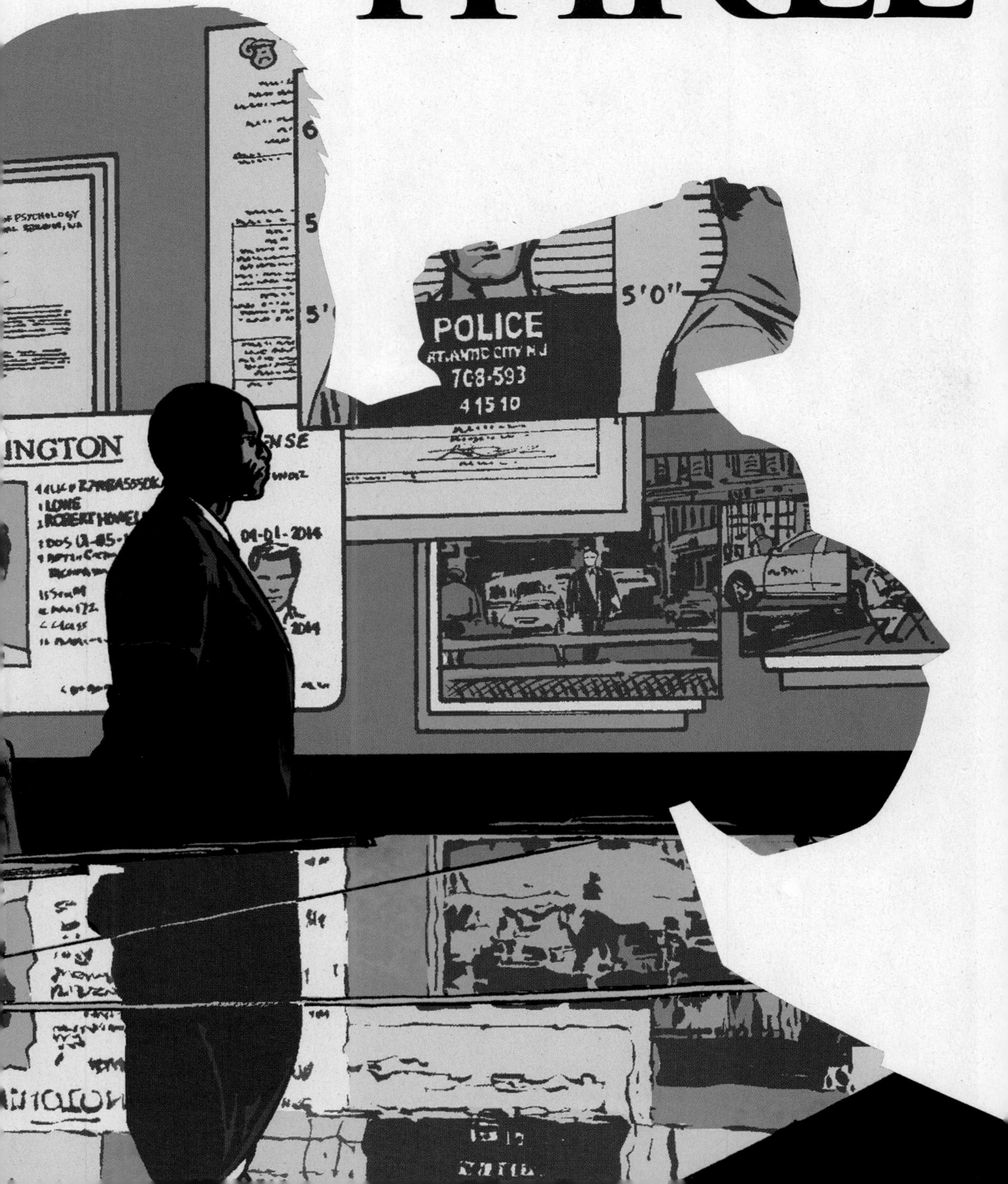
5'0"
POLICE
41510
INGTON

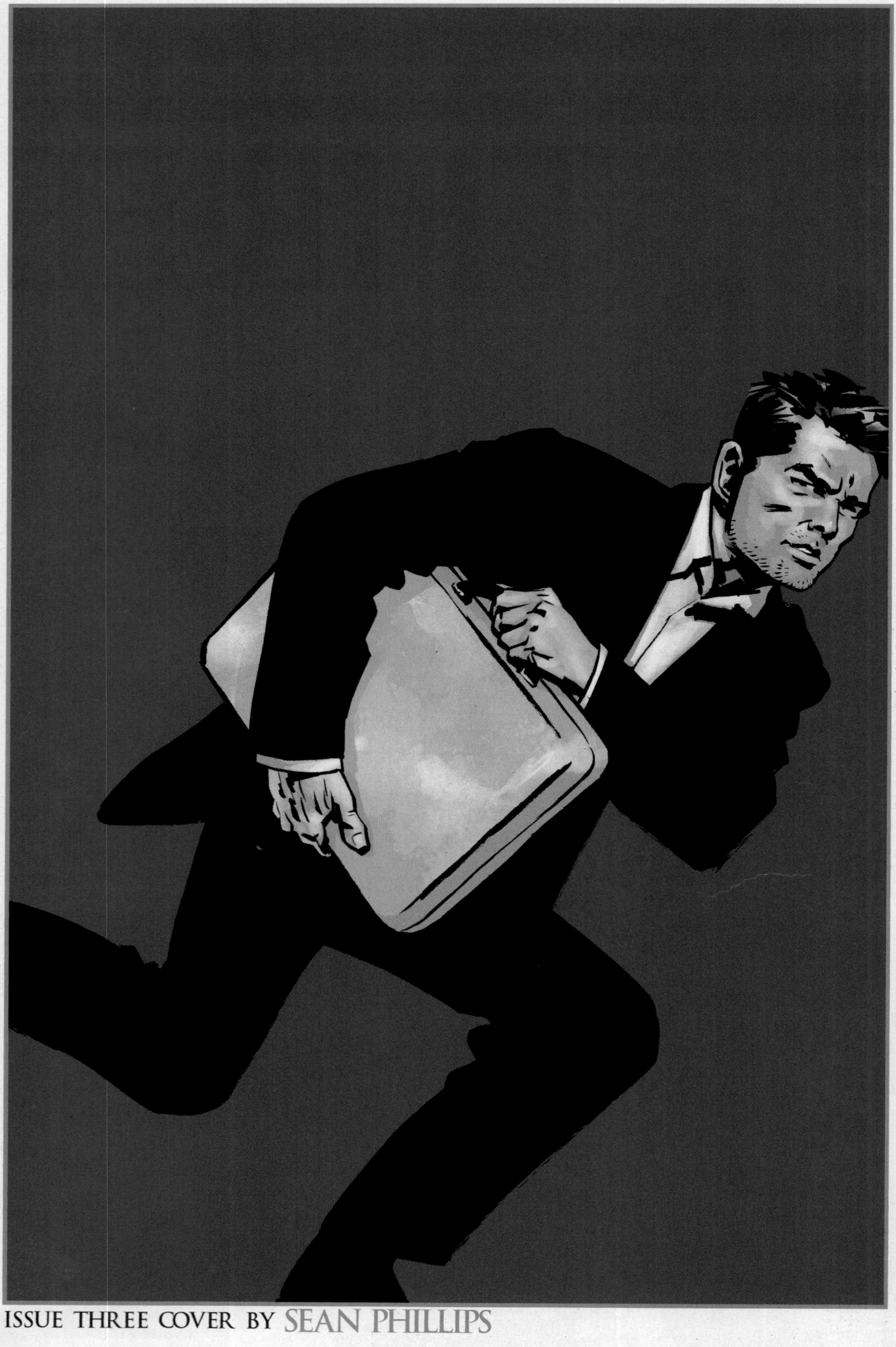

ISSUE THREE COVER BY SEAN PHILLIPS

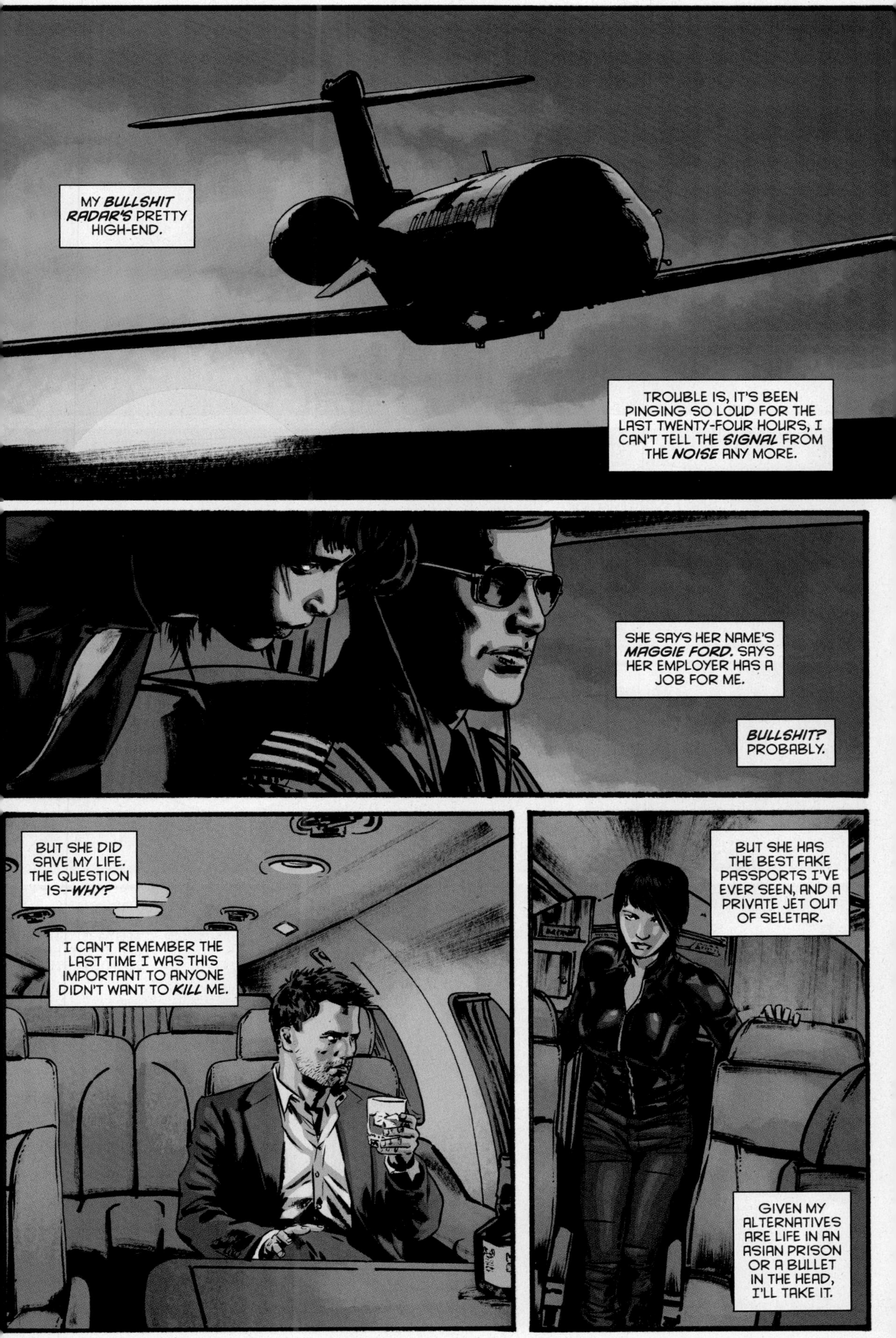
MY BULLSHIT RADAR'S PRETTY HIGH-END.
TROUBLE IS, IT'S BEEN PINGING SO LOUD FOR THE LAST TWENTY-FOUR HOURS, I CAN'T TELL THE SIGNAL FROM THE NOISE ANY MORE.
SHE SAYS HER NAME'S MAGGIE FORD. SAYS HER EMPLOYER HAS A JOB FOR ME.
BULLSHIT? PROBABLY.
BUT SHE DID SAVE MY LIFE. THE QUESTION IS--WHY?
I CAN'T REMEMBER THE LAST TIME I WAS THIS IMPORTANT TO ANYONE DIDN'T WANT TO KILL ME.
BUT SHE HAS THE BEST FAKE PASSPORTS I'VE EVER SEEN, AND A PRIVATE JET OUT OF SELETAR.
GIVEN MY ALTERNATIVES ARE LIFE IN AN ASIAN PRISON OR A BULLET IN THE HEAD, I'LL TAKE IT.

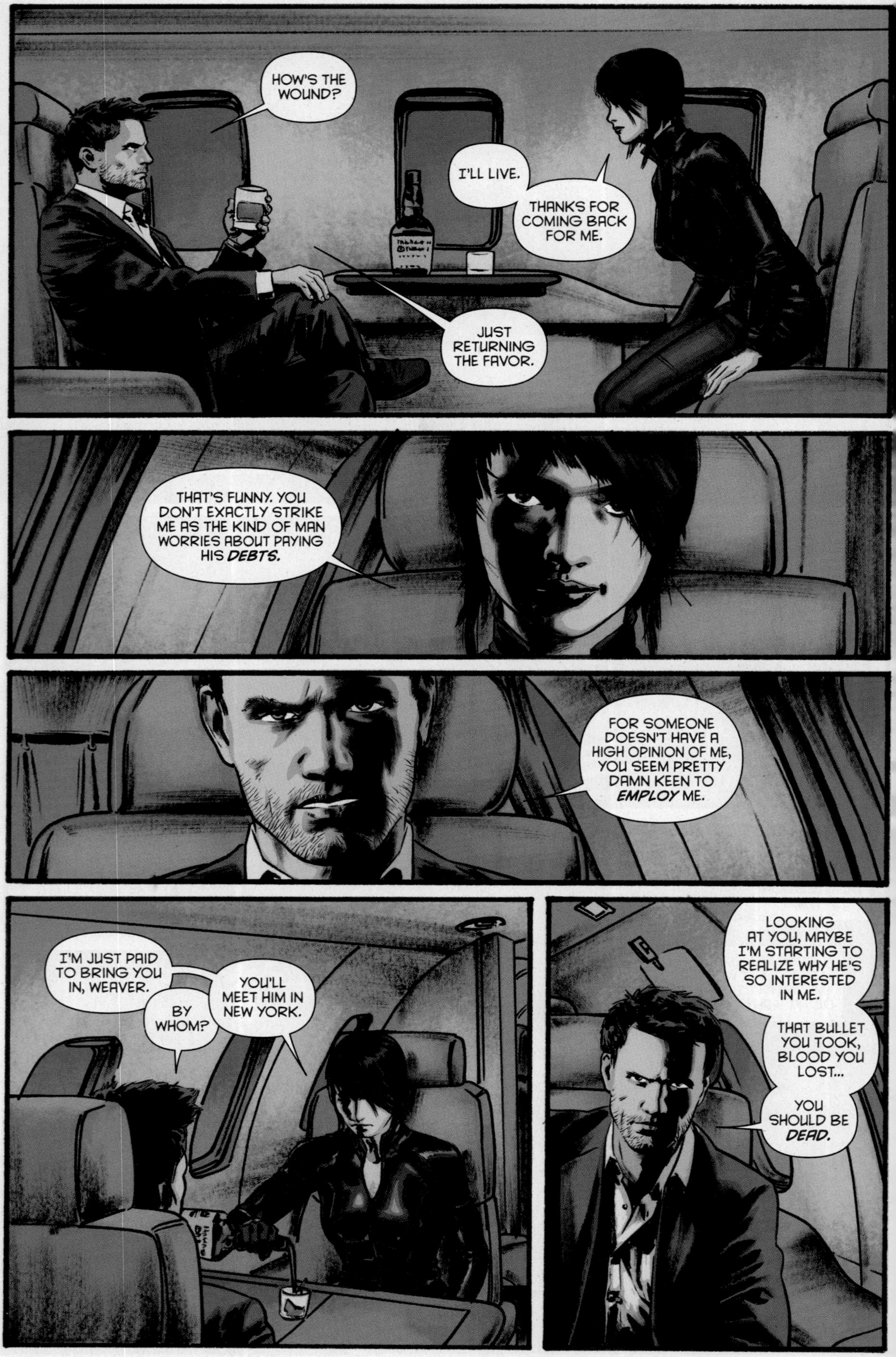
HOW'S THE WOUND?
I'LL LIVE.
THANKS FOR COMING BACK FOR ME.
JUST RETURNING THE FAVOR.
THAT'S FUNNY. YOU DON'T EXACTLY STRIKE ME AS THE KIND OF MAN WORRIES ABOUT PAYING HIS *DEBTS.*
FOR SOMEONE DOESN'T HAVE A HIGH OPINION OF ME, YOU SEEM PRETTY DAMN KEEN TO *EMPLOY* ME.
I'M JUST PAID TO BRING YOU IN, WEAVER.
BY WHOM?
YOU'LL MEET HIM IN NEW YORK.
LOOKING AT YOU, MAYBE I'M STARTING TO REALIZE WHY HE'S SO INTERESTED IN ME.
THAT BULLET YOU TOOK, BLOOD YOU LOST...
YOU SHOULD BE *DEAD.*

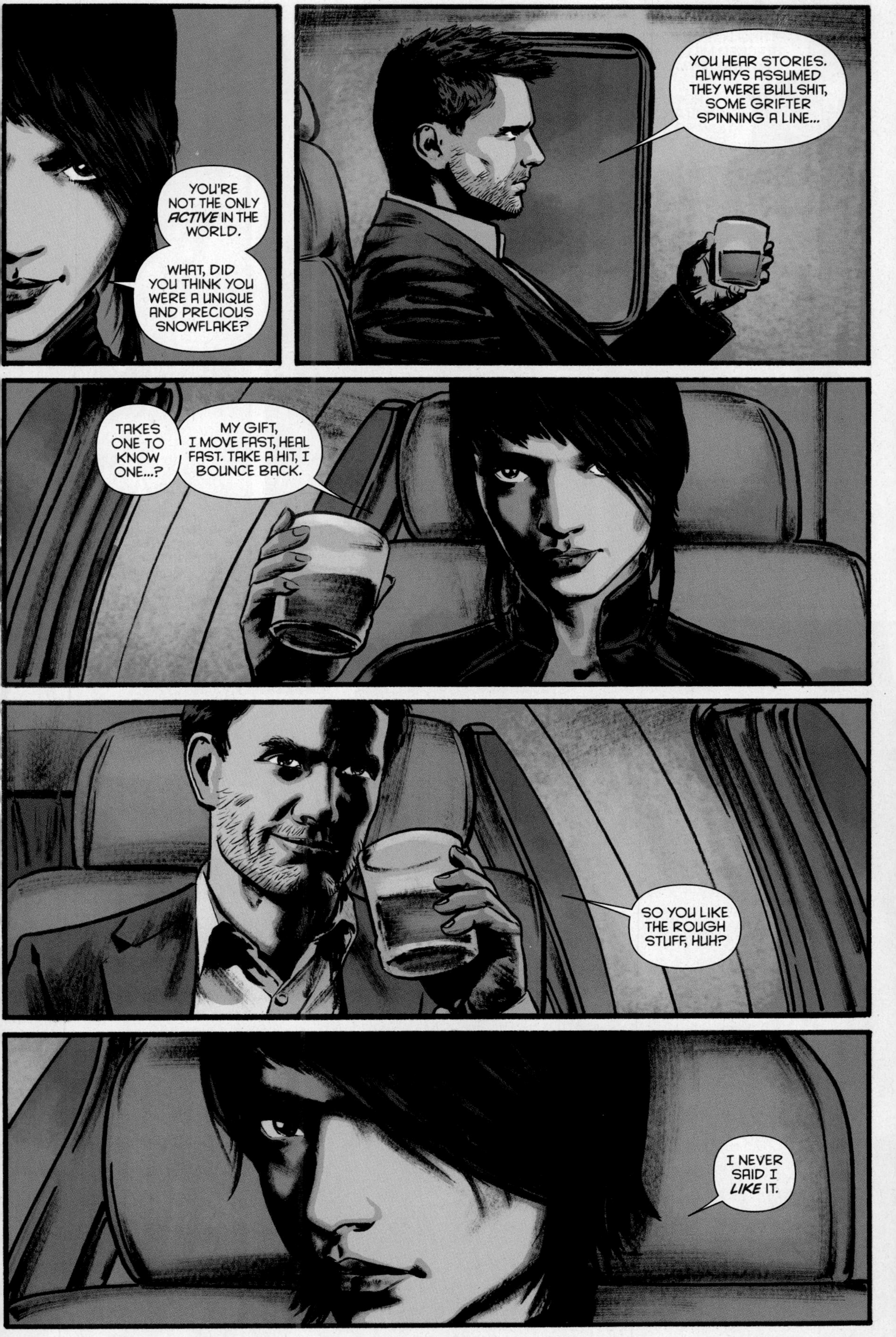

YOU'RE NOT THE ONLY *ACTIVE* IN THE WORLD.
WHAT, DID YOU THINK YOU WERE A UNIQUE AND PRECIOUS SNOWFLAKE?
YOU HEAR STORIES. ALWAYS ASSUMED THEY WERE BULLSHIT, SOME GRIFTER SPINNING A LINE...
TAKES ONE TO KNOW ONE...?
MY GIFT, I MOVE FAST, HEAL FAST. TAKE A HIT, I BOUNCE BACK.
SO YOU LIKE THE ROUGH STUFF, HUH?
I NEVER SAID I *LIKE* IT.

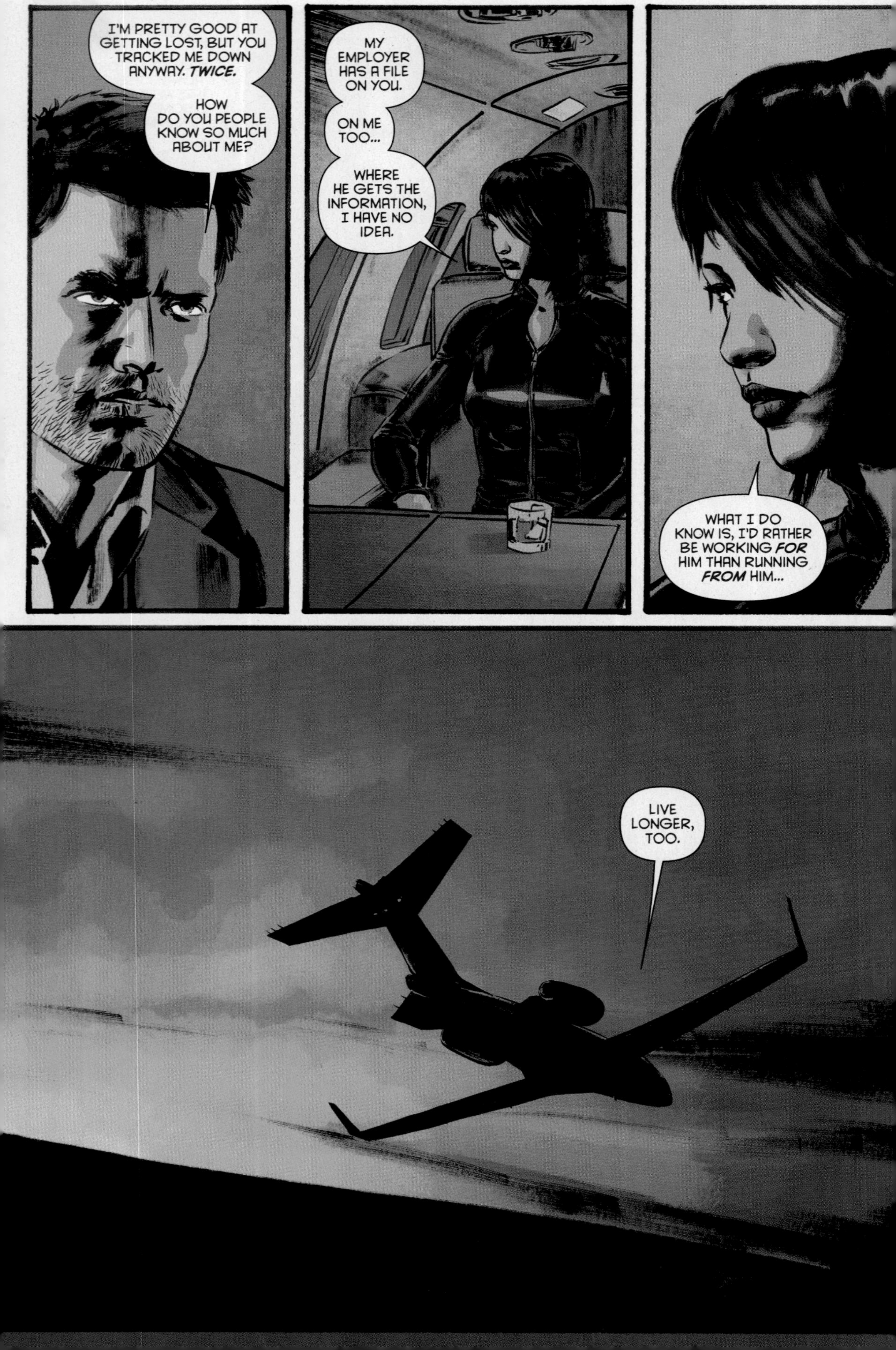
I'M PRETTY GOOD AT GETTING LOST, BUT YOU TRACKED ME DOWN ANYWAY. TWICE.
HOW DO YOU PEOPLE KNOW SO MUCH ABOUT ME?
MY EMPLOYER HAS A FILE ON YOU.
ON ME TOO...
WHERE HE GETS THE INFORMATION, I HAVE NO IDEA.
WHAT I DO KNOW IS, I'D RATHER BE WORKING FOR HIM THAN RUNNING FROM HIM...
LIVE LONGER, TOO.

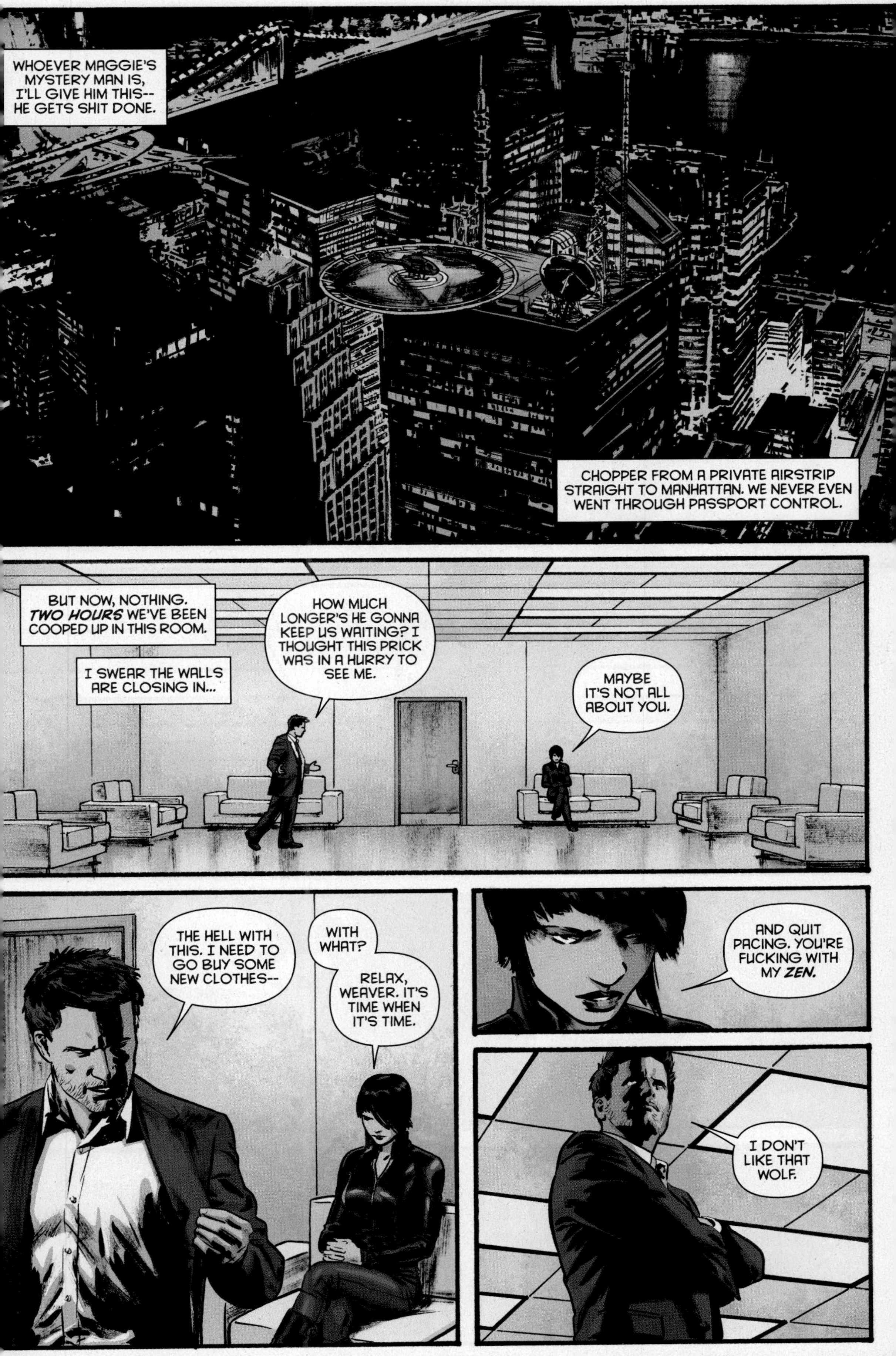
WHOEVER MAGGIE'S MYSTERY MAN IS, I'LL GIVE HIM THIS-- HE GETS SHIT DONE.
CHOPPER FROM A PRIVATE AIRSTRIP STRAIGHT TO MANHATTAN. WE NEVER EVEN WENT THROUGH PASSPORT CONTROL.
BUT NOW, NOTHING. *TWO HOURS* WE'VE BEEN COOPED UP IN THIS ROOM.
I SWEAR THE WALLS ARE CLOSING IN...
HOW MUCH LONGER'S HE GONNA KEEP US WAITING? I THOUGHT THIS PRICK WAS IN A HURRY TO SEE ME.
MAYBE IT'S NOT ALL ABOUT YOU.
THE HELL WITH THIS. I NEED TO GO BUY SOME NEW CLOTHES--
WITH WHAT?
RELAX, WEAVER. IT'S TIME WHEN IT'S TIME.
AND QUIT PACING. YOU'RE FUCKING WITH MY *ZEN.*
I DON'T LIKE THAT WOLF.

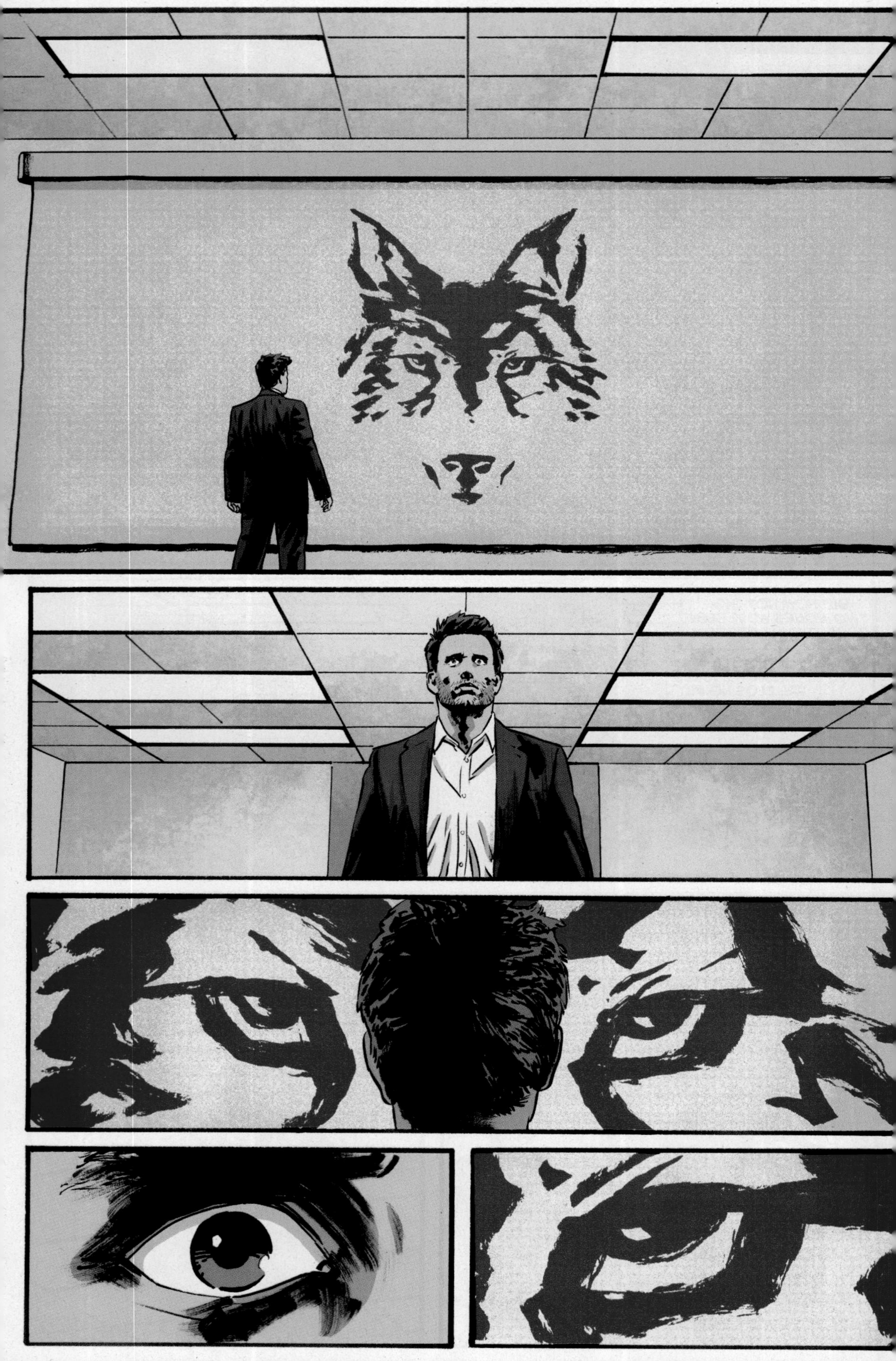

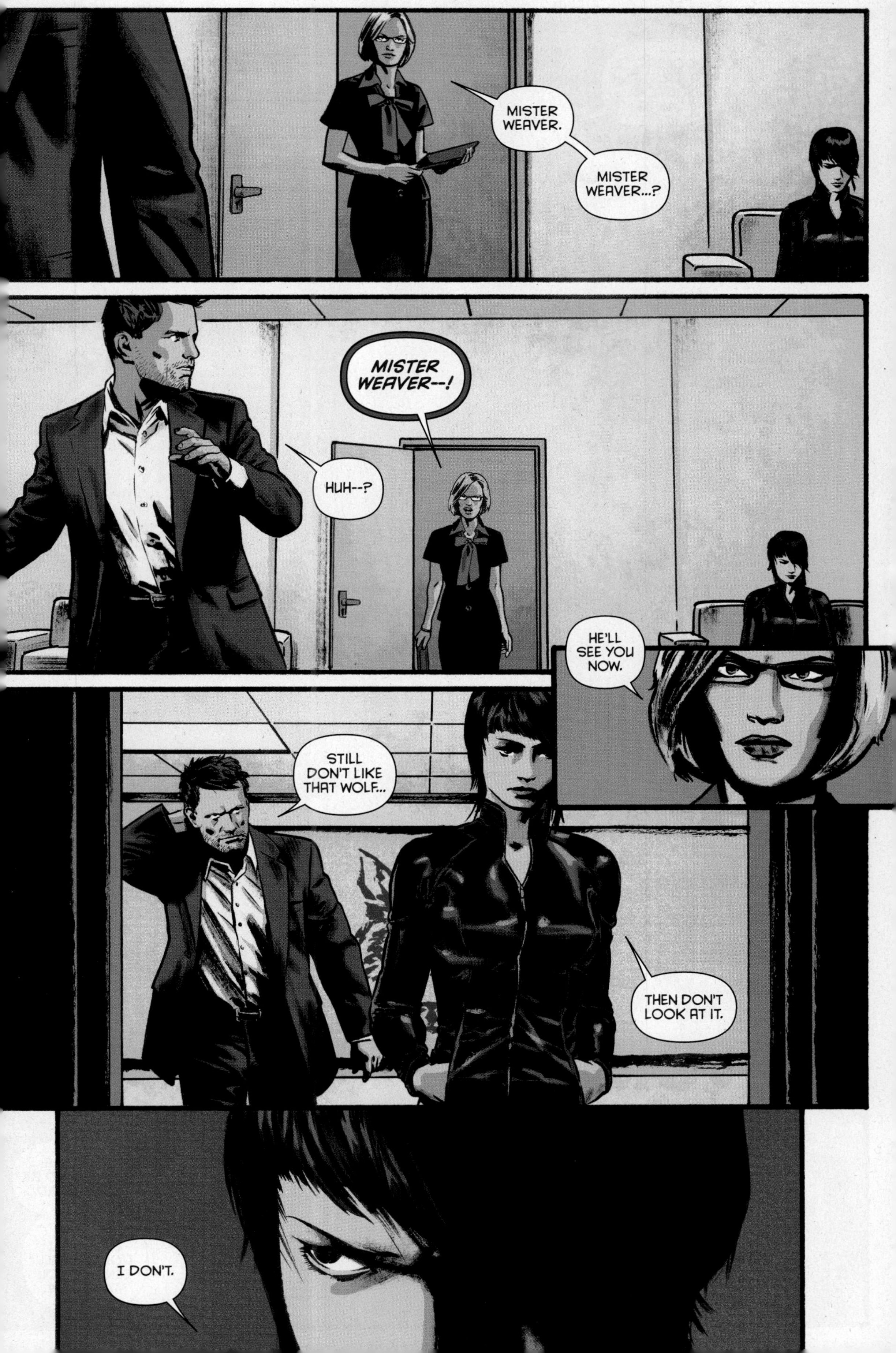
MISTER WEAVER.
MISTER WEAVER...?
MISTER WEAVER--!
HUH--?
HE'LL SEE YOU NOW.
STILL DON'T LIKE THAT WOLF...
THEN DON'T LOOK AT IT.
I DON'T.

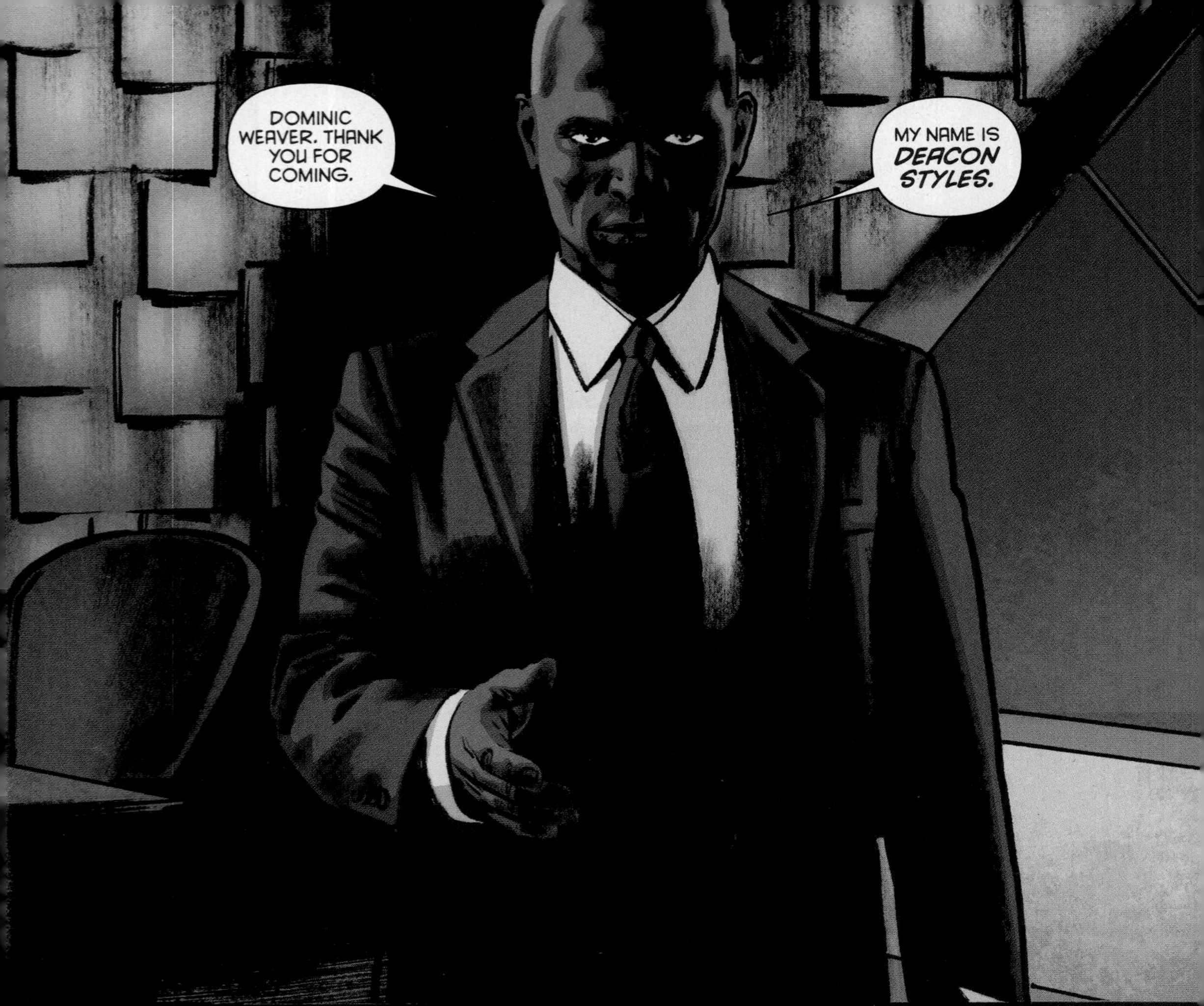
DOMINIC WEAVER. THANK YOU FOR COMING.
MY NAME IS *DEACON STYLES.*

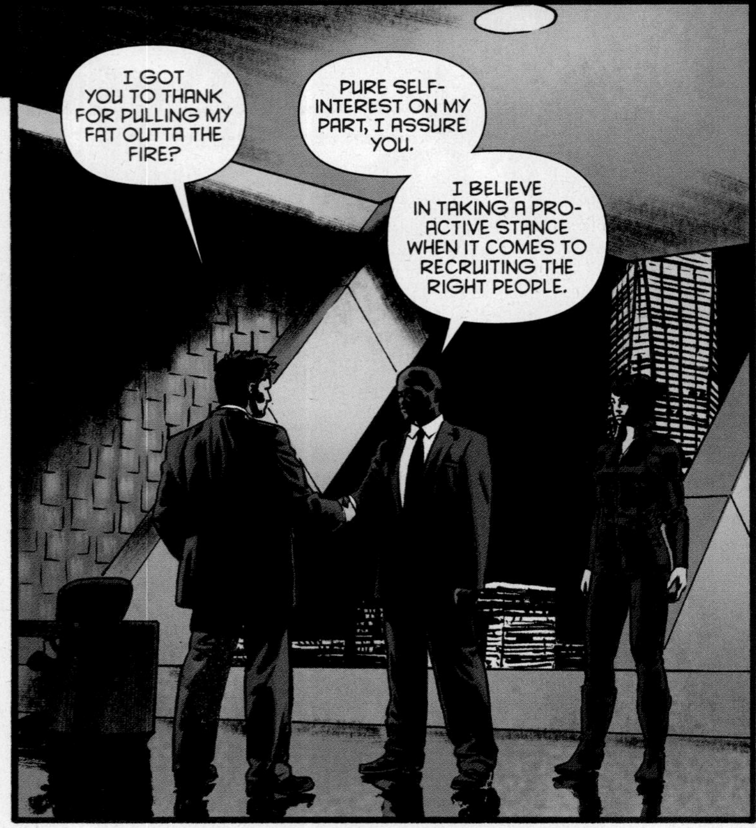
I GOT YOU TO THANK FOR PULLING MY FAT OUTTA THE FIRE?
PURE SELF-INTEREST ON MY PART, I ASSURE YOU.
I BELIEVE IN TAKING A PRO-ACTIVE STANCE WHEN IT COMES TO RECRUITING THE RIGHT PEOPLE.

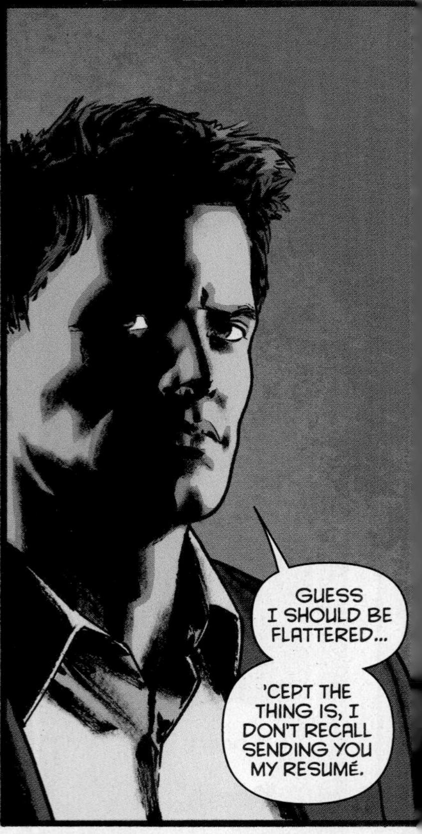
GUESS I SHOULD BE FLATTERED...
'CEPT THE THING IS, I DON'T RECALL SENDING YOU MY RESUMÉ.

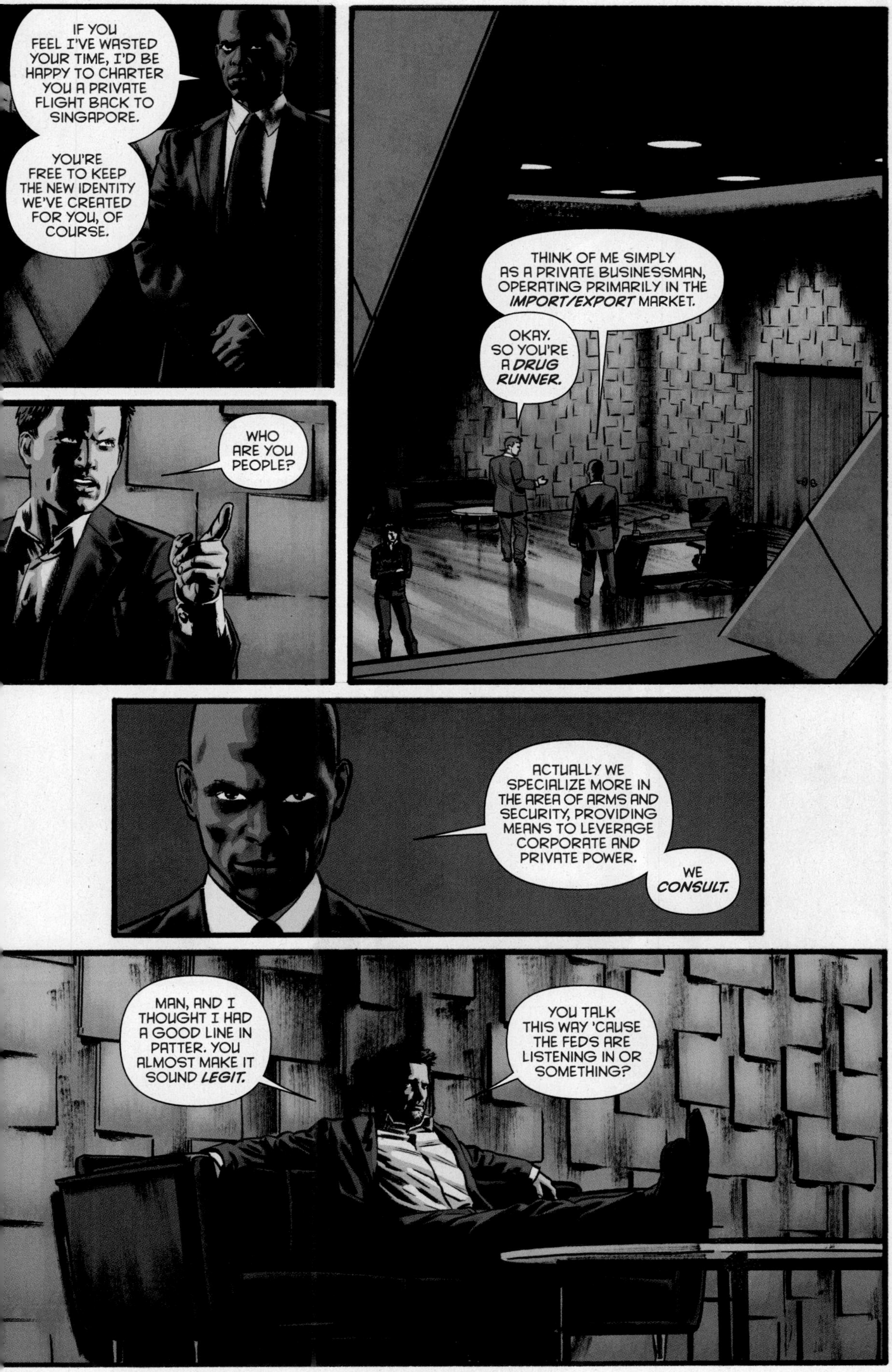
IF YOU FEEL I'VE WASTED YOUR TIME, I'D BE HAPPY TO CHARTER YOU A PRIVATE FLIGHT BACK TO SINGAPORE.
YOU'RE FREE TO KEEP THE NEW IDENTITY WE'VE CREATED FOR YOU, OF COURSE.
WHO ARE YOU PEOPLE?
THINK OF ME SIMPLY AS A PRIVATE BUSINESSMAN, OPERATING PRIMARILY IN THE IMPORT/EXPORT MARKET.
OKAY. SO YOU'RE A DRUG RUNNER.
ACTUALLY WE SPECIALIZE MORE IN THE AREA OF ARMS AND SECURITY, PROVIDING MEANS TO LEVERAGE CORPORATE AND PRIVATE POWER.
WE CONSULT.
MAN, AND I THOUGHT I HAD A GOOD LINE IN PATTER. YOU ALMOST MAKE IT SOUND LEGIT.
YOU TALK THIS WAY 'CAUSE THE FEDS ARE LISTENING IN OR SOMETHING?

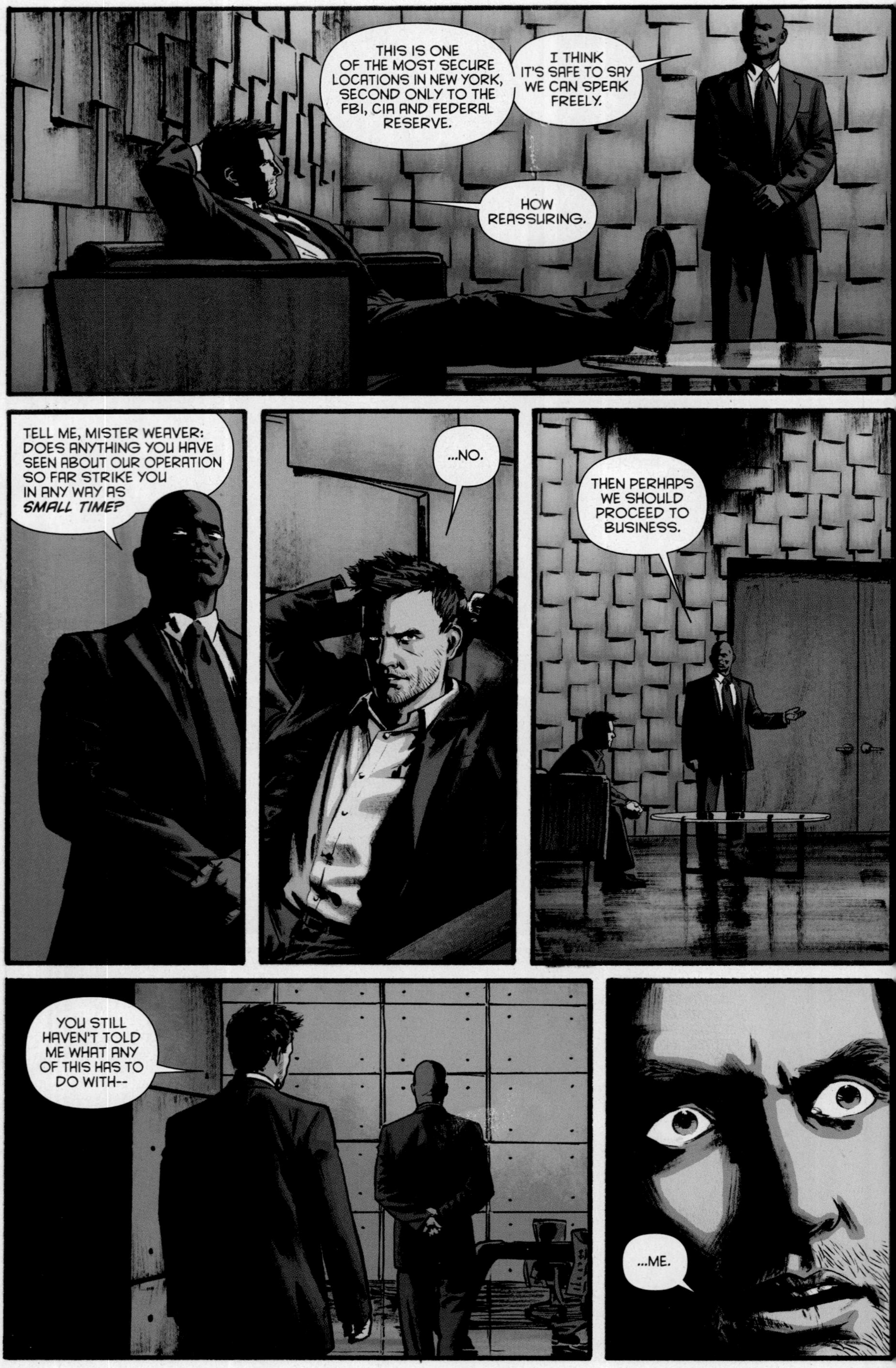
THIS IS ONE OF THE MOST SECURE LOCATIONS IN NEW YORK, SECOND ONLY TO THE FBI, CIA AND FEDERAL RESERVE.
I THINK IT'S SAFE TO SAY WE CAN SPEAK FREELY.
HOW REASSURING.
TELL ME, MISTER WEAVER: DOES ANYTHING YOU HAVE SEEN ABOUT OUR OPERATION SO FAR STRIKE YOU IN ANY WAY AS *SMALL TIME?*
...NO.
THEN PERHAPS WE SHOULD PROCEED TO BUSINESS.
YOU STILL HAVEN'T TOLD ME WHAT ANY OF THIS HAS TO DO WITH--
...ME.

IT HAS *EVERYTHING* TO DO WITH YOU.

NOT YOUR DOMINIC WEAVER IDENTITY, NOR THE ONE WE'VE JUST FURNISHED YOU WITH.

THE *REAL* YOU.

HOW DID YOU...?

YOU WERE BORN *ROBERT HOWELL LOWE* ON JANUARY 5th, 1975.

YOUR MOTHER, *ANNE HOWELL*, DIED GIVING BIRTH.

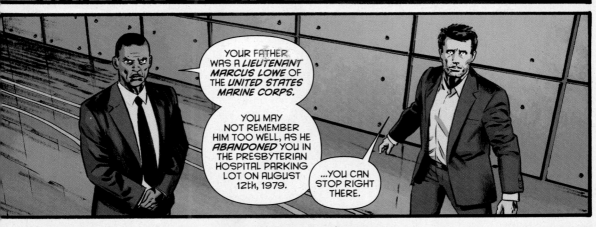

YOUR FATHER WAS A *LIEUTENANT MARCUS LOWE* OF THE *UNITED STATES MARINE CORPS.*

YOU MAY NOT REMEMBER HIM TOO WELL, AS HE *ABANDONED* YOU IN THE PRESBYTERIAN HOSPITAL PARKING LOT ON AUGUST 12th, 1979.

...YOU CAN STOP RIGHT THERE.

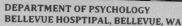
DEPARTMENT OF PSYCHOLOGY
BELLEVUE HOSPTIPAL, BELLEVUE, WA

Psychiatric Evaluation Form

Patient Name   Robert Howell Lowe

Patient Age   17

Observed Disorders   Borderline personality disorder
                      Acute stress disorder
                      Anxiety disorder
                      Schizophrenia
                      Shared psychotic disorder
                      Spontaneous unassociated "Delirium tremens"
                      Hallucinogen persisting perception disorder
                      Bouts of Depersonalization disorder
                      Cotard delusion
                      Fugue states
                      Narcissistic personality disorder
                      Panic disorder
                      Nightmare disorder

YOU WERE RAISED IN A SUCCESSION OF STATE FACILITIES, AFTER WHICH YOU SPENT THREE YEARS IN THE *BELLEVUE PSYCHIATRIC WING*--

ENOUGH!

WHY DON'T YOU TELL ME WHAT THE *FUCK* IT IS YOU *WANT* FROM ME?

I WANT TO KNOW WHY YOU'RE AN *ACTIVE*.

AND SO DO YOU.

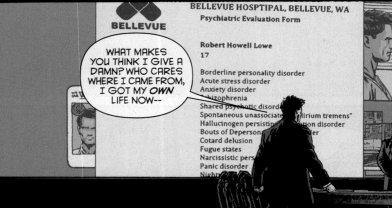

WHAT MAKES YOU THINK I GIVE A DAMN? WHO CARES WHERE I CAME FROM, I GOT MY *OWN* LIFE NOW--

BELLEVUE HOSPTIPAL, BELLEVUE, WA
Psychiatric Evaluation Form

Robert Howell Lowe
17

Borderline personality disorder
Acute stress disorder
Anxiety disorder
Schizophrenia
Shared psychotic disord
Spontaneous unassociate "Delirium tremens"
Hallucinogen persisti... tion disorder
Bouts of Depersona...
Cotard delusion
Fugue states
Narcissistic pers
Panic disorder
Night...

NO YOU DON'T. BUT THAT'S WHAT I'M OFFERING YOU.

A *LIFE*.

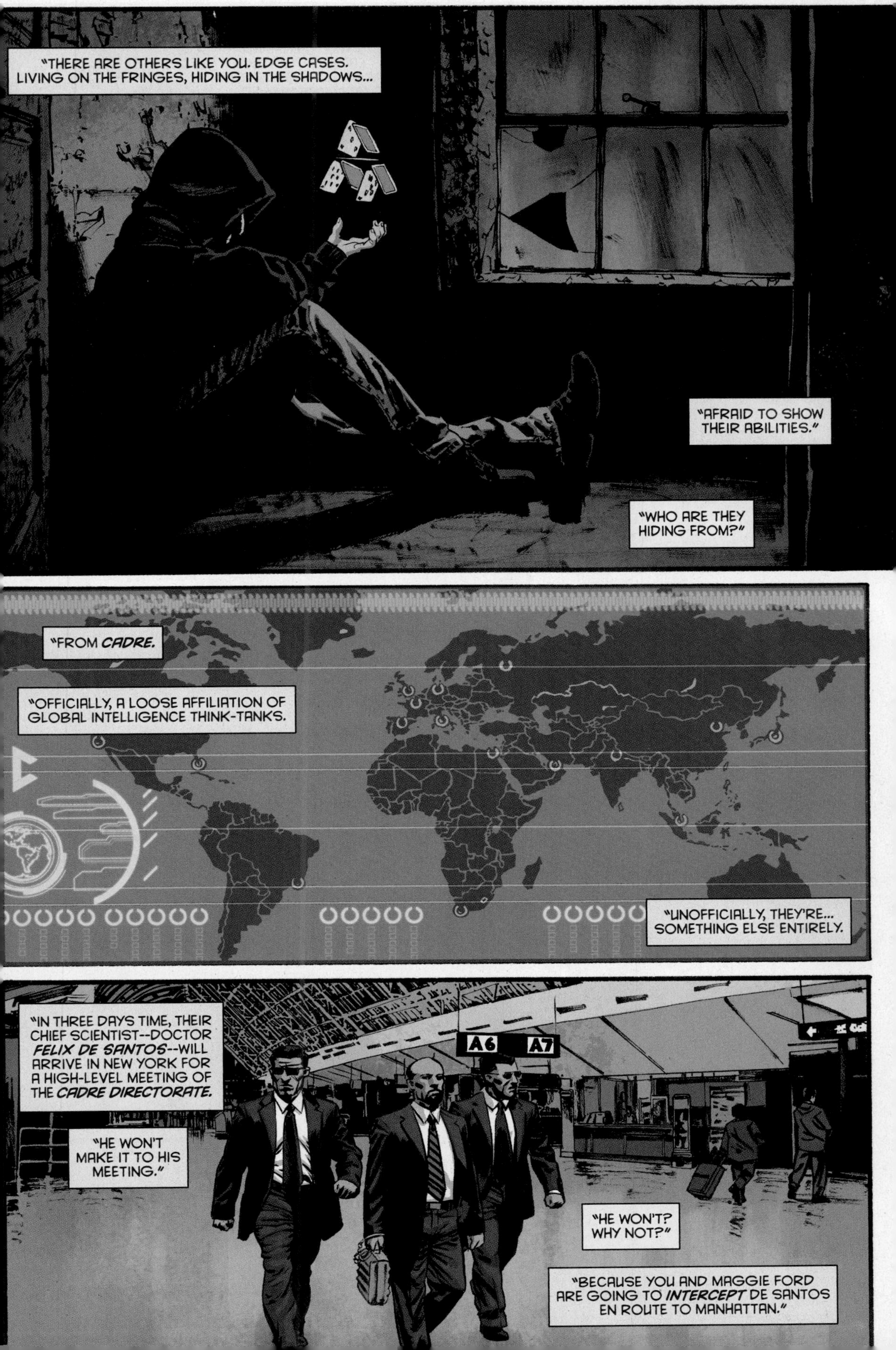
"THERE ARE OTHERS LIKE YOU. EDGE CASES. LIVING ON THE FRINGES, HIDING IN THE SHADOWS...
"AFRAID TO SHOW THEIR ABILITIES."
"WHO ARE THEY HIDING FROM?"
"FROM *CADRE*.
"OFFICIALLY, A LOOSE AFFILIATION OF GLOBAL INTELLIGENCE THINK-TANKS.
"UNOFFICIALLY, THEY'RE... SOMETHING ELSE ENTIRELY.
"IN THREE DAYS TIME, THEIR CHIEF SCIENTIST--DOCTOR ***FELIX DE SANTOS***--WILL ARRIVE IN NEW YORK FOR A HIGH-LEVEL MEETING OF THE ***CADRE DIRECTORATE***.
A6
A7
"HE WON'T MAKE IT TO HIS MEETING."
"HE WON'T? WHY NOT?"
"BECAUSE YOU AND MAGGIE FORD ARE GOING TO *INTERCEPT* DE SANTOS EN ROUTE TO MANHATTAN."

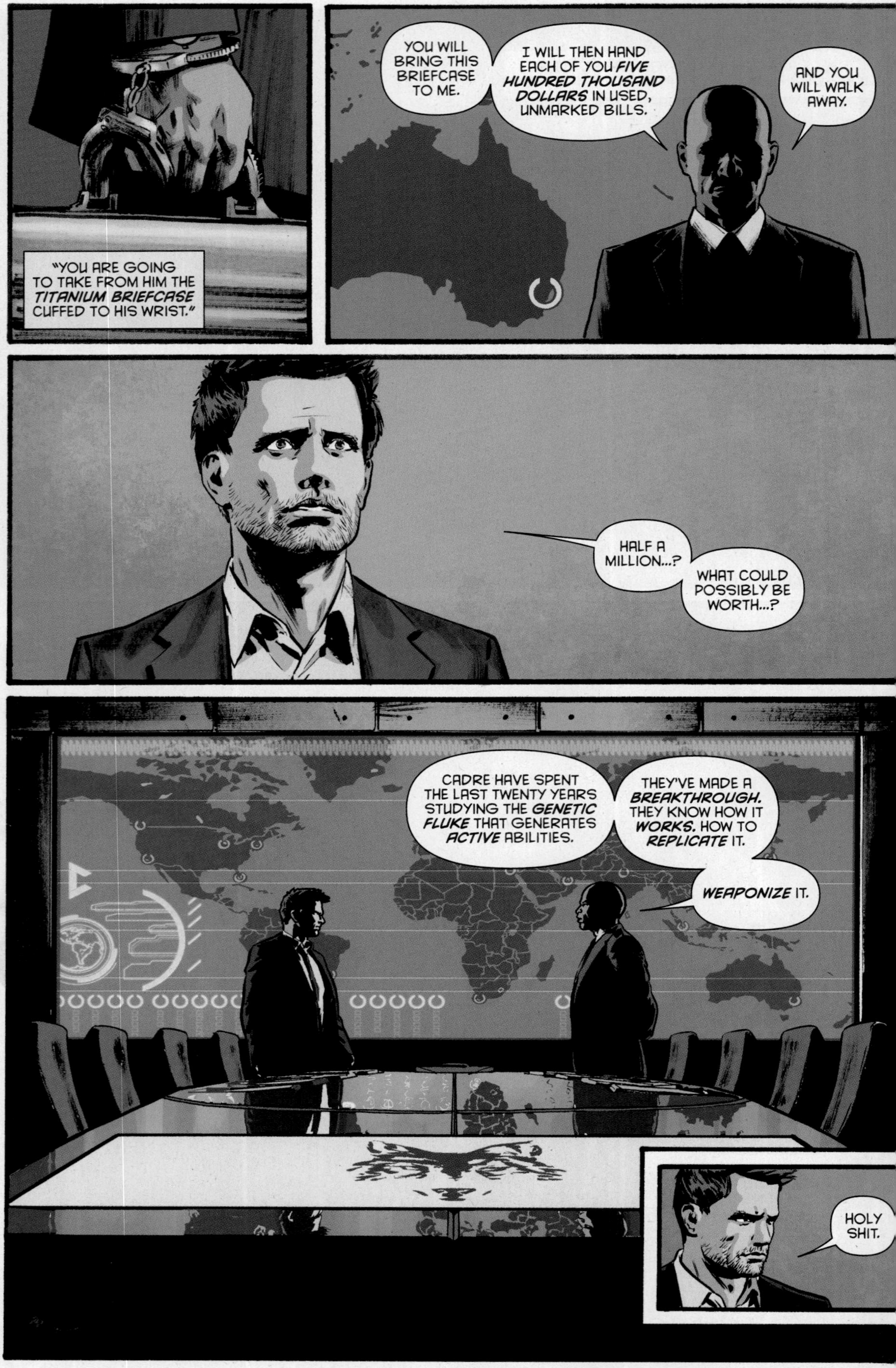
"YOU ARE GOING TO TAKE FROM HIM THE *TITANIUM BRIEFCASE* CUFFED TO HIS WRIST."
YOU WILL BRING THIS BRIEFCASE TO ME.
I WILL THEN HAND EACH OF YOU *FIVE HUNDRED THOUSAND DOLLARS* IN USED, UNMARKED BILLS.
AND YOU WILL WALK AWAY.
HALF A MILLION...?
WHAT COULD POSSIBLY BE WORTH...?
CADRE HAVE SPENT THE LAST TWENTY YEARS STUDYING THE *GENETIC FLUKE* THAT GENERATES *ACTIVE* ABILITIES.
THEY'VE MADE A *BREAKTHROUGH.* THEY KNOW HOW IT *WORKS.* HOW TO *REPLICATE* IT.
WEAPONIZE IT.
HOLY SHIT.

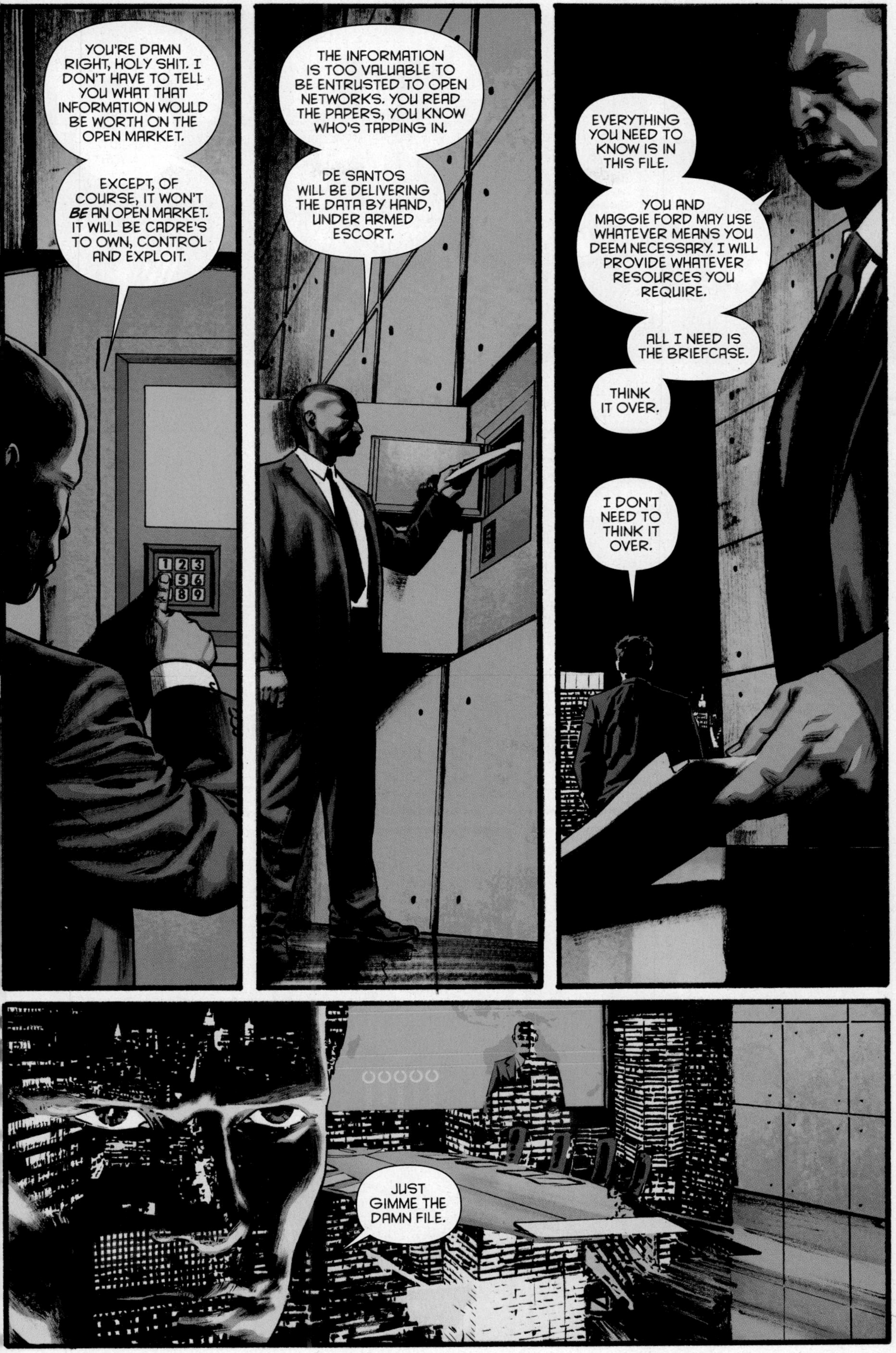
YOU'RE DAMN RIGHT, HOLY SHIT. I DON'T HAVE TO TELL YOU WHAT THAT INFORMATION WOULD BE WORTH ON THE OPEN MARKET.
EXCEPT, OF COURSE, IT WON'T *BE* AN OPEN MARKET. IT WILL BE CADRE'S TO OWN, CONTROL AND EXPLOIT.
THE INFORMATION IS TOO VALUABLE TO BE ENTRUSTED TO OPEN NETWORKS. YOU READ THE PAPERS, YOU KNOW WHO'S TAPPING IN.
DE SANTOS WILL BE DELIVERING THE DATA BY HAND, UNDER ARMED ESCORT.
EVERYTHING YOU NEED TO KNOW IS IN THIS FILE.
YOU AND MAGGIE FORD MAY USE WHATEVER MEANS YOU DEEM NECESSARY. I WILL PROVIDE WHATEVER RESOURCES YOU REQUIRE.
ALL I NEED IS THE BRIEFCASE.
THINK IT OVER.
I DON'T NEED TO THINK IT OVER.
JUST GIMME THE DAMN FILE.

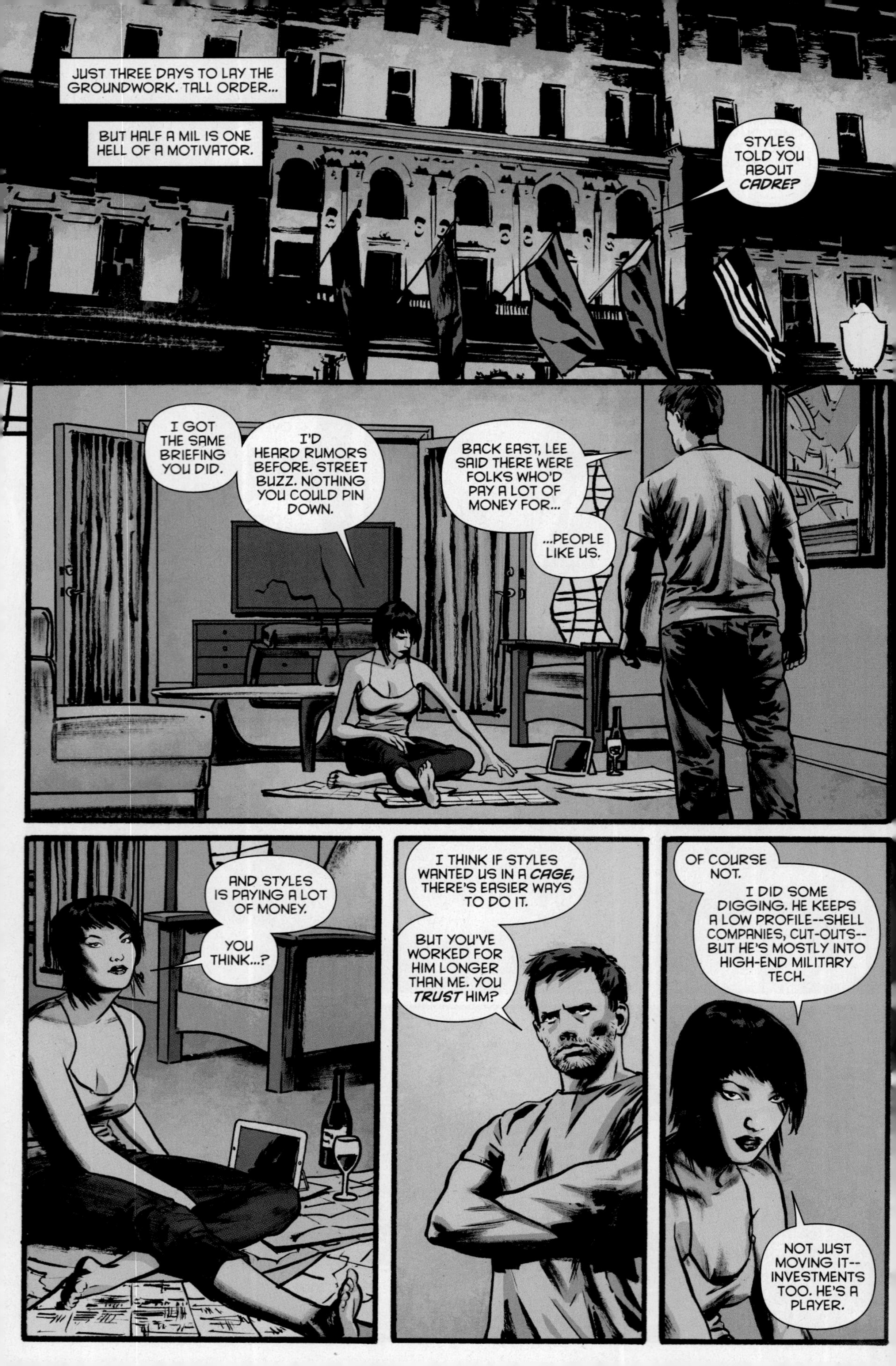
JUST THREE DAYS TO LAY THE GROUNDWORK. TALL ORDER...
BUT HALF A MIL IS ONE HELL OF A MOTIVATOR.
STYLES TOLD YOU ABOUT CADRE?
I GOT THE SAME BRIEFING YOU DID.
I'D HEARD RUMORS BEFORE. STREET BUZZ. NOTHING YOU COULD PIN DOWN.
BACK EAST, LEE SAID THERE WERE FOLKS WHO'D PAY A LOT OF MONEY FOR...
...PEOPLE LIKE US.
AND STYLES IS PAYING A LOT OF MONEY.
YOU THINK...?
I THINK IF STYLES WANTED US IN A CAGE, THERE'S EASIER WAYS TO DO IT.
BUT YOU'VE WORKED FOR HIM LONGER THAN ME. YOU TRUST HIM?
OF COURSE NOT.
I DID SOME DIGGING. HE KEEPS A LOW PROFILE--SHELL COMPANIES, CUT-OUTS--BUT HE'S MOSTLY INTO HIGH-END MILITARY TECH.
NOT JUST MOVING IT--INVESTMENTS TOO. HE'S A PLAYER.

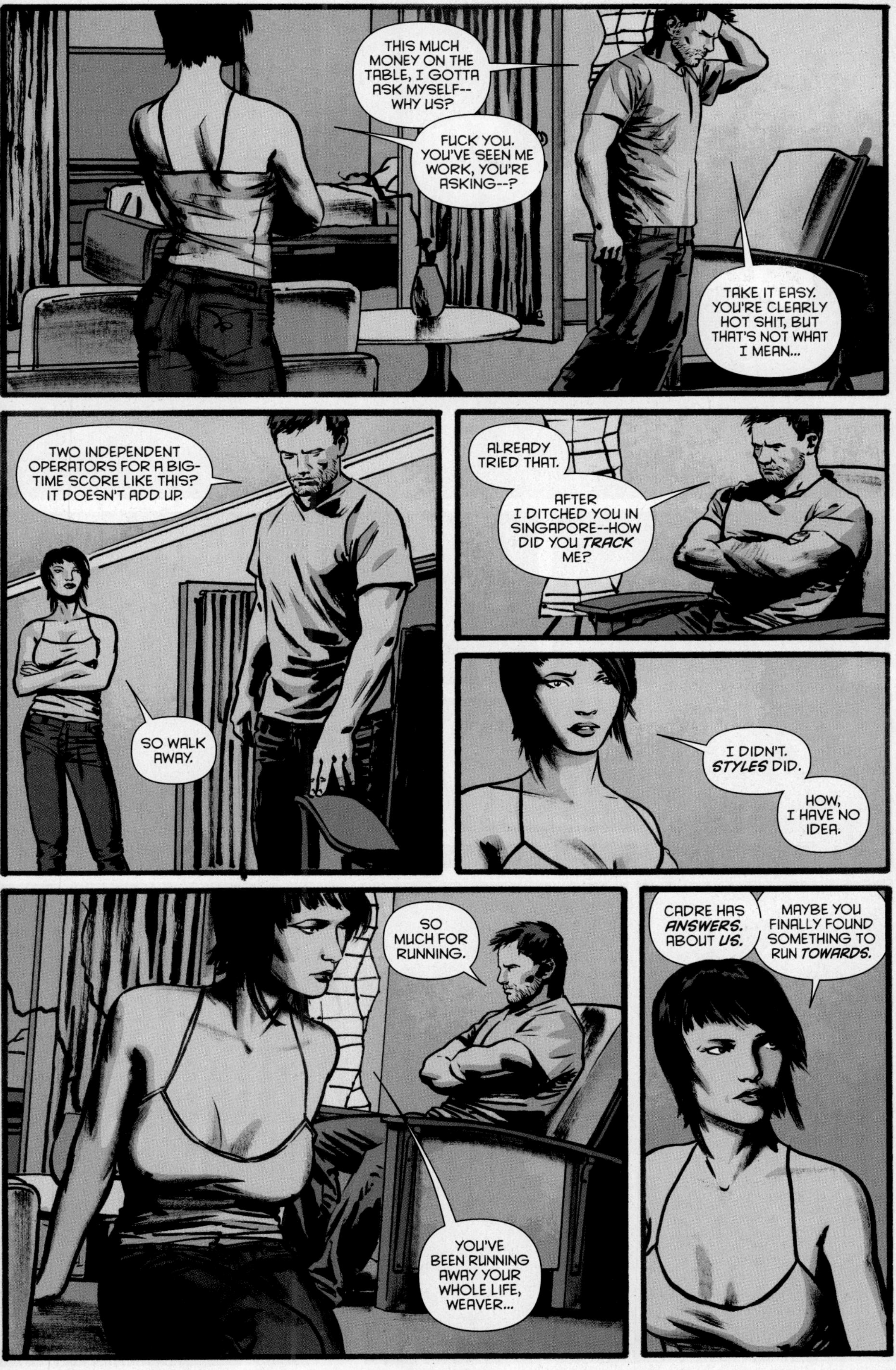
THIS MUCH MONEY ON THE TABLE, I GOTTA ASK MYSELF-- WHY US?
FUCK YOU. YOU'VE SEEN ME WORK, YOU'RE ASKING--?
TAKE IT EASY. YOU'RE CLEARLY HOT SHIT, BUT THAT'S NOT WHAT I MEAN...
TWO INDEPENDENT OPERATORS FOR A BIG-TIME SCORE LIKE THIS? IT DOESN'T ADD UP.
SO WALK AWAY.
ALREADY TRIED THAT.
AFTER I DITCHED YOU IN SINGAPORE--HOW DID YOU *TRACK* ME?
I DIDN'T. ***STYLES*** DID.
HOW, I HAVE NO IDEA.
SO MUCH FOR RUNNING.
YOU'VE BEEN RUNNING AWAY YOUR WHOLE LIFE, WEAVER...
CADRE HAS ***ANSWERS.*** ABOUT ***US.***
MAYBE YOU FINALLY FOUND SOMETHING TO RUN *TOWARDS.*

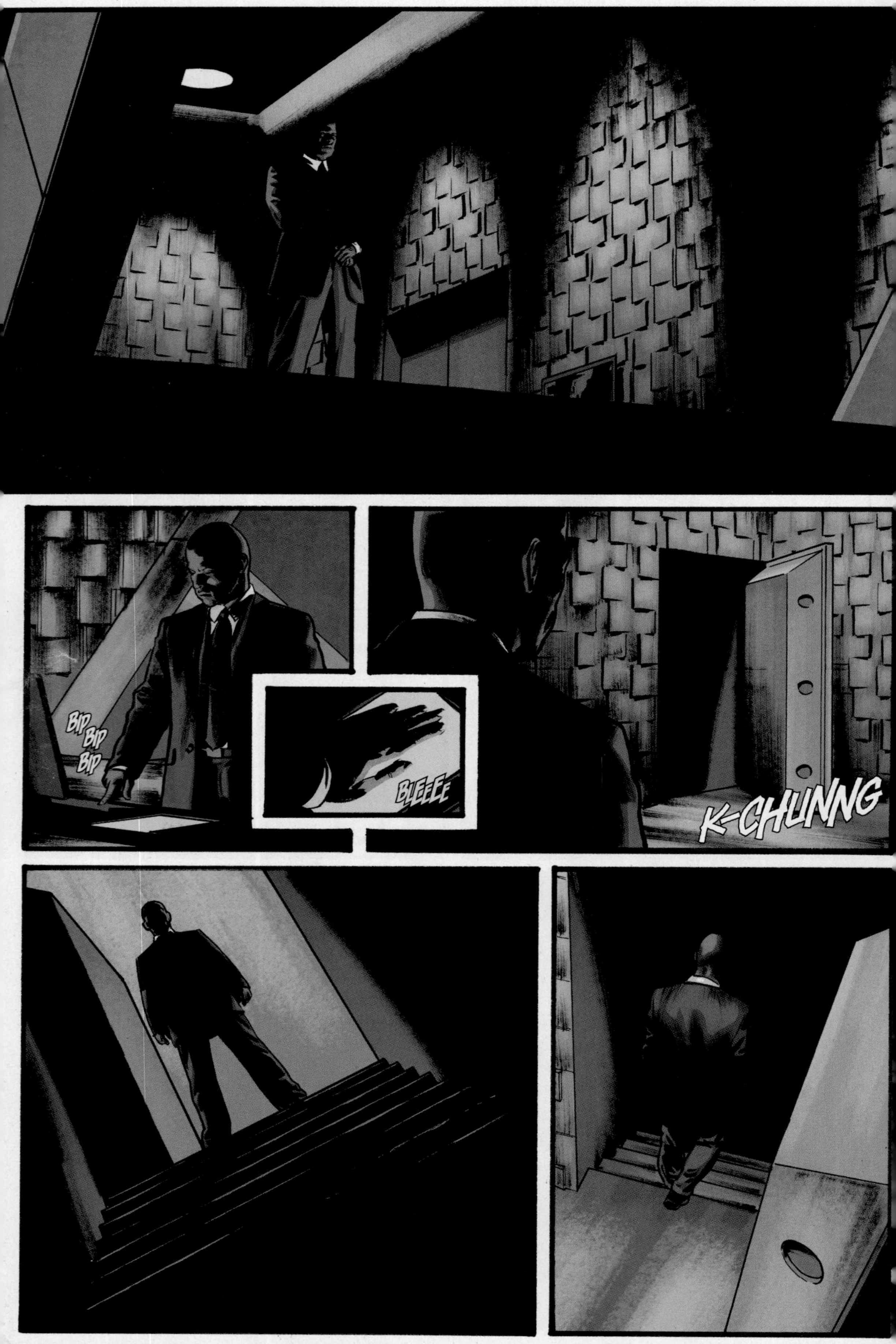
BIP BIP BIP
BLEEEE
K-CHUNNG

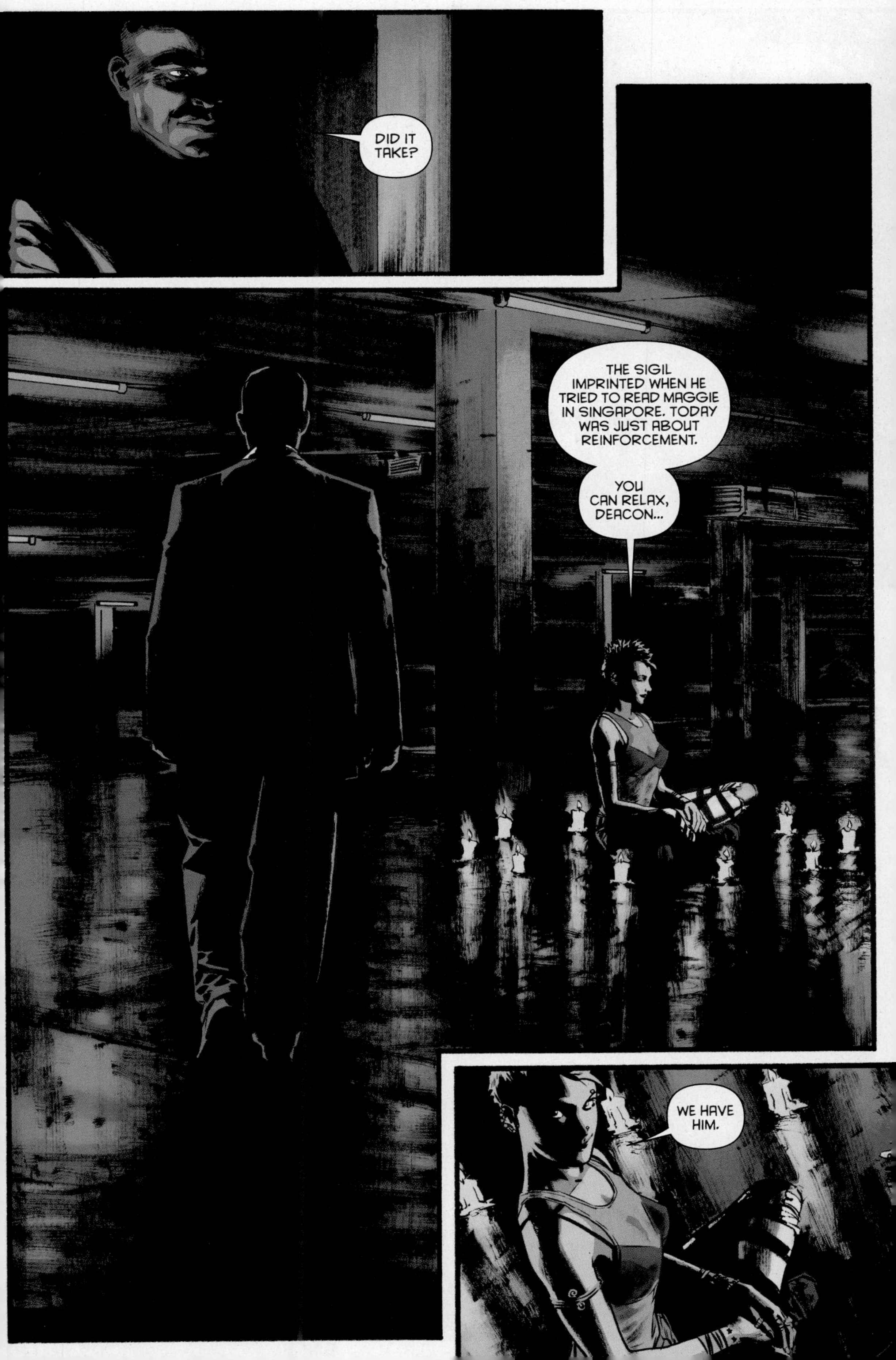
DID IT TAKE?
THE SIGIL IMPRINTED WHEN HE TRIED TO READ MAGGIE IN SINGAPORE. TODAY WAS JUST ABOUT REINFORCEMENT.
YOU CAN RELAX, DEACON...
WE HAVE HIM.

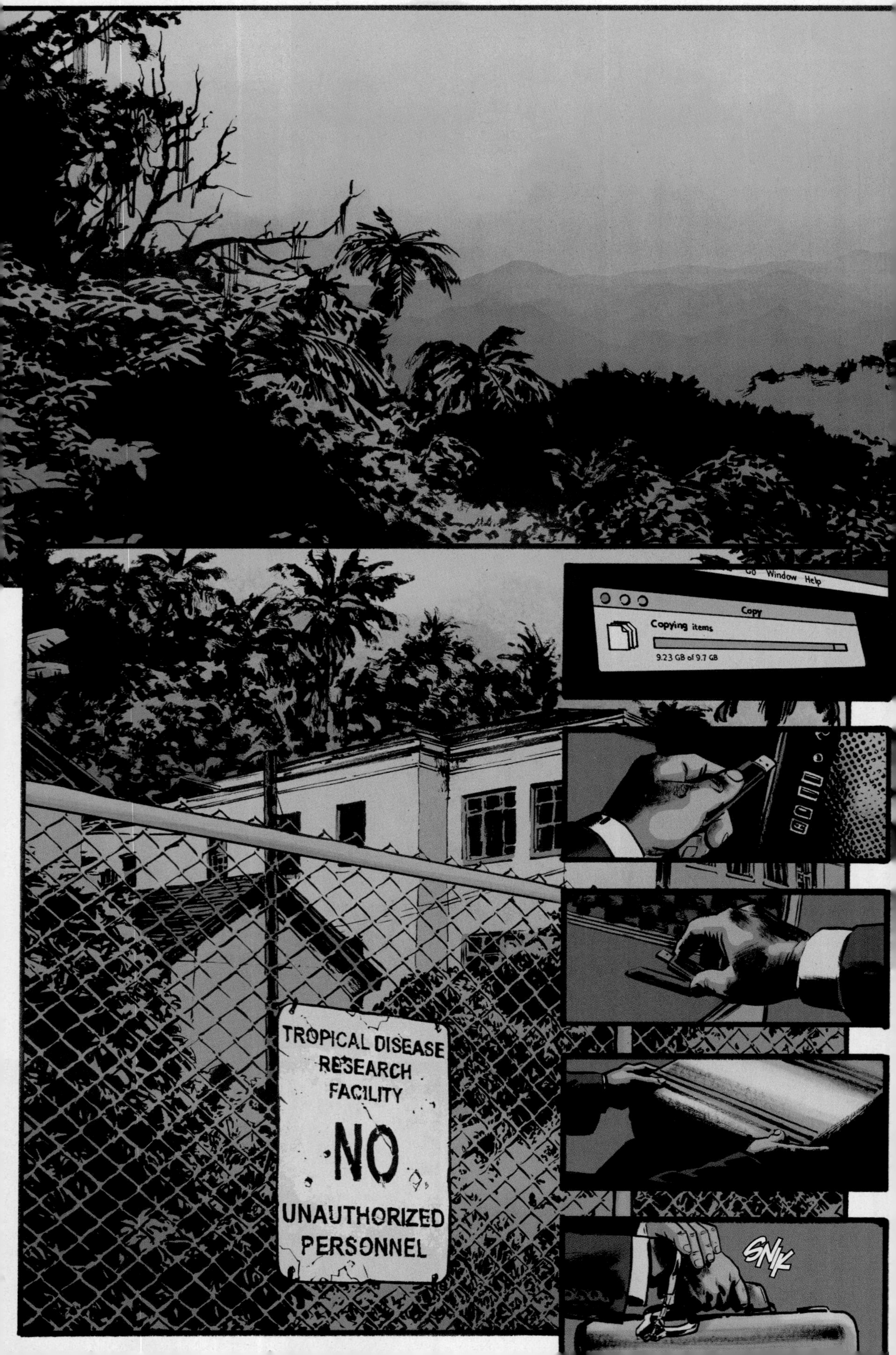

Go Window Help
Copy
Copying items
9.23 GB of 9.7 GB
TROPICAL DISEASE
RESEARCH
FACILITY
NO
UNAUTHORIZED
PERSONNEL
SNIK

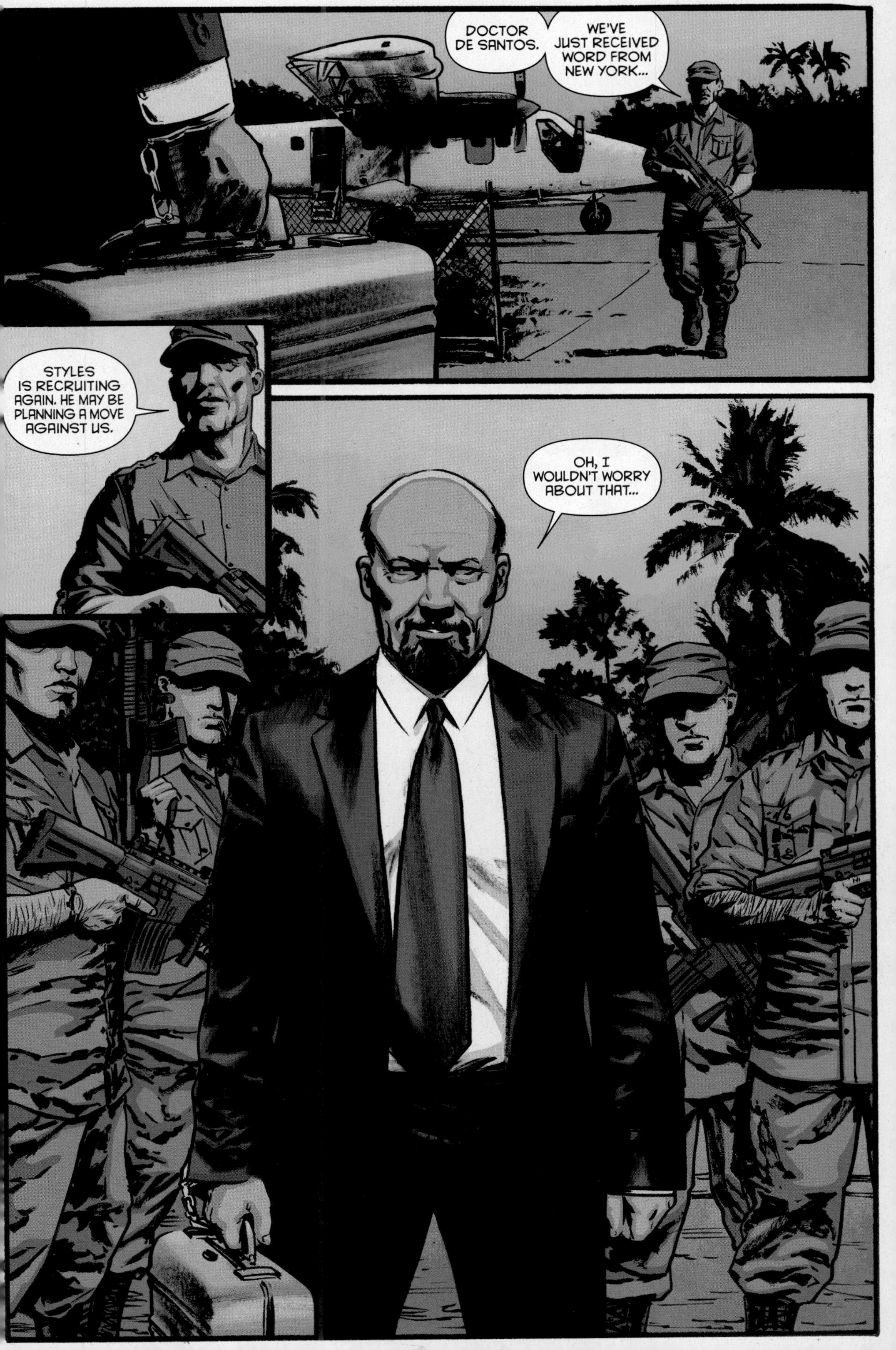
DOCTOR DE SANTOS.
WE'VE JUST RECEIVED WORD FROM NEW YORK...
STYLES IS RECRUITING AGAIN. HE MAY BE PLANNING A MOVE AGAINST US.
OH, I WOULDN'T WORRY ABOUT THAT...

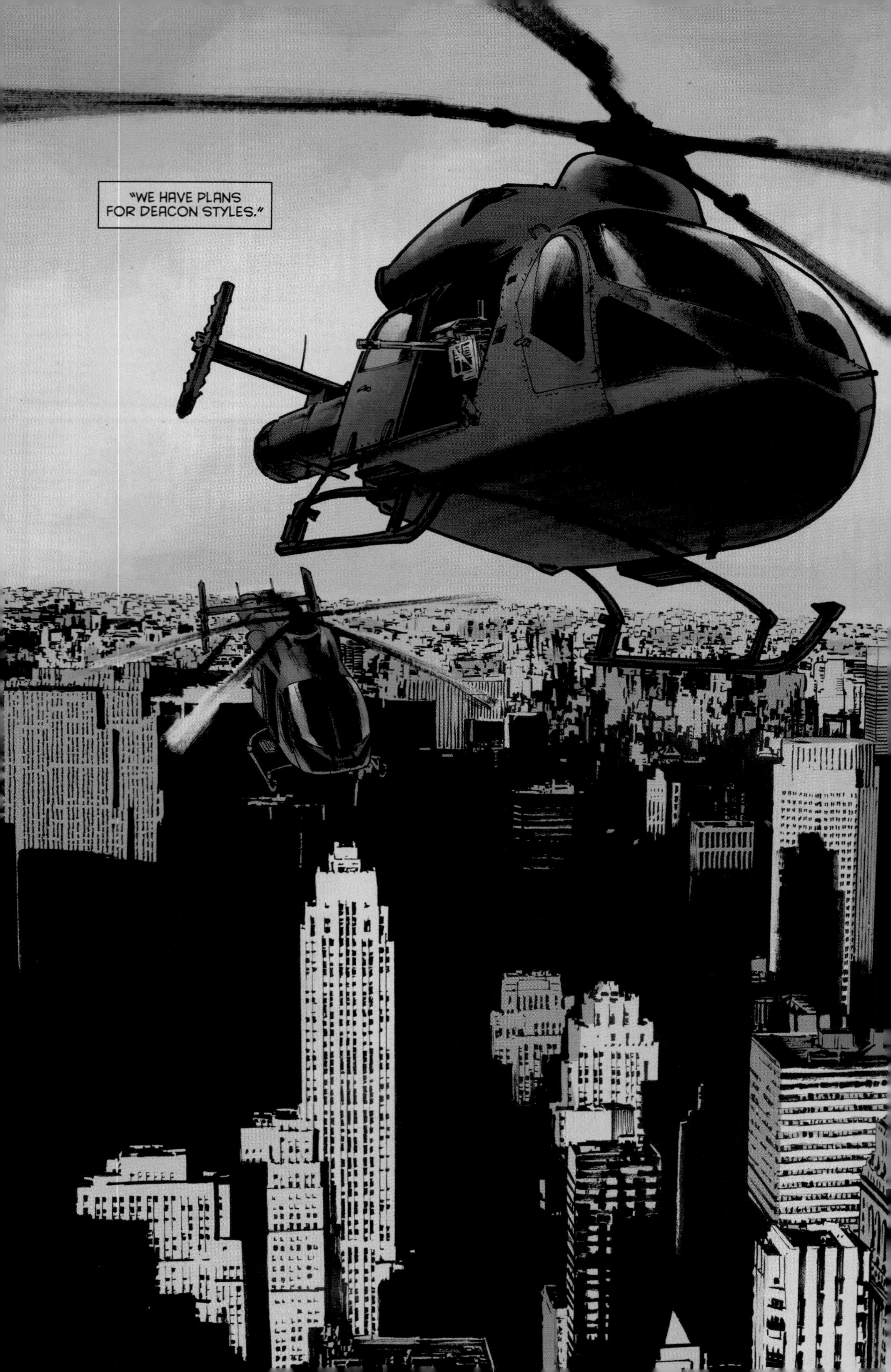
"WE HAVE PLANS FOR DEACON STYLES."

ISSUE FOUR

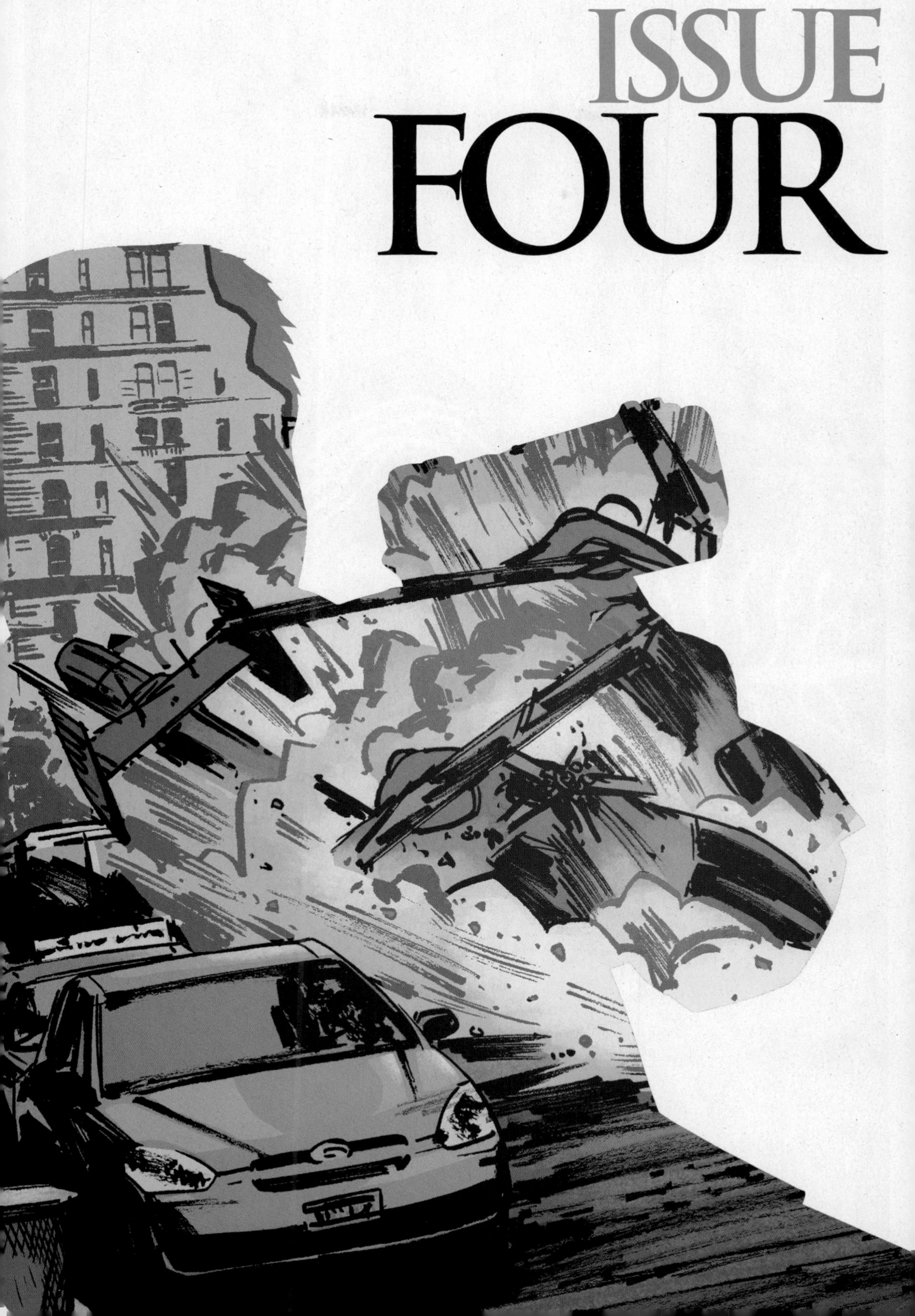

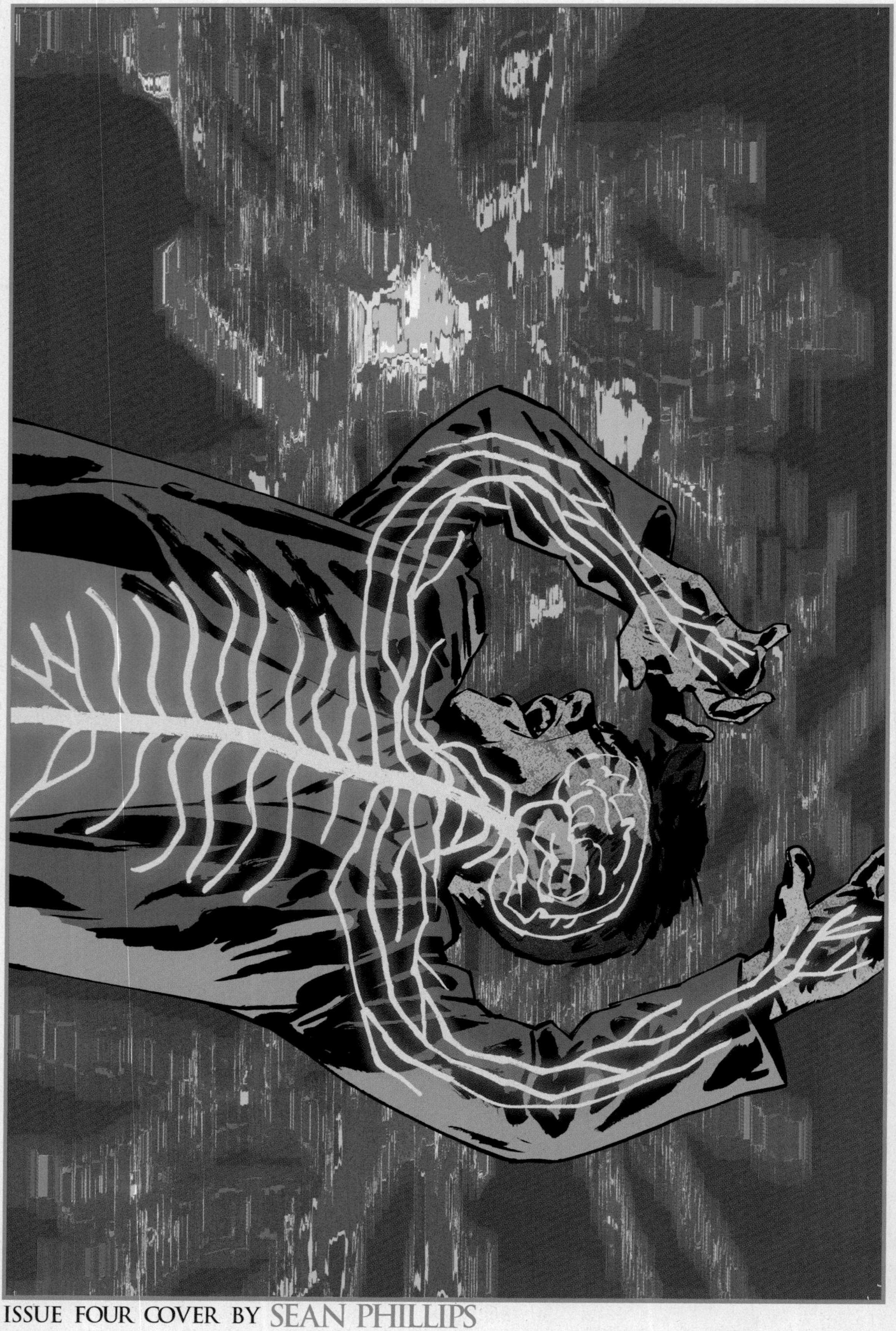

ISSUE FOUR COVER BY SEAN PHILLIPS

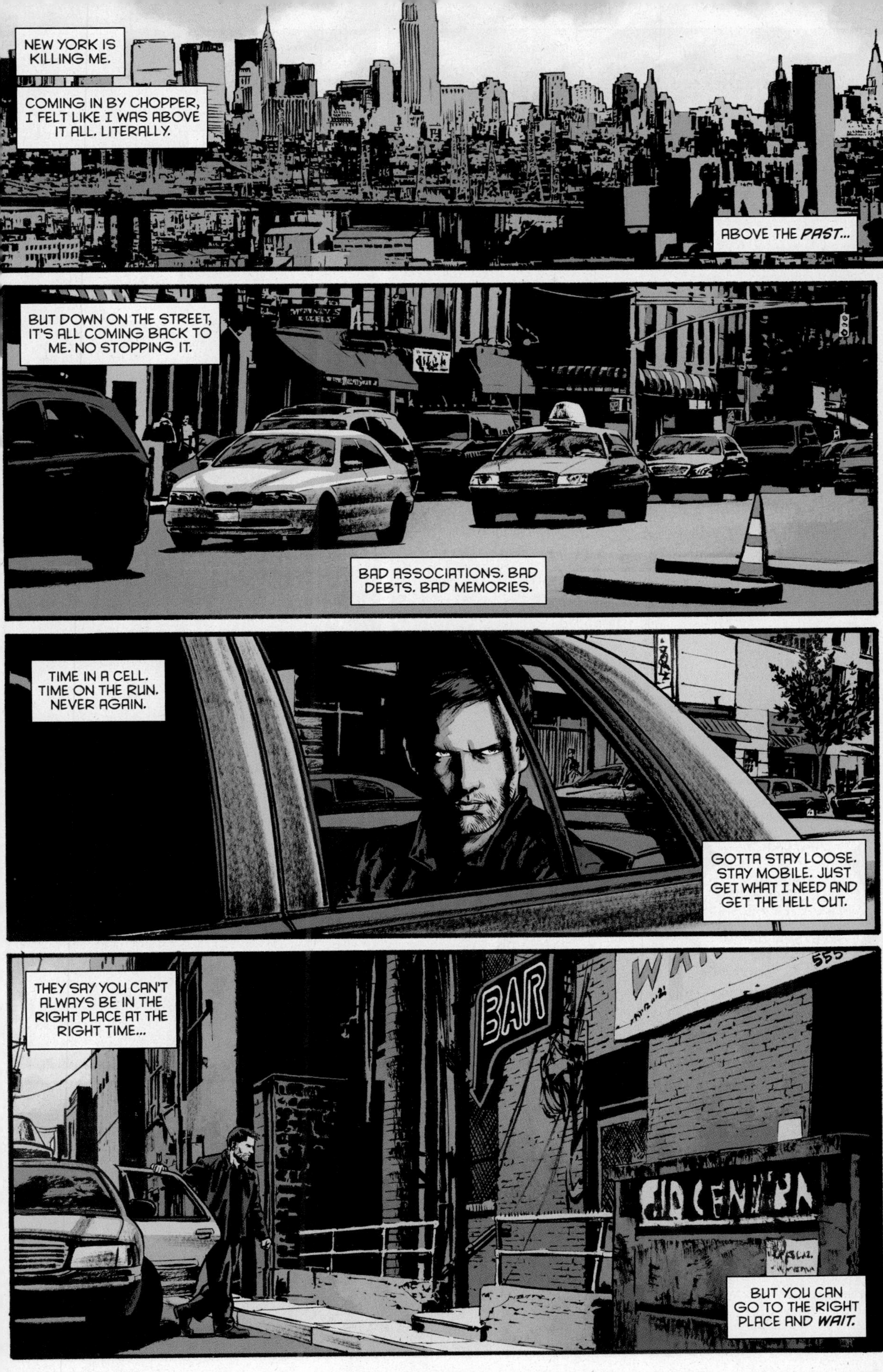
NEW YORK IS KILLING ME.
COMING IN BY CHOPPER, I FELT LIKE I WAS ABOVE IT ALL. LITERALLY.
ABOVE THE *PAST*...
BUT DOWN ON THE STREET, IT'S ALL COMING BACK TO ME. NO STOPPING IT.
BAD ASSOCIATIONS. BAD DEBTS. BAD MEMORIES.
TIME IN A CELL. TIME ON THE RUN. NEVER AGAIN.
GOTTA STAY LOOSE. STAY MOBILE. JUST GET WHAT I NEED AND GET THE HELL OUT.
BAR
THEY SAY YOU CAN'T ALWAYS BE IN THE RIGHT PLACE AT THE RIGHT TIME...
BUT YOU CAN GO TO THE RIGHT PLACE AND *WAIT.*

THREE DAYS PLANNING AND WE'RE ALMOST SET.

THREE DAYS HOLED UP WITH *MAGGIE*, PORING OVER THE MAPS AND SCHEDULES THAT *DEACON STYLES'* PEOPLE STOLE FROM CHRIST-KNOWS-WHERE.

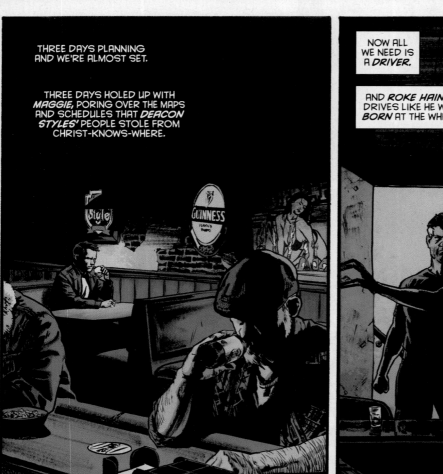

NOW ALL WE NEED IS A *DRIVER*.

AND *ROKE HAINES* DRIVES LIKE HE WAS *BORN* AT THE WHEEL.

WEAVER...

SON OF A BITCH.

GUESS IT MUST BE TRUE WHAT THEY SAY, HUH? YOU REALLY *ARE* CRAZY.

GOTTA BE, COMING BACK HERE AFTER THE SHIT WENT DOWN WITH THE *WESTERN UNION* SCORE.

BYGONES, ROKE.

SIT. I'M BUYING.

YOU SELL YOURSELF AS SOME KIND OF HOTSHOT. THEN WHEN PUSH COMES TO SHOVE, WHAT, YOU SUDDENLY *FORGET* HOW TO CRACK A SAFE?

TIMING WAS OFF. IT LED TO... COMPLICATIONS.

FORGET ABOUT IT. I HAVE SOMETHING NEW LINED UP, NEEDS A TOP-LINE WHEEL MAN. IF YOU'RE INTERESTED.

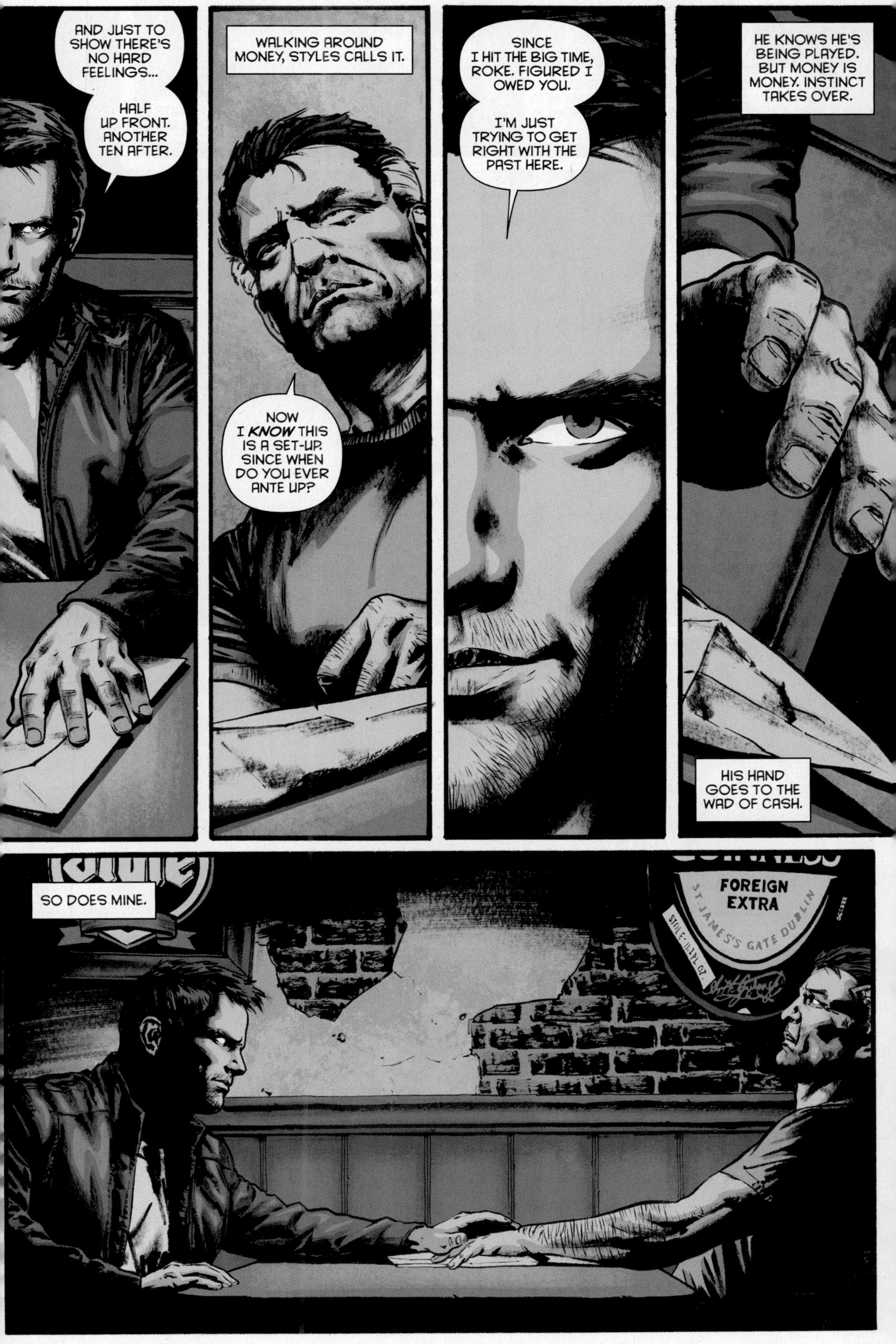
AND JUST TO SHOW THERE'S NO HARD FEELINGS...
HALF UP FRONT. ANOTHER TEN AFTER.
WALKING AROUND MONEY, STYLES CALLS IT.
NOW I *KNOW* THIS IS A SET-UP. SINCE WHEN DO YOU EVER ANTE UP?
SINCE I HIT THE BIG TIME, ROKE. FIGURED I OWED YOU.
I'M JUST TRYING TO GET RIGHT WITH THE PAST HERE.
HE KNOWS HE'S BEING PLAYED. BUT MONEY IS MONEY. INSTINCT TAKES OVER.
HIS HAND GOES TO THE WAD OF CASH.
SO DOES MINE.
FOREIGN EXTRA
ST. JAMES'S GATE DUBLIN

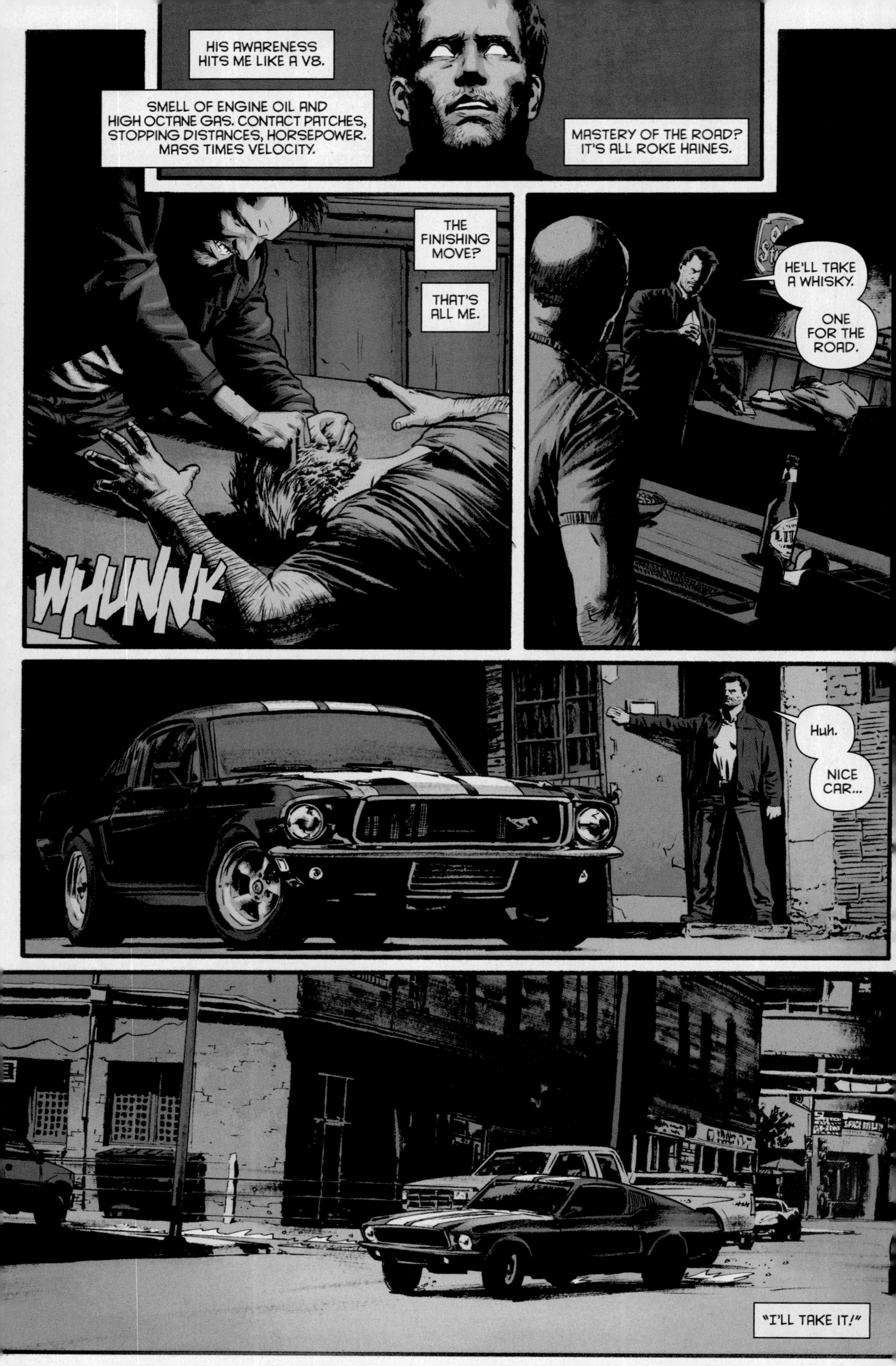

HIS AWARENESS HITS ME LIKE A V8.
SMELL OF ENGINE OIL AND HIGH OCTANE GAS. CONTACT PATCHES, STOPPING DISTANCES, HORSEPOWER. MASS TIMES VELOCITY.
MASTERY OF THE ROAD? IT'S ALL ROKE HAINES.
THE FINISHING MOVE?
THAT'S ALL ME.
WHUNNK
HE'LL TAKE A WHISKY.
ONE FOR THE ROAD.
Huh.
NICE CAR...
"I'LL TAKE IT!"

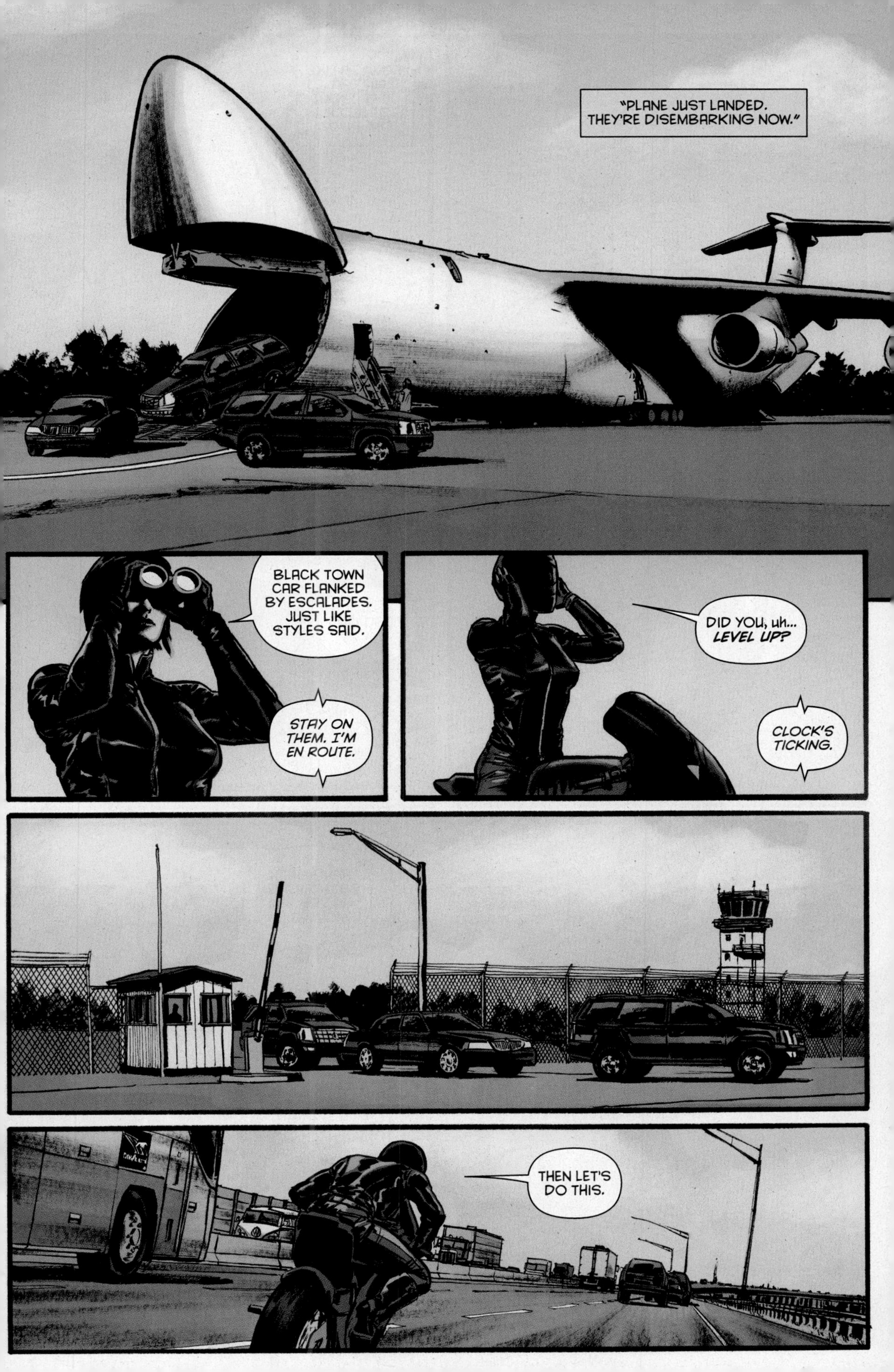
"PLANE JUST LANDED. THEY'RE DISEMBARKING NOW."
BLACK TOWN CAR FLANKED BY ESCALADES. JUST LIKE STYLES SAID.
STAY ON THEM. I'M EN ROUTE.
DID YOU, uh... LEVEL UP?
CLOCK'S TICKING.
THEN LET'S DO THIS.

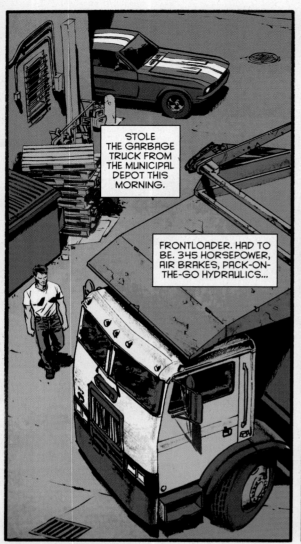

STOLE THE GARBAGE TRUCK FROM THE MUNICIPAL DEPOT THIS MORNING.

FRONTLOADER. HAD TO BE. 345 HORSEPOWER, AIR BRAKES, PACK-ON-THE-GO HYDRAULICS...

HANDLES LIKE SHIT, BUT I JUST ABOUT GOT IT OUT IN ONE PIECE.

EASIER NOW I'M CARRYING ROKE.

POSITION?

EASTBOUND ON 495. THEY'RE HEADING FOR THE TUNNEL.

HANG BACK, BUT KEEP THEM IN VIEW. I'M MOVING UP.

NICE AND EASY.

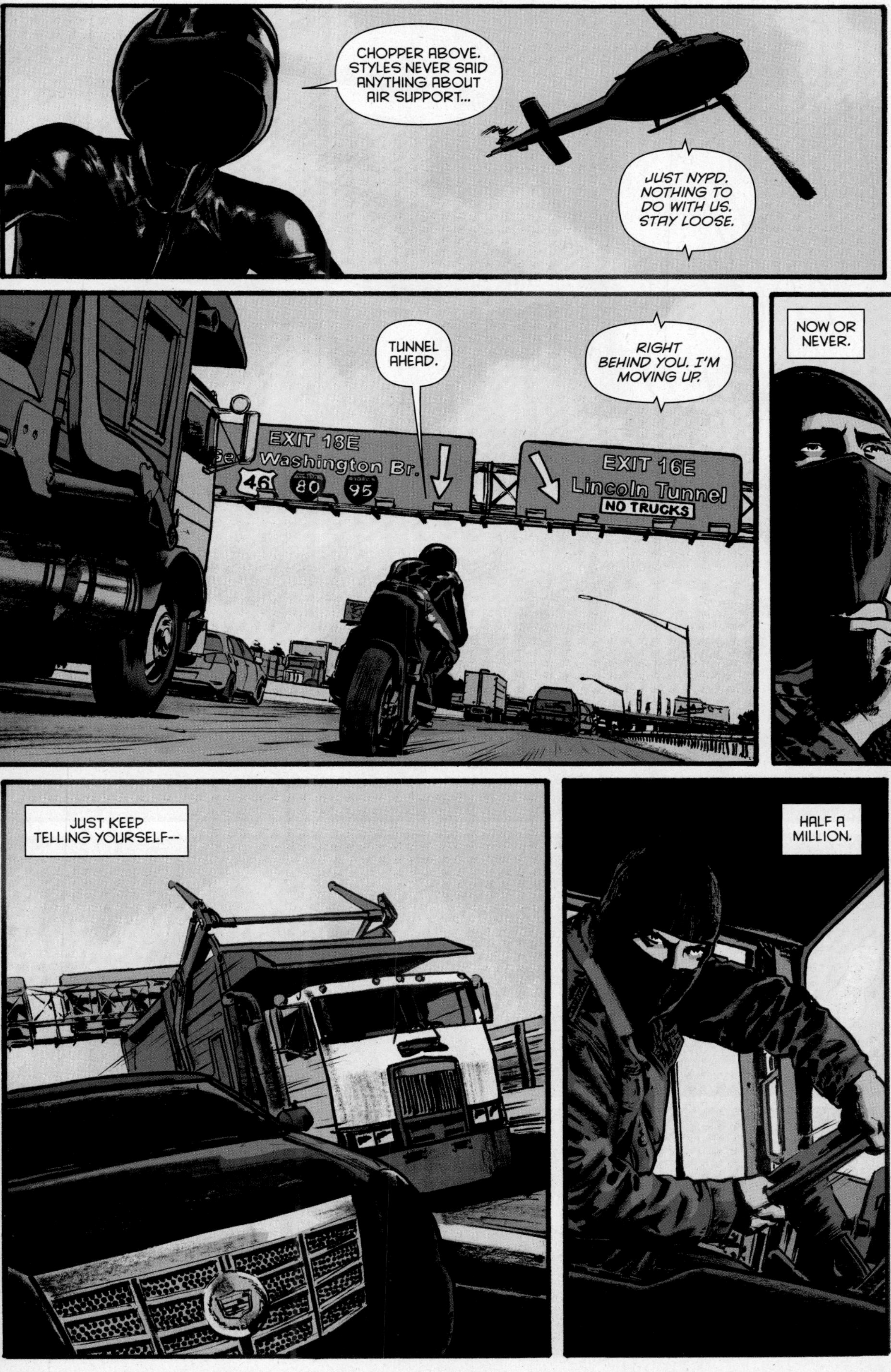
CHOPPER ABOVE. STYLES NEVER SAID ANYTHING ABOUT AIR SUPPORT...
JUST NYPD. NOTHING TO DO WITH US. STAY LOOSE.
TUNNEL AHEAD.
RIGHT BEHIND YOU. I'M MOVING UP.
EXIT 18E
Washington Br.
46
80
95
EXIT 16E
Lincoln Tunnel
NO TRUCKS
NOW OR NEVER.
JUST KEEP TELLING YOURSELF--
HALF A MILLION.

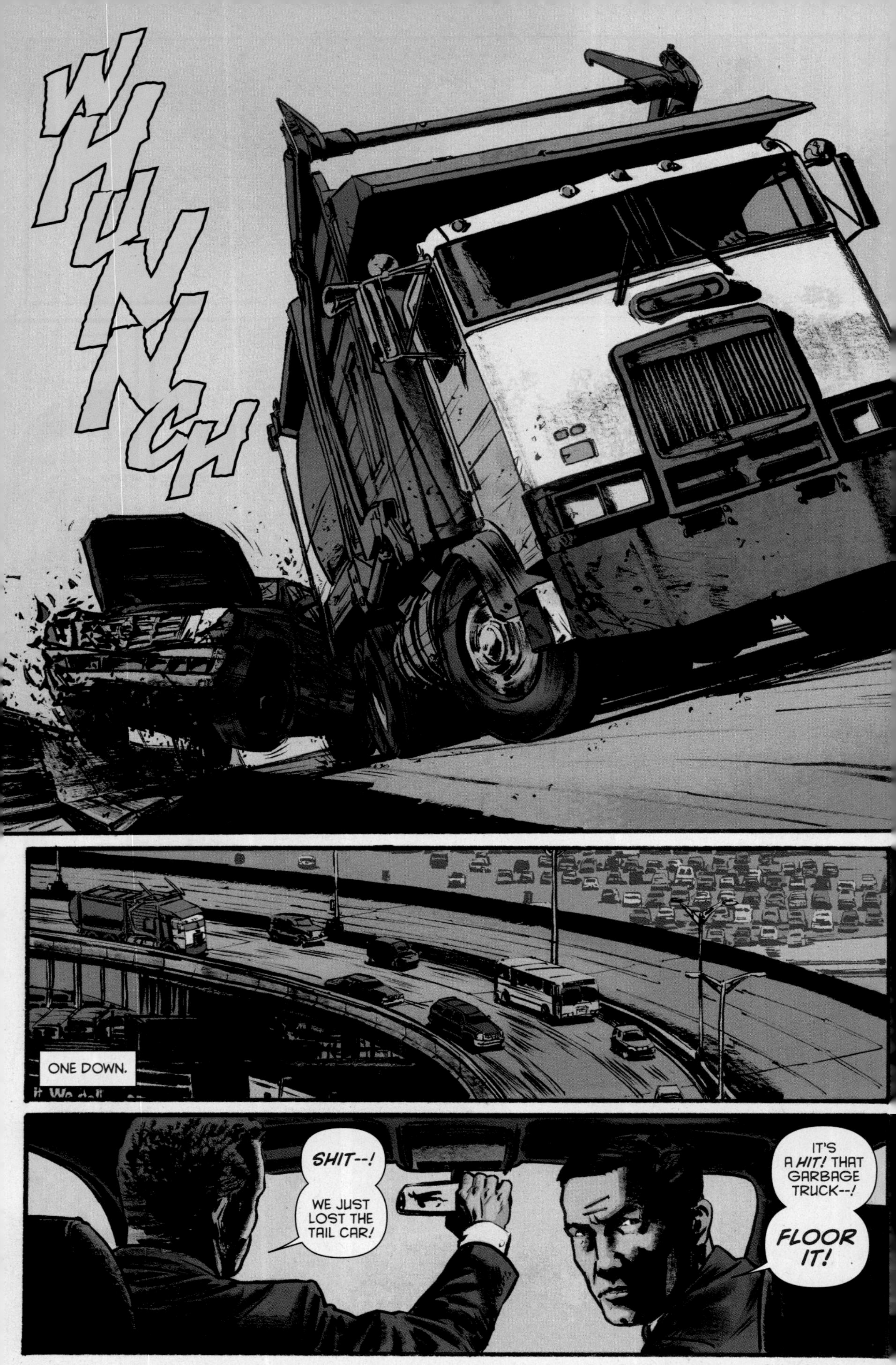
WHUNNCH
ONE DOWN.
SHIT--!
WE JUST LOST THE TAIL CAR!
IT'S A HIT! THAT GARBAGE TRUCK--!
FLOOR IT!

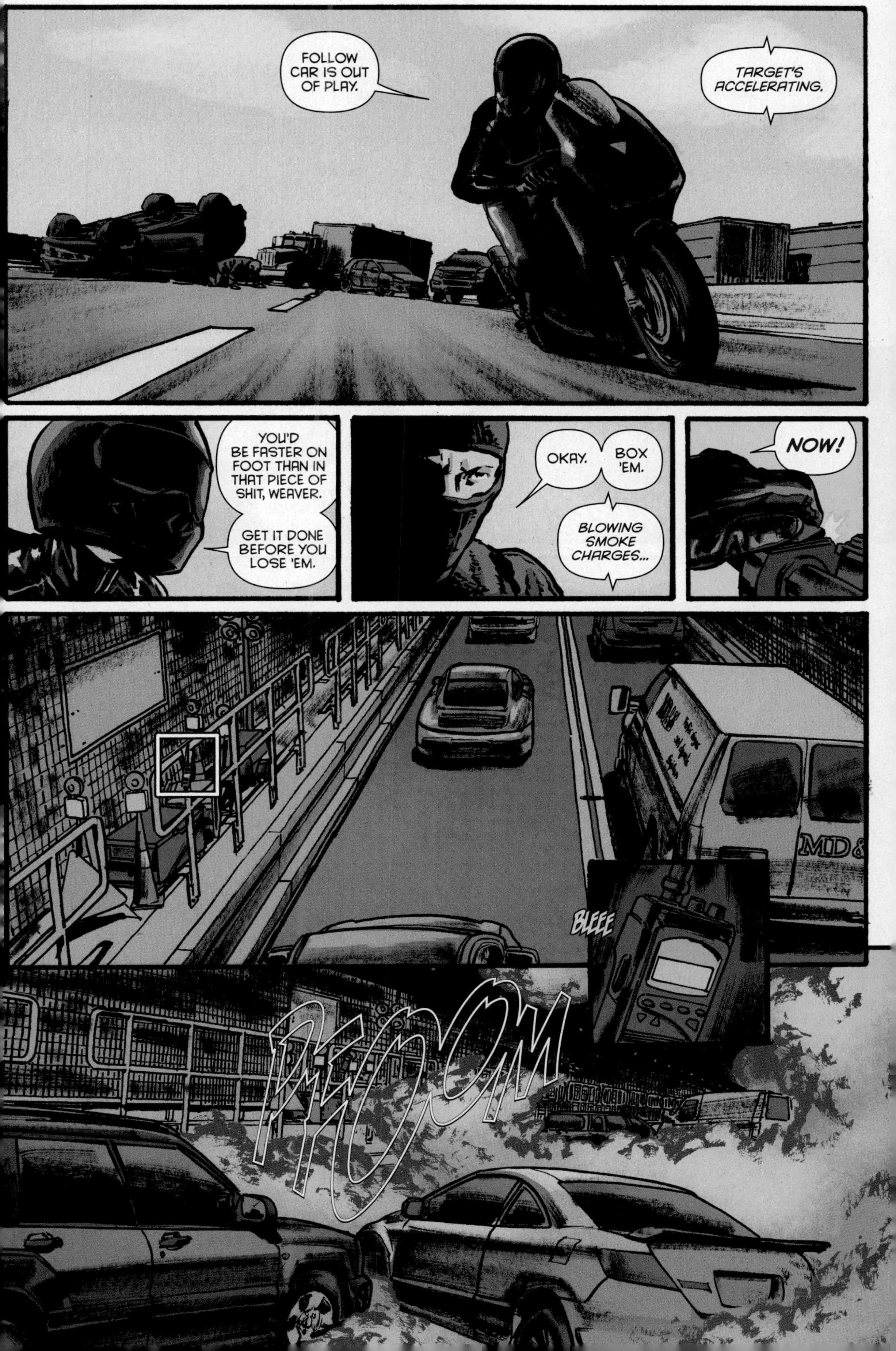
FOLLOW CAR IS OUT OF PLAY.
TARGET'S ACCELERATING.
YOU'D BE FASTER ON FOOT THAN IN THAT PIECE OF SHIT, WEAVER.
GET IT DONE BEFORE YOU LOSE 'EM.
OKAY.
BOX 'EM.
BLOWING SMOKE CHARGES...
NOW!
MD&
BLEEE
FFOOOM

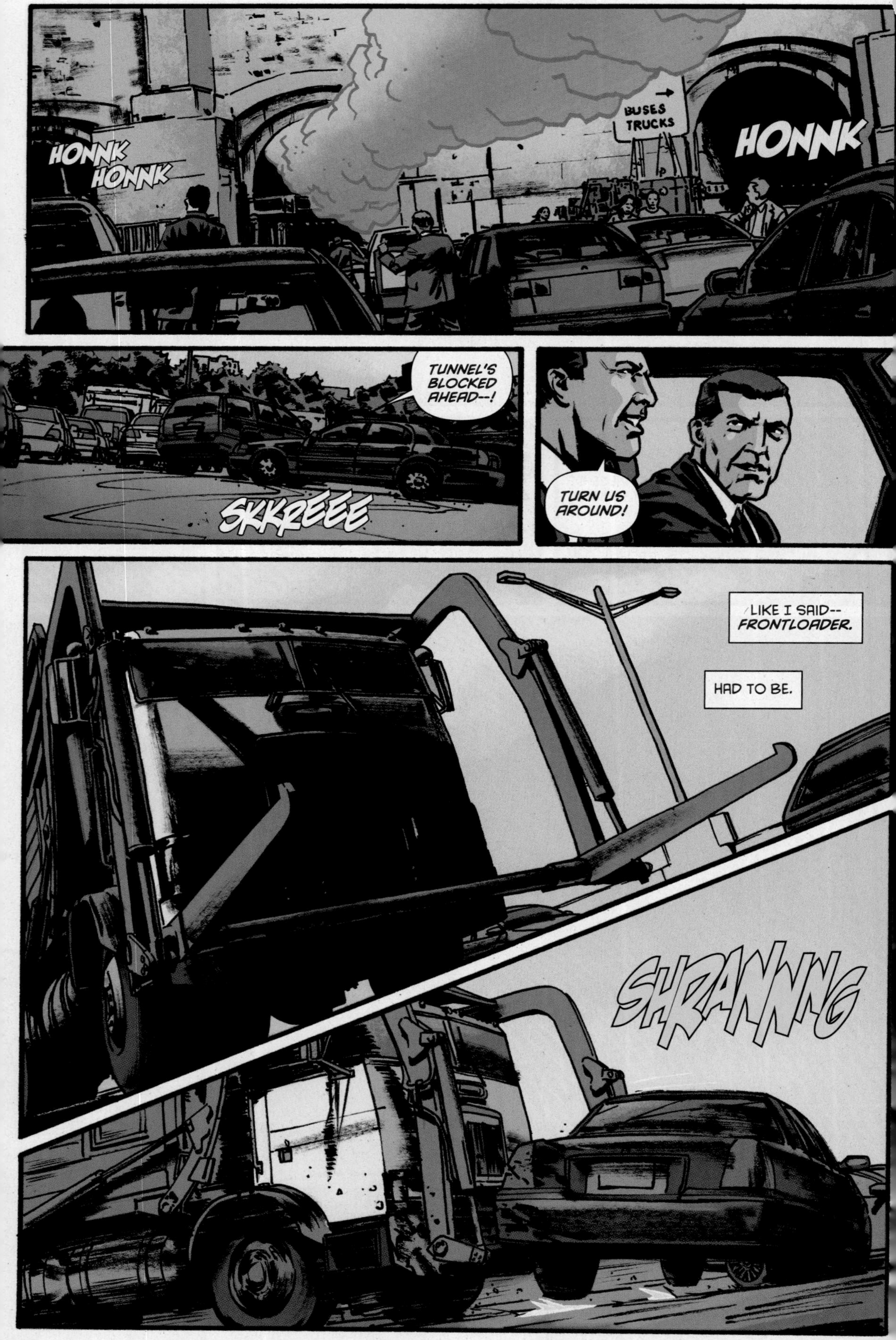
HONNK HONNK
BUSES TRUCKS
HONNK
TUNNEL'S BLOCKED AHEAD--!
SKKREEE
TURN US AROUND!
LIKE I SAID-- FRONTLOADER.
HAD TO BE.
SHRANNNG

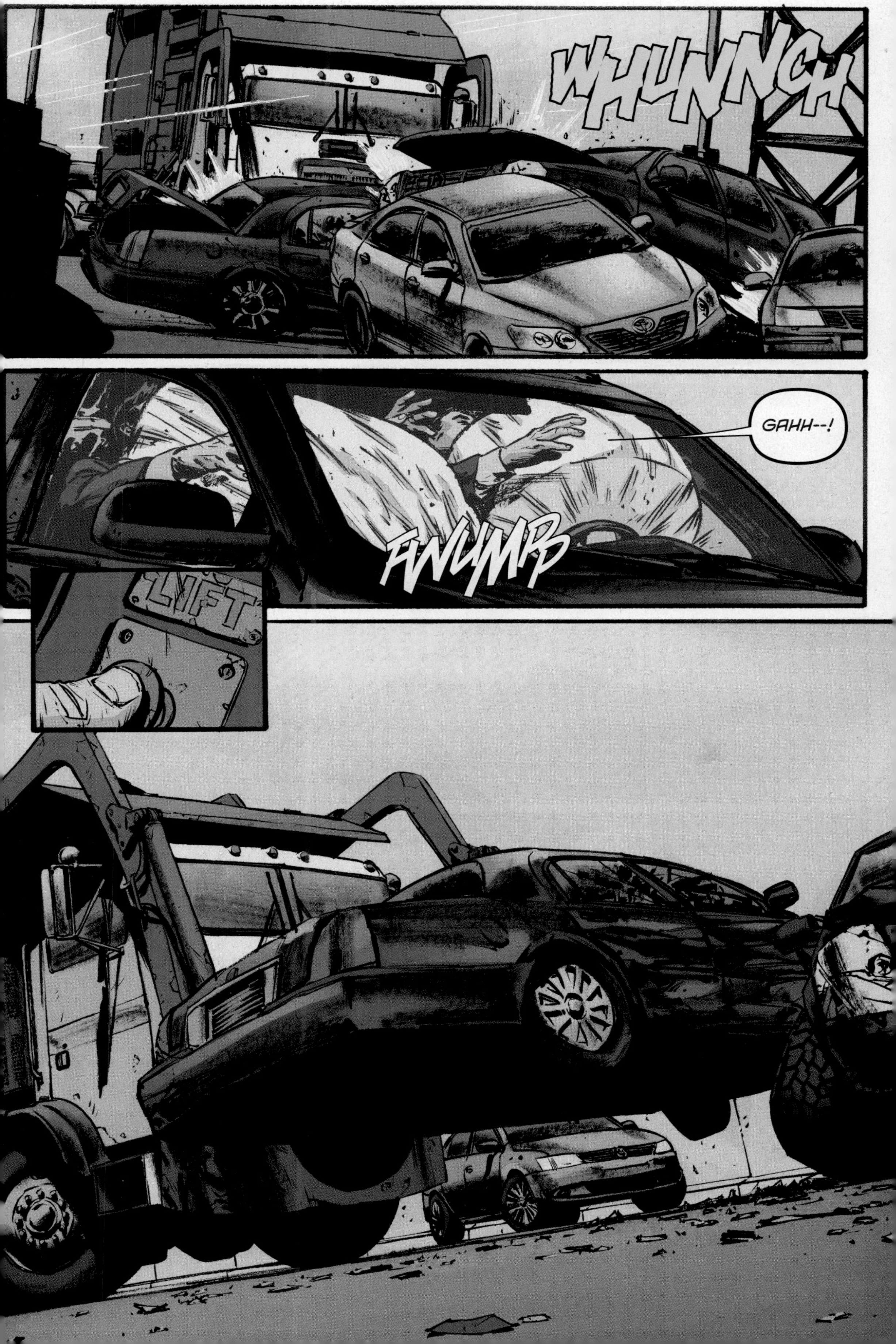
WHUNNCH
GAHH--!
FWUMP
LIFT

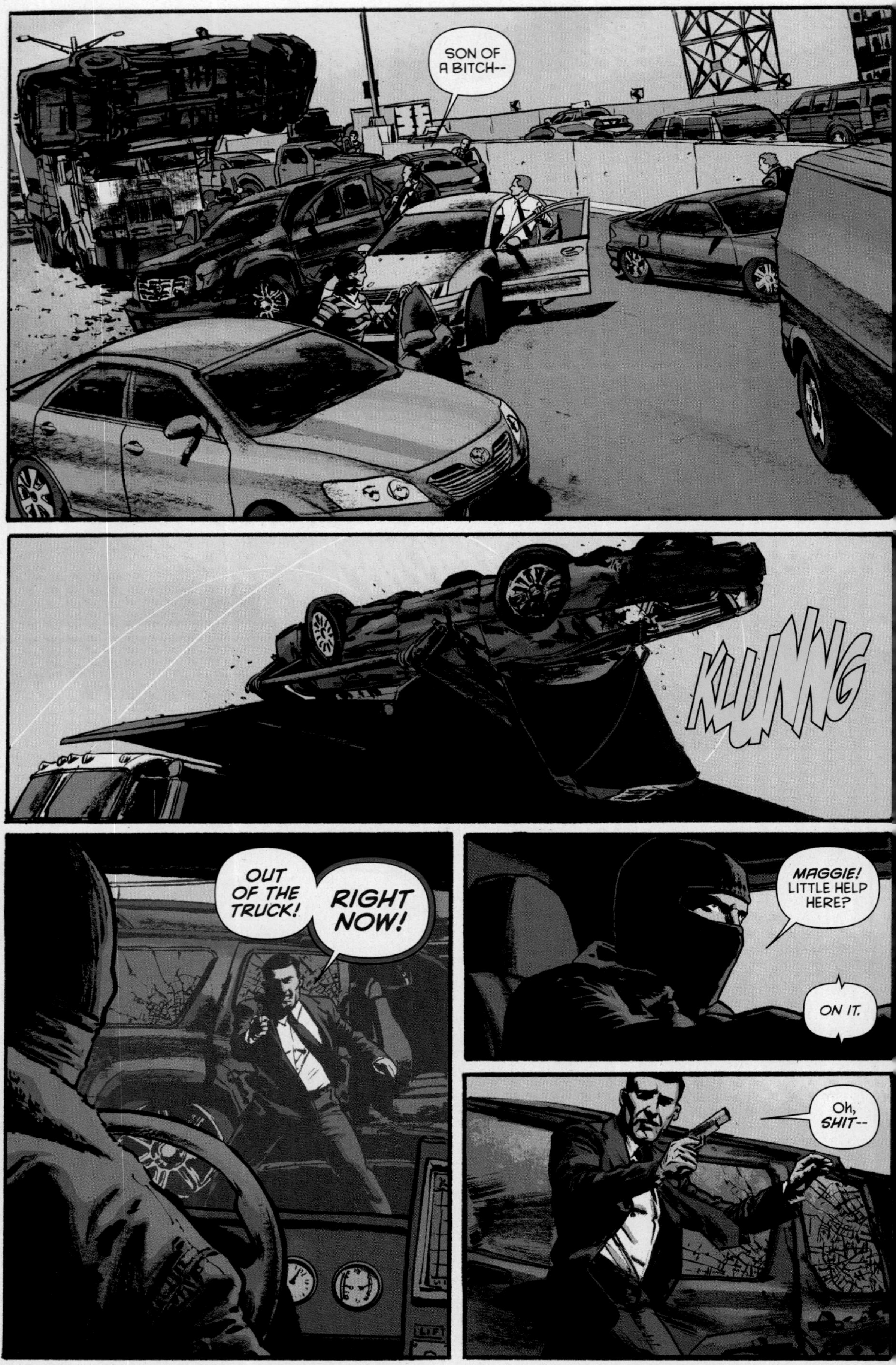
SON OF A BITCH--
KLUNNG
OUT OF THE TRUCK!
RIGHT NOW!
MAGGIE! LITTLE HELP HERE?
ON IT.
Oh, SHIT--

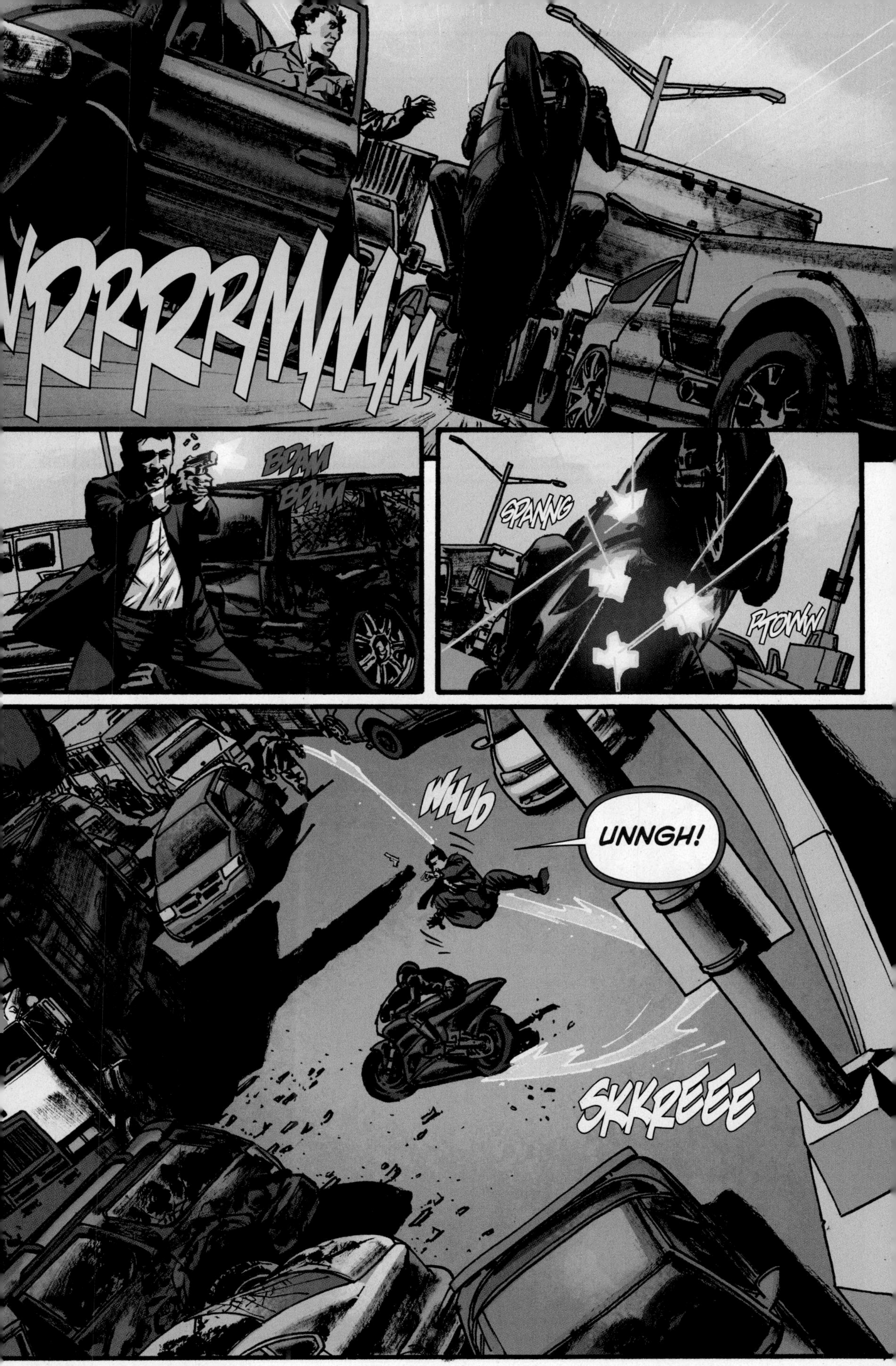
VRRRRMMMM
BDAM
BDAM
SPANNG
PTOWW
WHUD
UNNGH!
SKKREEE

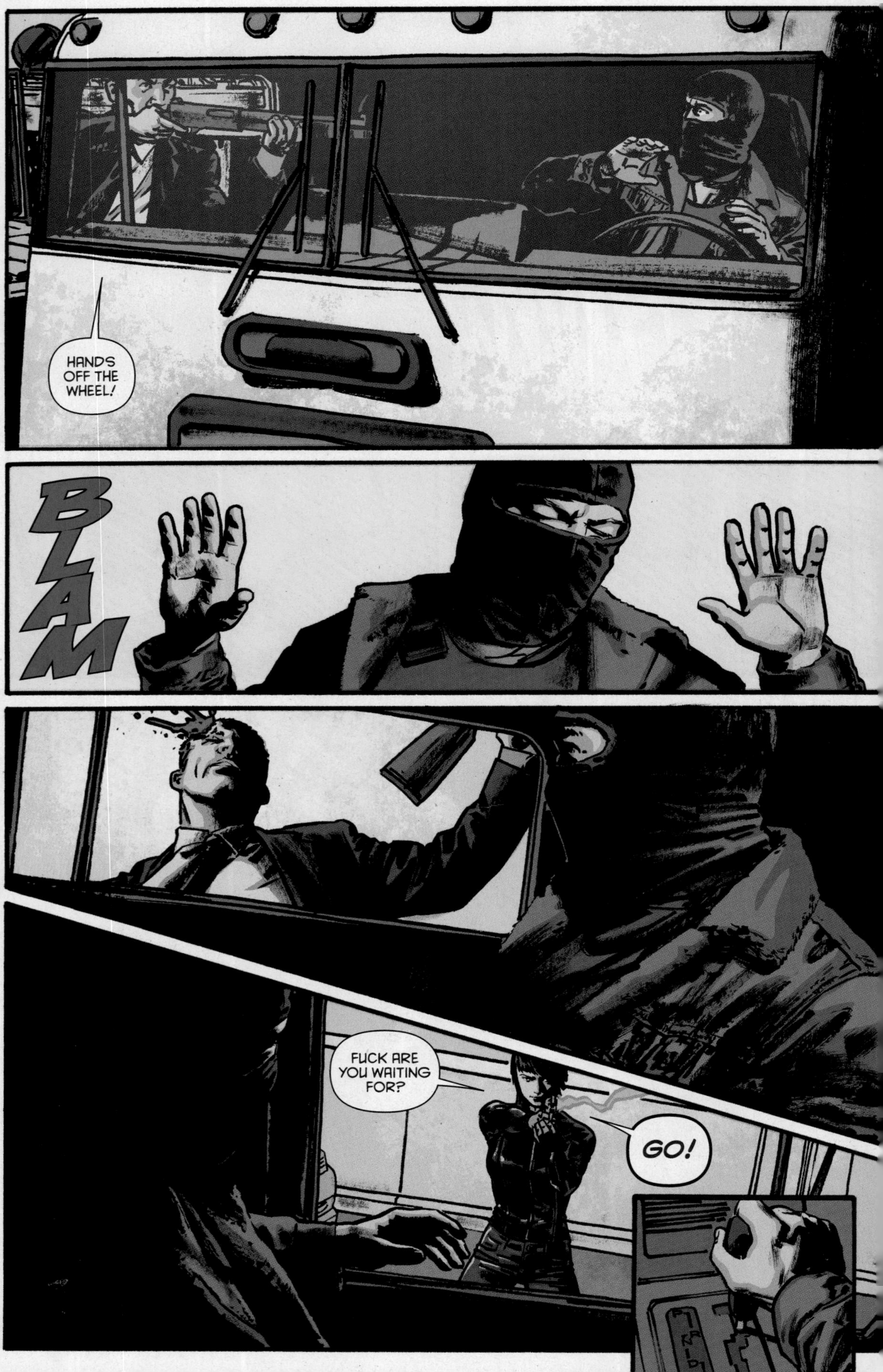
HANDS OFF THE WHEEL!
BLAM
FUCK ARE YOU WAITING FOR?
GO!

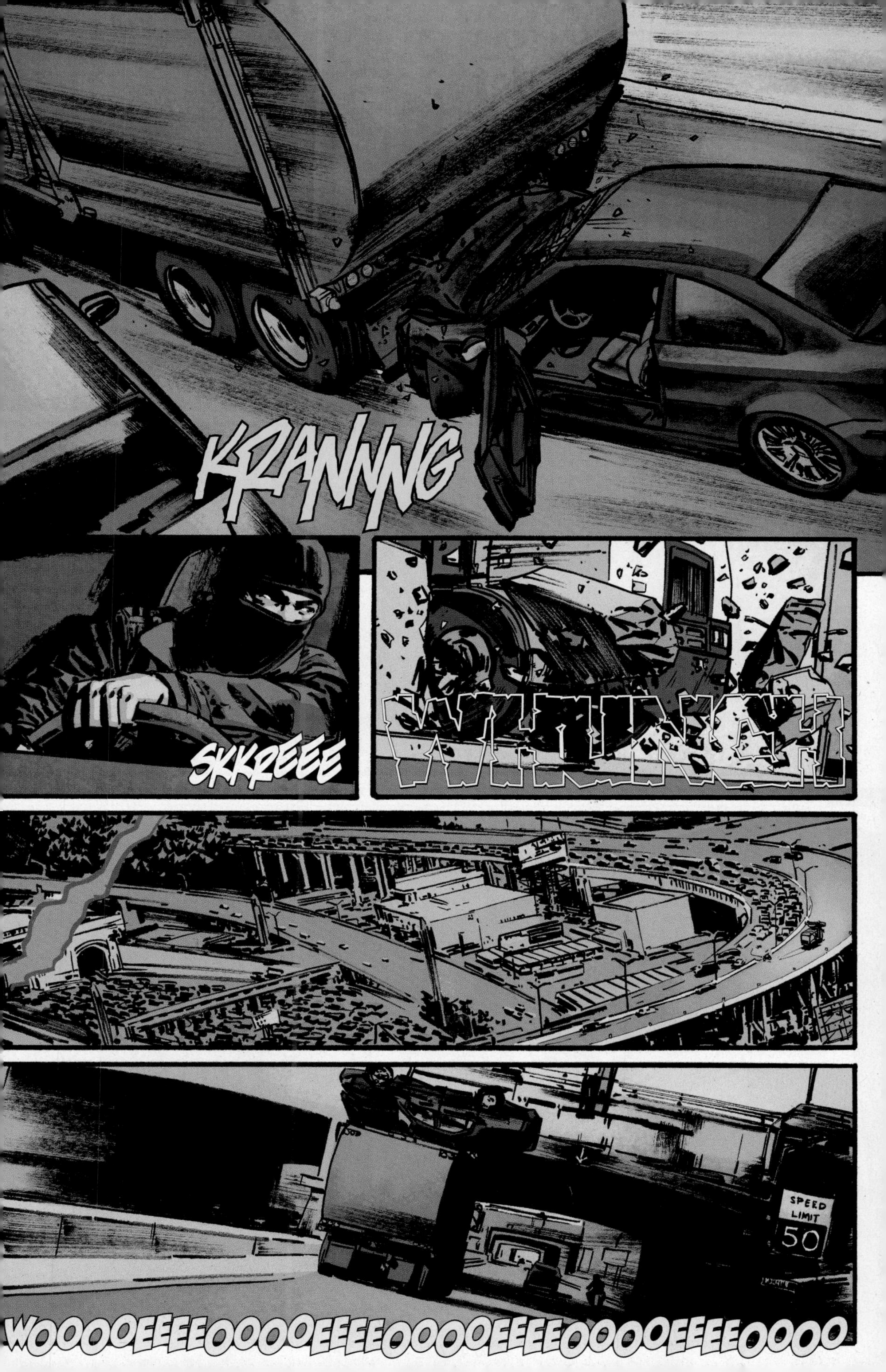
KRANNNG
SKKREEE
WHUNCH
SPEED LIMIT 50
WOOOOEEEEOOOOEEEEOOOOEEEEOOOOEEEEOOOO

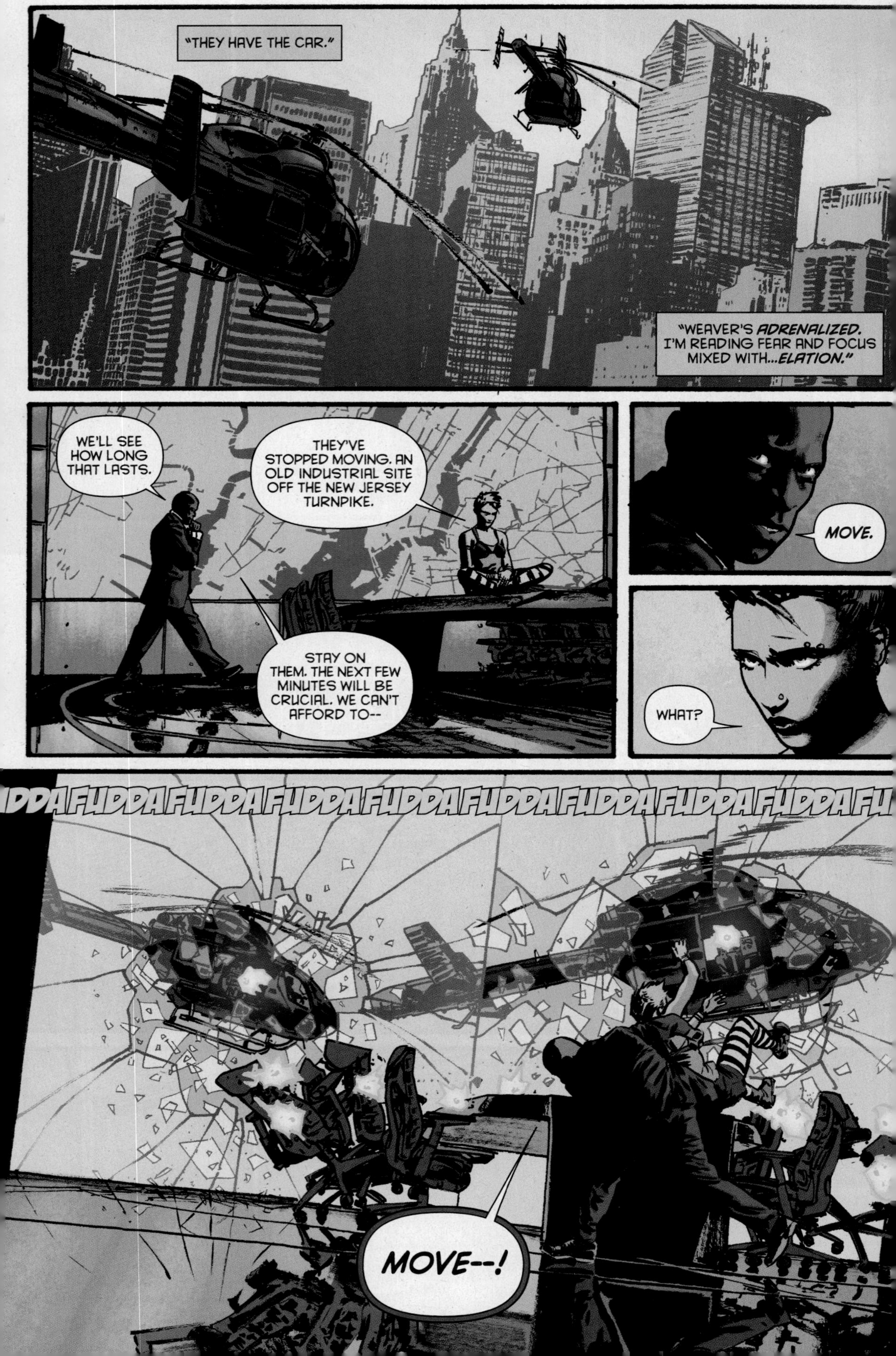
"THEY HAVE THE CAR."
"WEAVER'S ADRENALIZED. I'M READING FEAR AND FOCUS MIXED WITH...ELATION."
WE'LL SEE HOW LONG THAT LASTS.
THEY'VE STOPPED MOVING. AN OLD INDUSTRIAL SITE OFF THE NEW JERSEY TURNPIKE.
STAY ON THEM. THE NEXT FEW MINUTES WILL BE CRUCIAL. WE CAN'T AFFORD TO--
MOVE.
WHAT?
FUDDA FUDDA FUDDA FUDDA FUDDA FUDDA FUDDA FUDDA FUDDA
MOVE--!

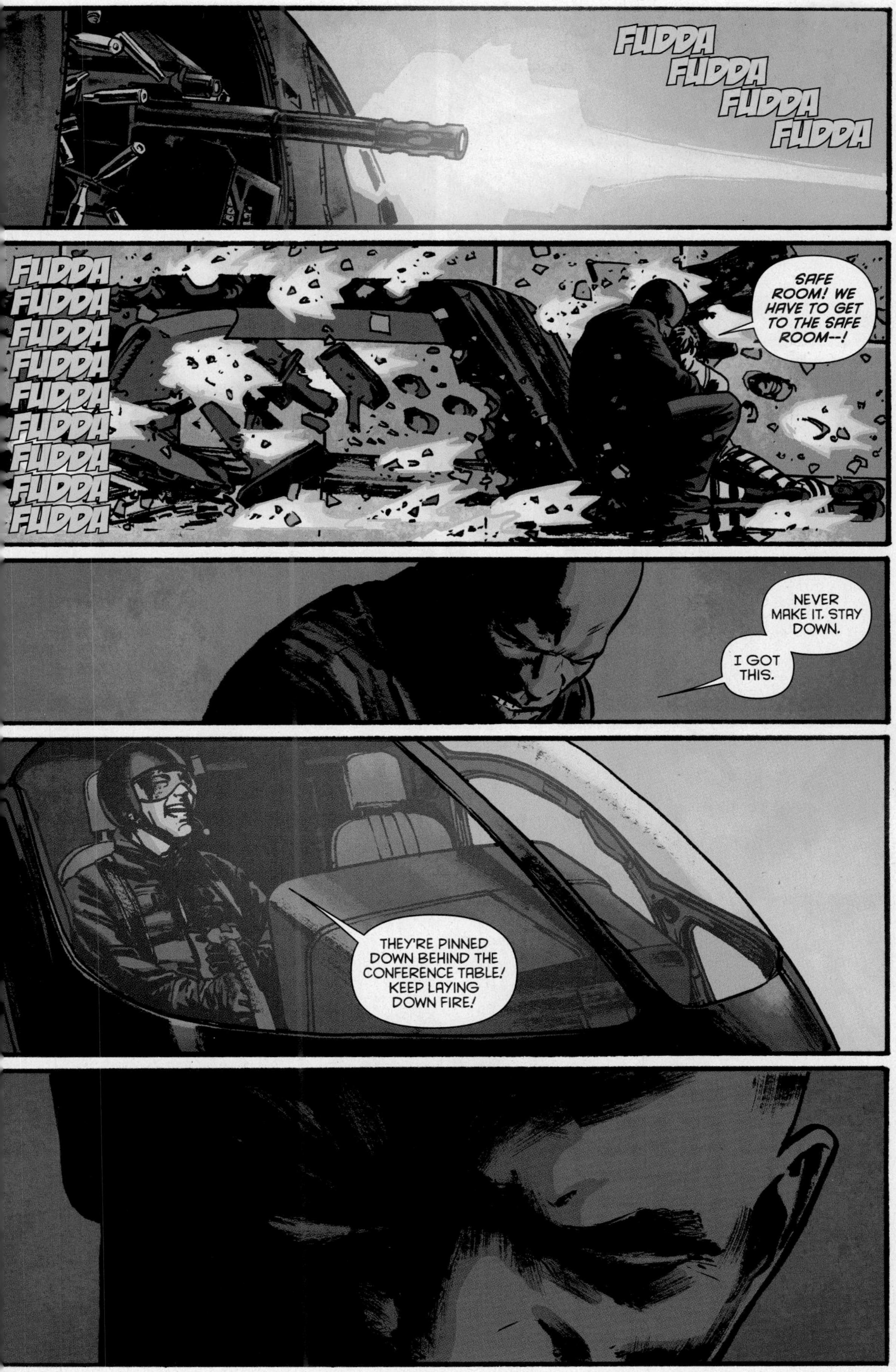
FUDDA FUDDA FUDDA FUDDA
FUDDA FUDDA FUDDA FUDDA FUDDA FUDDA FUDDA FUDDA FUDDA
SAFE ROOM! WE HAVE TO GET TO THE SAFE ROOM--!
NEVER MAKE IT. STAY DOWN.
I GOT THIS.
THEY'RE PINNED DOWN BEHIND THE CONFERENCE TABLE! KEEP LAYING DOWN FIRE!

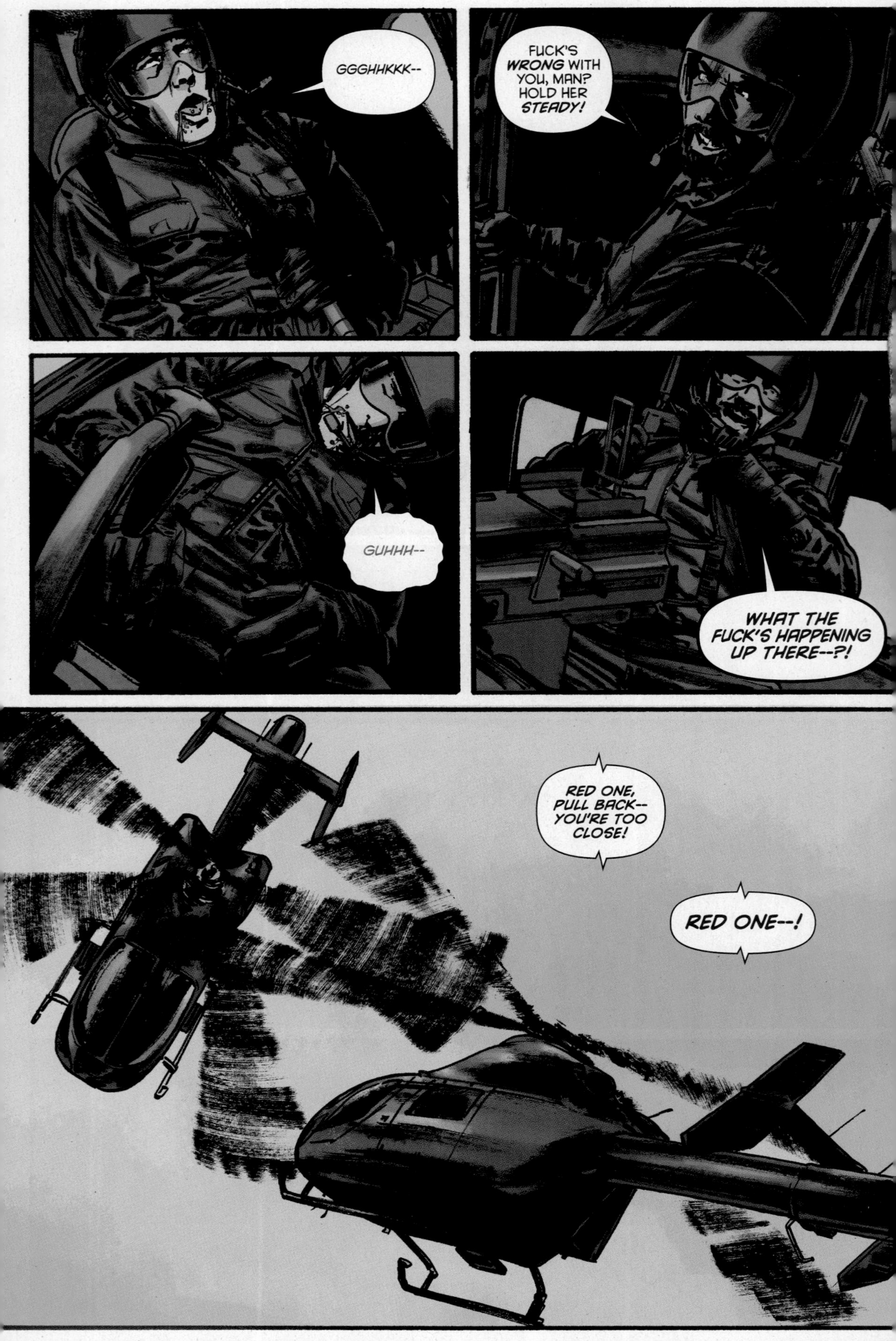
GGGHHKKK--
FUCK'S WRONG WITH YOU, MAN? HOLD HER STEADY!
GUHHH--
WHAT THE FUCK'S HAPPENING UP THERE--?!
RED ONE, PULL BACK-- YOU'RE TOO CLOSE!
RED ONE--!

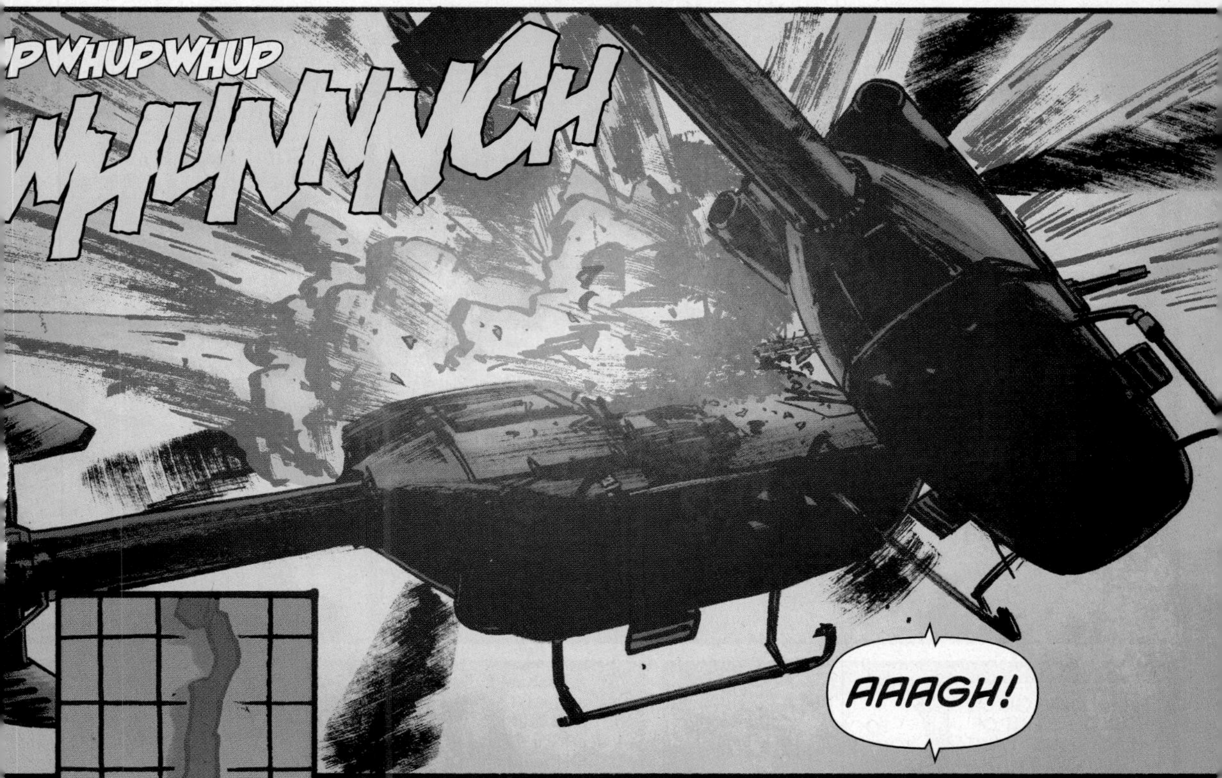
PWHUPWHUP
WHUNNNCH
AAAGH!
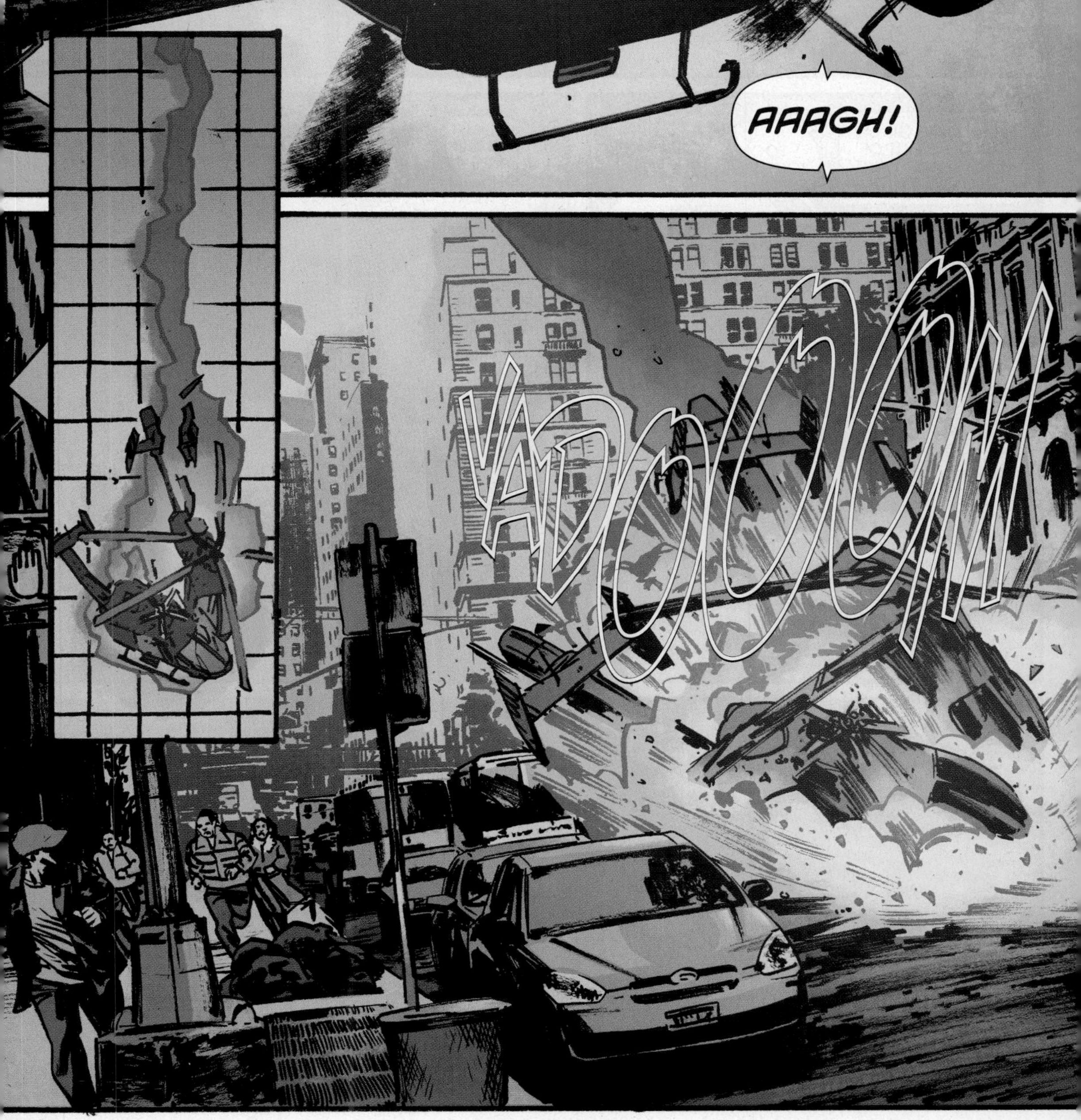
VADOOOM

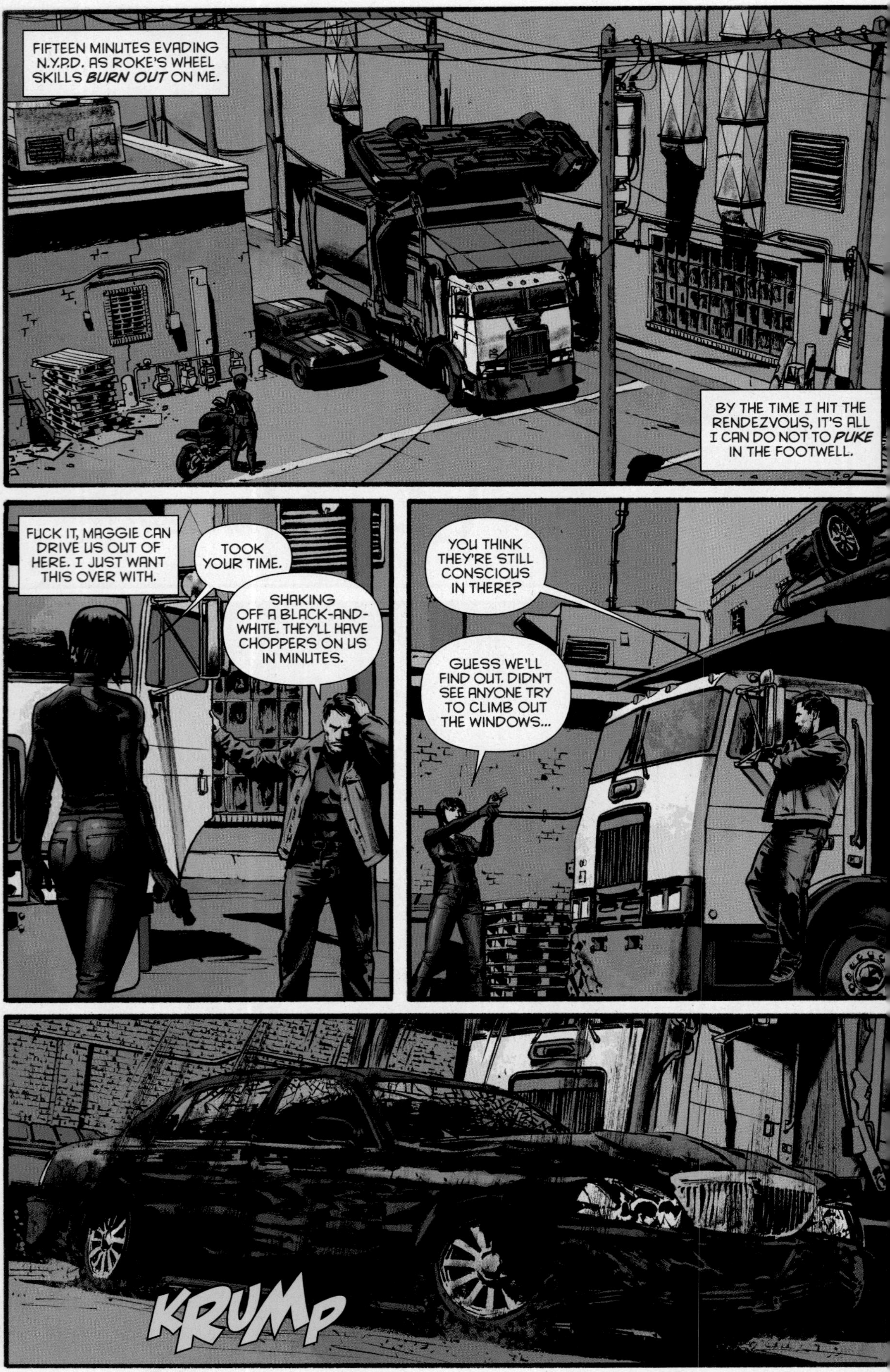
FIFTEEN MINUTES EVADING N.Y.P.D. AS ROKE'S WHEEL SKILLS *BURN OUT* ON ME.
BY THE TIME I HIT THE RENDEZVOUS, IT'S ALL I CAN DO NOT TO *PUKE* IN THE FOOTWELL.
FUCK IT, MAGGIE CAN DRIVE US OUT OF HERE. I JUST WANT THIS OVER WITH.
TOOK YOUR TIME.
SHAKING OFF A BLACK-AND-WHITE. THEY'LL HAVE CHOPPERS ON US IN MINUTES.
YOU THINK THEY'RE STILL CONSCIOUS IN THERE?
GUESS WE'LL FIND OUT. DIDN'T SEE ANYONE TRY TO CLIMB OUT THE WINDOWS...
KRUMP

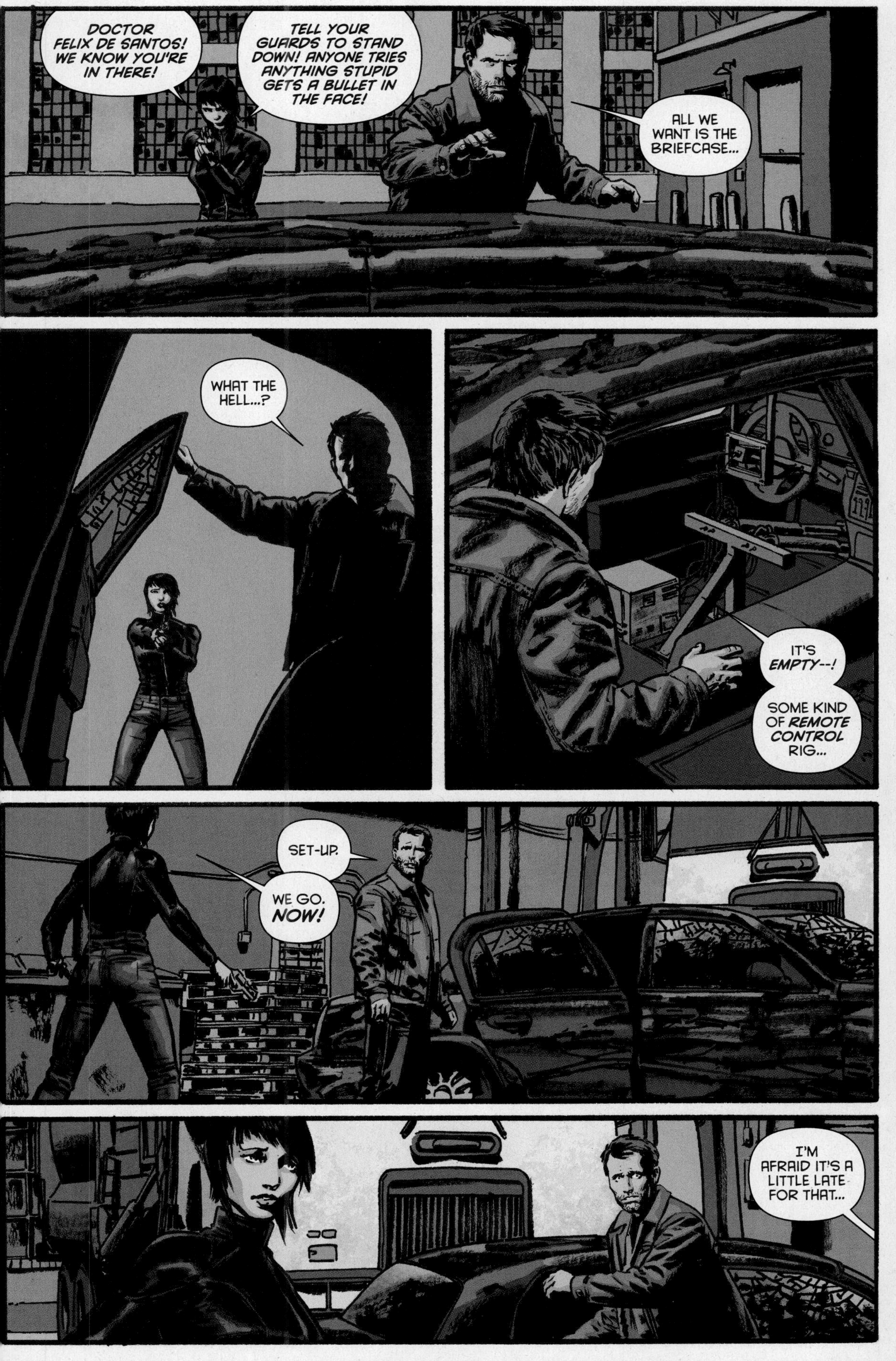
DOCTOR FELIX DE SANTOS! WE KNOW YOU'RE IN THERE!
TELL YOUR GUARDS TO STAND DOWN! ANYONE TRIES ANYTHING STUPID GETS A BULLET IN THE FACE!
ALL WE WANT IS THE BRIEFCASE...
WHAT THE HELL...?
IT'S *EMPTY*--!
SOME KIND OF *REMOTE CONTROL* RIG...
SET-UP.
WE GO. **NOW!**
I'M AFRAID IT'S A LITTLE LATE FOR THAT...

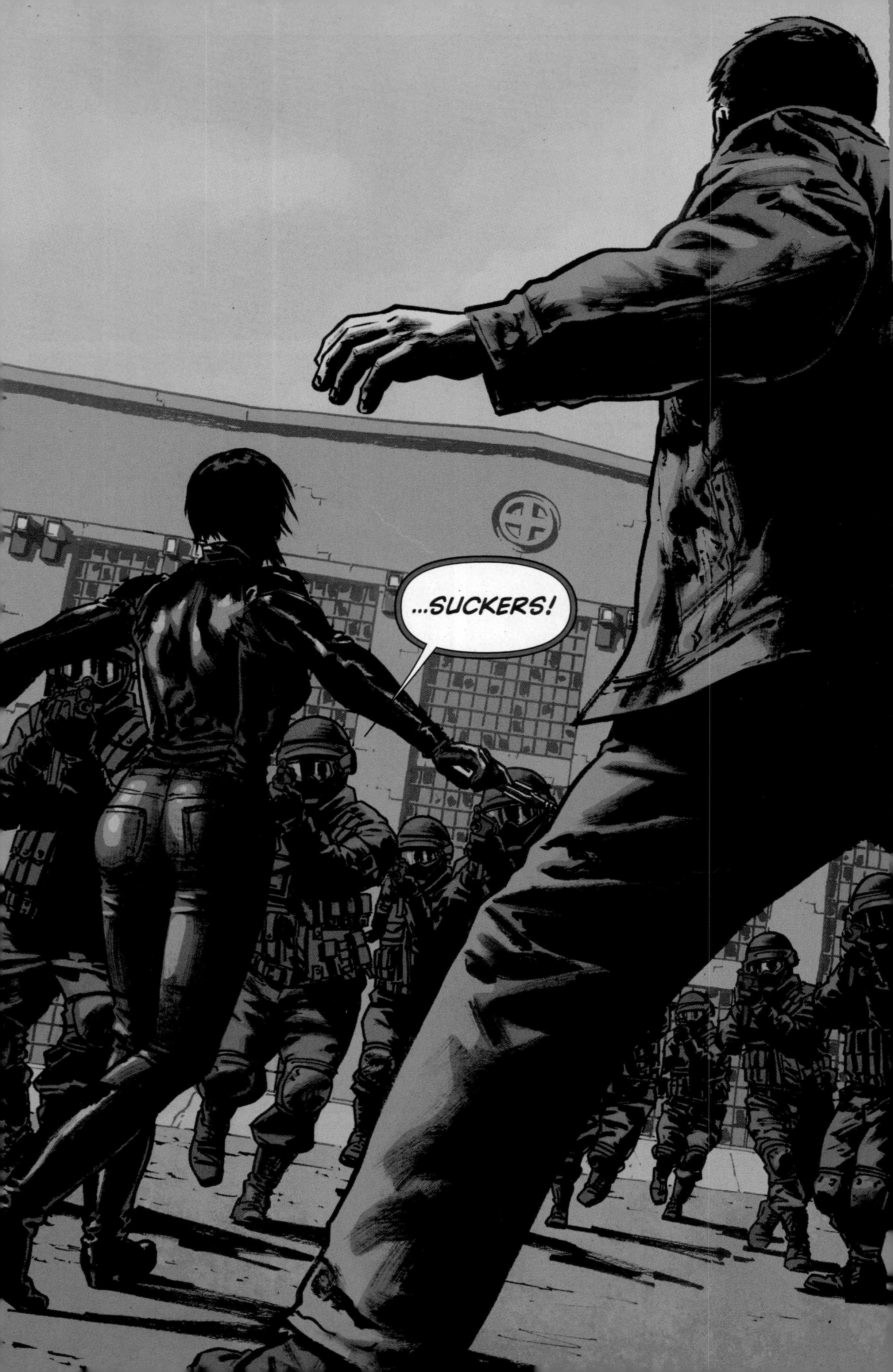
...SUCKERS!

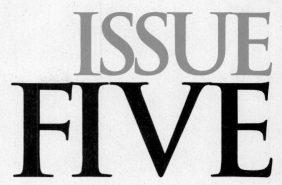

ISSUE FIVE

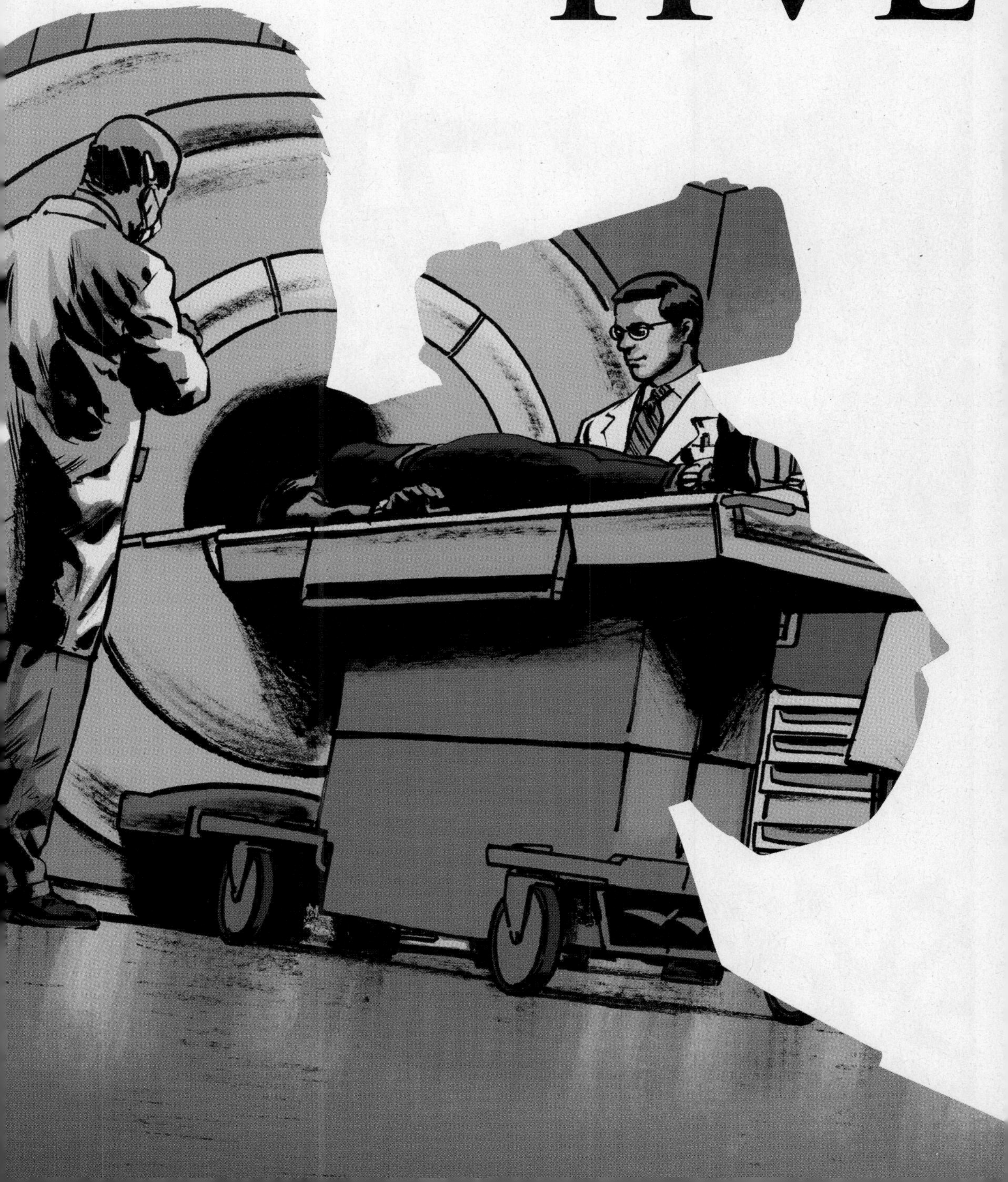

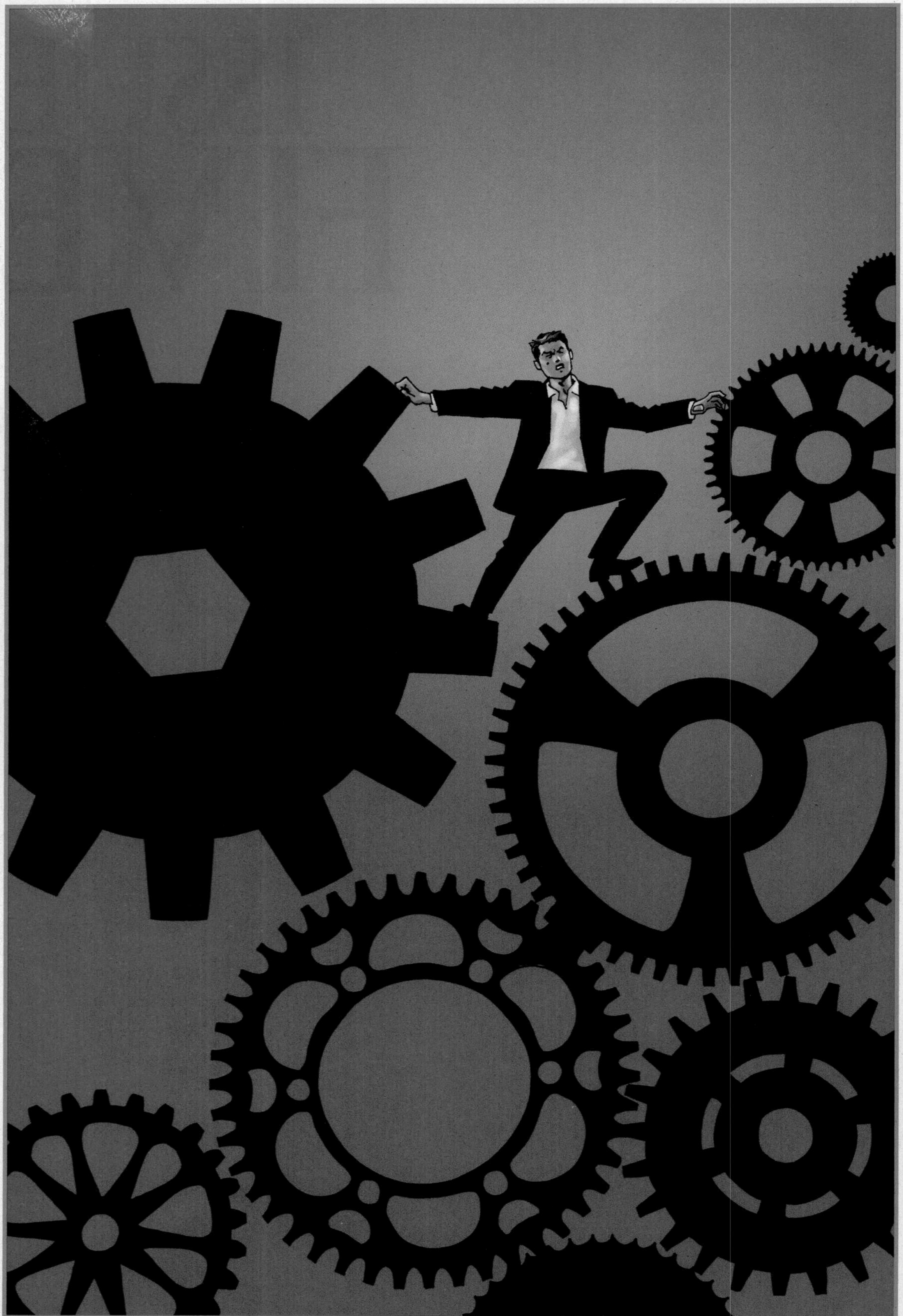

ISSUE FIVE COVER BY SEAN PHILLIPS

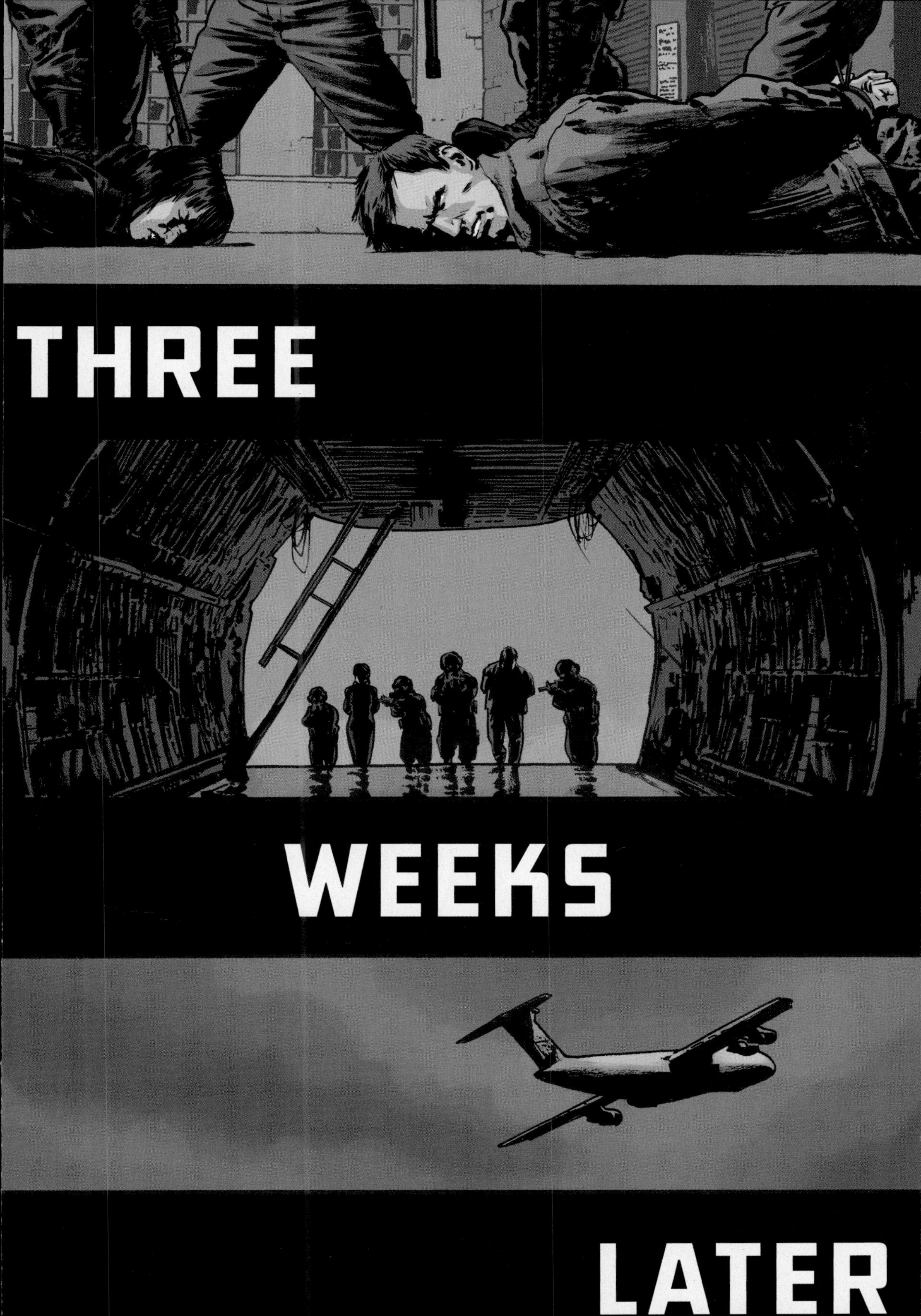
THREE
WEEKS
LATER

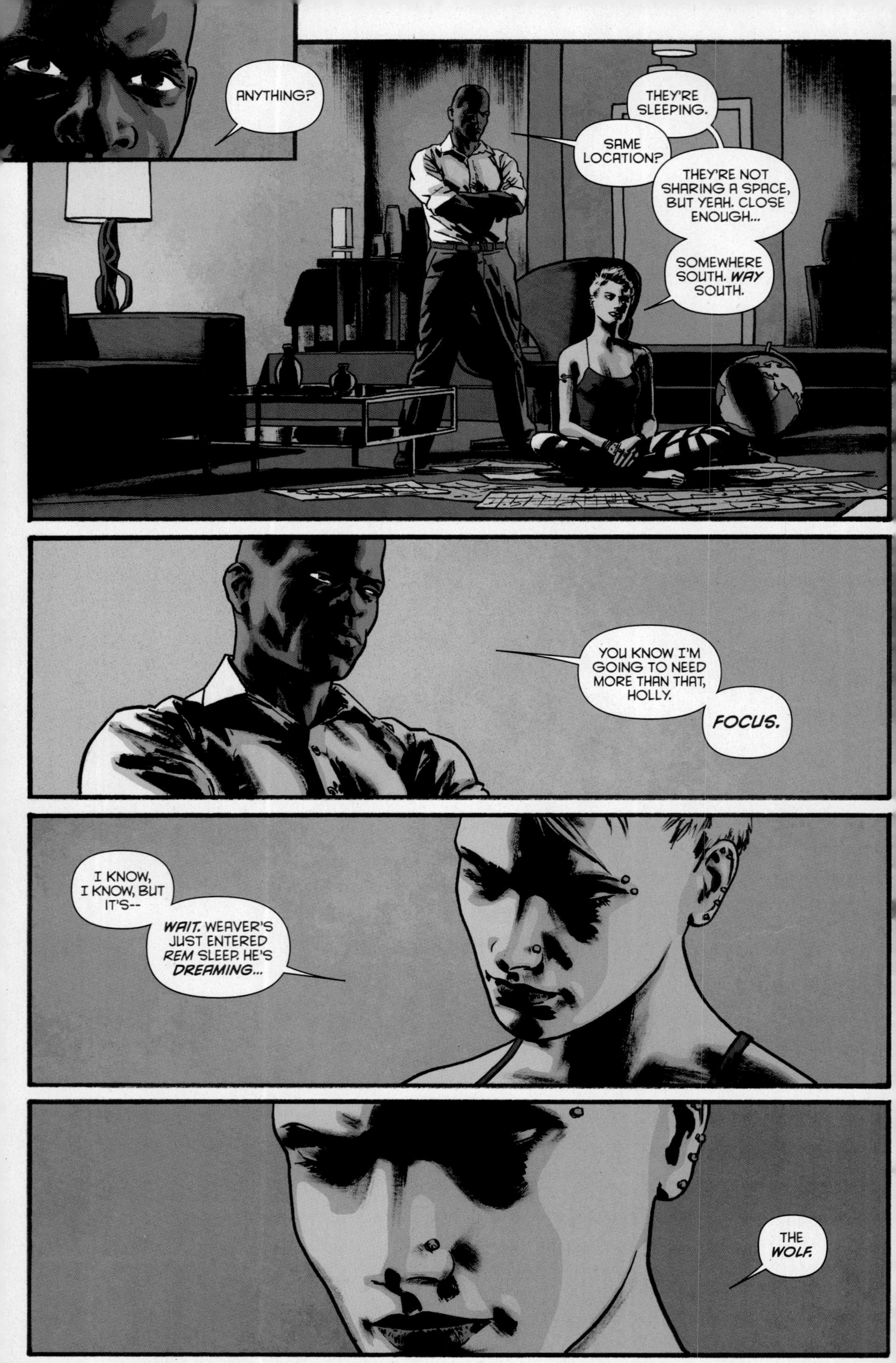
ANYTHING?
THEY'RE SLEEPING.
SAME LOCATION?
THEY'RE NOT SHARING A SPACE, BUT YEAH. CLOSE ENOUGH...
SOMEWHERE SOUTH. *WAY* SOUTH.
YOU KNOW I'M GOING TO NEED MORE THAN THAT, HOLLY.
FOCUS.
I KNOW, I KNOW, BUT IT'S--
WAIT. WEAVER'S JUST ENTERED *REM* SLEEP. HE'S *DREAMING...*
THE *WOLF.*

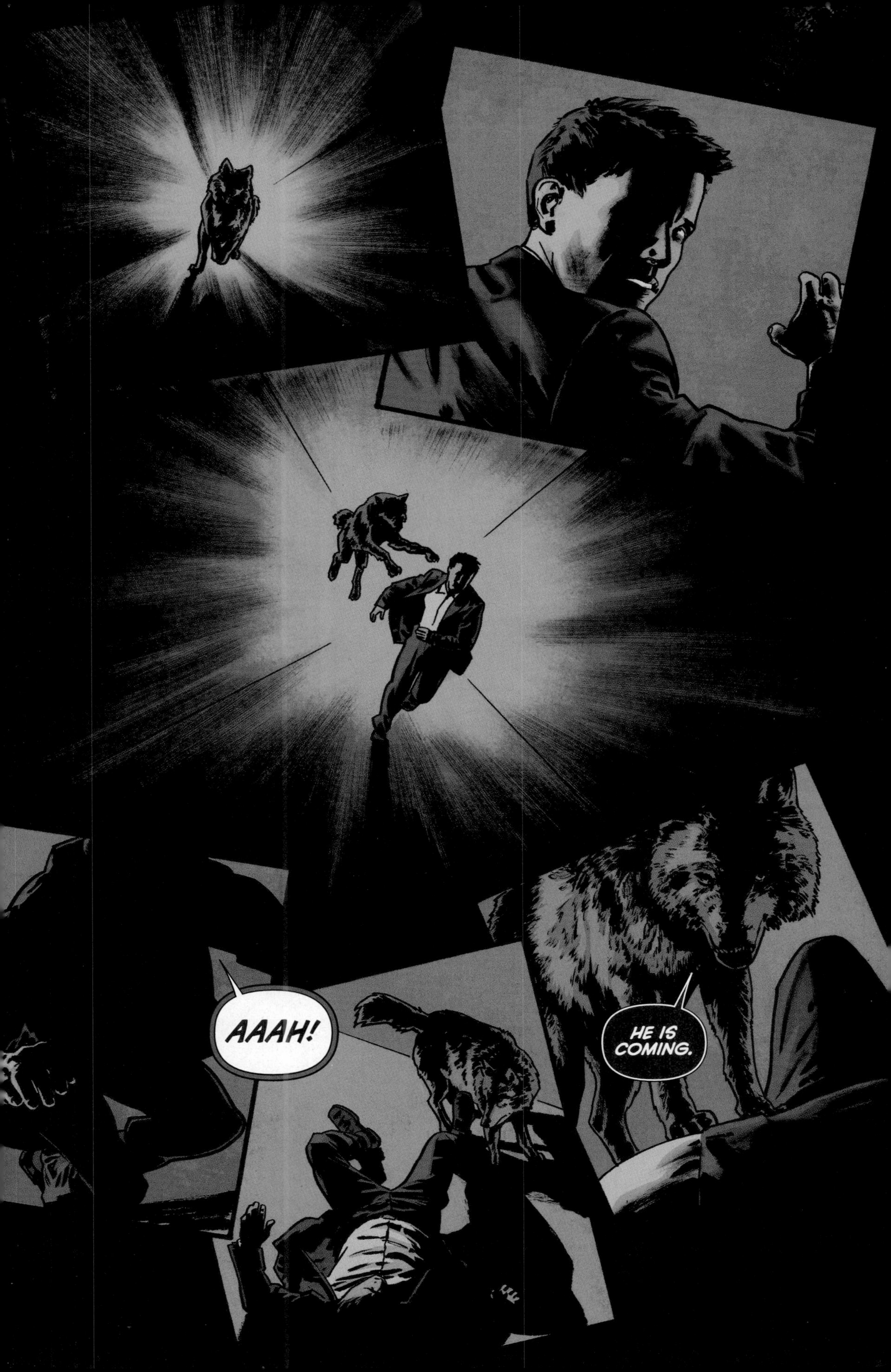
AAAH!
HE IS COMING.

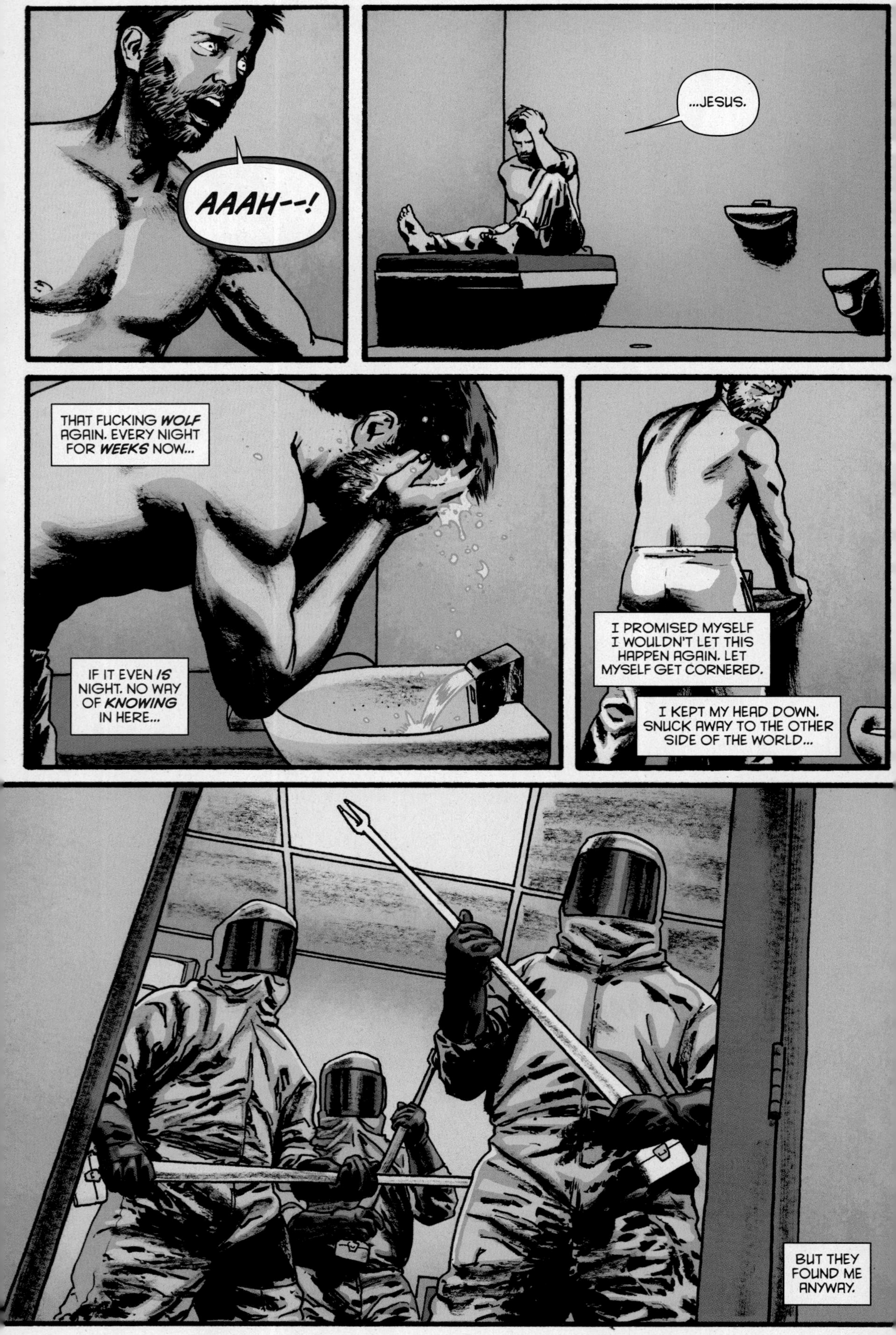
AAAH--!
...JESUS.
THAT FUCKING WOLF AGAIN. EVERY NIGHT FOR WEEKS NOW...
IF IT EVEN IS NIGHT. NO WAY OF KNOWING IN HERE...
I PROMISED MYSELF I WOULDN'T LET THIS HAPPEN AGAIN. LET MYSELF GET CORNERED.
I KEPT MY HEAD DOWN. SNUCK AWAY TO THE OTHER SIDE OF THE WORLD...
BUT THEY FOUND ME ANYWAY.

BUT THIS ISN'T LIKE BEFORE--THE YEARS WASTED IN THAT NEW YORK MENTAL HOSPITAL...

YEARS SPENT TRYING TO FIGURE OUT WHO I WAS...

WHAT I WAS.

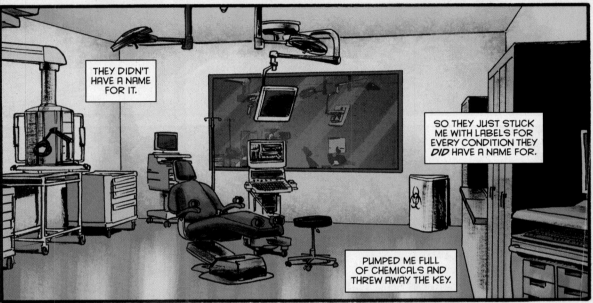

THEY DIDN'T HAVE A NAME FOR IT.

SO THEY JUST STUCK ME WITH LABELS FOR EVERY CONDITION THEY DID HAVE A NAME FOR.

PUMPED ME FULL OF CHEMICALS AND THREW AWAY THE KEY.

BUT THIS IS DIFFERENT. THESE PEOPLE--CADRE, STYLES CALLED THEM-- THEY KNOW WHAT I AM.

THAT'S WHY I'M HERE.

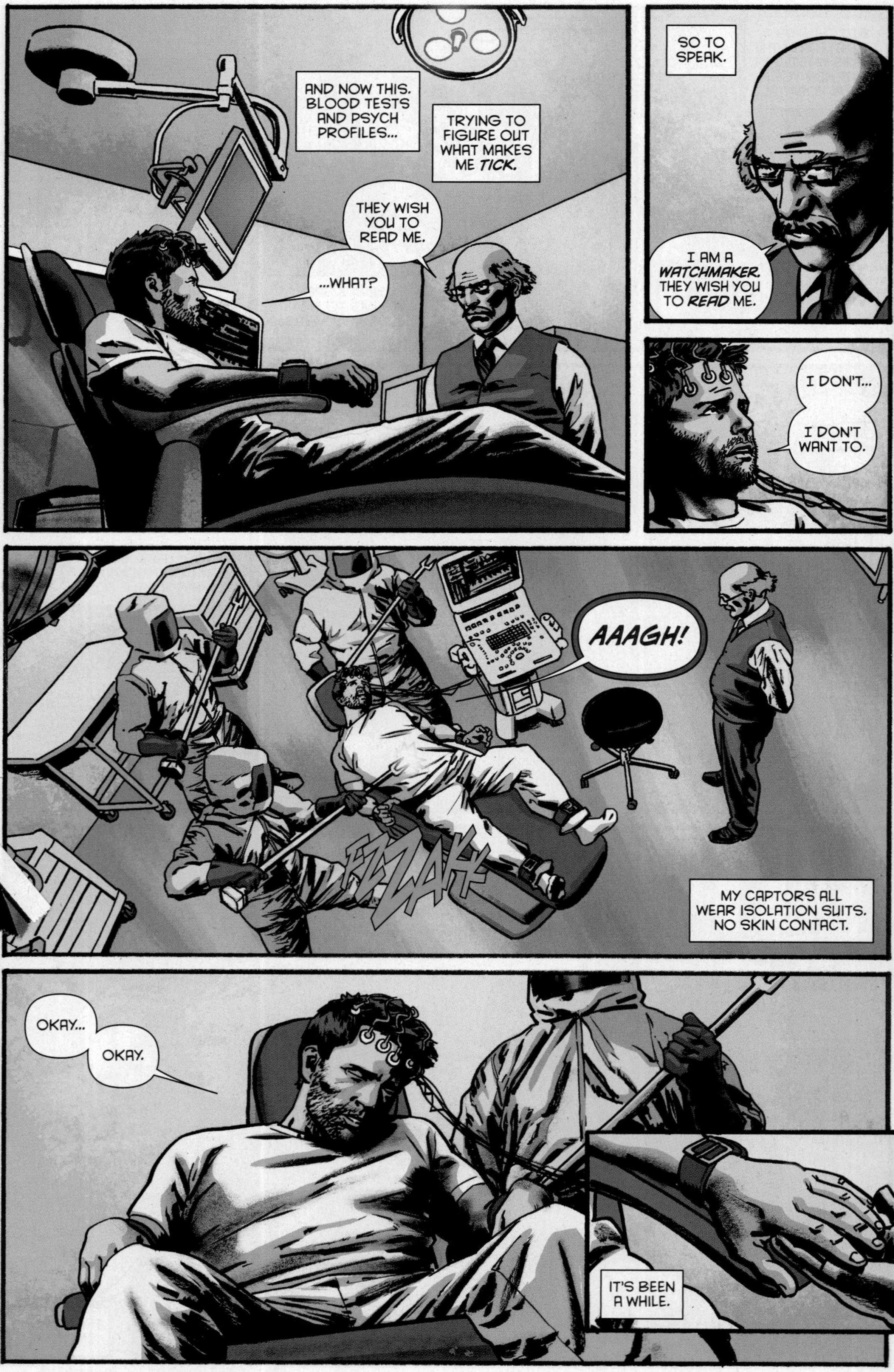
AND NOW THIS. BLOOD TESTS AND PSYCH PROFILES...
TRYING TO FIGURE OUT WHAT MAKES ME TICK.
THEY WISH YOU TO READ ME.
...WHAT?
SO TO SPEAK.
I AM A WATCHMAKER. THEY WISH YOU TO READ ME.
I DON'T...
I DON'T WANT TO.
AAAGH!
FZZAK!
MY CAPTORS ALL WEAR ISOLATION SUITS. NO SKIN CONTACT.
OKAY...
OKAY.
IT'S BEEN A WHILE.

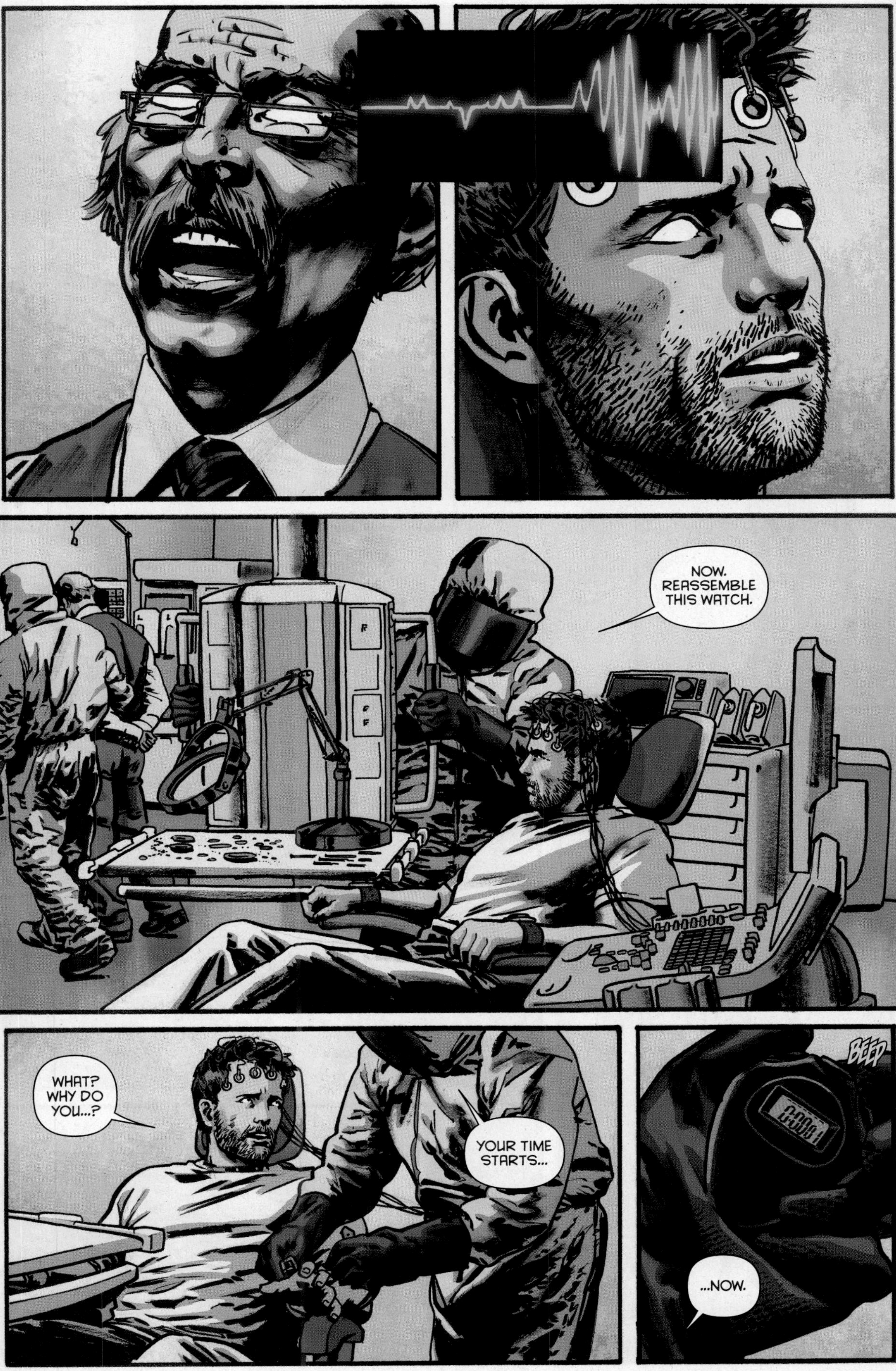
NOW. REASSEMBLE THIS WATCH.
WHAT? WHY DO YOU...?
YOUR TIME STARTS...
BEEP
...NOW.

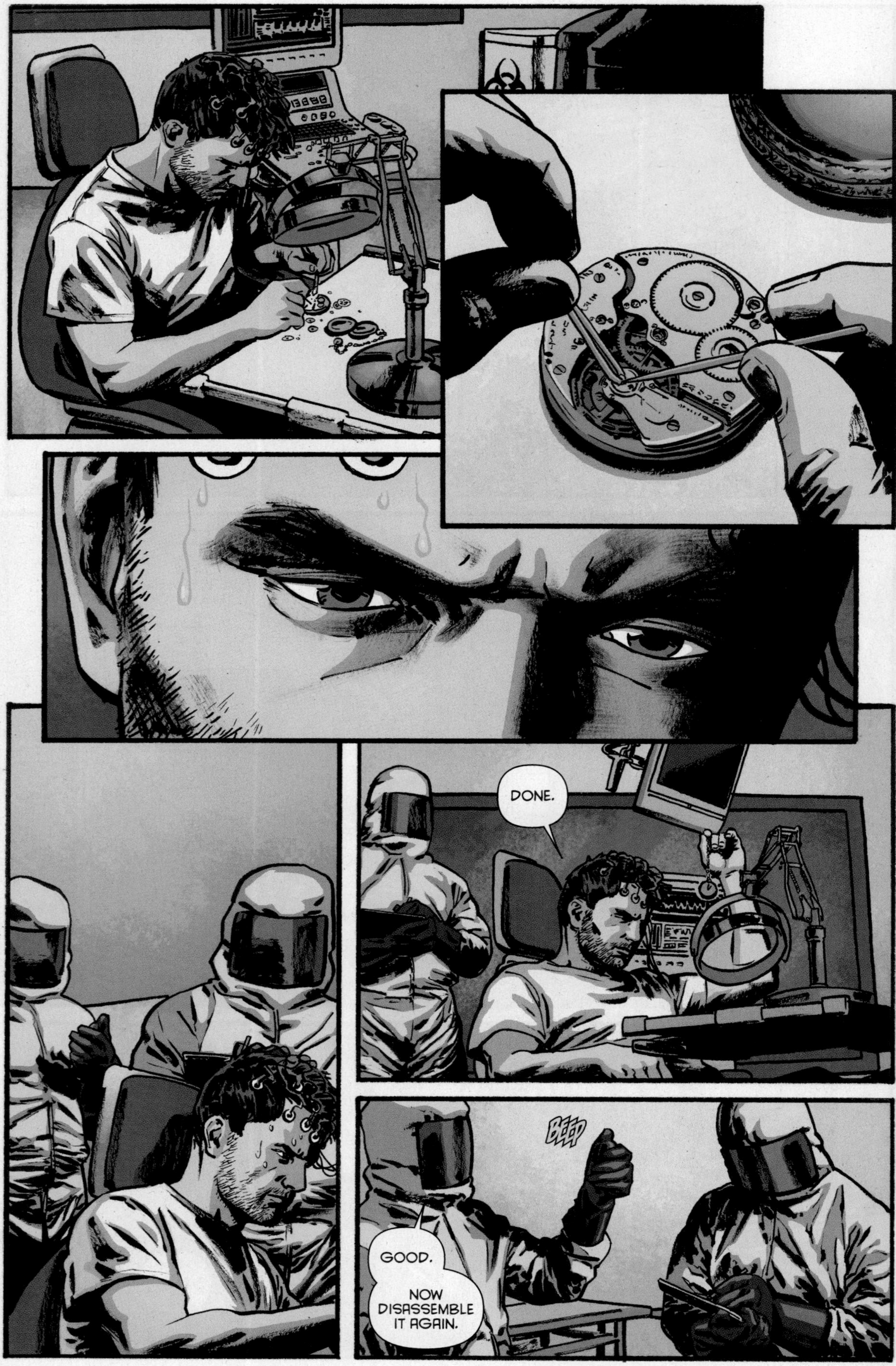
DONE.
BEEP
GOOD.
NOW DISASSEMBLE IT AGAIN.

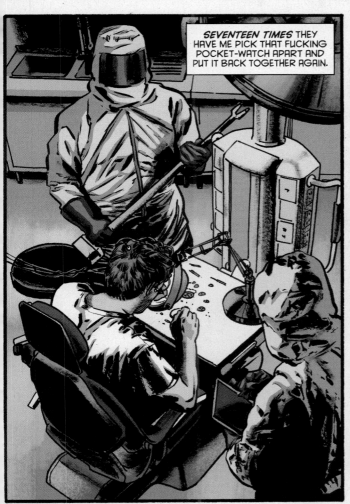

SEVENTEEN TIMES THEY HAVE ME PICK THAT FUCKING POCKET-WATCH APART AND PUT IT BACK TOGETHER AGAIN.

IT GETS HARDER EVERY TIME, AS THE OLD WATCHMAKER'S SKILL FADES, REPLACED WITH SUCKING EMPTINESS AND FRUSTRATION--

FUCK IT, I'M DONE. I DON'T KNOW WHAT I'M DOING ANY MORE.

FINISH IT.

I CAN'T FINISH IT! I DON'T KNOW WHAT I'M DOING.

IT'S JUST... GONE.

THEN BACK TO MY CELL TO STEW IN SELF-PITY.

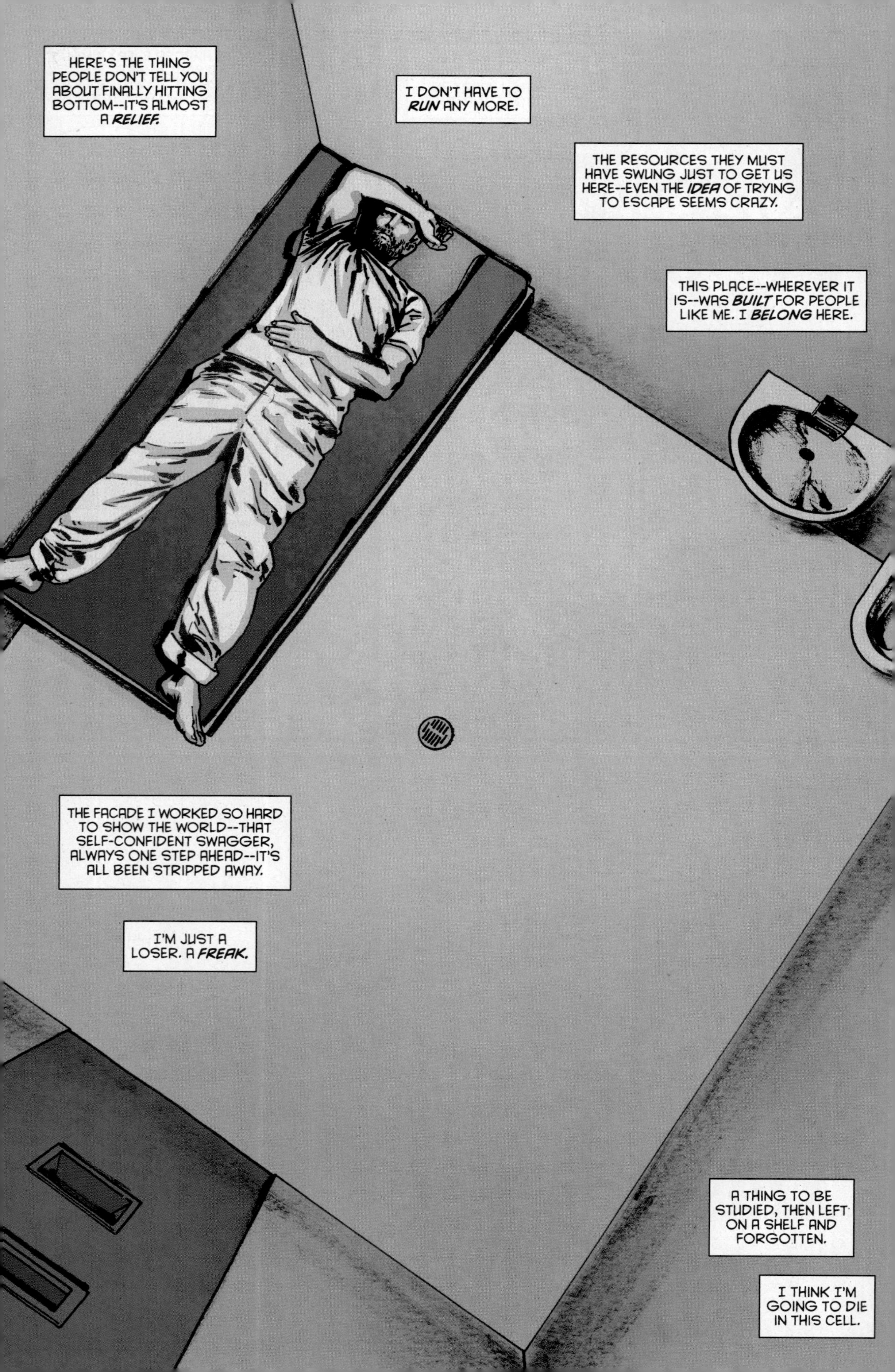
HERE'S THE THING PEOPLE DON'T TELL YOU ABOUT FINALLY HITTING BOTTOM--IT'S ALMOST A *RELIEF.*
I DON'T HAVE TO *RUN* ANY MORE.
THE RESOURCES THEY MUST HAVE SWUNG JUST TO GET US HERE--EVEN THE *IDEA* OF TRYING TO ESCAPE SEEMS CRAZY.
THIS PLACE--WHEREVER IT IS--WAS *BUILT* FOR PEOPLE LIKE ME. I *BELONG* HERE.
THE FACADE I WORKED SO HARD TO SHOW THE WORLD--THAT SELF-CONFIDENT SWAGGER, ALWAYS ONE STEP AHEAD--IT'S ALL BEEN STRIPPED AWAY.
I'M JUST A LOSER. A *FREAK.*
A THING TO BE STUDIED, THEN LEFT ON A SHELF AND FORGOTTEN.
I THINK I'M GOING TO DIE IN THIS CELL.

WEAVER'S E.E.G. YOU CAN SEE HOW THE HEIGHTENED BRAIN ACTIVITY DETERIORATES OVER TIME--

AS EXPECTED. THIS TELLS US NOTHING WE DON'T ALREADY KNOW.

E.E.G. IS TOO BLUNT A TOOL FOR THIS KIND OF FINESSE WORK. I NEED TO SEE WHICH *AREAS* OF THE BRAIN HE'S ACCESSING.

LINE HIM UP FOR AN M.R.I.

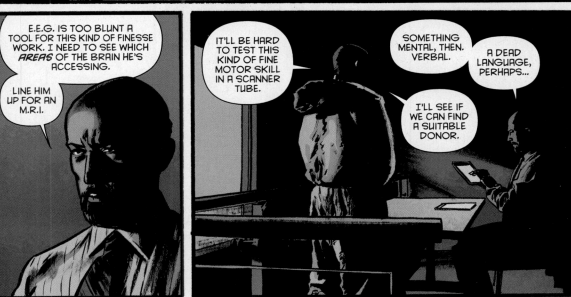

IT'LL BE HARD TO TEST THIS KIND OF FINE MOTOR SKILL IN A SCANNER TUBE.

SOMETHING MENTAL, THEN. VERBAL.

A DEAD LANGUAGE, PERHAPS...

I'LL SEE IF WE CAN FIND A SUITABLE DONOR.

AFTER WE'VE COMPLETED THE FORD WOMAN'S SET.

SHE'S SCHEDULED FOR TOMORROW. WHAT ARE WE TESTING FOR?

ENDURANCE.

CHRIST.

THIS JOB.

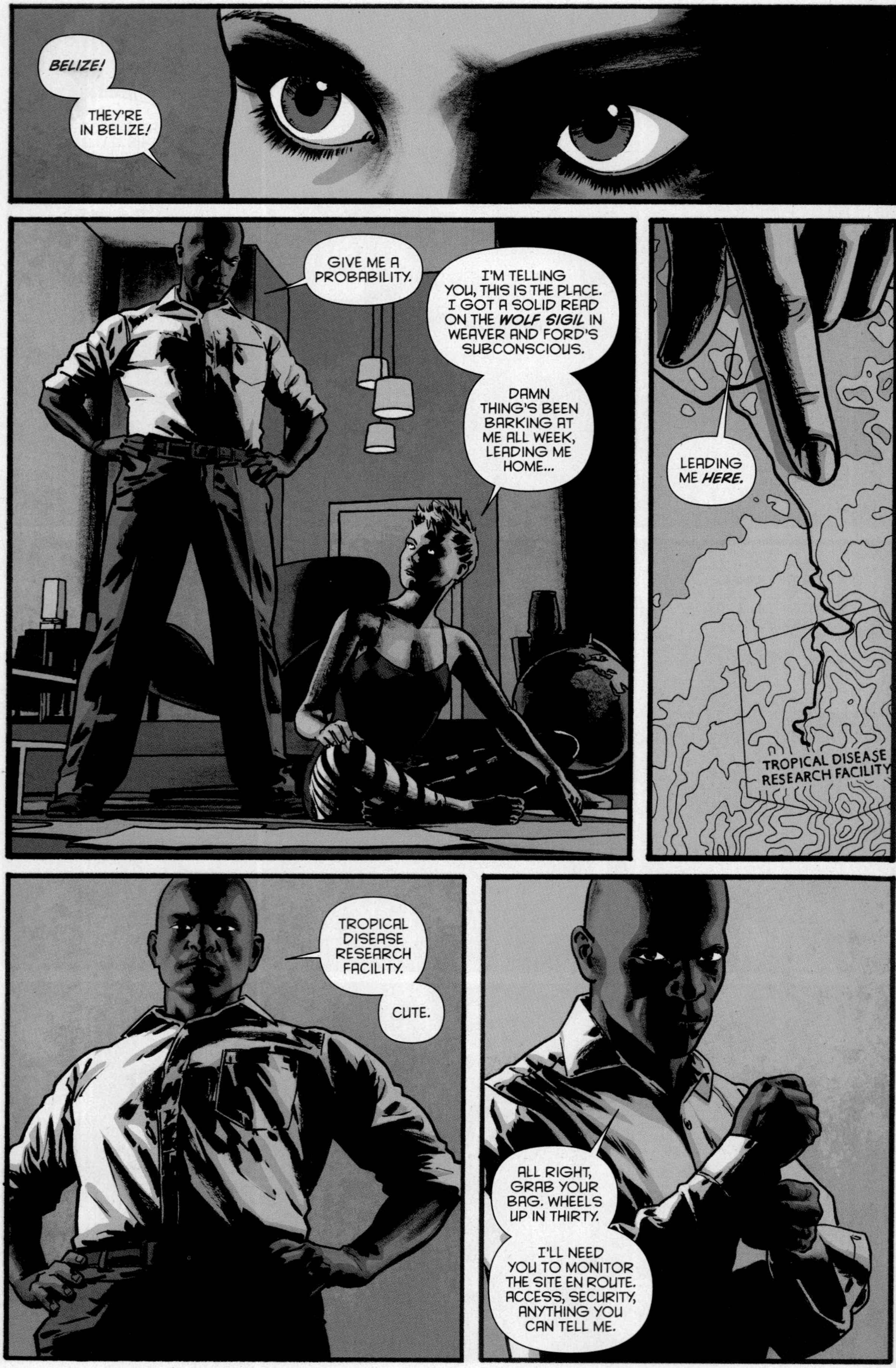

BELIZE!
THEY'RE IN BELIZE!
GIVE ME A PROBABILITY.
I'M TELLING YOU, THIS IS THE PLACE. I GOT A SOLID READ ON THE WOLF SIGIL IN WEAVER AND FORD'S SUBCONSCIOUS.
DAMN THING'S BEEN BARKING AT ME ALL WEEK, LEADING ME HOME...
LEADING ME HERE.
TROPICAL DISEASE RESEARCH FACILITY
TROPICAL DISEASE RESEARCH FACILITY.
CUTE.
ALL RIGHT, GRAB YOUR BAG. WHEELS UP IN THIRTY.
I'LL NEED YOU TO MONITOR THE SITE EN ROUTE. ACCESS, SECURITY, ANYTHING YOU CAN TELL ME.

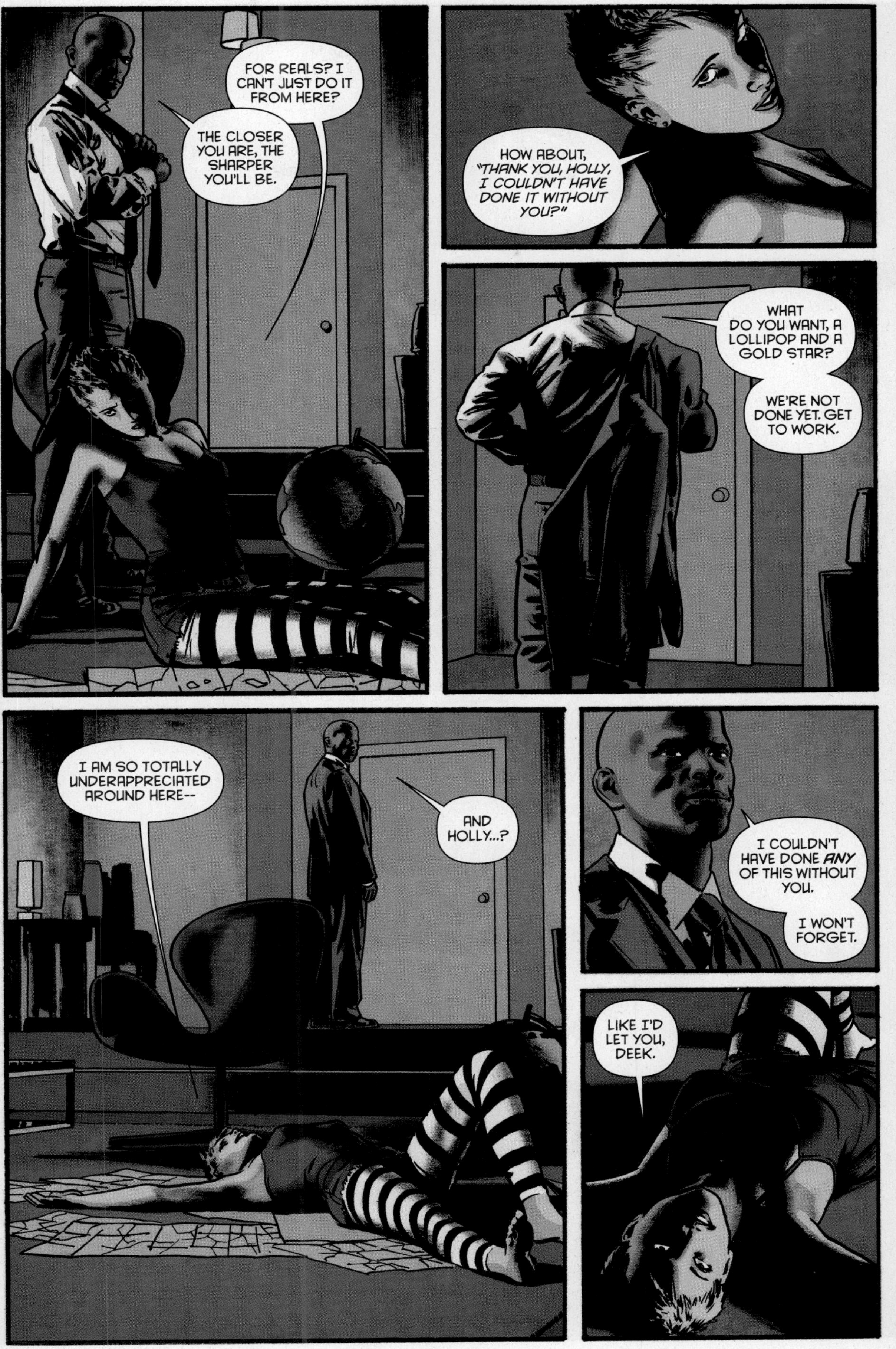
FOR REALS? I CAN'T JUST DO IT FROM HERE?
THE CLOSER YOU ARE, THE SHARPER YOU'LL BE.
HOW ABOUT, *"THANK YOU, HOLLY, I COULDN'T HAVE DONE IT WITHOUT YOU?"*
WHAT DO YOU WANT, A LOLLIPOP AND A GOLD STAR?
WE'RE NOT DONE YET. GET TO WORK.
I AM SO TOTALLY UNDERAPPRECIATED AROUND HERE--
AND HOLLY...?
I COULDN'T HAVE DONE *ANY* OF THIS WITHOUT YOU.
I WON'T FORGET.
LIKE I'D LET YOU, DEEK.

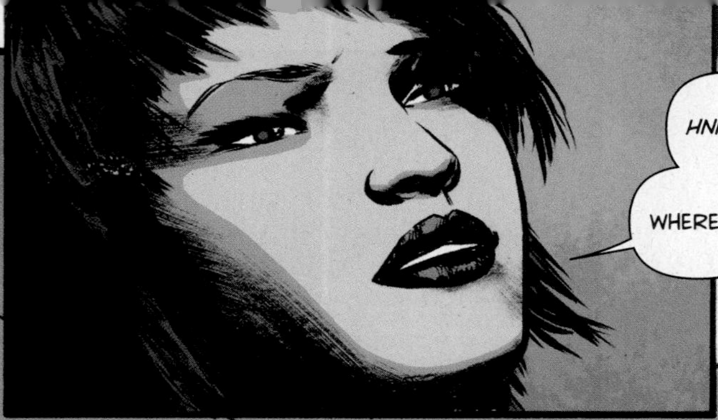
HNNGH...
WHERE...?

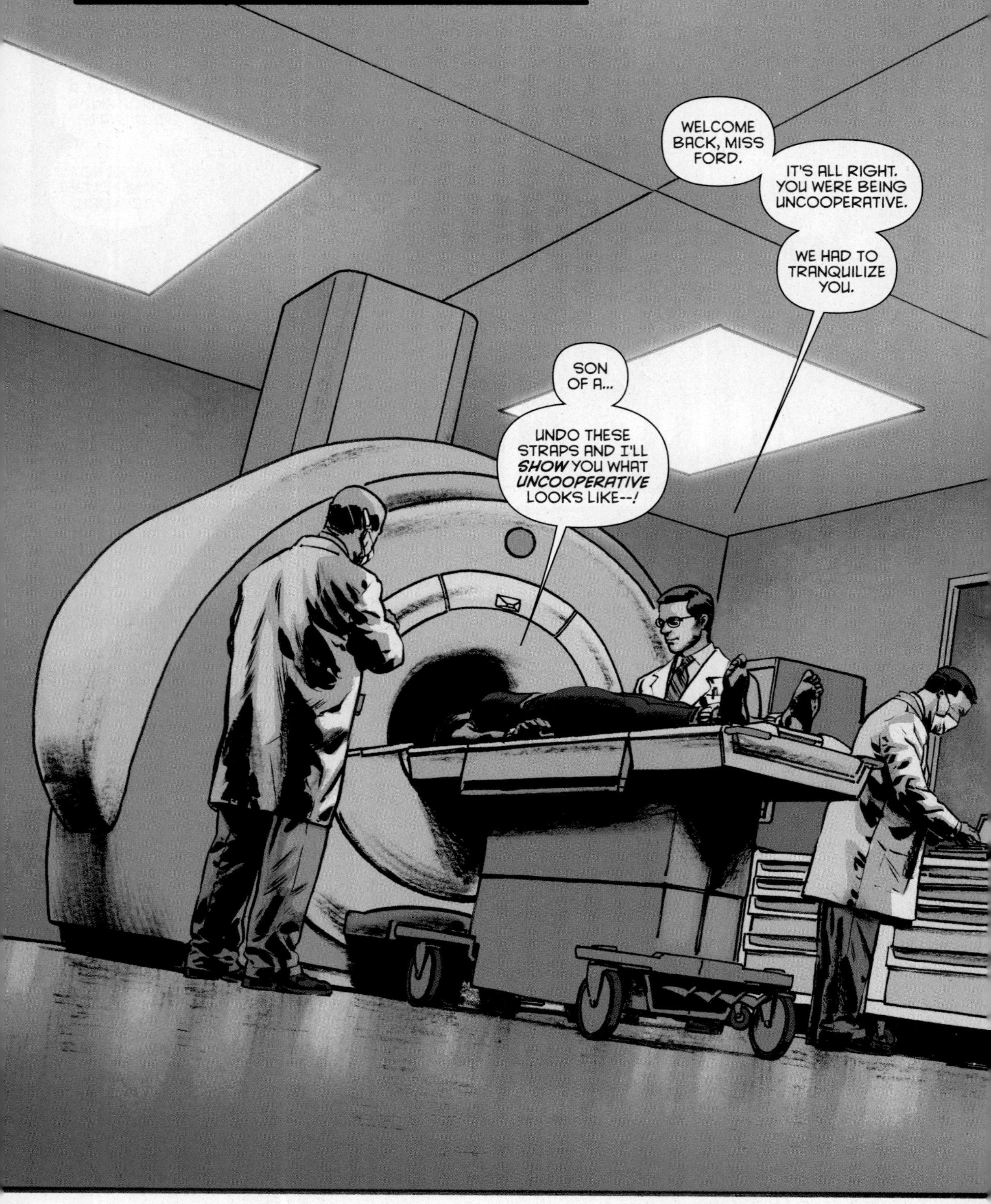
WELCOME BACK, MISS FORD.
IT'S ALL RIGHT. YOU WERE BEING UNCOOPERATIVE.
WE HAD TO TRANQUILIZE YOU.
SON OF A...
UNDO THESE STRAPS AND I'LL *SHOW* YOU WHAT *UNCOOPERATIVE* LOOKS LIKE--!

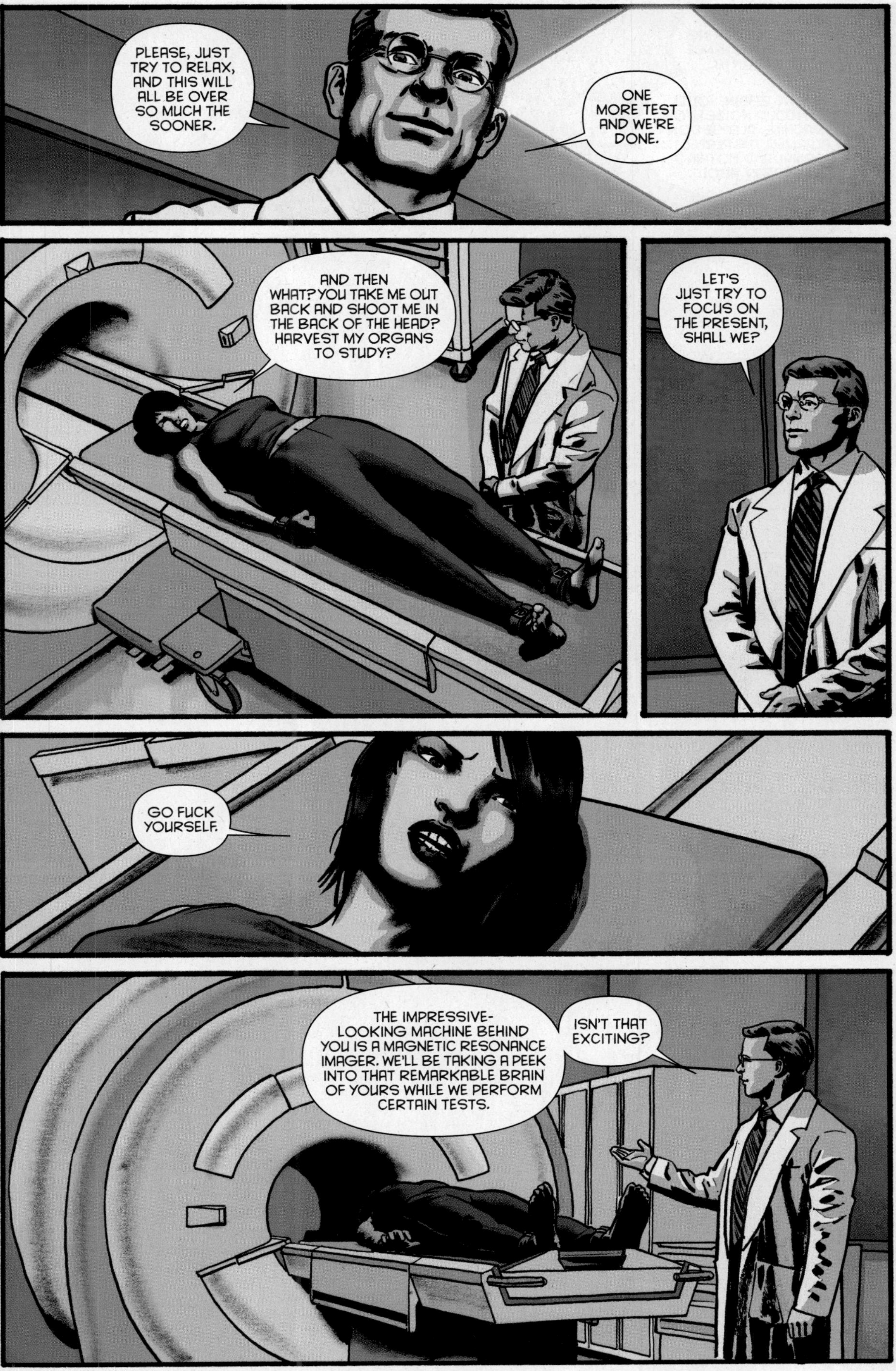
PLEASE, JUST TRY TO RELAX, AND THIS WILL ALL BE OVER SO MUCH THE SOONER.
ONE MORE TEST AND WE'RE DONE.
AND THEN WHAT? YOU TAKE ME OUT BACK AND SHOOT ME IN THE BACK OF THE HEAD? HARVEST MY ORGANS TO STUDY?
LET'S JUST TRY TO FOCUS ON THE PRESENT, SHALL WE?
GO FUCK YOURSELF.
THE IMPRESSIVE-LOOKING MACHINE BEHIND YOU IS A MAGNETIC RESONANCE IMAGER. WE'LL BE TAKING A PEEK INTO THAT REMARKABLE BRAIN OF YOURS WHILE WE PERFORM CERTAIN TESTS.
ISN'T THAT EXCITING?

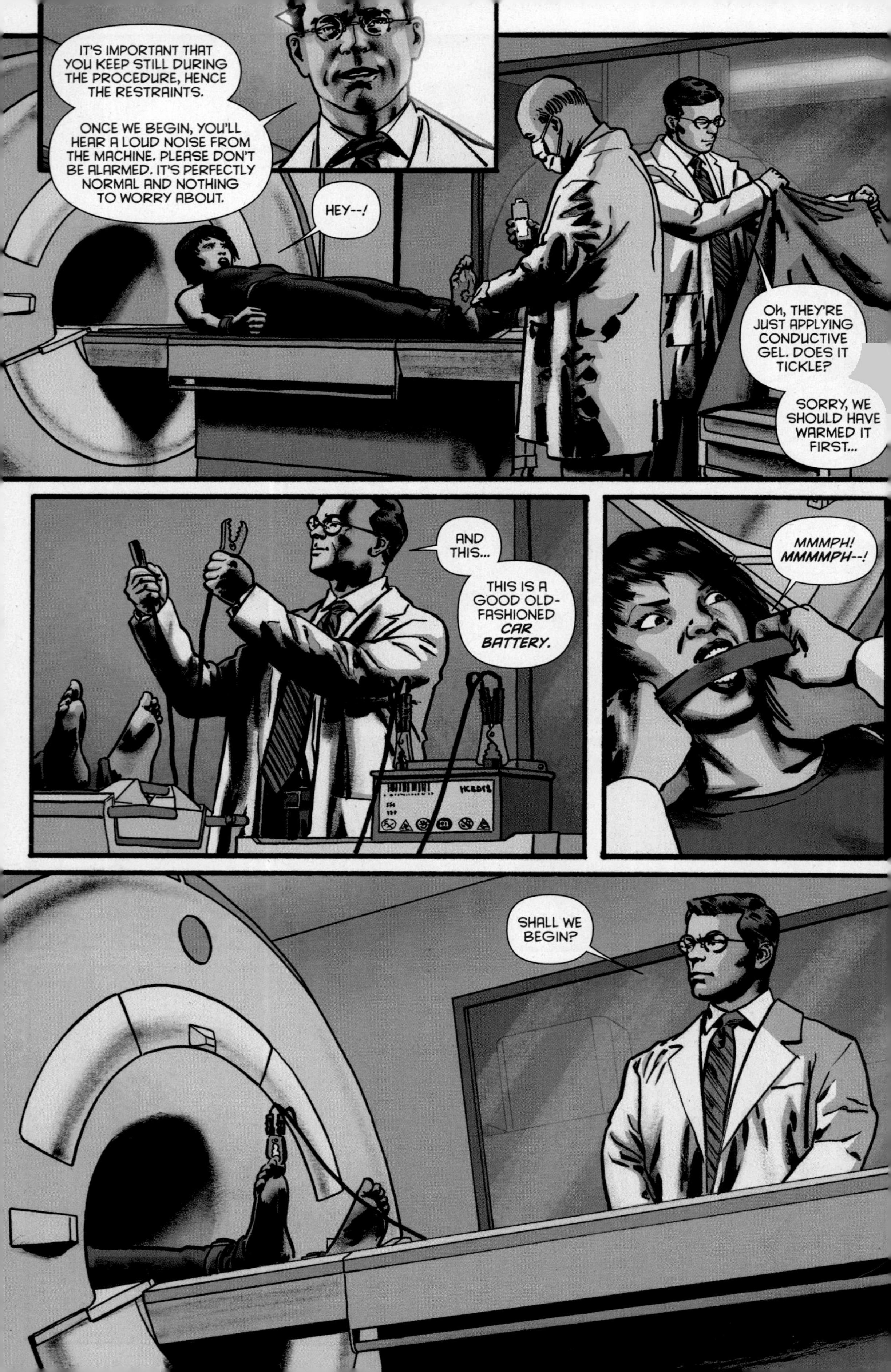
IT'S IMPORTANT THAT YOU KEEP STILL DURING THE PROCEDURE, HENCE THE RESTRAINTS.
ONCE WE BEGIN, YOU'LL HEAR A LOUD NOISE FROM THE MACHINE. PLEASE DON'T BE ALARMED. IT'S PERFECTLY NORMAL AND NOTHING TO WORRY ABOUT.
HEY--!
OH, THEY'RE JUST APPLYING CONDUCTIVE GEL. DOES IT TICKLE?
SORRY, WE SHOULD HAVE WARMED IT FIRST...
AND THIS...
THIS IS A GOOD OLD-FASHIONED *CAR BATTERY.*
MMMPH! MMMMPH--!
SHALL WE BEGIN?

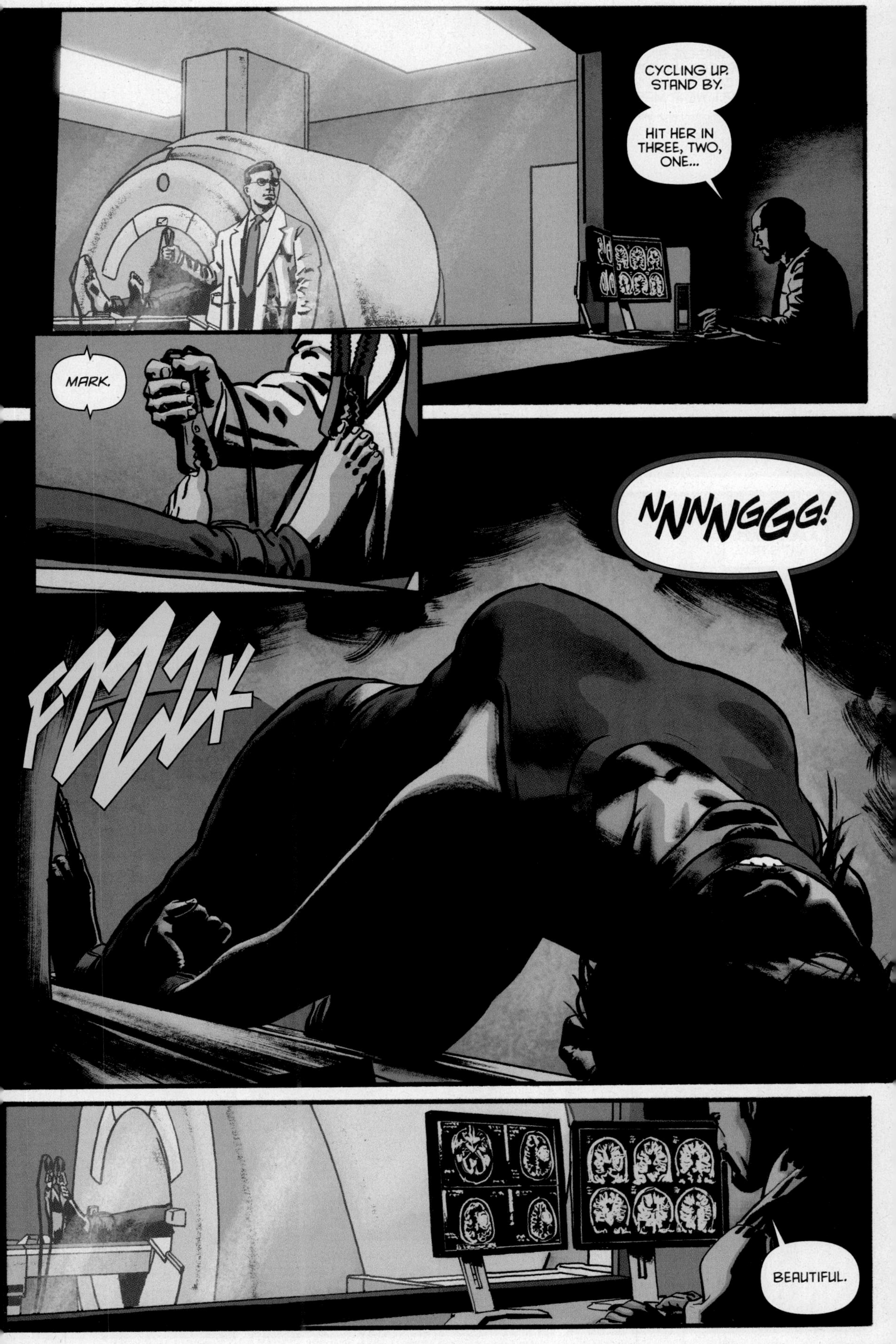
CYCLING UP. STAND BY.
HIT HER IN THREE, TWO, ONE...
MARK.
NNNNGGG!
FZZZK
BEAUTIFUL.

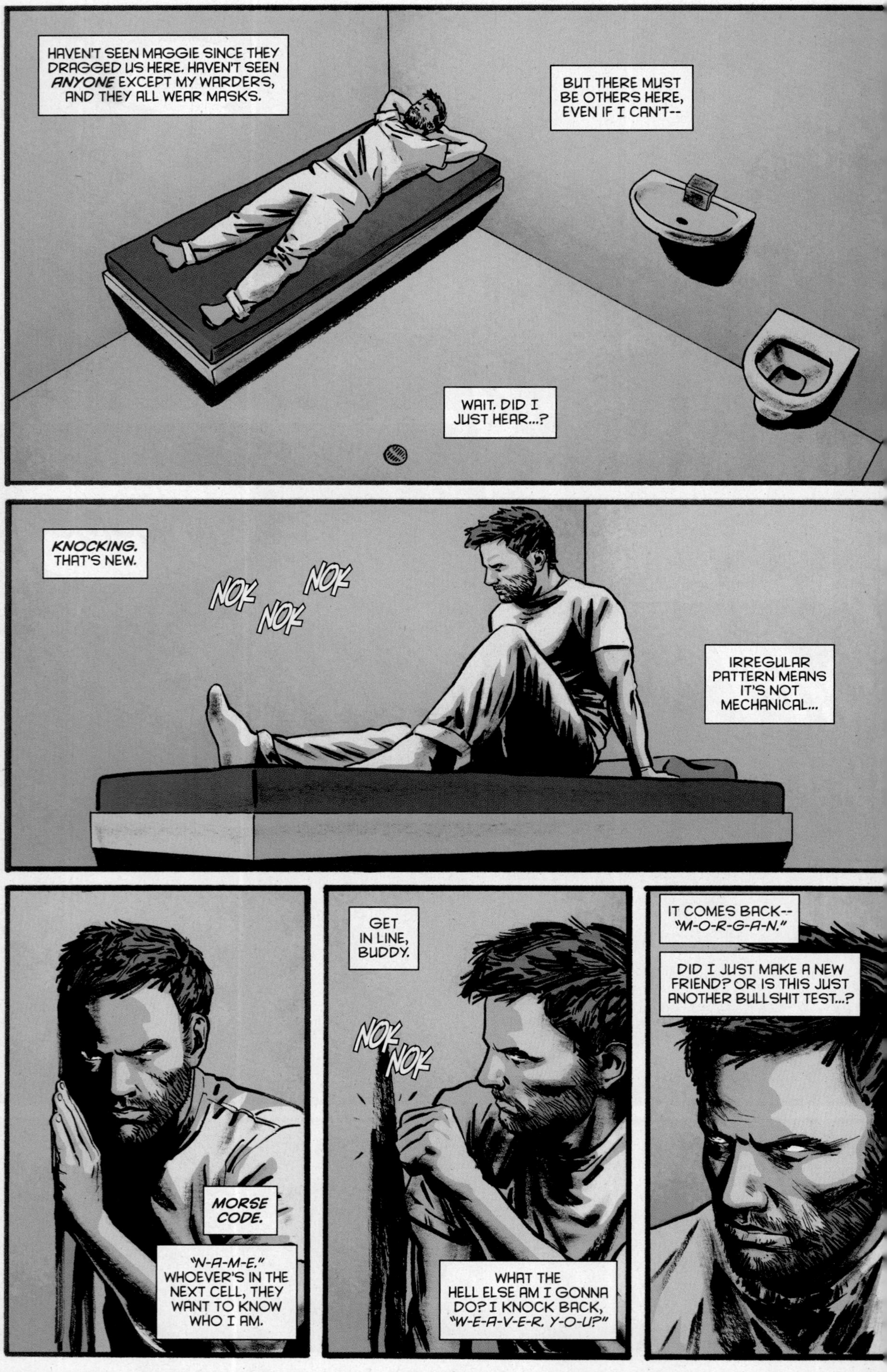
HAVEN'T SEEN MAGGIE SINCE THEY DRAGGED US HERE. HAVEN'T SEEN *ANYONE* EXCEPT MY WARDERS, AND THEY ALL WEAR MASKS.
BUT THERE MUST BE OTHERS HERE, EVEN IF I CAN'T--
WAIT. DID I JUST HEAR...?
KNOCKING. THAT'S NEW.
NOK NOK NOK
IRREGULAR PATTERN MEANS IT'S NOT MECHANICAL...
MORSE CODE.
"N-A-M-E." WHOEVER'S IN THE NEXT CELL, THEY WANT TO KNOW WHO I AM.
GET IN LINE, BUDDY.
NOK NOK
WHAT THE HELL ELSE AM I GONNA DO? I KNOCK BACK, *"W-E-A-V-E-R. Y-O-U?"*
IT COMES BACK-- *"M-O-R-G-A-N."*
DID I JUST MAKE A NEW FRIEND? OR IS THIS JUST ANOTHER BULLSHIT TEST...?

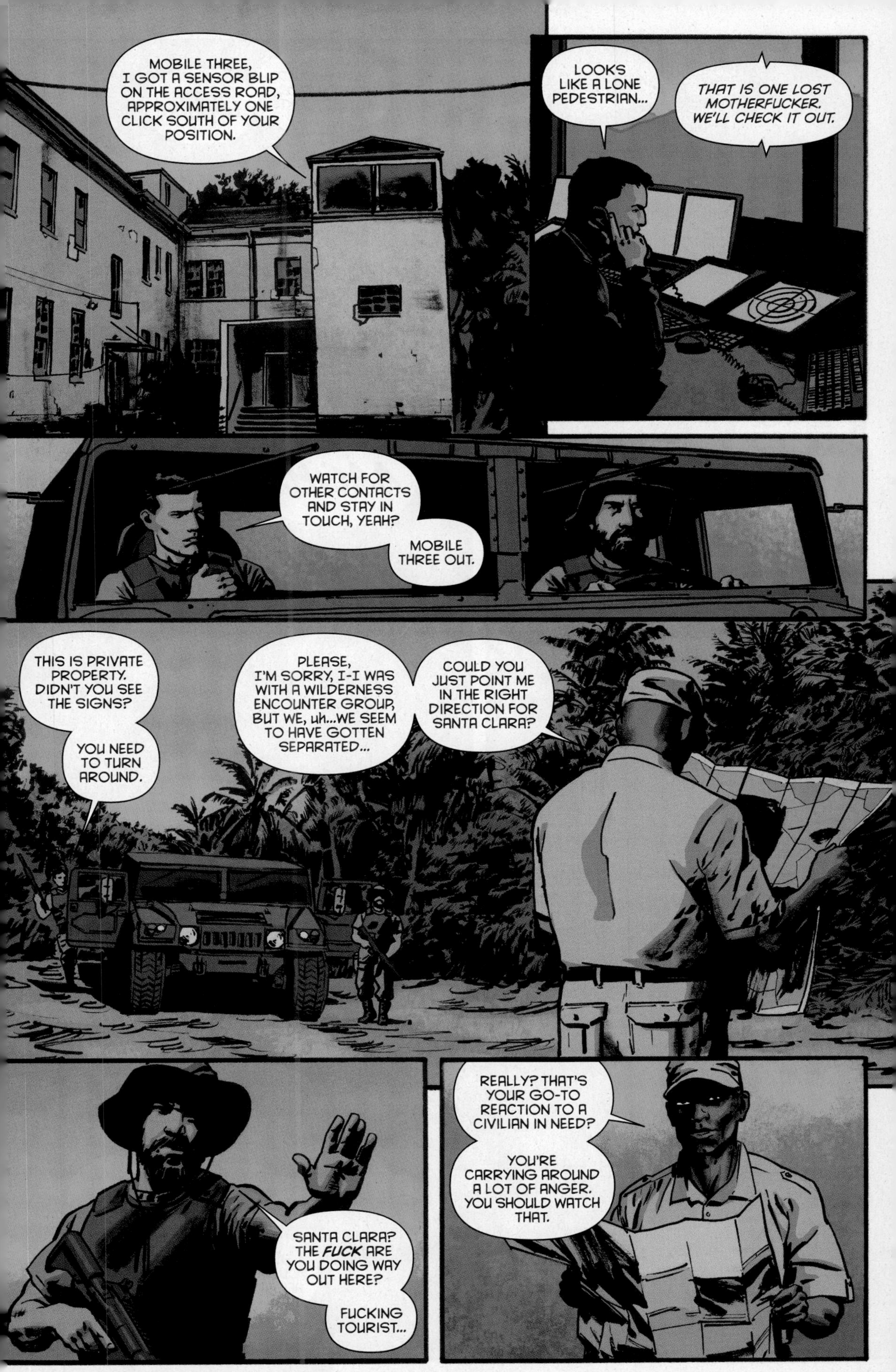
MOBILE THREE, I GOT A SENSOR BLIP ON THE ACCESS ROAD, APPROXIMATELY ONE CLICK SOUTH OF YOUR POSITION.
LOOKS LIKE A LONE PEDESTRIAN...
THAT IS ONE LOST MOTHERFUCKER. WE'LL CHECK IT OUT.
WATCH FOR OTHER CONTACTS AND STAY IN TOUCH, YEAH?
MOBILE THREE OUT.
THIS IS PRIVATE PROPERTY. DIDN'T YOU SEE THE SIGNS?
YOU NEED TO TURN AROUND.
PLEASE, I'M SORRY, I-I WAS WITH A WILDERNESS ENCOUNTER GROUP, BUT WE, uh...WE SEEM TO HAVE GOTTEN SEPARATED...
COULD YOU JUST POINT ME IN THE RIGHT DIRECTION FOR SANTA CLARA?
SANTA CLARA? THE *FUCK* ARE YOU DOING WAY OUT HERE?
FUCKING TOURIST...
REALLY? THAT'S YOUR GO-TO REACTION TO A CIVILIAN IN NEED?
YOU'RE CARRYING AROUND A LOT OF ANGER. YOU SHOULD WATCH THAT.

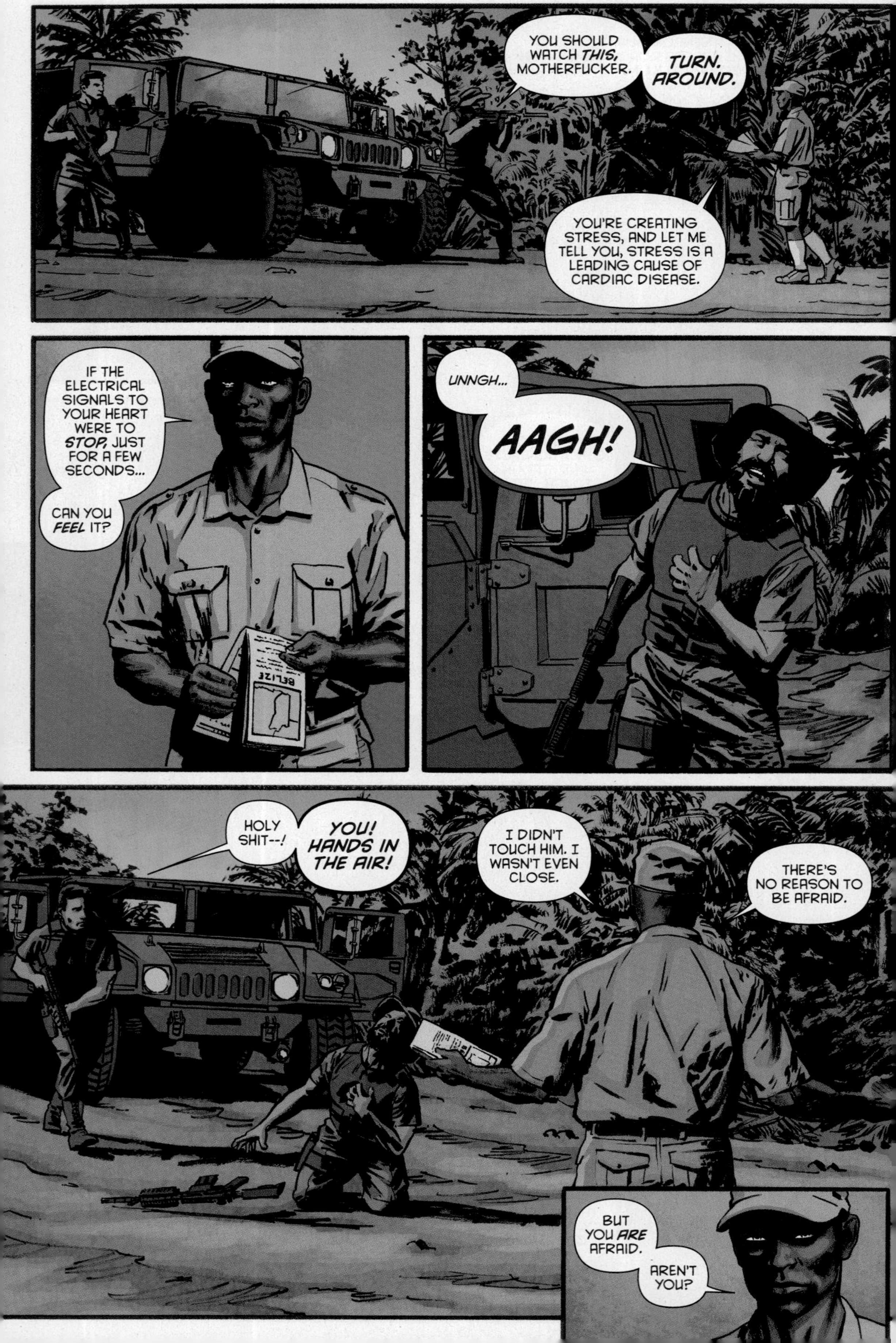
YOU SHOULD WATCH THIS, MOTHERFUCKER.
TURN. AROUND.
YOU'RE CREATING STRESS, AND LET ME TELL YOU, STRESS IS A LEADING CAUSE OF CARDIAC DISEASE.
IF THE ELECTRICAL SIGNALS TO YOUR HEART WERE TO STOP, JUST FOR A FEW SECONDS...
CAN YOU FEEL IT?
BELIZE
UNNGH...
AAGH!
HOLY SHIT--!
YOU! HANDS IN THE AIR!
I DIDN'T TOUCH HIM. I WASN'T EVEN CLOSE.
THERE'S NO REASON TO BE AFRAID.
BUT YOU ARE AFRAID.
AREN'T YOU?

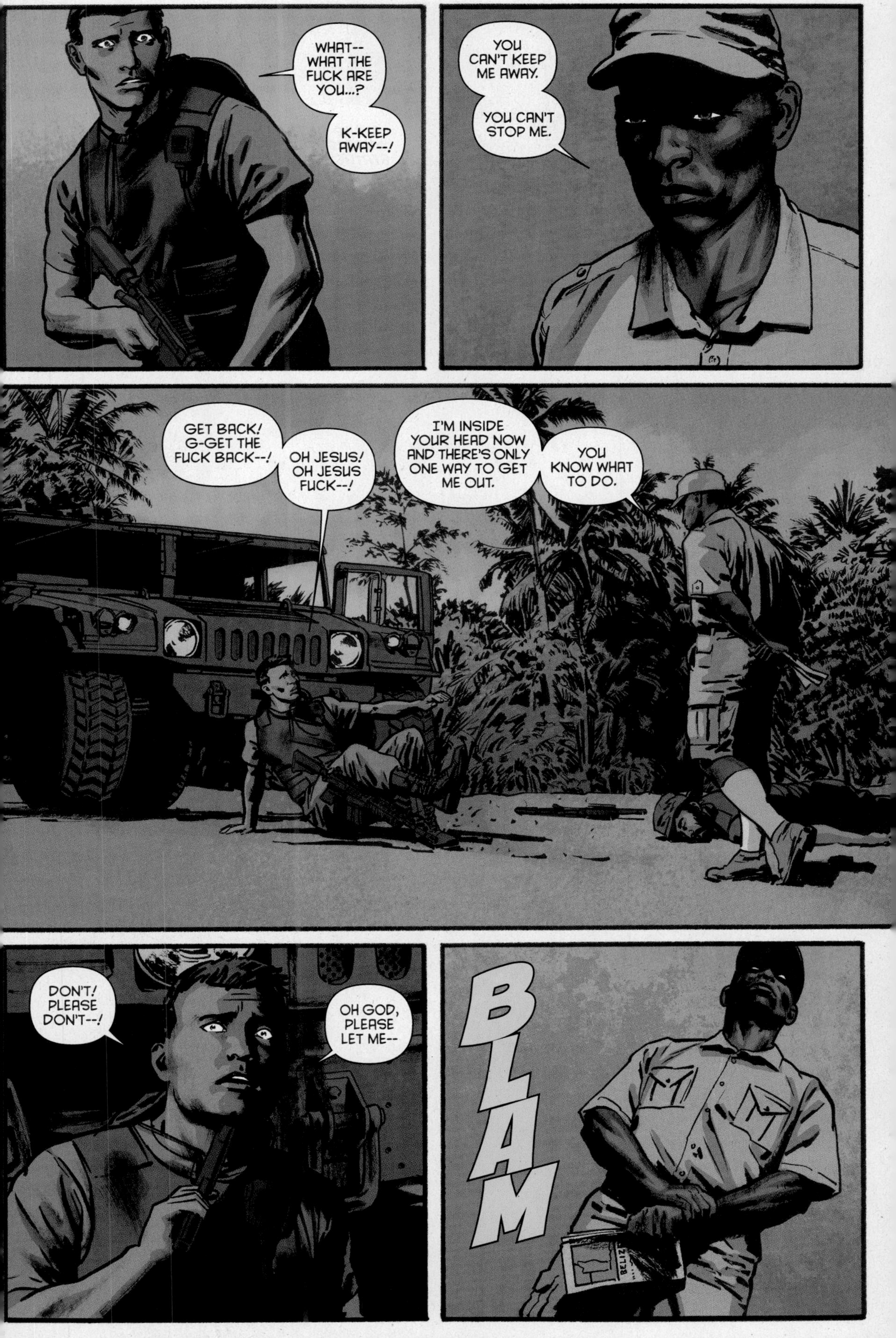
WHAT--
WHAT THE
FUCK ARE
YOU...?
K-KEEP
AWAY--!
YOU
CAN'T KEEP
ME AWAY.
YOU CAN'T
STOP ME.
GET BACK!
G-GET THE
FUCK BACK--!
OH JESUS!
OH JESUS
FUCK--!
I'M INSIDE
YOUR HEAD NOW
AND THERE'S ONLY
ONE WAY TO GET
ME OUT.
YOU
KNOW WHAT
TO DO.
DON'T!
PLEASE
DON'T--!
OH GOD,
PLEASE
LET ME--
BLAM

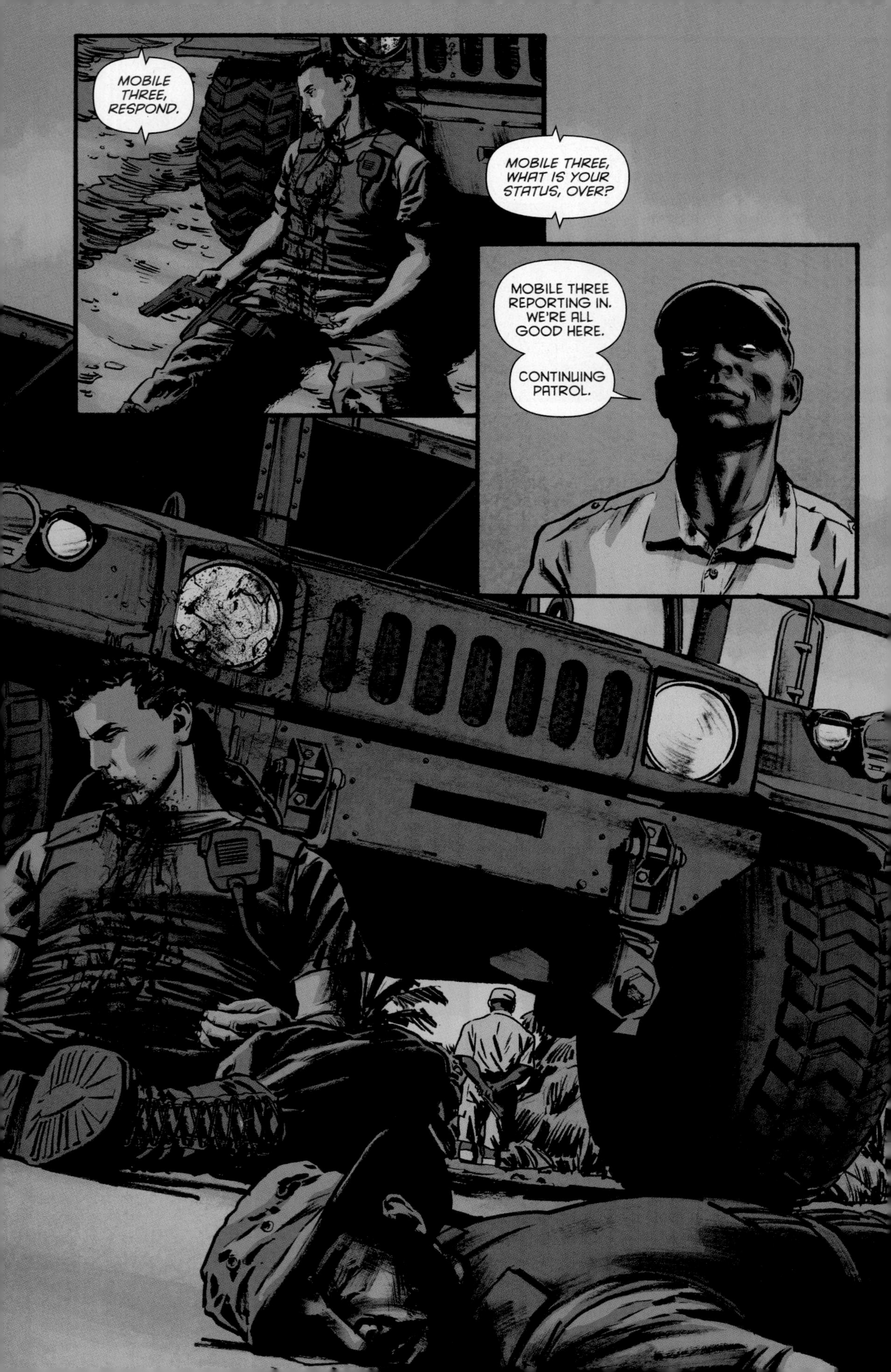
MOBILE THREE, RESPOND.
MOBILE THREE, WHAT IS YOUR STATUS, OVER?
MOBILE THREE REPORTING IN. WE'RE ALL GOOD HERE.
CONTINUING PATROL.

ISSUE SIX

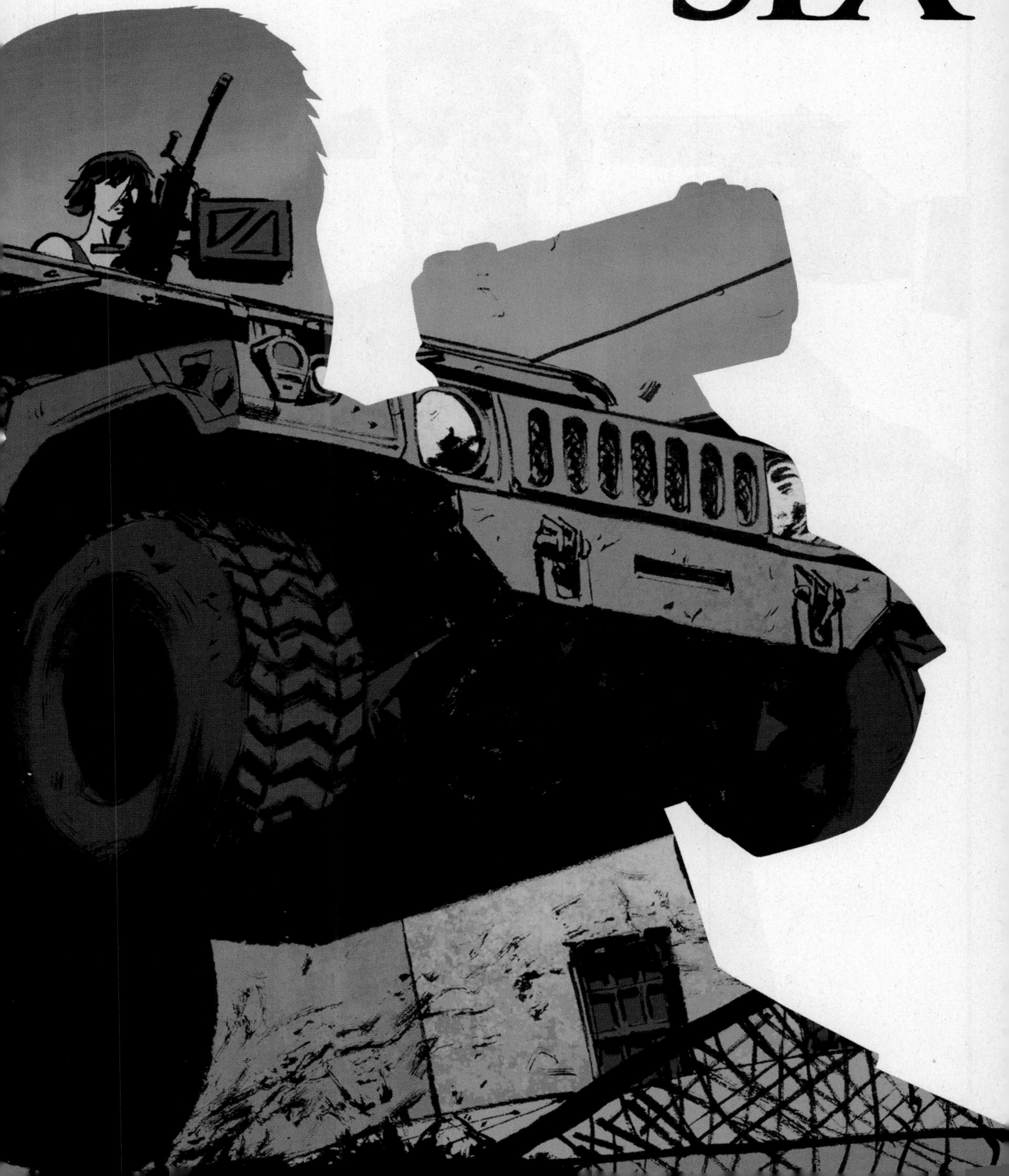

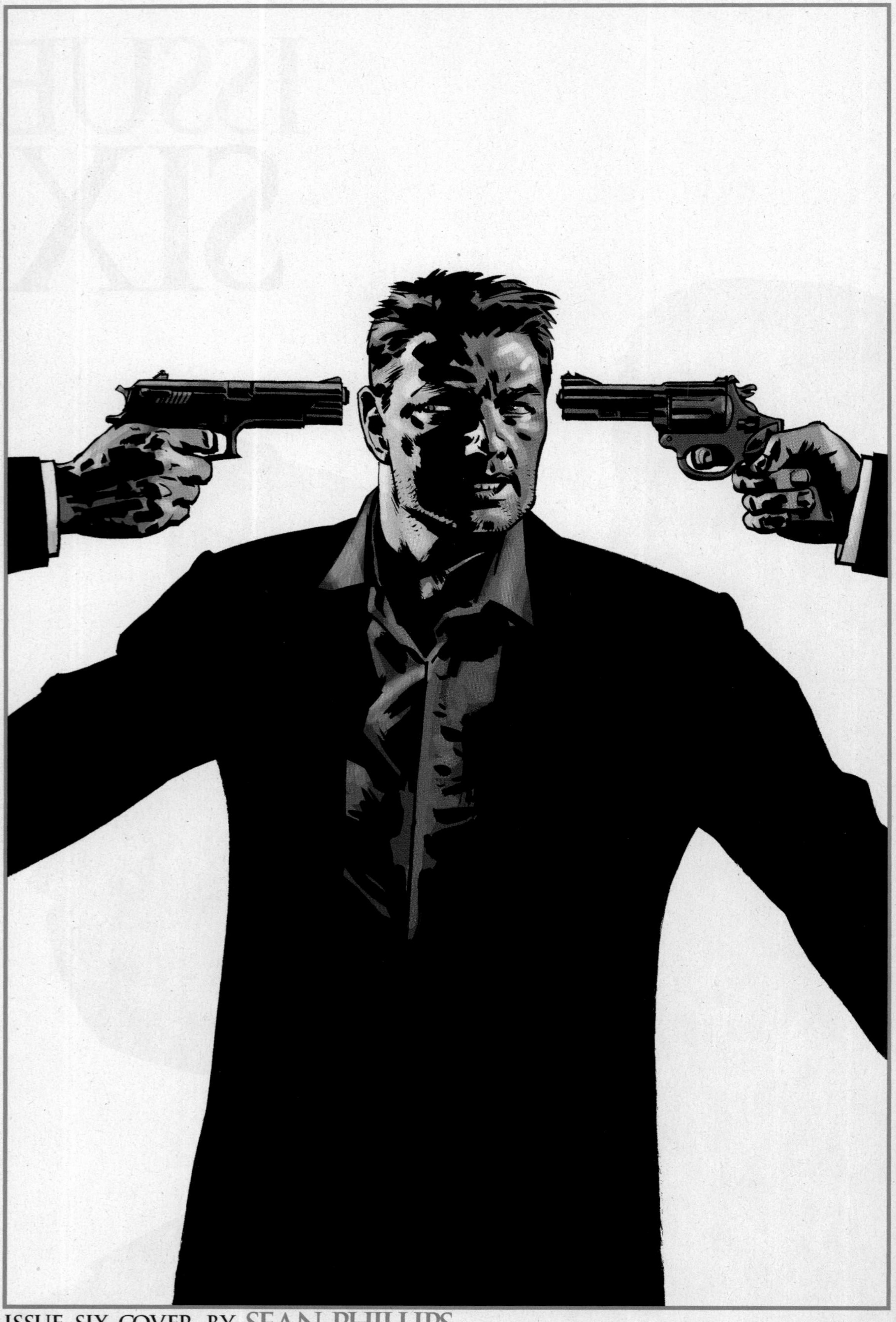

ISSUE SIX COVER BY SEAN PHILLIPS

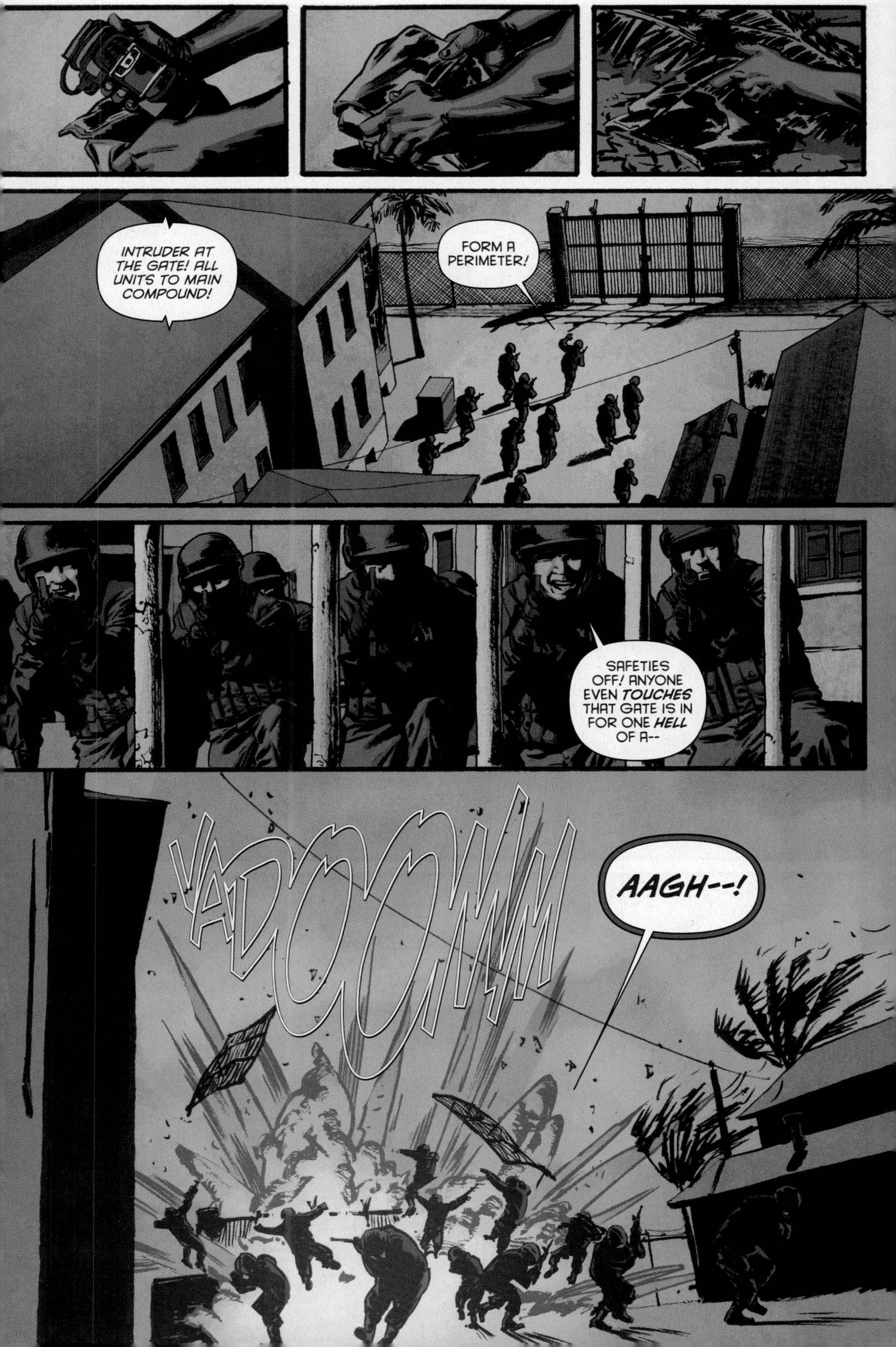
INTRUDER AT THE GATE! ALL UNITS TO MAIN COMPOUND!
FORM A PERIMETER!
SAFETIES OFF! ANYONE EVEN *TOUCHES* THAT GATE IS IN FOR ONE *HELL* OF A--
VADOOOMM
AAGH--!

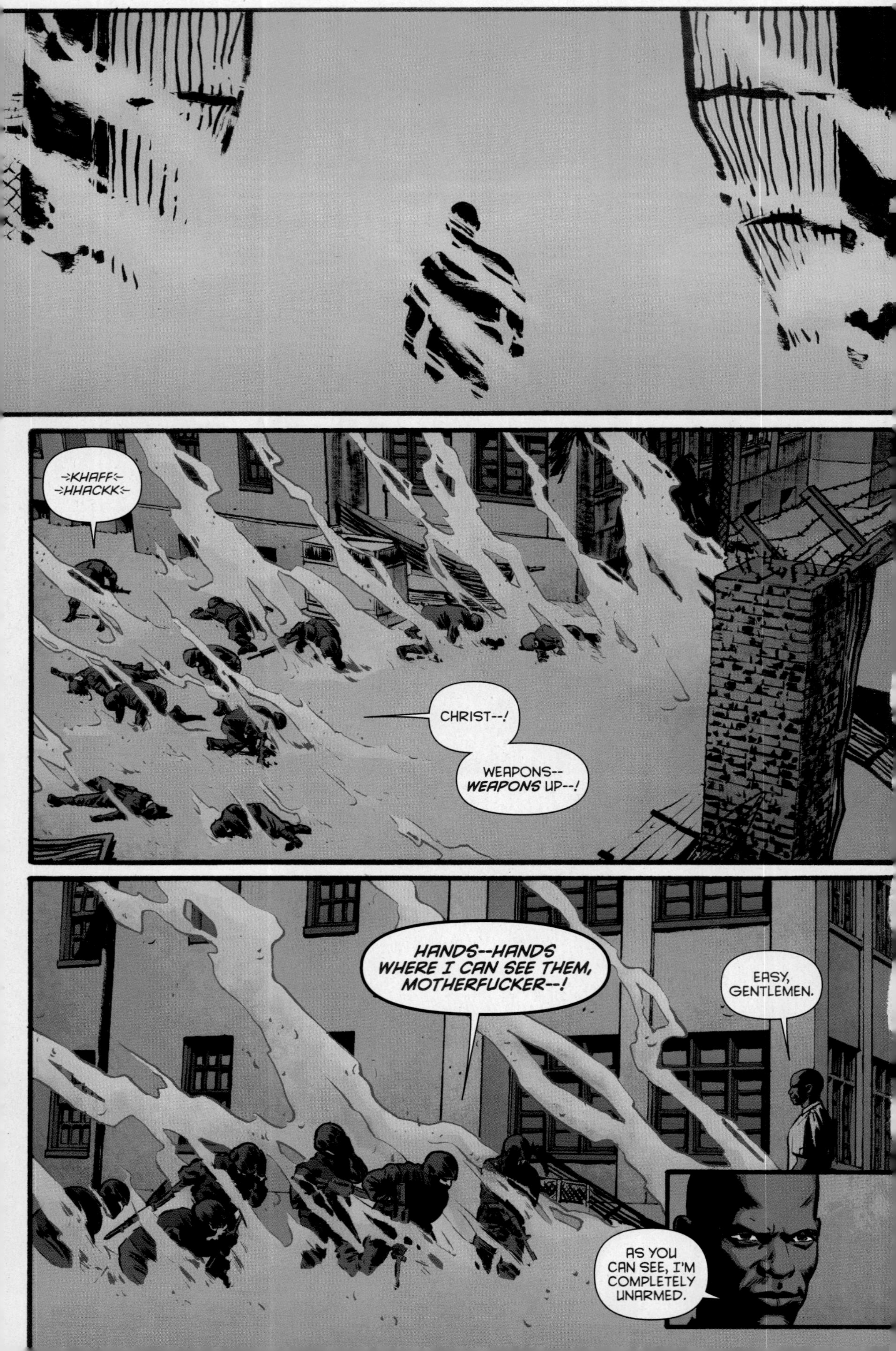
KHAFF
HHACKK
CHRIST--!
WEAPONS-- WEAPONS UP--!
HANDS--HANDS WHERE I CAN SEE THEM, MOTHERFUCKER--!
EASY, GENTLEMEN.
AS YOU CAN SEE, I'M COMPLETELY UNARMED.

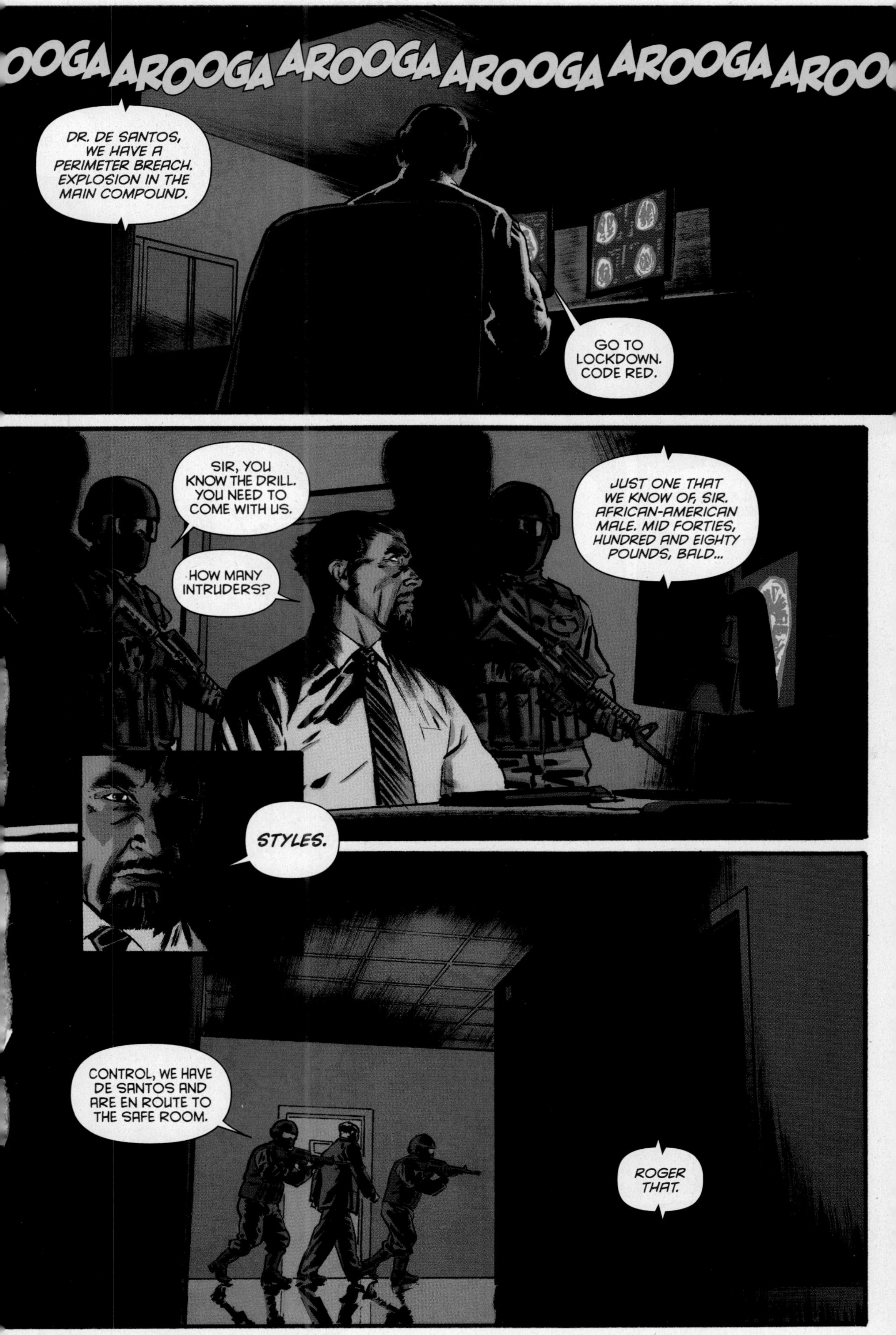
AROOGA AROOGA AROOGA AROOGA AROOGA AROO
DR. DE SANTOS, WE HAVE A PERIMETER BREACH. EXPLOSION IN THE MAIN COMPOUND.
GO TO LOCKDOWN. CODE RED.
SIR, YOU KNOW THE DRILL. YOU NEED TO COME WITH US.
HOW MANY INTRUDERS?
JUST ONE THAT WE KNOW OF, SIR. AFRICAN-AMERICAN MALE. MID FORTIES, HUNDRED AND EIGHTY POUNDS, BALD...
STYLES.
CONTROL, WE HAVE DE SANTOS AND ARE EN ROUTE TO THE SAFE ROOM.
ROGER THAT.

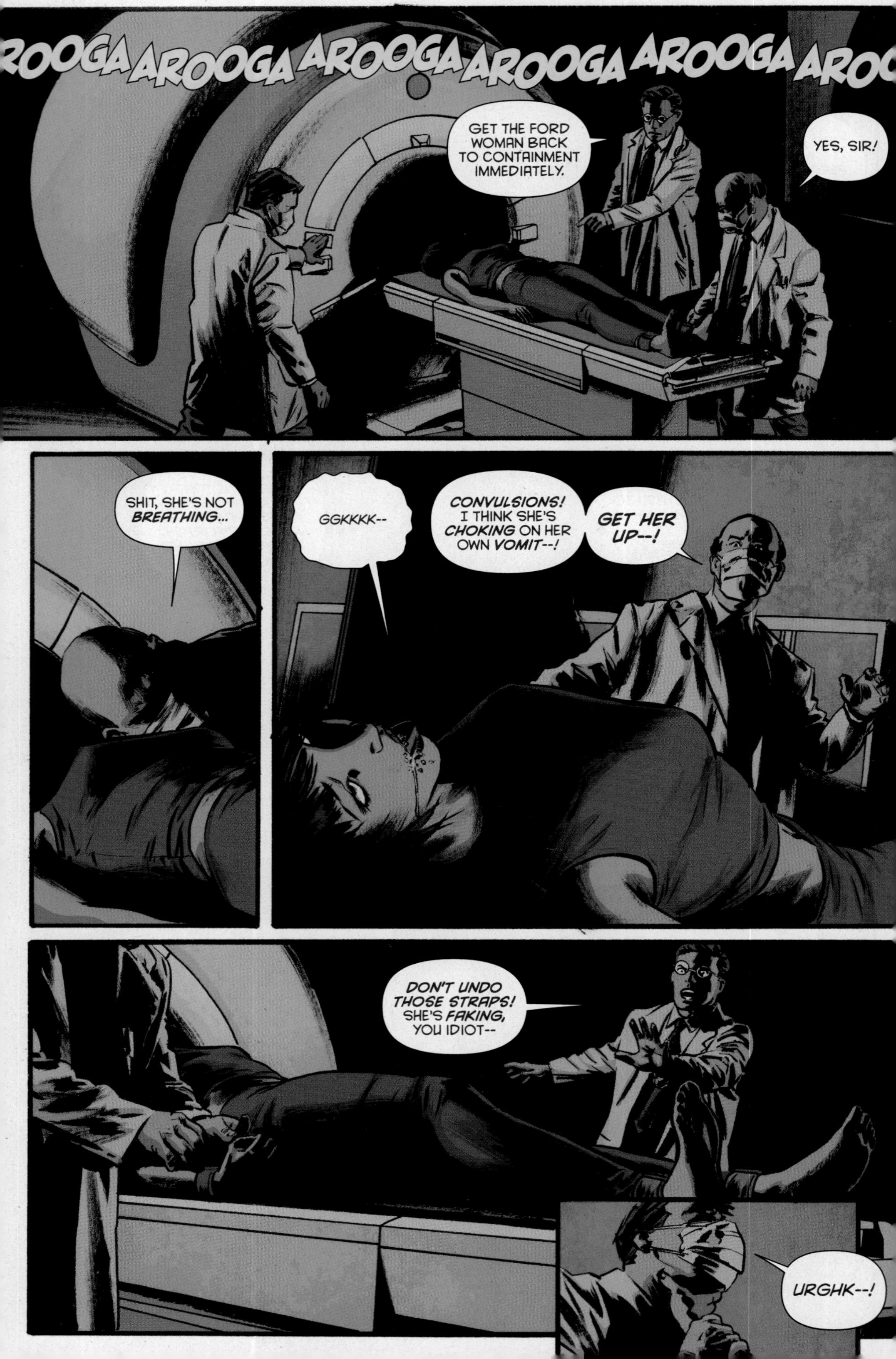
ROOGA AROOGA AROOGA AROOGA AROOGA AROO
GET THE FORD WOMAN BACK TO CONTAINMENT IMMEDIATELY.
YES, SIR!
SHIT, SHE'S NOT BREATHING...
GGKKKK--
CONVULSIONS! I THINK SHE'S CHOKING ON HER OWN VOMIT--!
GET HER UP--!
DON'T UNDO THOSE STRAPS! SHE'S FAKING, YOU IDIOT--
URGHK--!

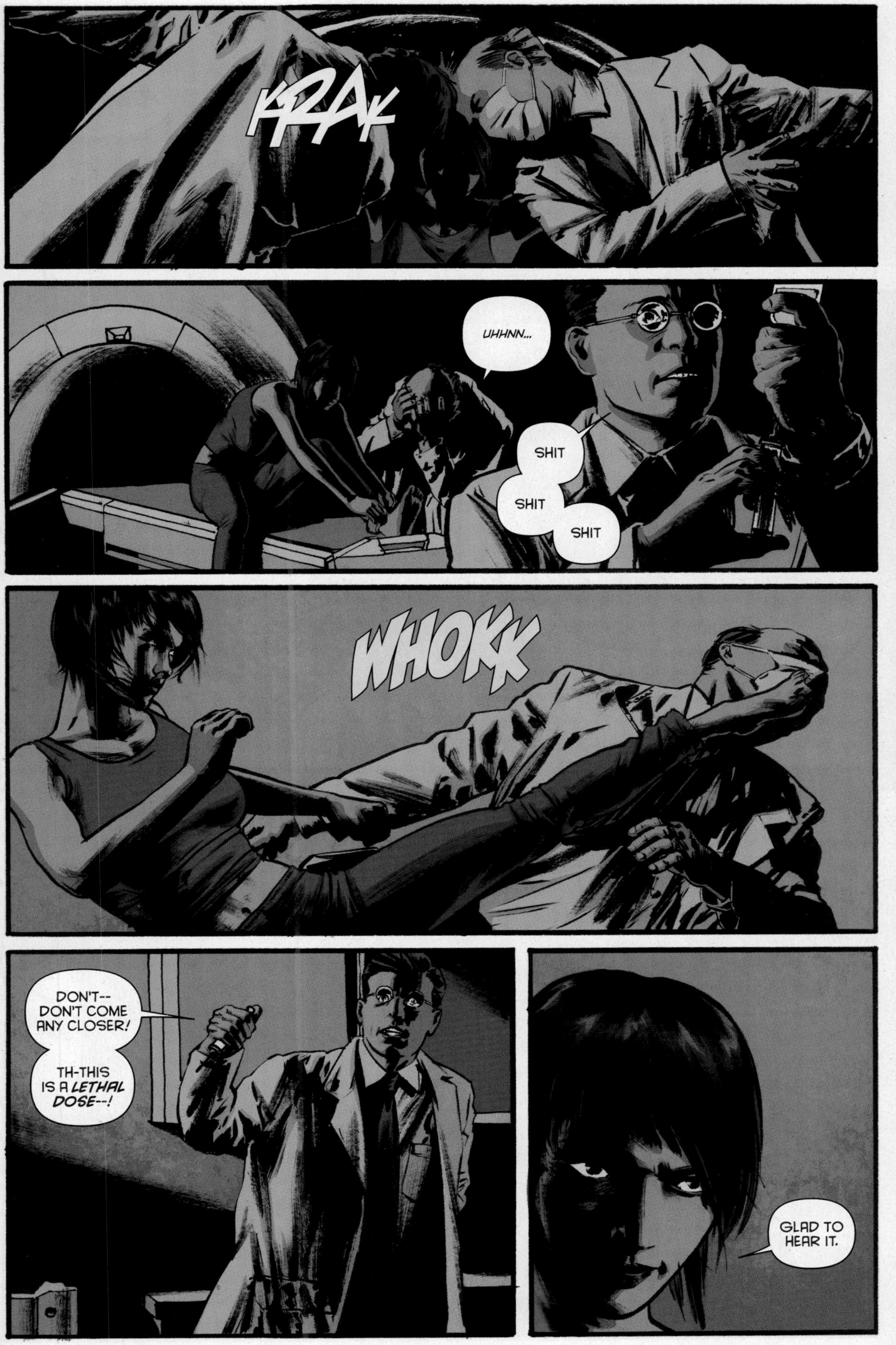
KRAK
UHHNN...
SHIT
SHIT
SHIT
WHOKK
DON'T-- DON'T COME ANY CLOSER!
TH-THIS IS A *LETHAL DOSE*--!
GLAD TO HEAR IT.

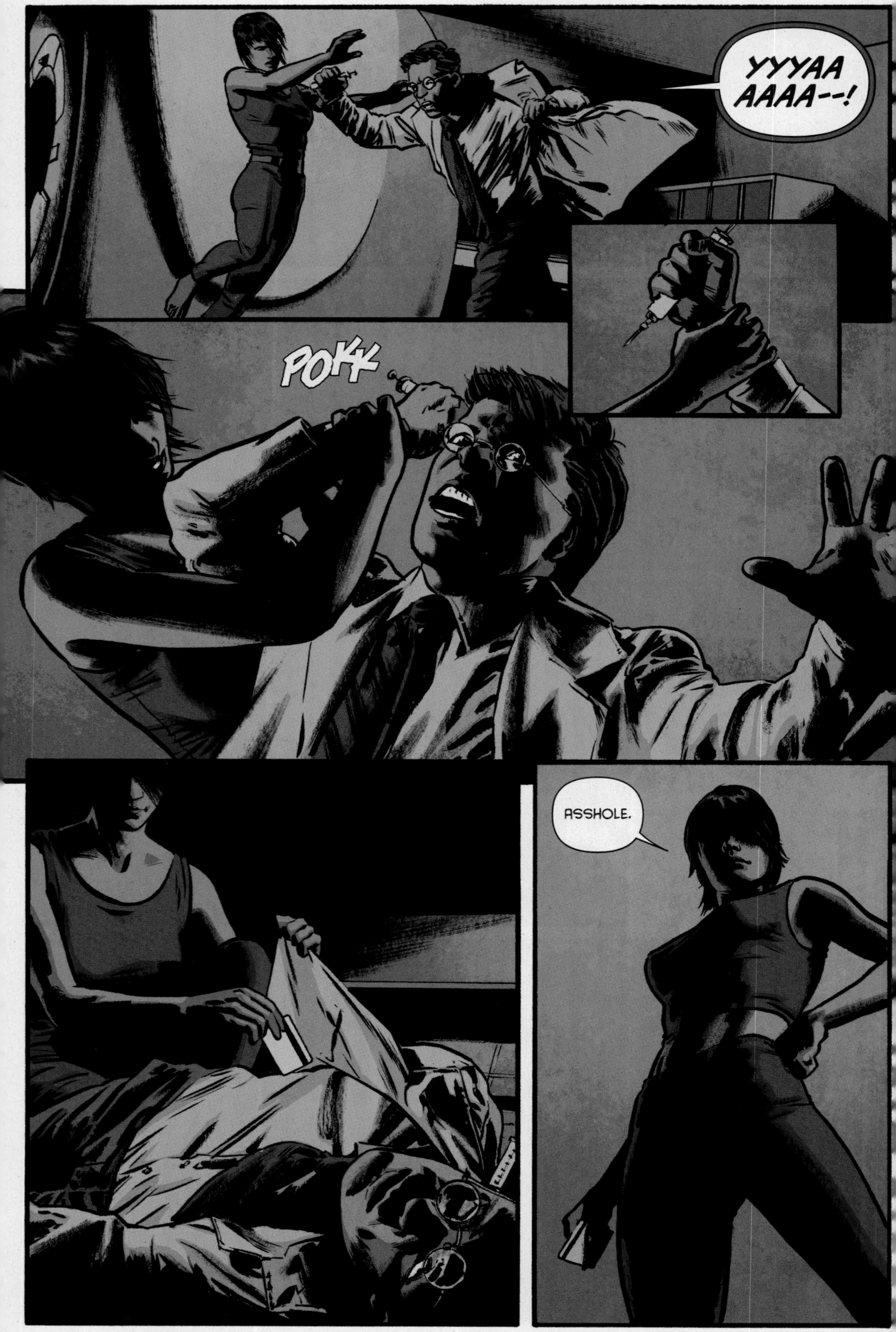
YYYAA AAAA--!
POKK
ASSHOLE.

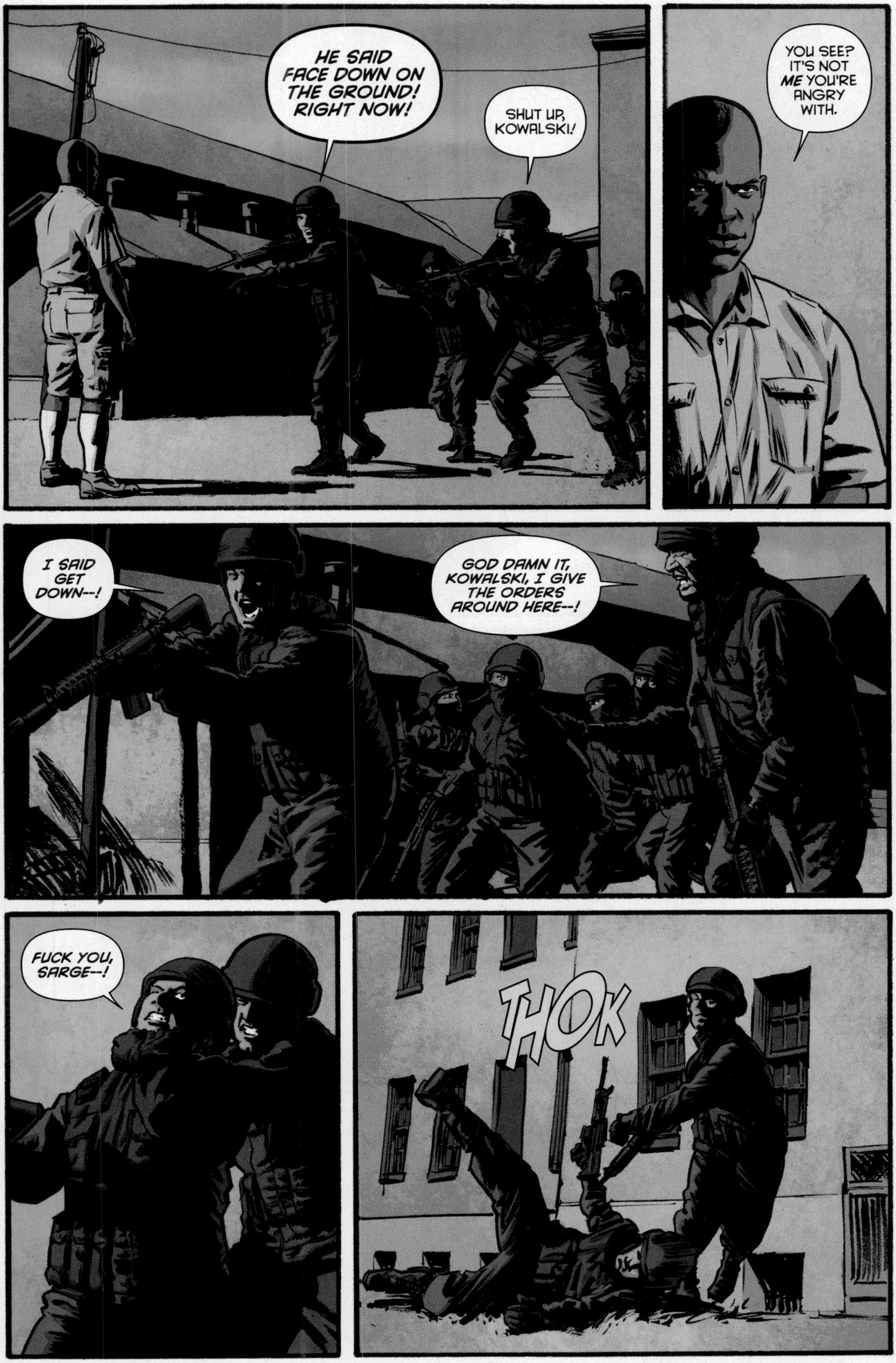
HE SAID FACE DOWN ON THE GROUND! RIGHT NOW!
SHUT UP, KOWALSKI!
YOU SEE? IT'S NOT *ME* YOU'RE ANGRY WITH.
I SAID GET DOWN--!
GOD DAMN IT, KOWALSKI, I GIVE THE ORDERS AROUND HERE--!
FUCK YOU, SARGE--!
THOK

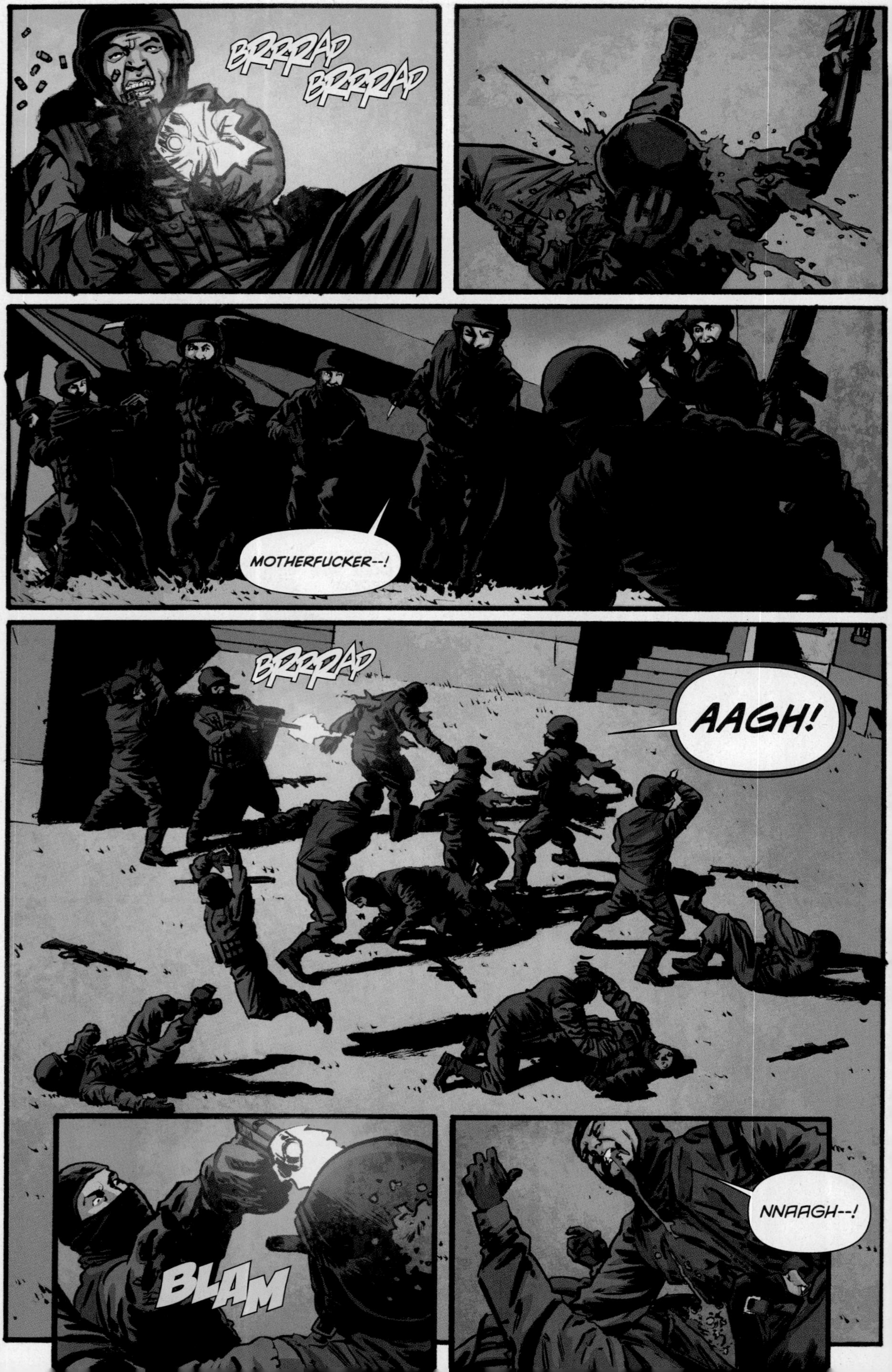
BRRRAP
BRRRAP
MOTHERFUCKER--!
BRRRAP
AAGH!
BLAM
NNAAGH--!

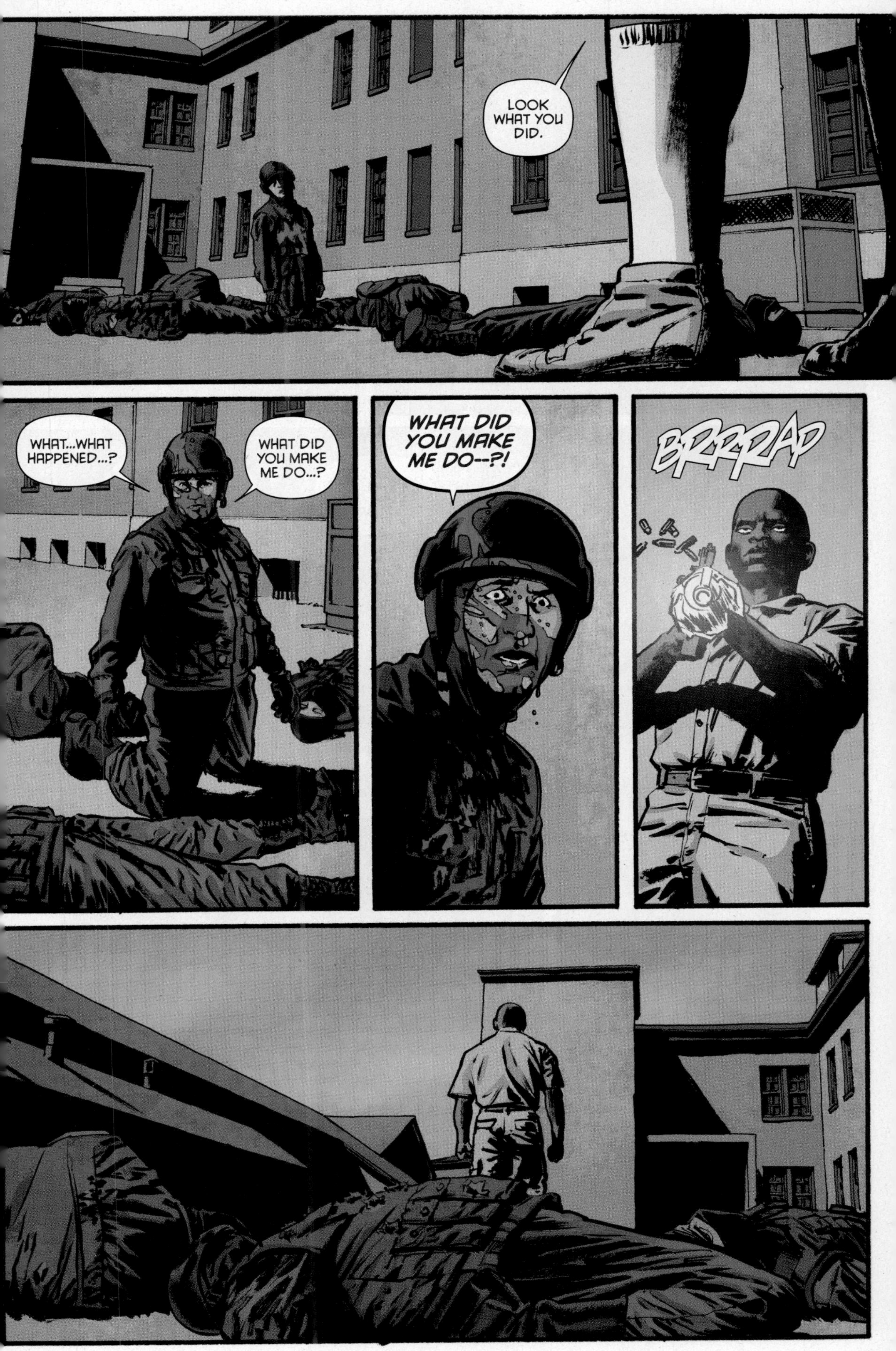
LOOK WHAT YOU DID.
WHAT...WHAT HAPPENED...?
WHAT DID YOU MAKE ME DO...?
WHAT DID YOU MAKE ME DO--?!
BRRRRAP

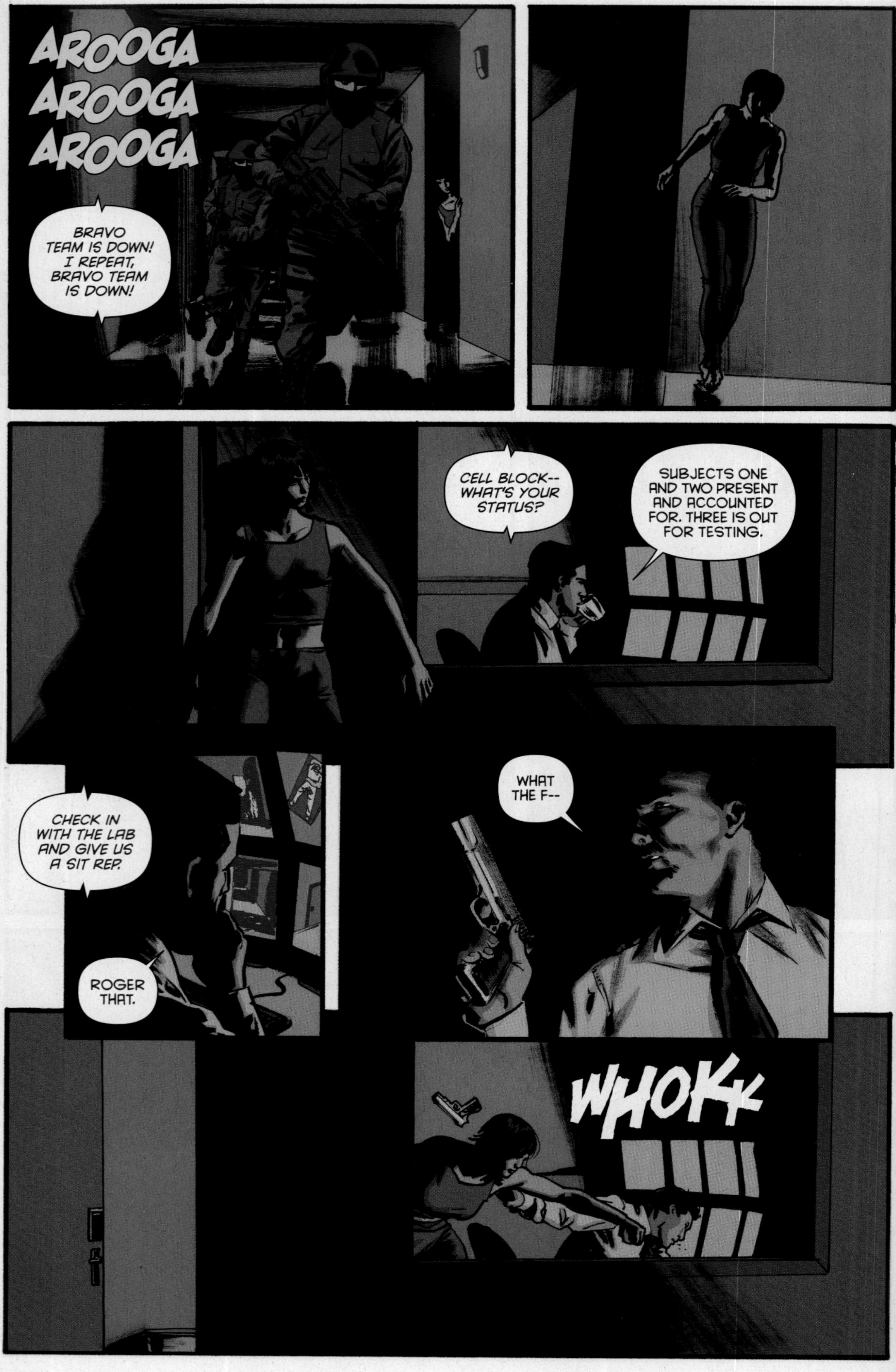
AROOGA
AROOGA
AROOGA
BRAVO TEAM IS DOWN! I REPEAT, BRAVO TEAM IS DOWN!
CELL BLOCK-- WHAT'S YOUR STATUS?
SUBJECTS ONE AND TWO PRESENT AND ACCOUNTED FOR. THREE IS OUT FOR TESTING.
CHECK IN WITH THE LAB AND GIVE US A SIT REP.
ROGER THAT.
WHAT THE F--
WHOKK

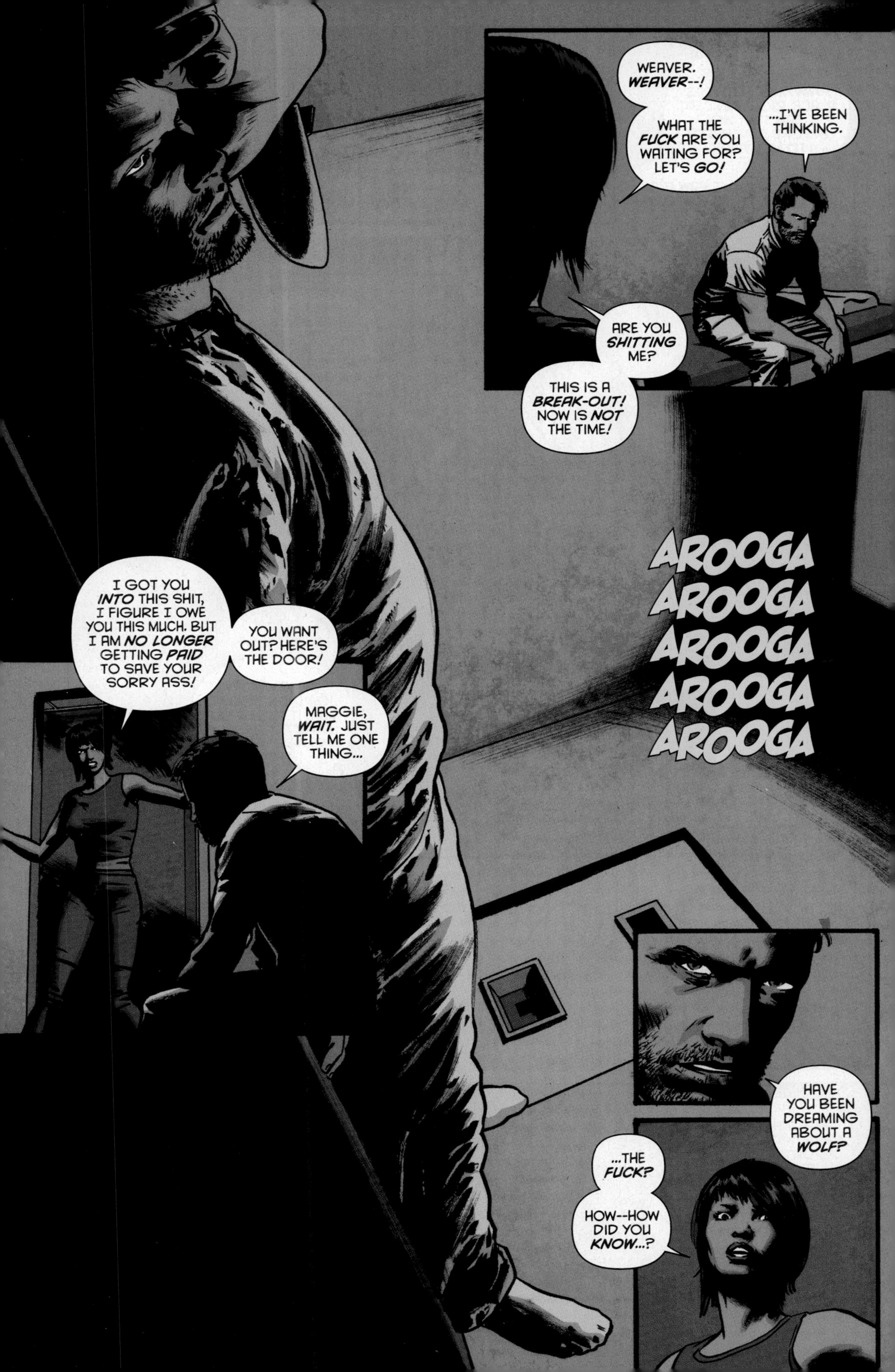

WEAVER. WEAVER--!
WHAT THE FUCK ARE YOU WAITING FOR? LET'S GO!
...I'VE BEEN THINKING.
ARE YOU SHITTING ME?
THIS IS A BREAK-OUT! NOW IS NOT THE TIME!
AROOGA AROOGA AROOGA AROOGA AROOGA
I GOT YOU INTO THIS SHIT, I FIGURE I OWE YOU THIS MUCH. BUT I AM NO LONGER GETTING PAID TO SAVE YOUR SORRY ASS!
YOU WANT OUT? HERE'S THE DOOR!
MAGGIE, WAIT. JUST TELL ME ONE THING...
HAVE YOU BEEN DREAMING ABOUT A WOLF?
...THE FUCK?
HOW--HOW DID YOU KNOW...?

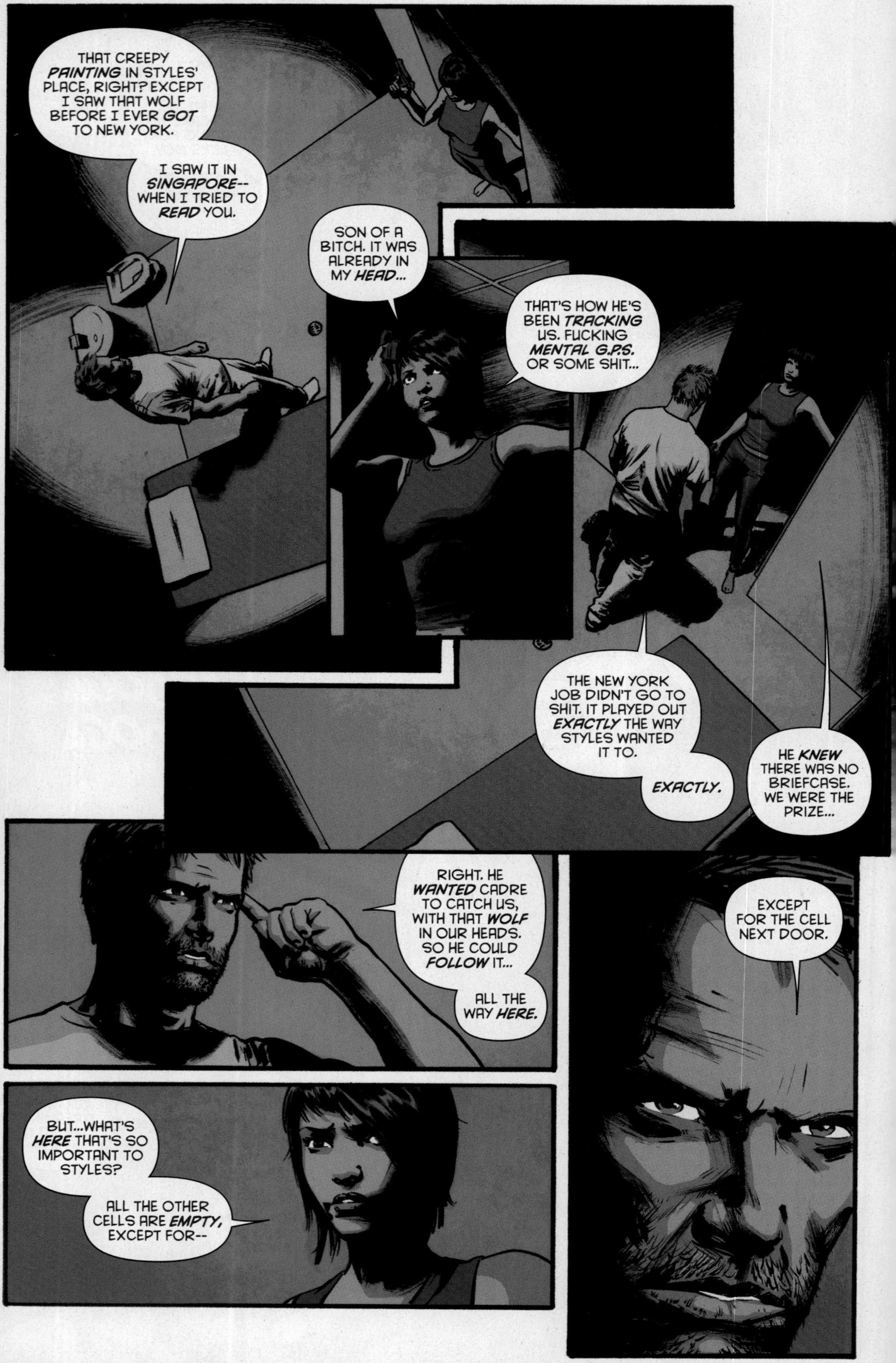
THAT CREEPY PAINTING IN STYLES' PLACE, RIGHT? EXCEPT I SAW THAT WOLF BEFORE I EVER GOT TO NEW YORK.
I SAW IT IN SINGAPORE-- WHEN I TRIED TO READ YOU.
SON OF A BITCH. IT WAS ALREADY IN MY HEAD...
THAT'S HOW HE'S BEEN TRACKING US. FUCKING MENTAL G.P.S. OR SOME SHIT...
THE NEW YORK JOB DIDN'T GO TO SHIT. IT PLAYED OUT EXACTLY THE WAY STYLES WANTED IT TO.
EXACTLY.
HE KNEW THERE WAS NO BRIEFCASE. WE WERE THE PRIZE...
RIGHT. HE WANTED CADRE TO CATCH US, WITH THAT WOLF IN OUR HEADS. SO HE COULD FOLLOW IT...
ALL THE WAY HERE.
BUT...WHAT'S HERE THAT'S SO IMPORTANT TO STYLES?
ALL THE OTHER CELLS ARE EMPTY, EXCEPT FOR--
EXCEPT FOR THE CELL NEXT DOOR.

BDEEP

K-CHUNNG

IT'S *MORGAN*, RIGHT?

WEAVER.

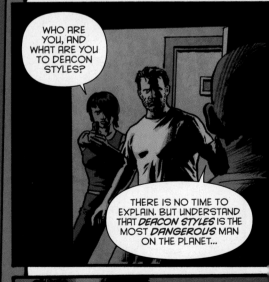

WHO ARE YOU, AND WHAT ARE YOU TO DEACON STYLES?

THERE IS NO TIME TO EXPLAIN. BUT UNDERSTAND THAT *DEACON STYLES* IS THE MOST *DANGEROUS* MAN ON THE PLANET...

NO.

YOUR NAME IS *LOWE.*

AND IF YOU VALUE YOUR LIVES, YOU WOULD DO WELL TO BE SOMEWHERE ELSE WHEN HE GETS HERE.

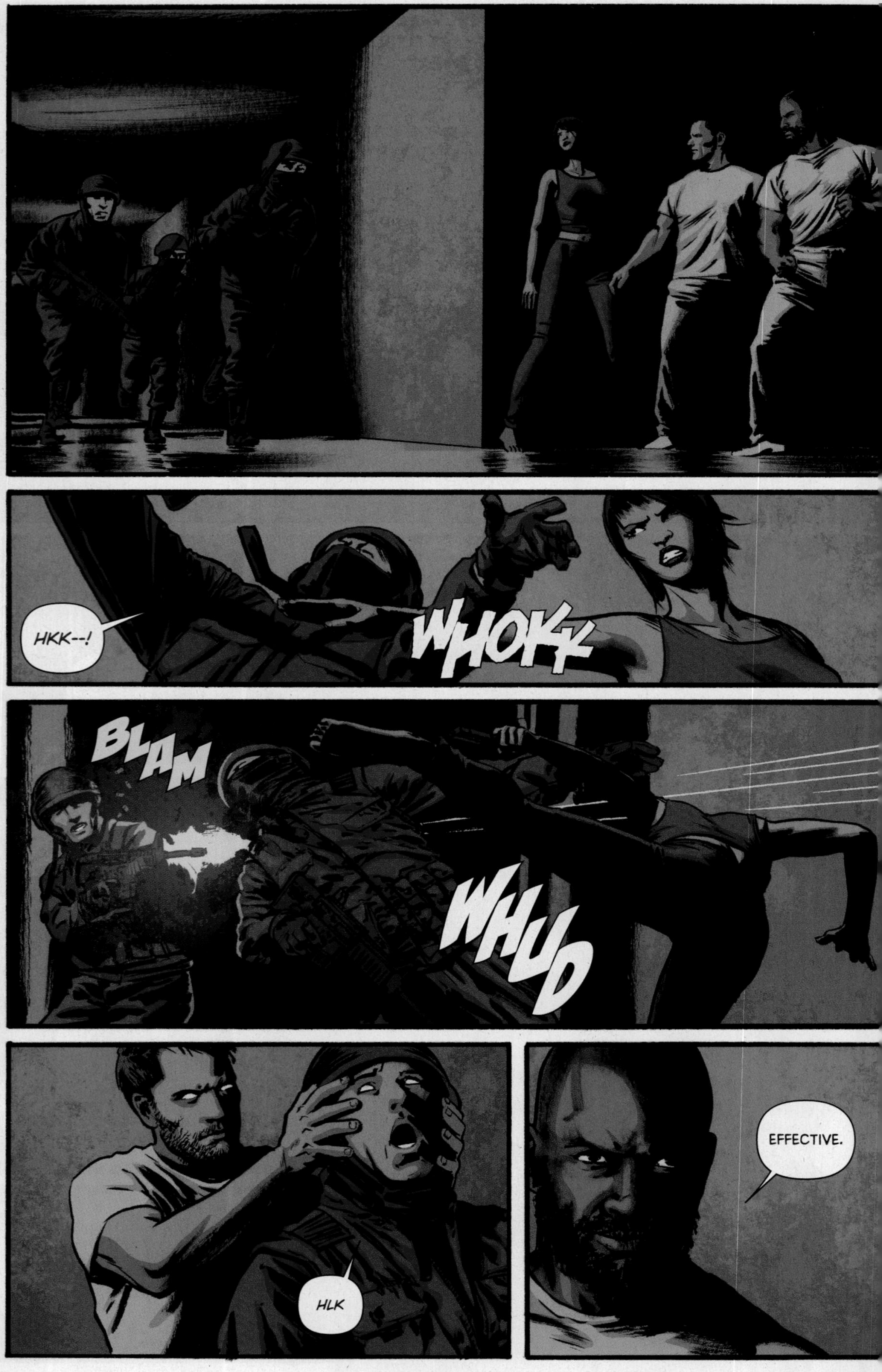
HKK--!
WHOKK
BLAM
WHUD
HLK
EFFECTIVE.

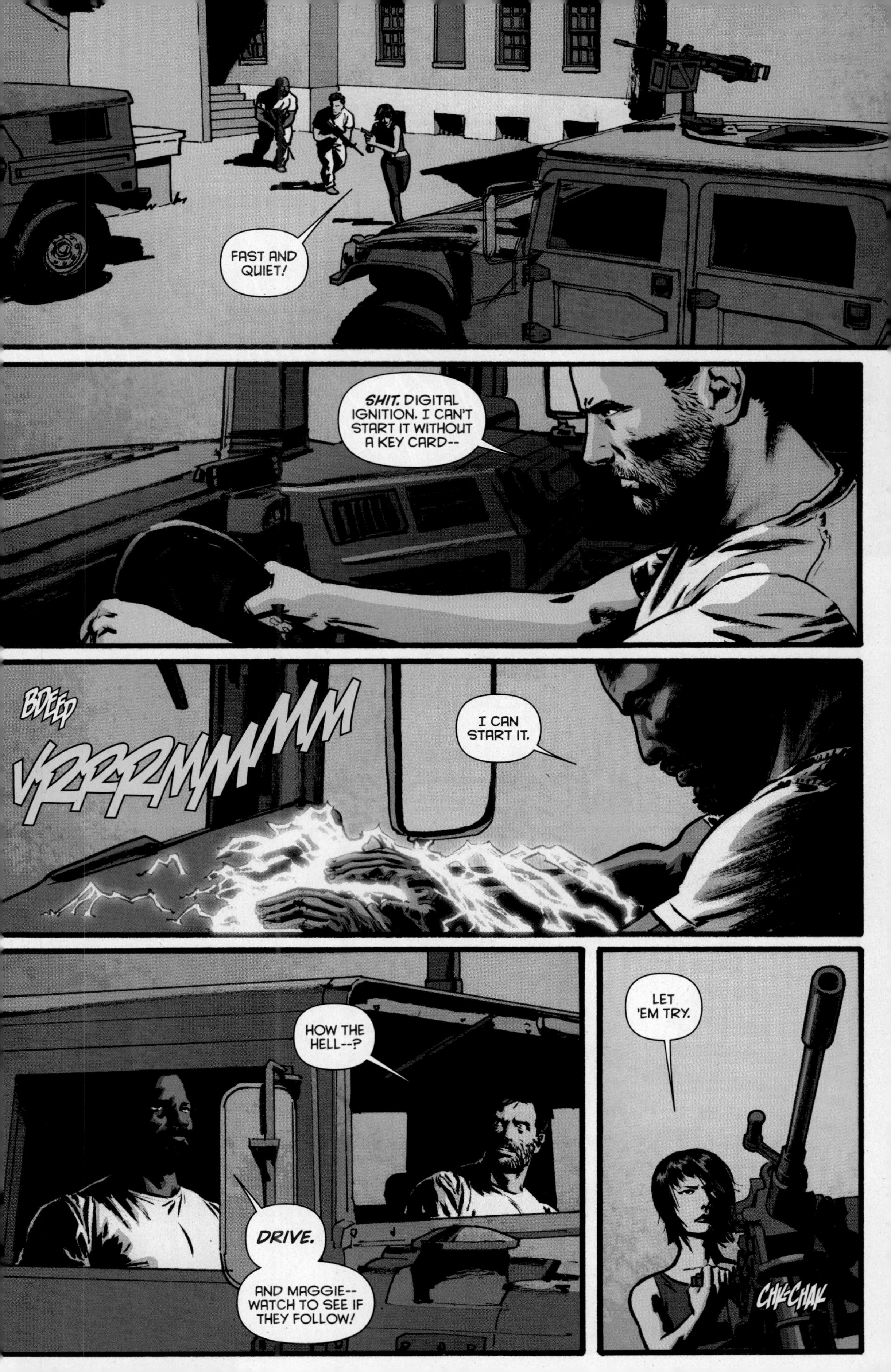
FAST AND QUIET!
SHIT. DIGITAL IGNITION. I CAN'T START IT WITHOUT A KEY CARD--
BDEEP
VRRRMMMMM
I CAN START IT.
HOW THE HELL--?
DRIVE.
AND MAGGIE-- WATCH TO SEE IF THEY FOLLOW!
LET 'EM TRY.
CHK-CHAK

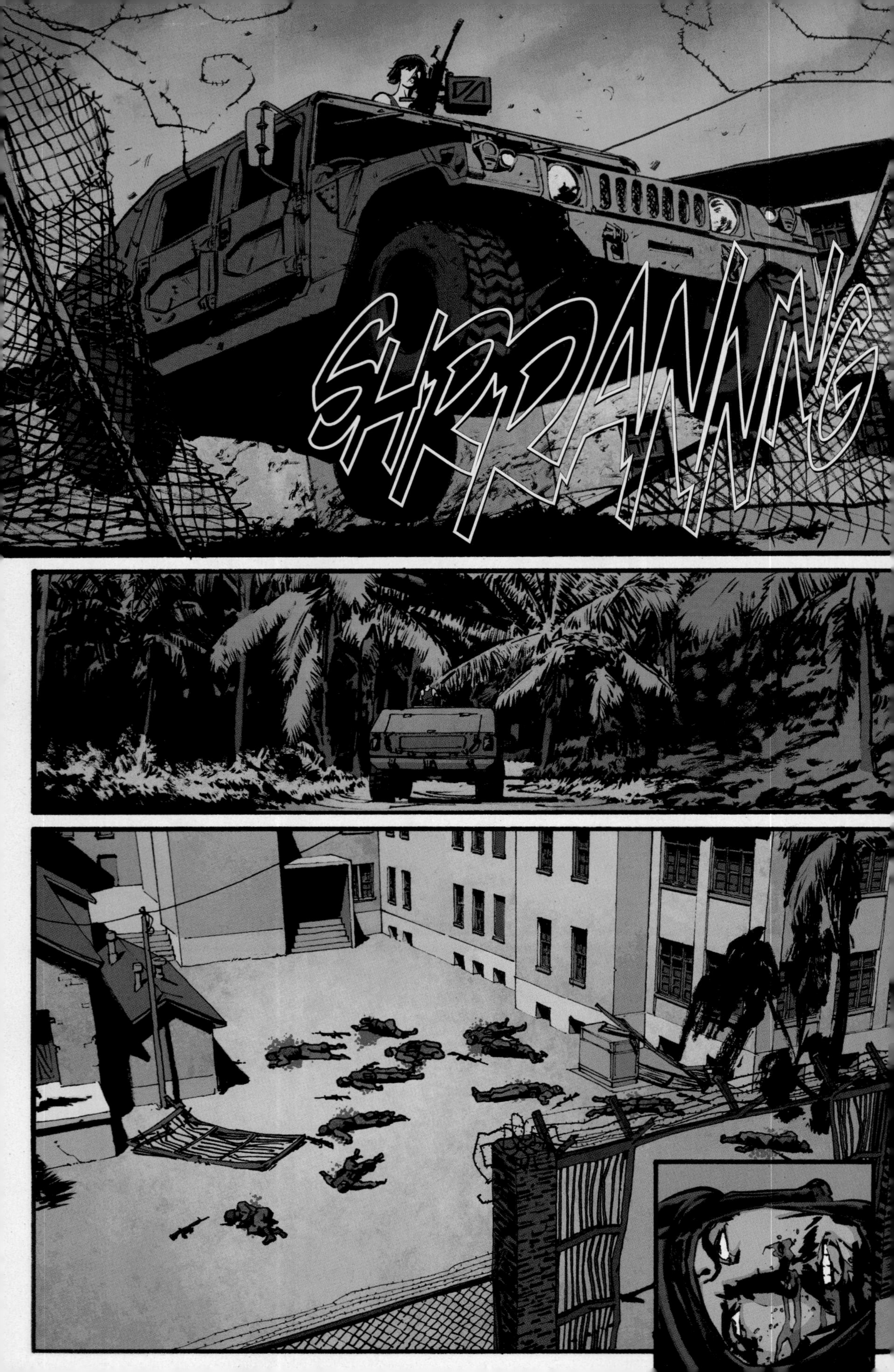
SHRRANNNG

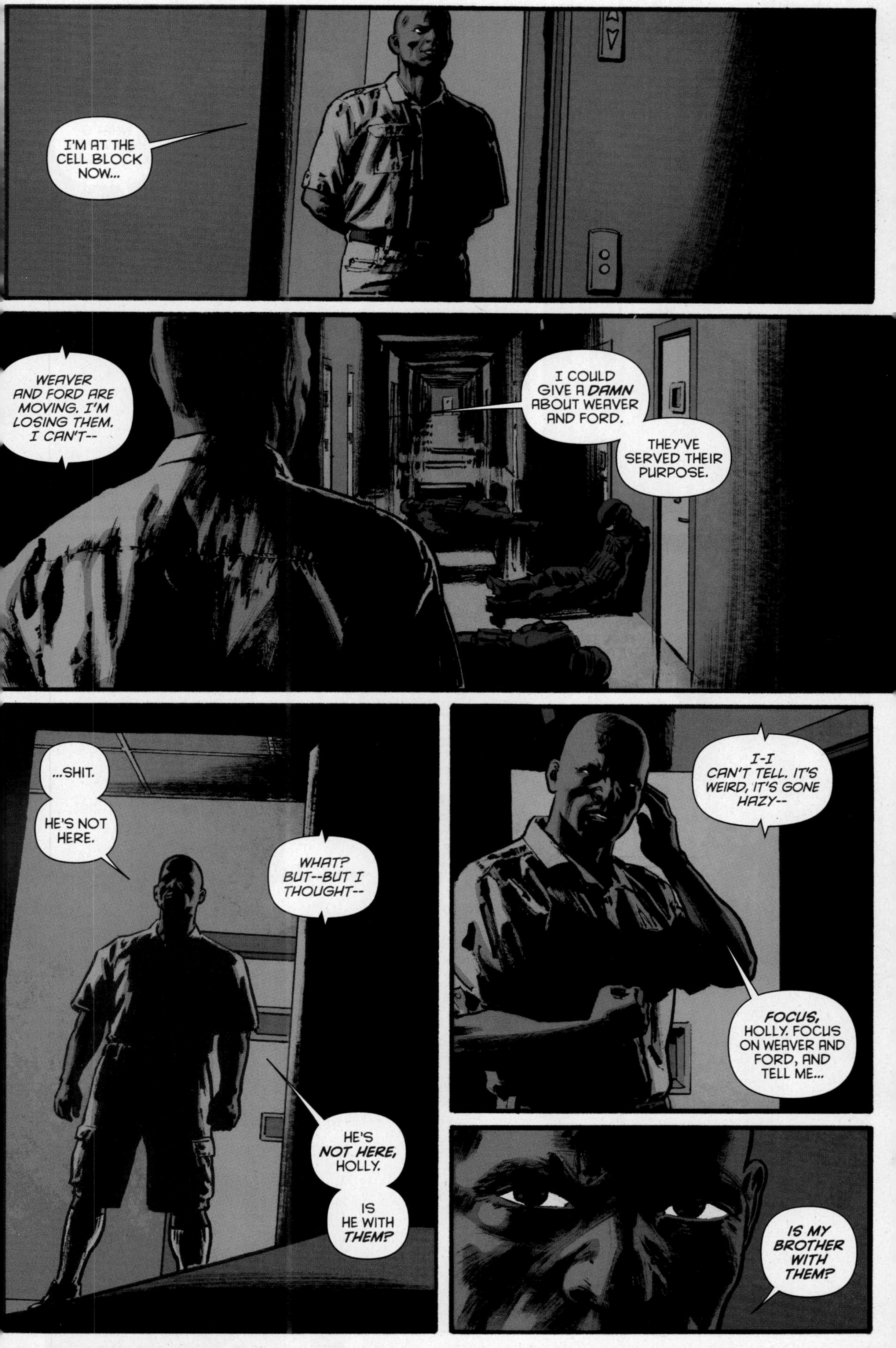
I'M AT THE CELL BLOCK NOW...
WEAVER AND FORD ARE MOVING. I'M LOSING THEM. I CAN'T--
I COULD GIVE A DAMN ABOUT WEAVER AND FORD.
THEY'VE SERVED THEIR PURPOSE.
...SHIT.
HE'S NOT HERE.
WHAT? BUT--BUT I THOUGHT--
HE'S NOT HERE, HOLLY.
IS HE WITH THEM?
I-I CAN'T TELL. IT'S WEIRD, IT'S GONE HAZY--
FOCUS, HOLLY. FOCUS ON WEAVER AND FORD, AND TELL ME...
IS MY BROTHER WITH THEM?

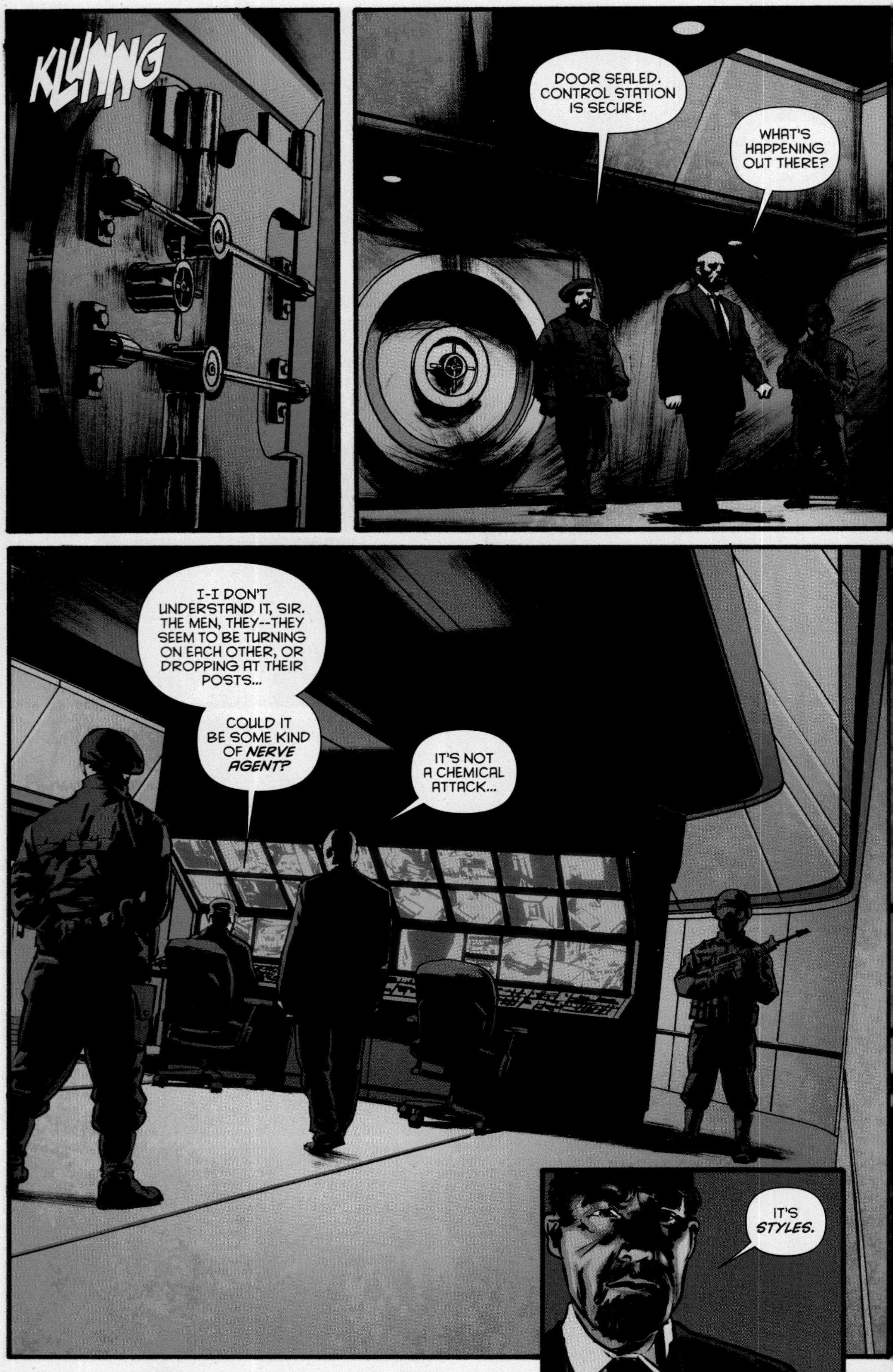
KLUNNG
DOOR SEALED. CONTROL STATION IS SECURE.
WHAT'S HAPPENING OUT THERE?
I-I DON'T UNDERSTAND IT, SIR. THE MEN, THEY--THEY SEEM TO BE TURNING ON EACH OTHER, OR DROPPING AT THEIR POSTS...
COULD IT BE SOME KIND OF *NERVE AGENT?*
IT'S NOT A CHEMICAL ATTACK...
IT'S *STYLES.*

SIR, WE SHOULD GET YOU OUT OF HERE. WE CAN HAVE A BLACKHAWK ON SITE IN THIRTY MINUTES.

WELL, YOU CAN REST EASY HERE, SIR. THESE WALLS ARE SIX-FOOT THICK REINFORCED CONCRETE. NOTHING GETS IN HERE WITHOUT OUR SAY-SO. WE CAN HOLD OUT IN HERE FOR *WEEKS* IF WE HAVE TO.

NO, CAPTAIN. BELIEVE ME, A HELICOPTER IS JUST ABOUT THE *LEAST* SAFE PLACE I COULD BE RIGHT NOW.

IF YOU SAW WHAT HE DID IN NEW YORK...

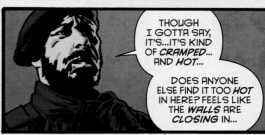

THOUGH I GOTTA SAY, IT'S...IT'S KIND OF *CRAMPED*... AND *HOT*...

DOES ANYONE ELSE FIND IT TOO *HOT* IN HERE? FEELS LIKE THE *WALLS* ARE *CLOSING* IN...

CHRIST. Oh CHRIST...I CAN'T *BREATHE*...

I GOTTA GET *OUT* OF HERE--!

RESTRAIN HIM!

QUICKLY! BEFORE--

WHAT--?

G-GET BACK! GET THE FUCK BACK!

I GOTTA GET OUT OF HERE! I GOTTA GET OUT OF THIS ROOM--!

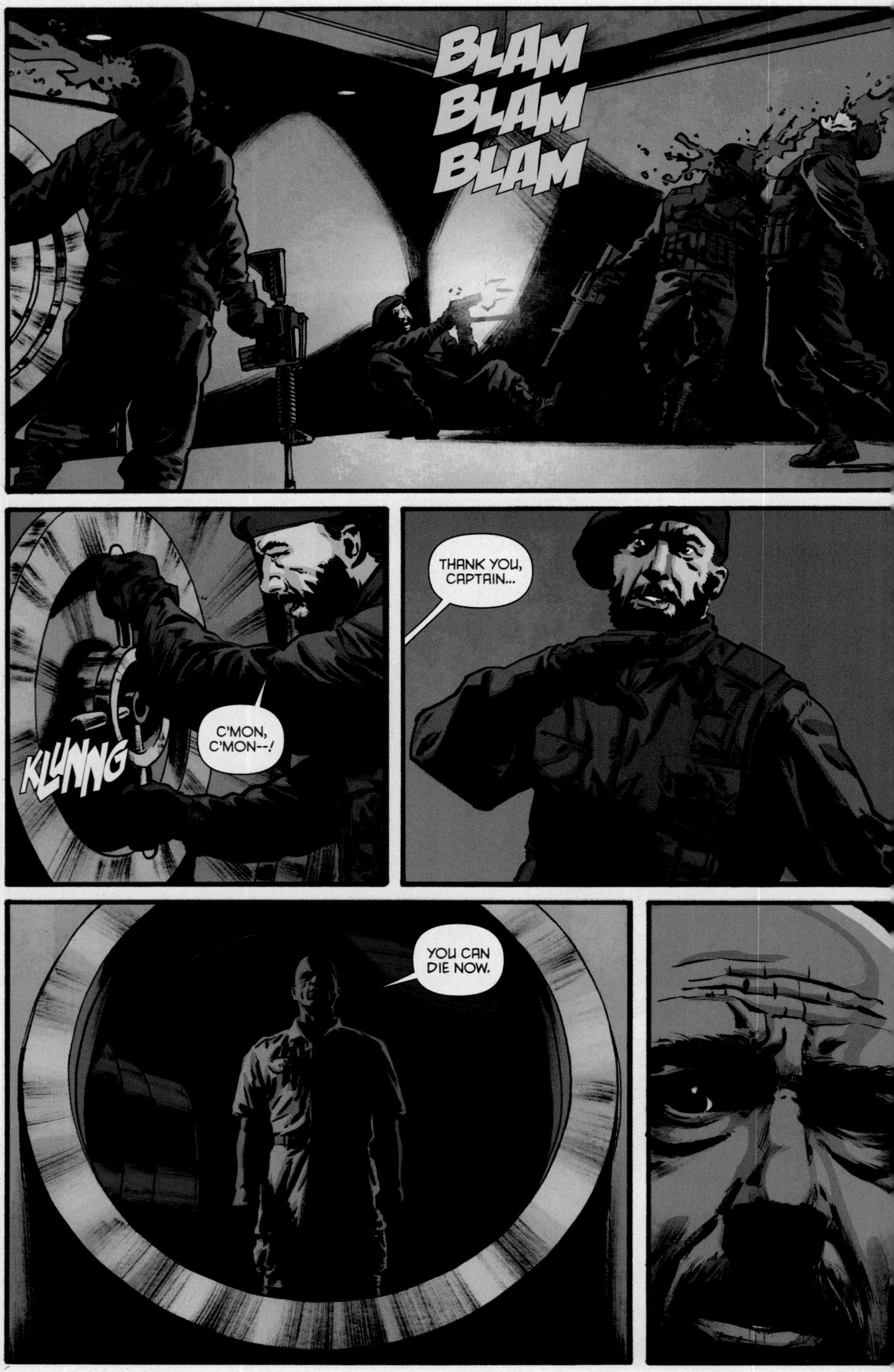
BLAM
BLAM
BLAM
KLUNNG
C'MON, C'MON--!
THANK YOU, CAPTAIN...
YOU CAN DIE NOW.

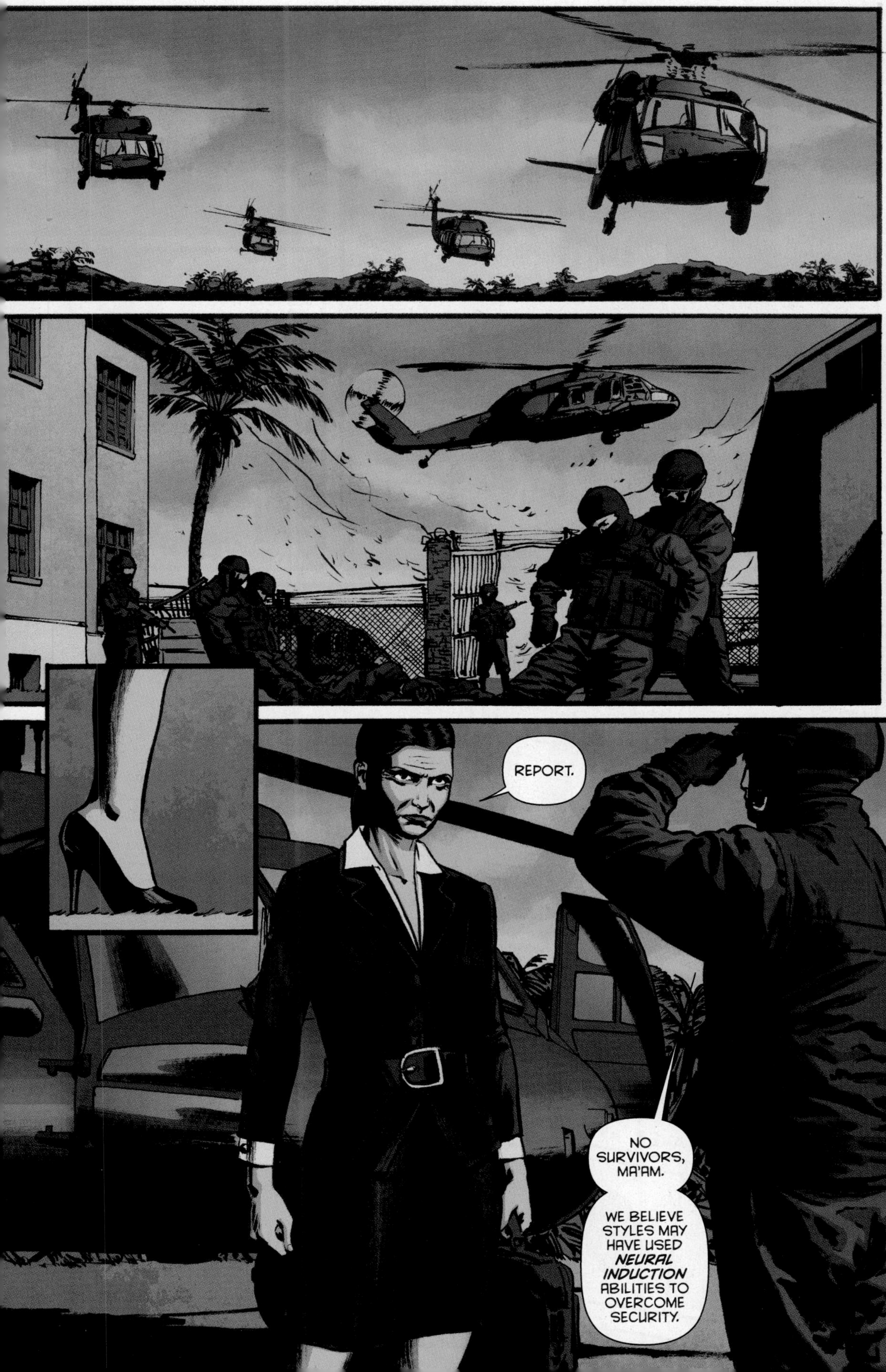
REPORT.
NO SURVIVORS, MA'AM.
WE BELIEVE STYLES MAY HAVE USED ***NEURAL INDUCTION*** ABILITIES TO OVERCOME SECURITY.

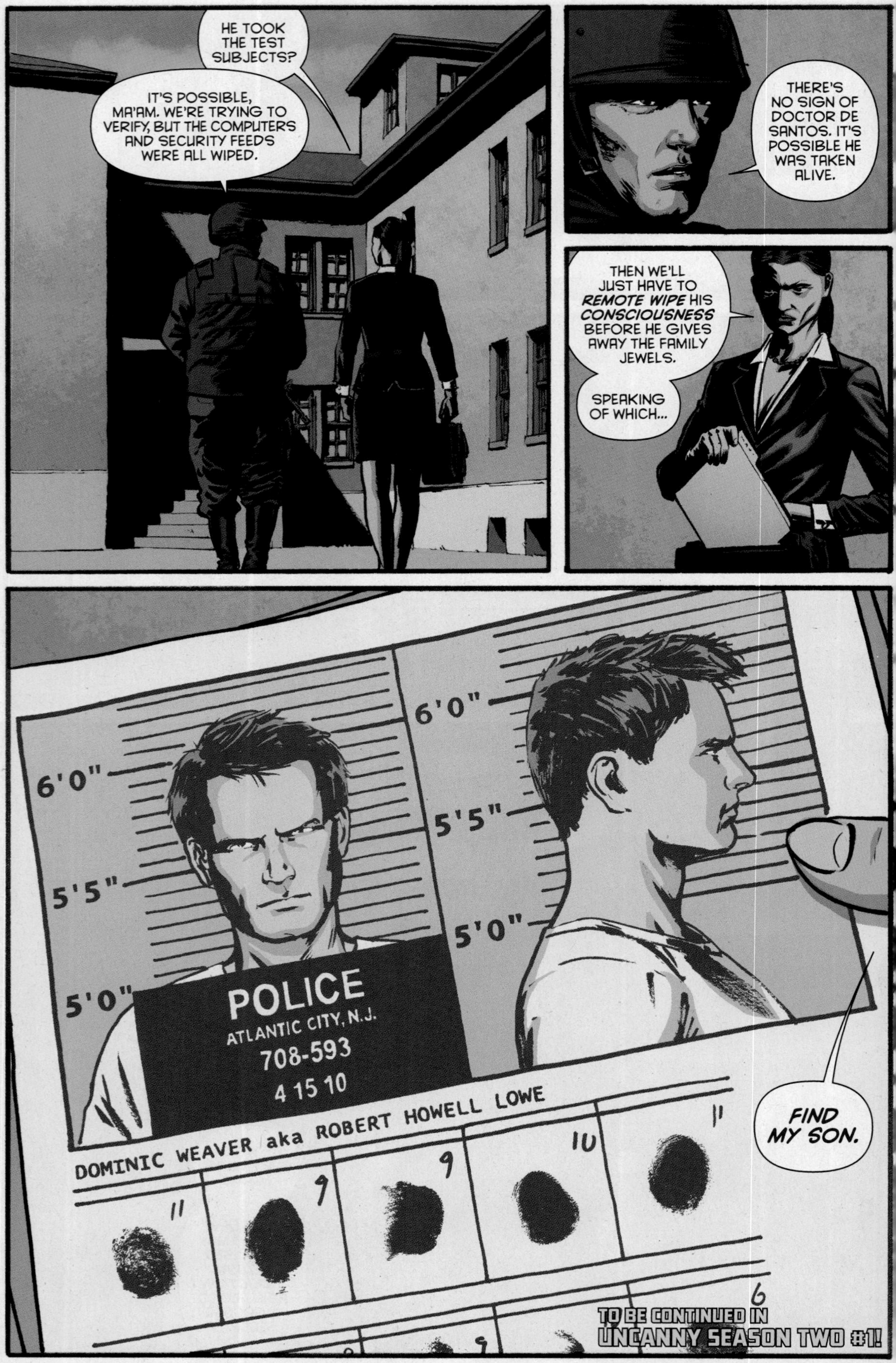
HE TOOK THE TEST SUBJECTS?
IT'S POSSIBLE, MA'AM. WE'RE TRYING TO VERIFY, BUT THE COMPUTERS AND SECURITY FEEDS WERE ALL WIPED.
THERE'S NO SIGN OF DOCTOR DE SANTOS. IT'S POSSIBLE HE WAS TAKEN ALIVE.
THEN WE'LL JUST HAVE TO *REMOTE WIPE* HIS *CONSCIOUSNESS* BEFORE HE GIVES AWAY THE FAMILY JEWELS.
SPEAKING OF WHICH...
6'0"
5'5"
5'0"
POLICE
ATLANTIC CITY, N.J.
708-593
4 15 10
6'0"
5'5"
5'0"
DOMINIC WEAVER aka ROBERT HOWELL LOWE
11
9
9
10
11
6
FIND MY SON.
TO BE CONTINUED IN
UNCANNY SEASON TWO #1!

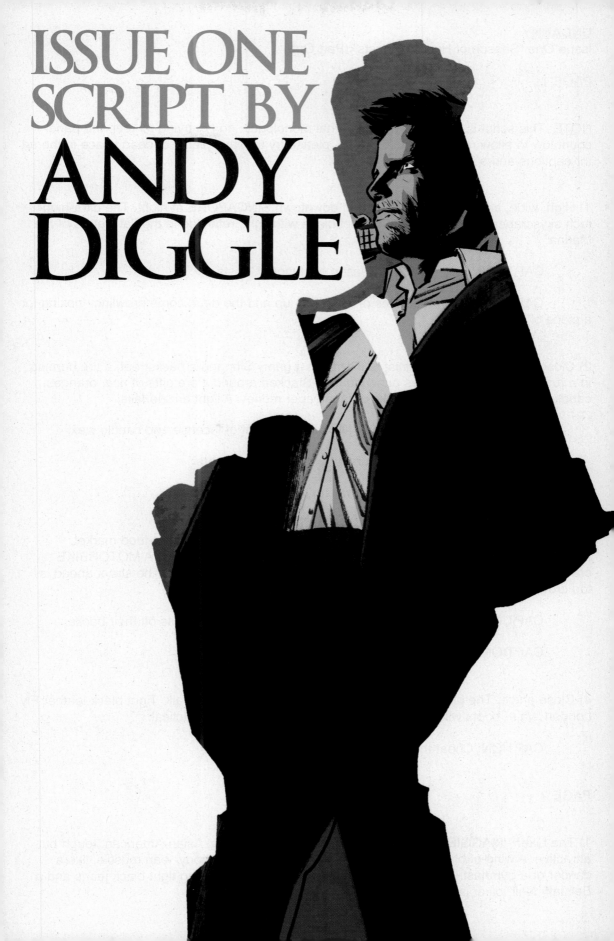

ISSUE ONE
SCRIPT BY
ANDY
DIGGLE

UNCANNY

Issue One "Season of Hungry Ghosts" (Part One)

<u>PAGE 1</u>

<u>NOTE</u>: This script is pretty heavy on internal monologue, so I'm trying to keep the panel count low to allow room for text. Even so, please try to leave plenty of dead space in the art for captions and speech balloons. Thanks!

1) High, wide, aerial establishing shot of downtown SINGAPORE at night. The ultra-high-tech skyscrapers of the Financial District blaze with light, reflected in the flat waters of the Marina.

      CAPTION: They call it the <u>Season of Hungry Ghosts</u>.

      CAPTION: When the gates of Hell open up and the dead come prowling, looking for a piece of the action.

2) Close on a makeshift Buddhist SHRINE on a grimy Singapore backstreet; a fire burning in a rusted oil drum with holes punched in it. Stacked around it are gifts of rice, oranges, candles, incense sticks, and stacks of fake paper money. A light drizzle falls.

      CAPTION: The warm night air fills with the scent of incense and candle wax.

      CAPTION: Oil-drum altars burning on the street corners.

      CAPTION: Fake paper money wilting in the Singapore rain.

3) Widen to show the street scene. A bustling, low-rent, open-air street-food market. Hawkers selling skewers of meat and bowls of rice and soup noodles. A MOTORBIKE crawls into the lower corner of the panel. Female rider, black helmet. The street ahead is too crowded for it to continue.

      CAPTION: The locals leave these offerings to keep the spirits off their backs.

      CAPTION: Buy a little peace.

4) Close angle. The biker's BOOT steps down onto the wet sidewalk. Tight black leather Fly London "Vale" boots with a thick rubber wedge heel. Sexy but practical.

      CAPTION: Cheat the dead.

<u>PAGE 2</u>

1) The biker - MAGGIE - pulls off her helmet. She's early 30s, Asian-American, tough but attractive. A wing of black hair semi-obscuring one eye. Lithe body, lean muscle, like a dancer or a gymnast. Gina Carano meets Lucy Liu. She's wearing tight black jeans and a Belstaff "Nail" biker jacket or similar.

CAPTION: No wonder the ghosts stay hungry. It's all fake.

CAPTION: So they have to keep hunting for the next hit. The next mark.

2) Low angle, worm's eye POV. Maggie walks towards a gleaming building. A huge illuminated sign reveals it as the LEE CASINO.

CAPTION: Anything to make them feel alive.

CAPTION: Until it's time to go back to the shadows.

3) BIG reveal of our American anti-hero - WEAVER. He sits at a two-player poker table inside the casino, cards in hand. A Josh Holloway/Leo DiCaprio/Bradley Cooper type. Wolfishly handsome. Flinty eyes. An urban predator; a hunter, ever alert to being hunted. Gray suit, white shirt open at the collar, no tie. He's surrounded by affluent and glamorous Asians, including MIKO, a beautiful escort in a sleek dress, standing close behind him.

CAPTION: I can relate.

TITLE & CREDITS: *Season of Hungry Ghosts (Part 1)*

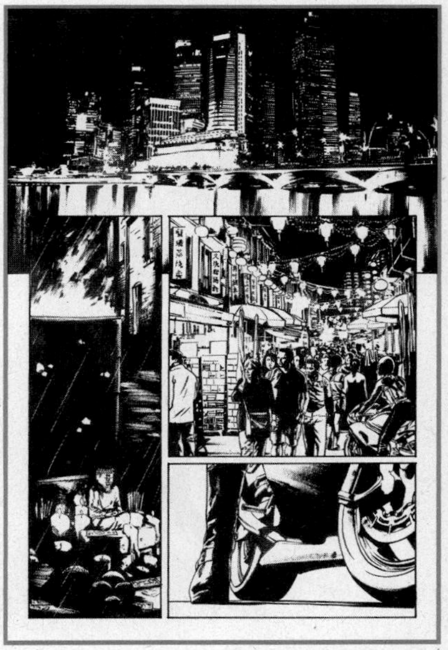

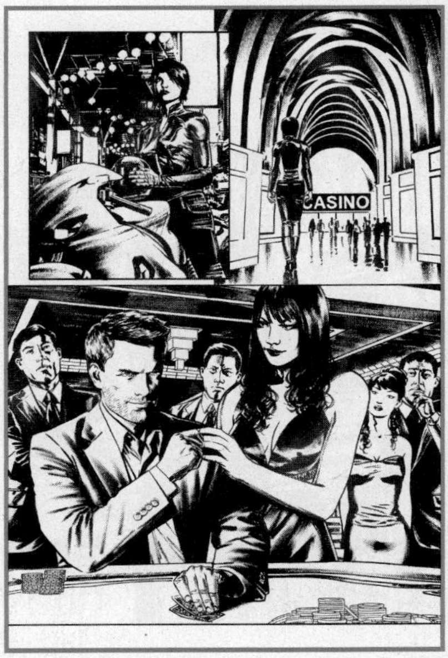
CASINO

PAGE 3

1) Move in on Weaver, scowling at his cards.

CAPTION: Festival of the Dead means I've been in Singapore a year now. Figures.

CAPTION: Getting too comfortable. Getting stale.

2) Angle on the man sitting opposite him - LEE, a fat, smug-looking Chinese businessman. Lee grins nastily at us.

CAPTION: But the Asian tiger makes for rich pickings for a man in my line of work...

CAPTION: And this smug fuck is ready to fall.

LEE: Hoping your hand will sprout aces if you stare at it long enough?
(link)
The bet is for your last fifty thousand, Mr. Weaver.

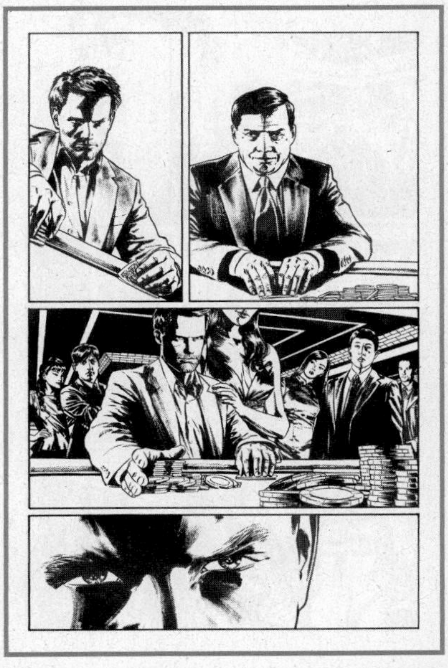

Meet me or fold.

3) Weaver lays his cards face down. He pushes his <u>last</u> remaining stack of poker chips out onto the table.

> CAPTION: I <u>read</u> him before the game. He's a bluffer with more money than sense.

> CAPTION: Been luring him into a false sense of security all night. Letting him think he's winning...

WEAVER: I'll meet you and <u>raise</u>.

4) Close angle on Weaver's eyes, narrowed, nailing us with a flinty look.

> WEAVER: <u>Two hundred and fifty thousand</u>.

> CAPTION: ... Before I spring the <u>trap</u>.

PAGE 4

1) Weaver sits back in his chair with a cold smile. He and Lee regard each other coolly across the table. The other patrons look on, wondering how it'll play out...

> CAPTION: Time to clean up and move on.

> LEE: You don't have it.

> WEAVER: I don't need it. Put up or shut up.

2) Close. LEE lays his cards on the table, face up. A ROYAL FLUSH!

> LEE (off panel above): Very well.
> (link)
> <u>Royal flush</u>.

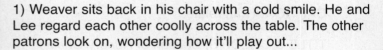

3) On Weaver, stunned into silence. Trying to keep his shit together.

> CAPTION: Fuck.

> CAPTION: He wasn't bluffing.

> CAPTION: <u>Fuck</u>.

4) On Lee. Cold menace. Eye contact.

LEE: You owe me two hundred thousand dollars, American.

PAGE 5

1) Weaver rises from his seat, smiling. Trying to play it cool, even though he's gut-sick inside. His escort MIKO turns to him, wondering how he's going to react.

> WEAVER: Kudos, Mr. Lee. I can see how you won the casino.
> (link)
> Guess I'd better go write you a <u>check</u>.

2) Still seated, Lee gestures for the hulking bodyguard behind him, XIONG, to get moving.

> LEE: Xiong, my head of security, will accompany you.

3) Weaver smiles as he half-turns to us, casual —

> WEAVER: No trust left in this town, huh?

4) Weaver's smile vanishes as he takes MIKO by the upper arm and maneuvers her out through the crowd surrounding the table. Everyone's looking at him. He just lost big.

> CAPTION: I don't have two hundred thousand dollars.

> WEAVER: Walk.

5) Weaver and Miko move towards us across the casino floor, Weaver still holding her upper arm. Xiong follows on behind, just out of earshot. Miko plays along, laughing. Weaver stony-faced.

> CAPTION: Hell, I didn't have the <u>fifty</u>. Bought the chips on stolen credit.:

> WEAVER: Smile and laugh, like I just said something means I don't give a shit.

> MIKO: *Ha ha!*

PAGE 6

1) FLASHBACK. Before the game, Weaver and Lee stand at the table, shaking hands, friendly, smiling.

> CAPTION: How the fuck did I get Lee so wrong...?

> CAPTION: I shook his hand before the game. Got a good solid <u>read</u> on him.

2) FLASHBACK. On Lee, his smile fading slightly, his expression slackening, as if he's a little spaced out. In this panel only, Lee's eyes have turned COMPLETELY WHITE.

CAPTION: His head was full of angles, every one of them a bluff.

CAPTION: I saw it. I took it in. Turned it against him.

3) Wide shot, back to the present. Weaver, Miko and Xiong are stepping into one of several elevators in mid background. Miko shrugs Weaver's hand off her arm. He's too preoccupied with his own thoughts to notice or care. A SILHOUETTED FIGURE leans against a pillar in the close foreground, panel right, watching them...

CAPTION: Unless somehow he <u>knows</u> what I can do. Prepared for it...

4) Reveal the figure watching. It's MAGGIE.

CAPTION: ... and played me like a violin.

PAGE 7

1) Low angle. The three of them stand in the elevator. Xiong towers behind Weaver, menacing. Miko takes a tiny smartphone out of her purse.

CAPTION: And if Lee knows, does that mean his gorilla knows too?

MIKO: Excuse me, my phone is buzzing...

2) Casino hotel corridor. Weaver swipes his key-card across his room lock. He turns as Miko says to him —

CAPTION: Guess I'll find out once he sees there's nothing in my room safe but fake passports and stolen credit cards...

MIKO: That was the agency.
(link)
Thank you for a wonderful few days, but I'm afraid I have to leave now.

WEAVER: What? That wasn't the arrangement...

3) Miko half turns to give us a sour look and a dismissive wave as she strolls off down the corridor, heading back to the elevators.

MIKO: You get the company you <u>pay</u> for, Mr. Weaver...
(link)
And your credit just dried up.

4) Xiong raises one eyebrow. His expression blank.

5) Weaver shrugs it off, smiling awkwardly, embarrassed.

WEAVER: Like I gotta pay for it.

PAGE 8

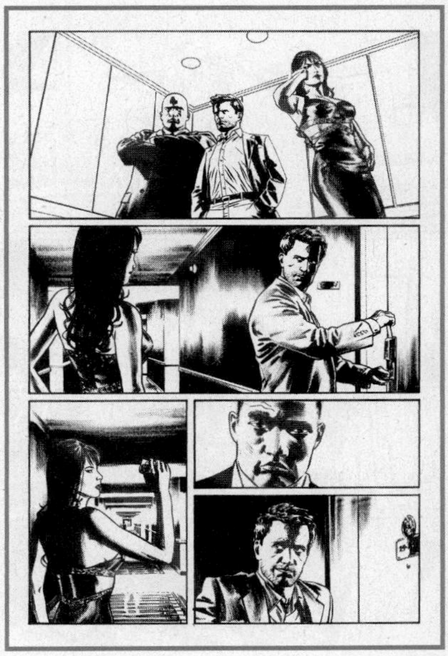

1) Wide establishing shot. A luxury suite. Our POV from the bay window. Wall closet at rear, panel left; door on the back wall, mid-panel; bar at panel right, with a cut-crystal whisky decanter and glasses. A large open lounge space in the foreground with a glass coffee table in the middle. Weaver walks in, gesturing towards the decanter. He's heading towards the closet. Xiong follows him in, implacable.

WEAVER: Make yourself at home. Drinks over there.

XIONG: I am only here for the check.

2) POV over Weaver's shoulder as he opens the key-code digital safe inside the closet. Inside is a long leather travel wallet, nothing else. He turns to us with feigned anger —

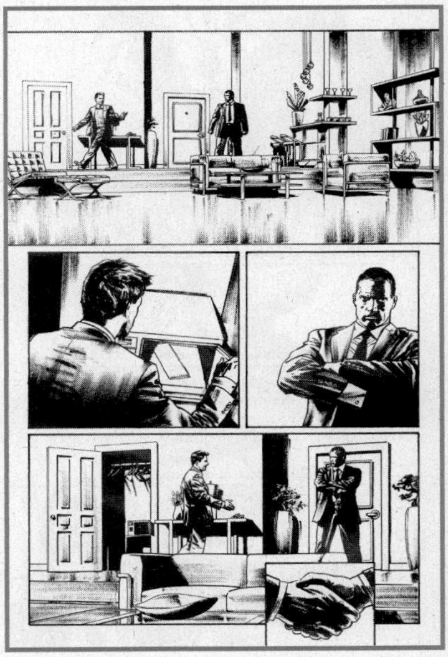

WEAVER: Hey, what the hell kind of place are you guys running here?
(link)
My safe's been ripped off!

3) Xiong, implacable.

XIONG: Mr. Lee said you would try to cheat me.
(link)
He will not be pleased to be proved correct.

4) Weaver walks towards Xiong, holding out his hand to shake...

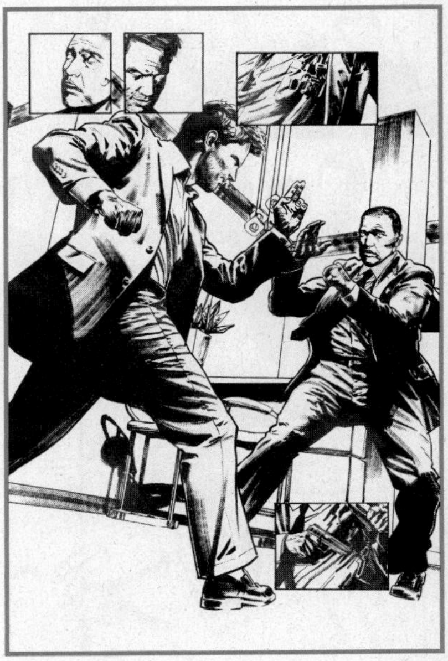

WEAVER: Hey listen, you got me all wrong, Xiong.
(link)
You'll get your money...

5) Close inset. Weaver and Xiong shake hands.

WEAVER (off-panel above): I give you my word.

PAGE 9

Lots of small inset panels floating on a full-page panel 4, as we go into WEAVER-VISON. He has absorbed some of Xiong's knowledge, perceptions and abilities. We jump

in close to take in lots of little details...

1) Close inset. On Xiong, slack-featured. His eyes turn COMPLETELY WHITE.

CAPTION: And suddenly I <u>know</u> him.

2) Close inset. On WEAVER - his eyes have turned white too.

CAPTION: For the next few minutes, I know him better than I know myself.

3) Close inset. On Xiong's jacket hanging slightly open, revealing a glimpse of HANDGUN grip in a shoulder holster.

CAPTION: I know he's wearing a gun in a shoulder rig under his left armpit.

4) Widen. Xiong takes a step back, gathering himself. A serious, predatory look on Weaver's face now. Their eyes return to normal. Both of them tensing, coiled, dynamic tension —

CAPTION: I know it's a NORINCO Model 77B with a 3-pound trigger pull.

CAPTION: And because he's also a black-belt in *taekwondo*...

5) Close inset. Xiong pulls open his jacket with his left hand, reaching for the gun with his right —

CAPTION: ... I know how to take it off him.

PAGE 10

Fight! Let's go fairly wide on the imagery to give the reader a clear sense of the geography/choreography —

1) Weaver executes a perfect, head-height, straight-leg roundhouse KICK to Xiong's hand that sends the gun FLYING! Xiong's gun-arm is knocked out wide, a look of surprise on his face —

2) Xiong throws an expert KICK. Weaver DUCKS and

Xiong's shoe just misses his head —

3) Weaver drops to one knee and PUNCHES the side of Xiong's KNEE, snapping the joint sideways —

      XIONG (jagged): *AAGH!*

4) Xiong has collapsed to one knee, supporting himself with one hand on the floor, in agony. His broken leg hangs at a sickening angle. Weaver skips back, defensive stance —

PAGE 11

1) Close. Xiong flicks his free arm out straight and a KNIFE pops out of his suit sleeve into his waiting hand.

      CAPTION: Oh, great.

2) The two men circle each other, taut, defensive. Xiong supporting his weight on his one good leg, knife in his right hand...

3) Xiong LUNGES with the knife —

4) Close. Fast as a striking snake, Weaver GRABS Xiong's wrist —

5) Weaver has spun around so he's now standing close behind Xiong, holding Xiong's knife-arm out straight. With his left hand, Xiong scrabbles for Weaver's eyes. Both men struggling, teeth gritted, desperate —

PAGE 12

1) Weaver slams Xiong's arm down hard and brings his knee up sharply, SNAPPING Xiong's arm backwards at the elbow! Xiong screams, dropping the knife —

2) BIG! Weaver SPINS into a straight leg KICK! Xiong's head SNAPS back and he flies backwards —

3) Xiong SMASHES into the glass coffee table and it EXPLODES —

4) Wide shot. Xiong lies unconscious in the shattered remains of the table. Weaver picks up the fallen gun.

      CAPTION: Hadn't seen the knife.

      CAPTION: Like I said. Getting stale.

1) Close, Weaver's POV. He looks down at the NORINCO 77B handgun lying in the palm of his hand.

> CAPTION: Tempting as it is, the gun's a cop magnet. Especially in a town as uptight as this one.

2) Weaver DISASSEMBLES the gun without even looking at it. Grip in one hand, slide and magazine in the other...

> CAPTION: Fortunately, Xiong knows how to field strip a 77B blindfolded.

3) Gun parts lie scattered at Weaver's feet.

> CAPTION: I keep the firing pin. Just in case.

4) Close. Weaver turns to look back at us as he reaches in to take the travel wallet from the open safe...

> CAPTION: One last thing...

5) Weaver crouches beside Xiong, checking Xiong's pockets...

6) Waver holds up a CAR KEY, dangling it from the beeper keyring. He smiles thinly; grim satisfaction.

> CAPTION: Paydirt.

1) Wide. Weaver stands in an underground car park, foreground panel left, holding out the key-ring beeper. Parked cars recede into the distance. Mid-way down the row, the headlights flash on one of the cars, lighting up the gloom...

> CAPTION: By the time I find Xiong's car, there's not much of him left.

> CAPTION: His repertoire of kicks, punches and disarm maneuvers fading like a waking dream.

2) Side-on view. On Weaver, driving through the night streets of Singapore. One hand on the wheel; the other massaging his shoulder, wincing as he squeezes a knotted muscle.

> CAPTION: Always hate the comedown. That hollowed-out feeling mixed with sour adrenaline.

> CAPTION: That and muscle burn. It's not like I had time to stretch.

3) Angle from low behind Weaver, strolling up to the glass facade of Singapore's CHANGI AIRPORT.

CAPTION: The fact that he shook my hand means he didn't know what was coming. If Lee knew, why didn't he warn him?

CAPTION: If Lee <u>didn't</u> know, then what the hell...?

4) In the ticket hall, Weaver casts a wary, narrow-eyed sideways glance at two black-clothed BORDER POLICE carrying SMGs.

CAPTION: Too many angles. Too many <u>guns</u>...

CAPTION: Now's not the time. <u>Focus</u>, asshole.

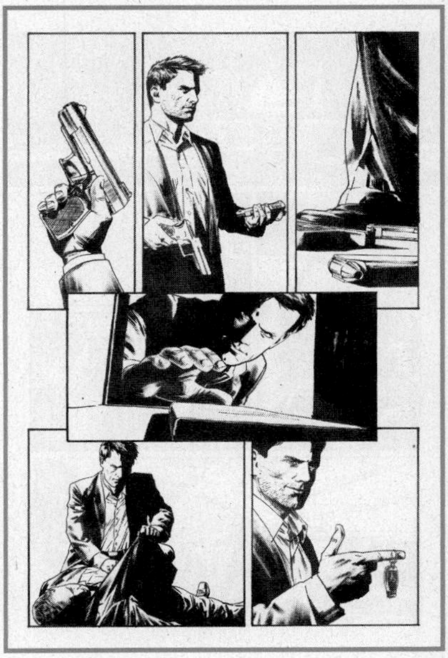

PAGE 15

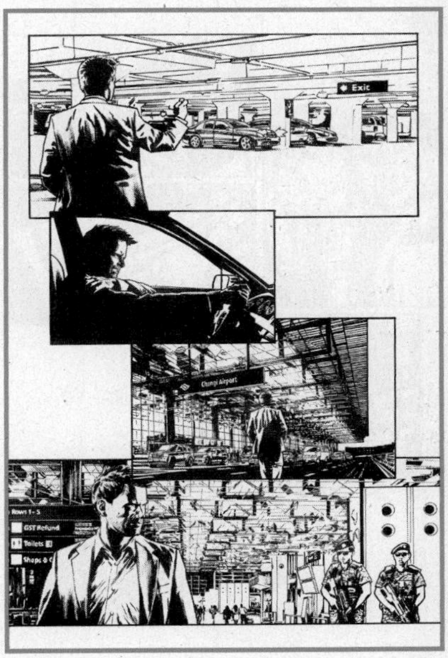
Exit
Changi Airport

1) Close. Weaver's POV. He pulls several gold CREDIT CARDS out of the leather travel wallet. His U.S. PASSPORT stays in there.

CAPTION: What I do know for sure is that my credit's burned.

CAPTION: Do I have Lee to thank for that?

2) Close. Weaver's hand drops the credit cards into a TRASH BIN.

CAPTION: If so, he won't have spiked my black-market passport. He'd rather keep me in town so he can deal with me personally.

CAPTION: At least, that's what I keep telling myself.

3) Weaver buys a smallish shoulder bag at an airport store. Paying cash.

CAPTION: Enough cash left to buy a ticket back Stateside - just - and an empty bag.

4) A pretty Clerk hands Weaver his boarding pass at the ticketing desk, smiling —

CAPTION: No bags raises flags.

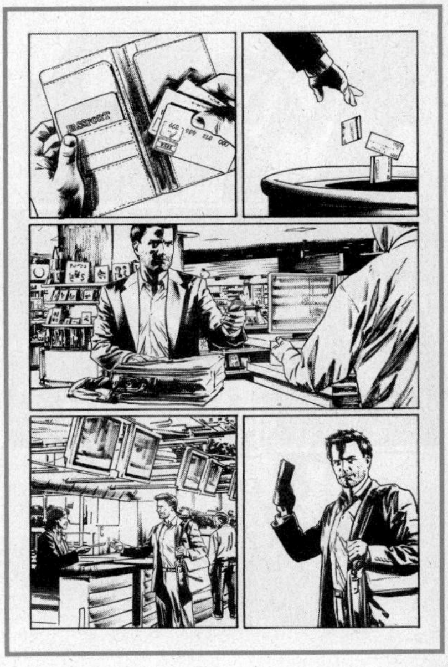
PASSPORT

TICKET CLERK: Enjoy your flight, Mr. Jones.
(link)
We hope to see you back in Singapore soon.

5) Her POV. Weaver gestures with the pass, like a hat-tip. Bag over his shoulder. Dryly —

WEAVER: Don't count on it.

PAGE 16

1) Wide. A Singapore Airlines 747 taxis towards the runway. Night.

ANNOUNCEMENT (jagged; no tail): *Ladies and gentlemen, we are cleared for takeoff. We hope you enjoy the flight.*
(link)
Flight crew, doors to manual and cross-check.

2) Weaver sits back in a huge, comfortable-looking Business Class seat, nursing a tumbler of whisky on his arm rest. He looks tense.

CAPTION: Business class. Fuck it.

CAPTION: If they're gonna grab me, might as well be out of a comfortable seat.

3) Close on his. He leans his head back, closes his eyes, forcing himself to be calm.

CAPTION: Relax. Let the whisky do its work.

CAPTION: Nobody knows. Nobody suspects a—

ANNOUNCEMENT (jagged; no tail): *Ladies and gentlemen, I'm afraid I have some bad news.*
(link)
We've just been asked to return to the gate.

4) Alarmed now, Weaver cranes round in his seat, peering down the aisle behind him —

CAPTION: Shit.

ANNOUNCEMENT (jagged; no tail): *Our apologies for the delay.*
(link)
We will of course keep you updated as we receive

more information.

5) Weaver's POV. Further down the aisle, one of the pretty flight attendants stoops to whisper to a tough-looking Asian civilian in his seat - an undercover Air Marshal. <u>Both of them are looking right back at us</u>.

        CAPTION: Air marshal.

PAGE 17

1) Weaver is up out of his seat, moving fast, heading forward towards the curtained-off stewardesses area. He pushes past another stewardess —

        CAPTION: He'll be armed...

        STEWARDESS: Sir, you have to return to your seat—

        WEAVER: It's okay. Security.

2) Close. Weaver is throwing the big metal lever on the emergency exit!

        CAPTION: ... but so will the border cops waiting for me back at the gate.:

        CAPTION: And there'll be a lot more of 'em.

        STEWARDESS (jagged): <u>Sir</u>—!

3) Exterior. The inflatable slide DEPLOYS! Weaver silhouetted in the open doorway —

4) The Air Marshal RUNS towards us down the aisle. The passengers look alarmed —

        AIR MARSHAL: <u>Stay in your seats!</u>

5) Weaver SLIDES down the emergency slide!

PAGE 18

1) The Air Marshal stands in the aircraft doorway, half concealed, speaking into a phone. He holds his HANDGUN close, pointing upwards for safety.

        AIR MARSHAL: Suspect has deployed the slide! Am in pursuit!

2) Beneath the plane. Weaver hides, standing with his back pressed against one of the landing wheels. We might see that Weaver holds a small coin in one hand. Behind him and off to one side, the Air Marshal emerges from the bottom of the slide, gun out, cautious. We're in the middle of the runway, darkness all around...

3) Close inset. Weaver FLICKS a COIN off his thumb —

4) Close inset. The coin PINGS off the asphalt —

5) The Air Marshal pivots and AIMS at the sound, gun held in the straight-arm, two-handed "Weaver Stance" —

1) BIG! Weaver DIVES into the Air Marshal from behind! Grabbing him in an ugly, messy, brutal flying tackle —

2) Weaver's POV. The Air Marshal on his back, snarling; Weaver's hand at his throat. The Air Marshal's eyes turn WHITE —

    CAPTION: I only take what I need.

    CAPTION: His gun. His phone. His key-code...

3) Air Marshal's POV, from the ground. Weaver stands TOWERING over us in steep perspective, speaking into the phone which he took. Weaver holds the Marshal's gun in one hand, hanging loose at his side. He doesn't want to kill anyone.

    CAPTION: ... and the complete security protocols for Changi International Airport.

    WEAVER: <u>Code 9!</u> Suspect is heading for the <u>cargo terminal</u>!
    (link)
    Blue overalls - he's dressed as a <u>maintenance worker</u>!
    (link)
    We need him alive! Do <u>not</u> open fire!

1) Wide. Weaver RUNS out onto the grassy field surrounding the runway, heading into deep black shadow - i.e. <u>away</u> from the terminal. He's some distance from us here...

    CAPTION: Desperation move.

    CAPTION: But it should keep 'em chasing their tails long enough for me to reach the blind spot on the south perimeter...

2) Close. Weaver crouches close to a runway marker, peeking out. Out in the blank darkness surrounding the airfield, a single headlight is approaching...

    CAPTION: ... or not.

3) BIG! Maggie's MOTORBIKE slews to a halt, digging up grass.

CAPTION: The fuck...?

MAGGIE: Weaver!

4) Weaver stands, nonplussed.

WEAVER: Who the fuck are you?

5) Maggie flips up her helmet faceplate.

MAGGIE: Right now, your only friend in the world.
(link)
Get on.

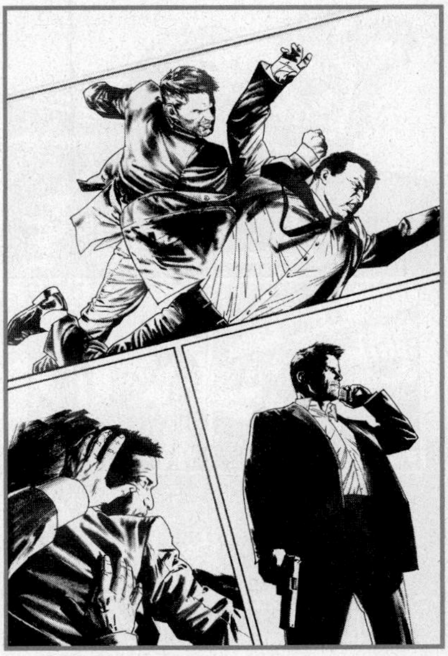

PAGE 21

1) Two shot. Weaver, his back to us, faces Maggie, facing us.

WEAVER: I don't know you, lady.
(link)
Did Lee send you?

MAGGIE: I'm with some people want to offer you a job. Like the kind that pays.
(link)
Unless you'd rather take your chances with them....?

2) Over-the-shoulder shot. Weaver turns to see a line of FLASHING LIGHTS approaching from the direction of the terminal building, which is maybe half a mile off in the background. A dozen POLICE CARS rushing towards us...

CAPTION: Shit.

3) Weaver climbs onto the back of the bike behind Maggie. She guns the engine, faceplate down.

WEAVER: Gotta be out of my mind...

4) The bike ROARS off across the grass, heading straight towards the 12-foot high chain-link PERIMETER FENCE. Weaver hangs onto a hand-grip at the back of the bike seat.

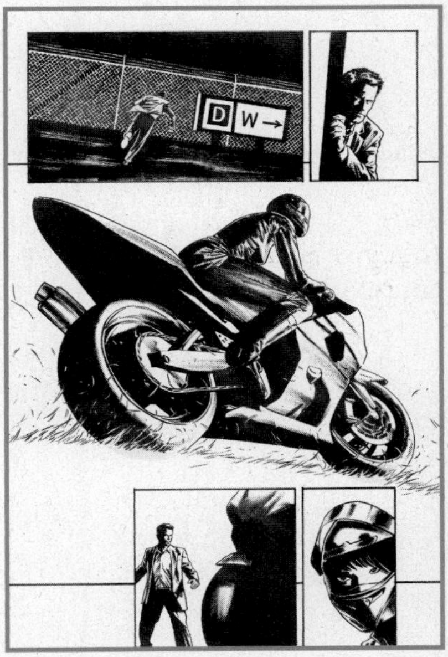
D
W →

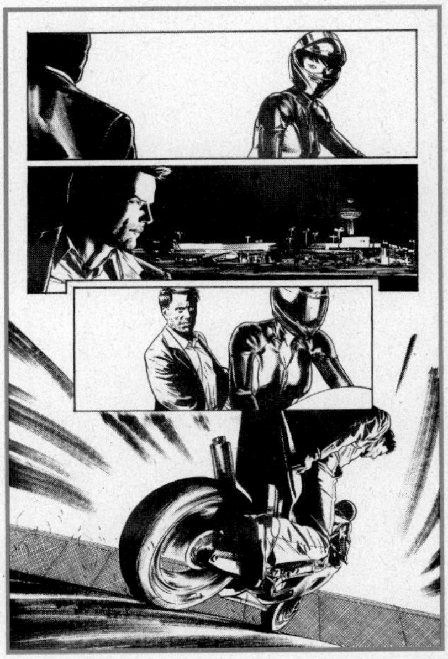

WEAVER: Watch out, you're heading straight for the <u>fence</u>!
(link)
The <u>fence</u>—!

PAGE 22

1) Maggie crouches low over the handlebars. Weaver hangs on for dear life, his arms around her waist —

    MAGGIE: Put your head down.

    WEAVER: Are you <u>shitting</u> me—?!

2) The bike PUNCHES through a vertical slit in the chain-link fence, flapping it open like a pair of curtains —

3) The Bike screeches to a halt on the road beyond - a empty airport maintenance area. Warehouses, loading bays, yellow sodium lighting...

    MAGGIE: I already cut it. How'd you think I got in?

    WEAVER: You are one crazy bitch, you know that, lady?

4) Maggie half turns towards Weaver sat behind her.

    MAGGIE: I don't like being called a bitch.
    (link)
    The name's <u>Maggie</u>.

    WEAVER: Fine, whatever. Any other points of etiquette you want I should know about?

    MAGGIE: Yeah...

5) High angle, looking straight down the service road from high above. The bike ROARS away from us into the night, Weaver still on the back. If he's not too far away to see this detail, we might see that he's now hanging onto the hand-grip at the back of the saddle instead of Maggie's waist...

    CAPTION: *"Keep those hands to yourself."*

    FOOTER: TO BE CONTINUED...

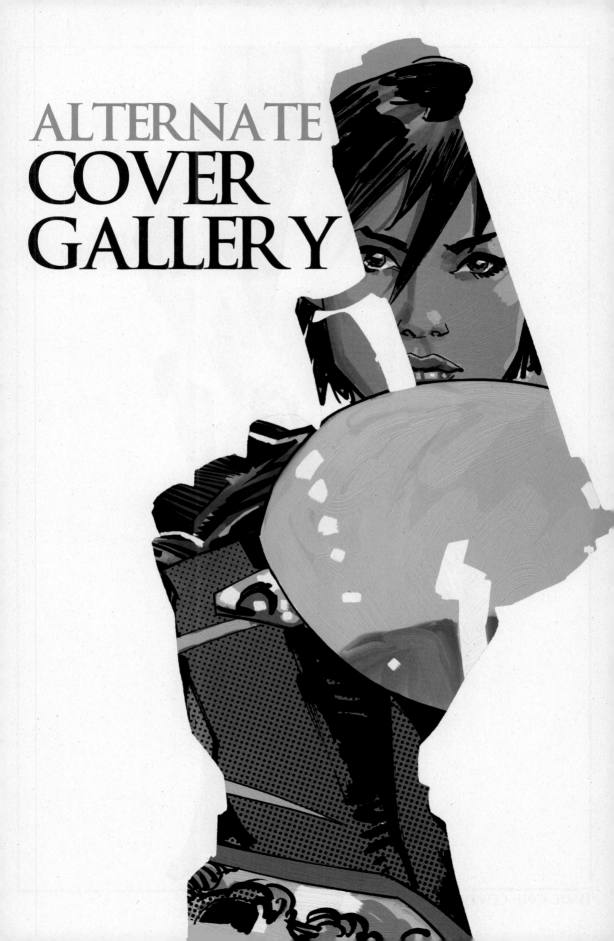

ALTERNATE
COVER
GALLERY

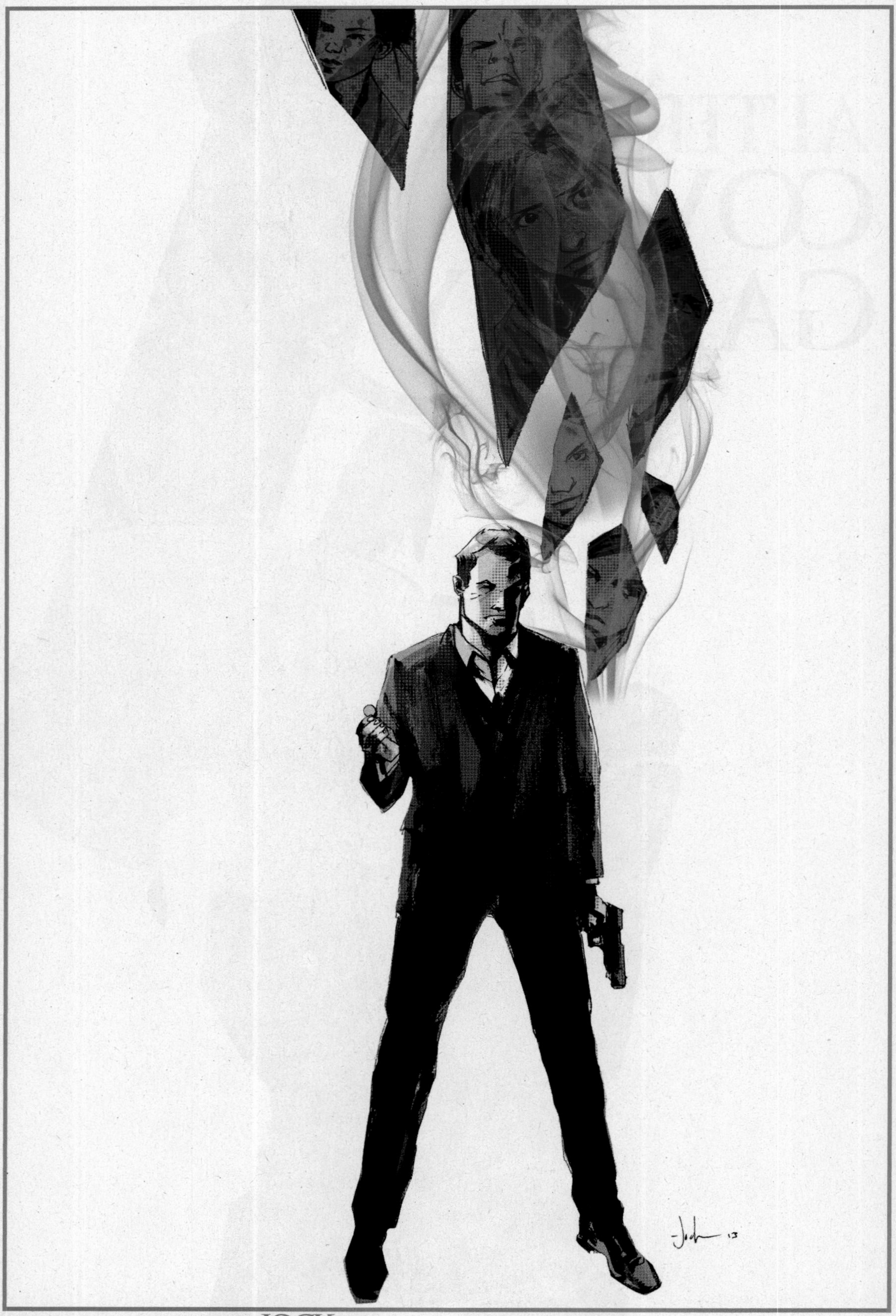

ISSUE ONE COVER BY JOCK

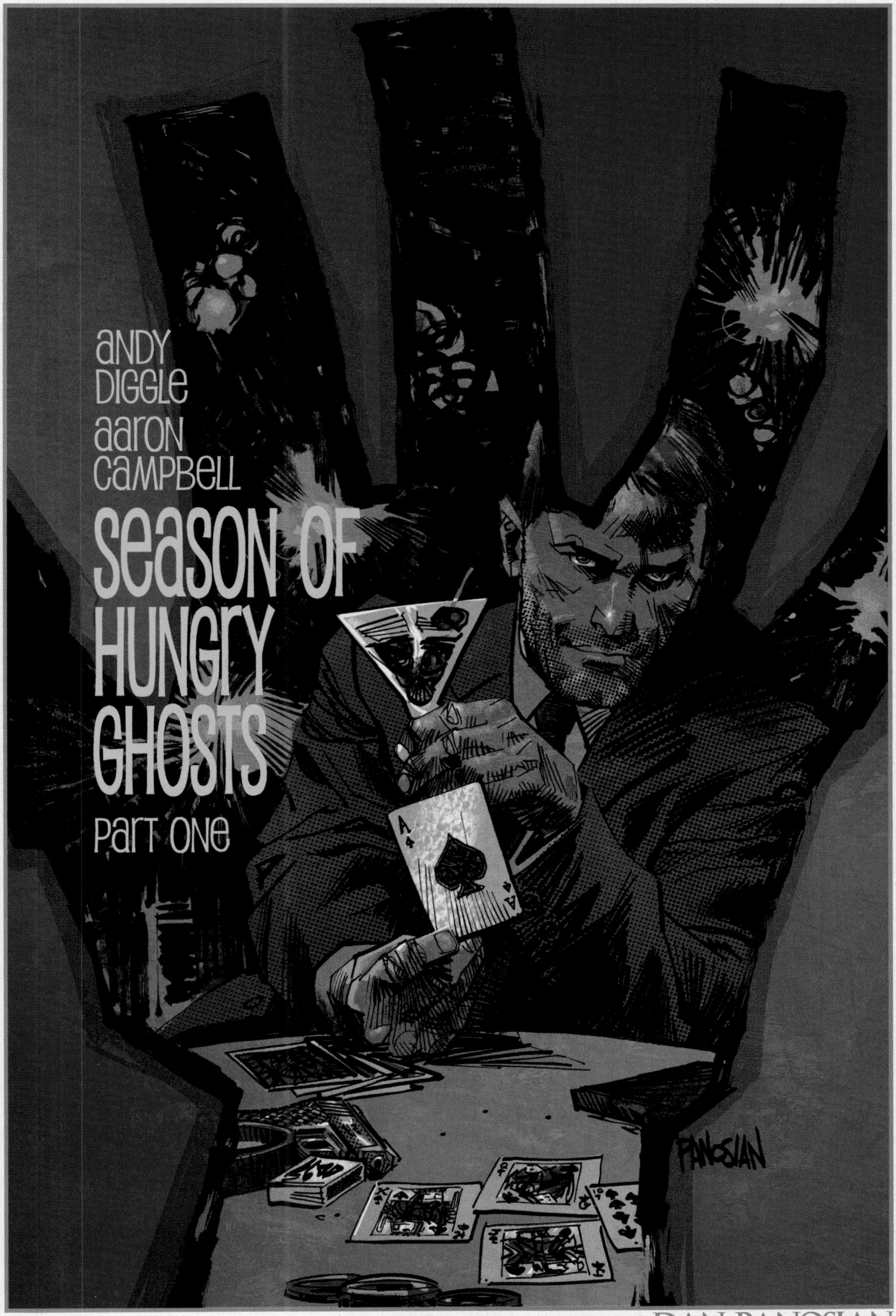
ANDY
DIGGLE
AARON
CAMPBELL
SEASON OF
HUNGRY
GHOSTS
PART ONE
PANOSIAN

ISSUE ONE COVER BY DAN PANOSIAN

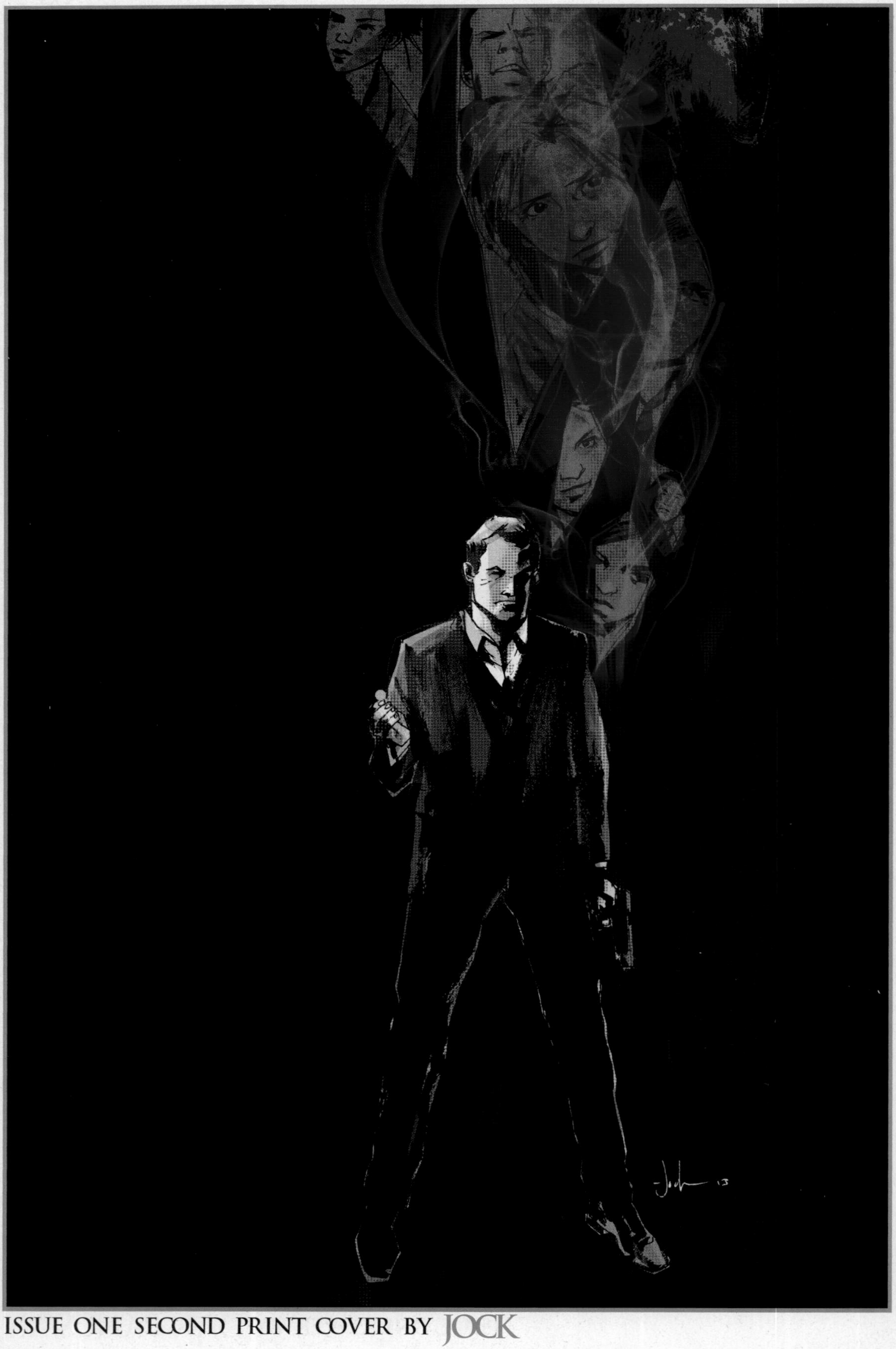

ISSUE ONE SECOND PRINT COVER BY JOCK

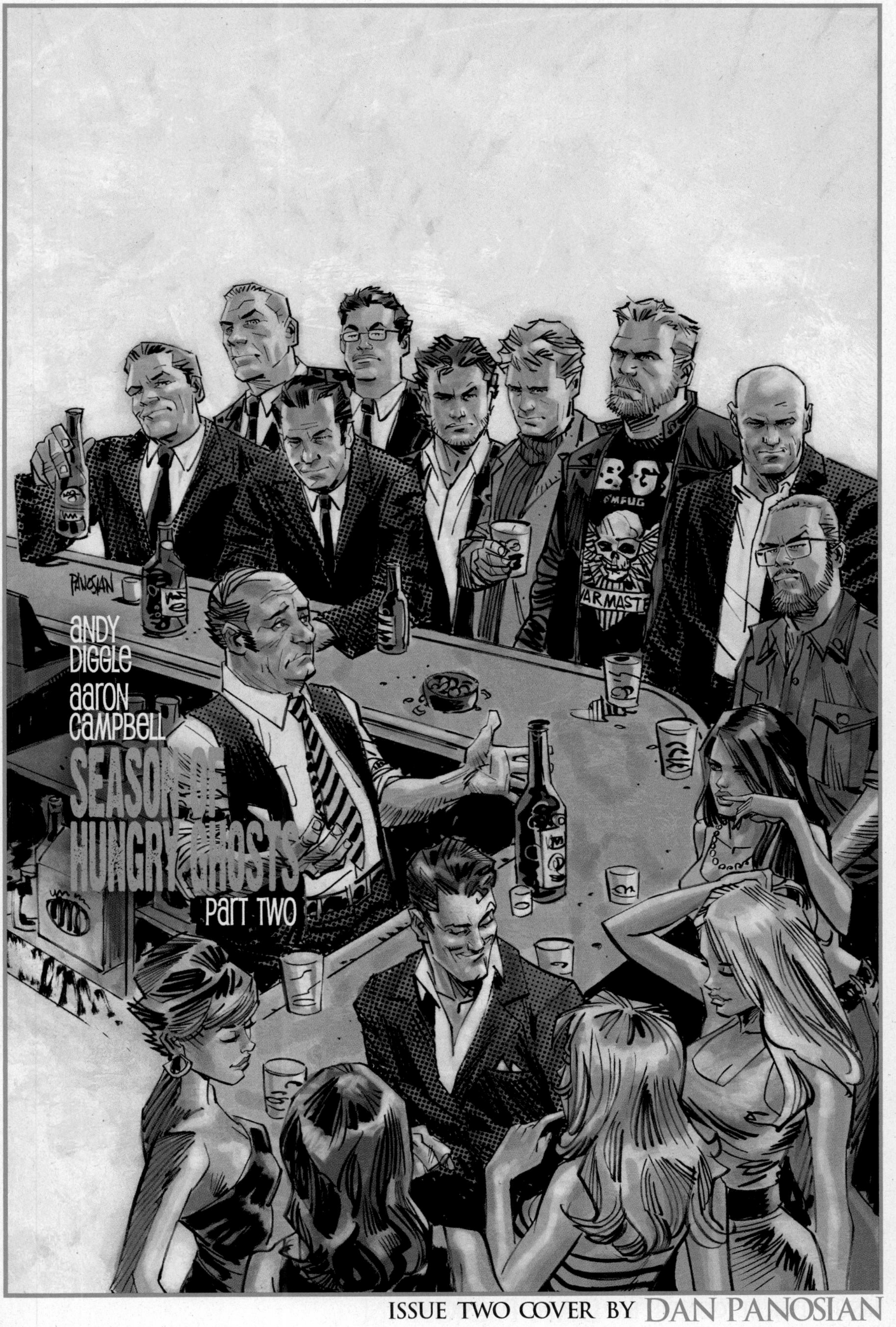
PANOSIAN
andy
diggle
aaron
campbell
SEASON OF
HUNGRY GHOSTS
part two

ISSUE TWO COVER BY DAN PANOSIAN

ISSUE THREE COVER BY DAN PANOSIAN

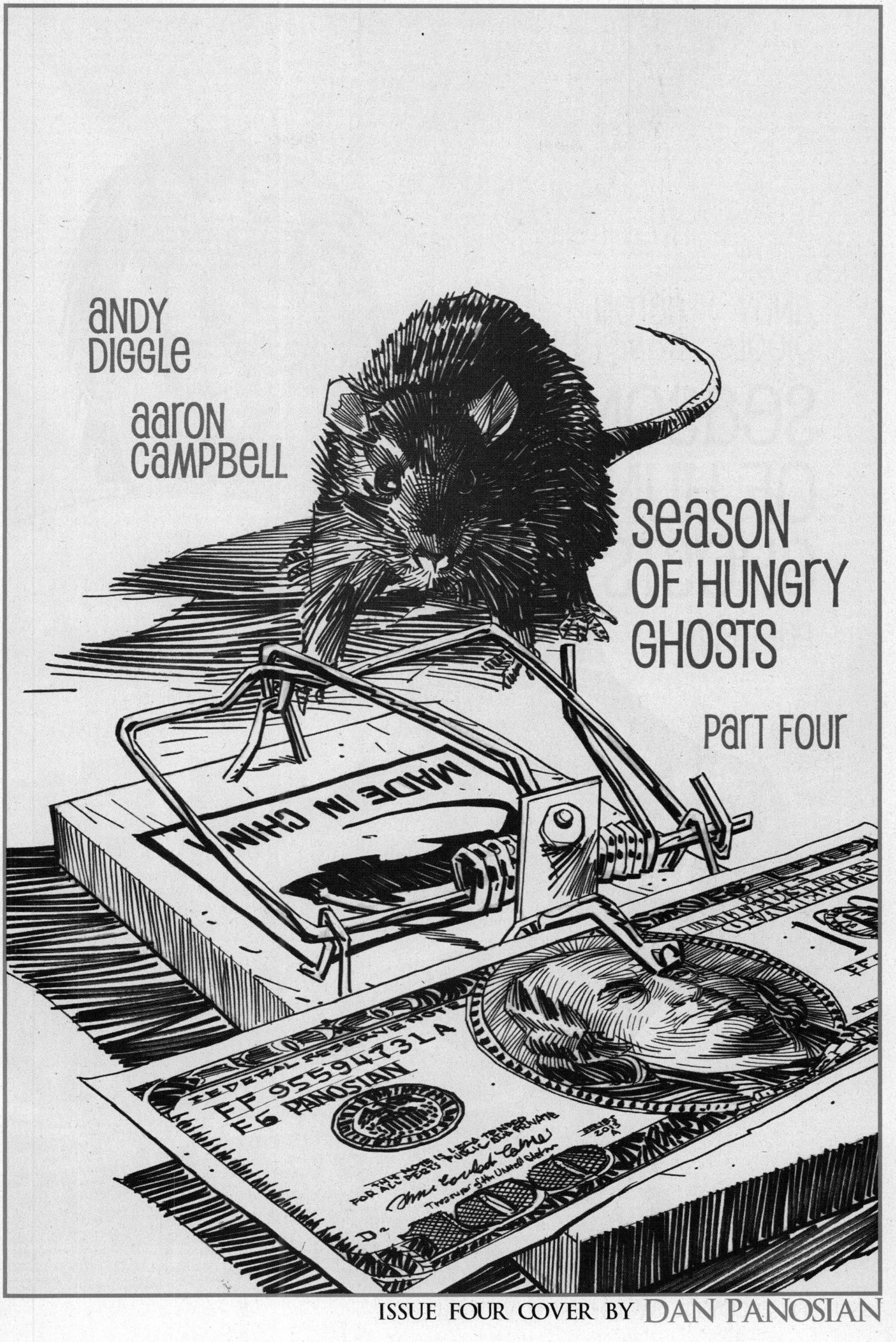
andy
diggle
aaron
campbell
season
of hungry
ghosts
part four
MADE IN CHINA
FEDERAL RESERVE NOTE
FF 95594731A
F6 PANOSIAN

ISSUE FOUR COVER BY DAN PANOSIAN

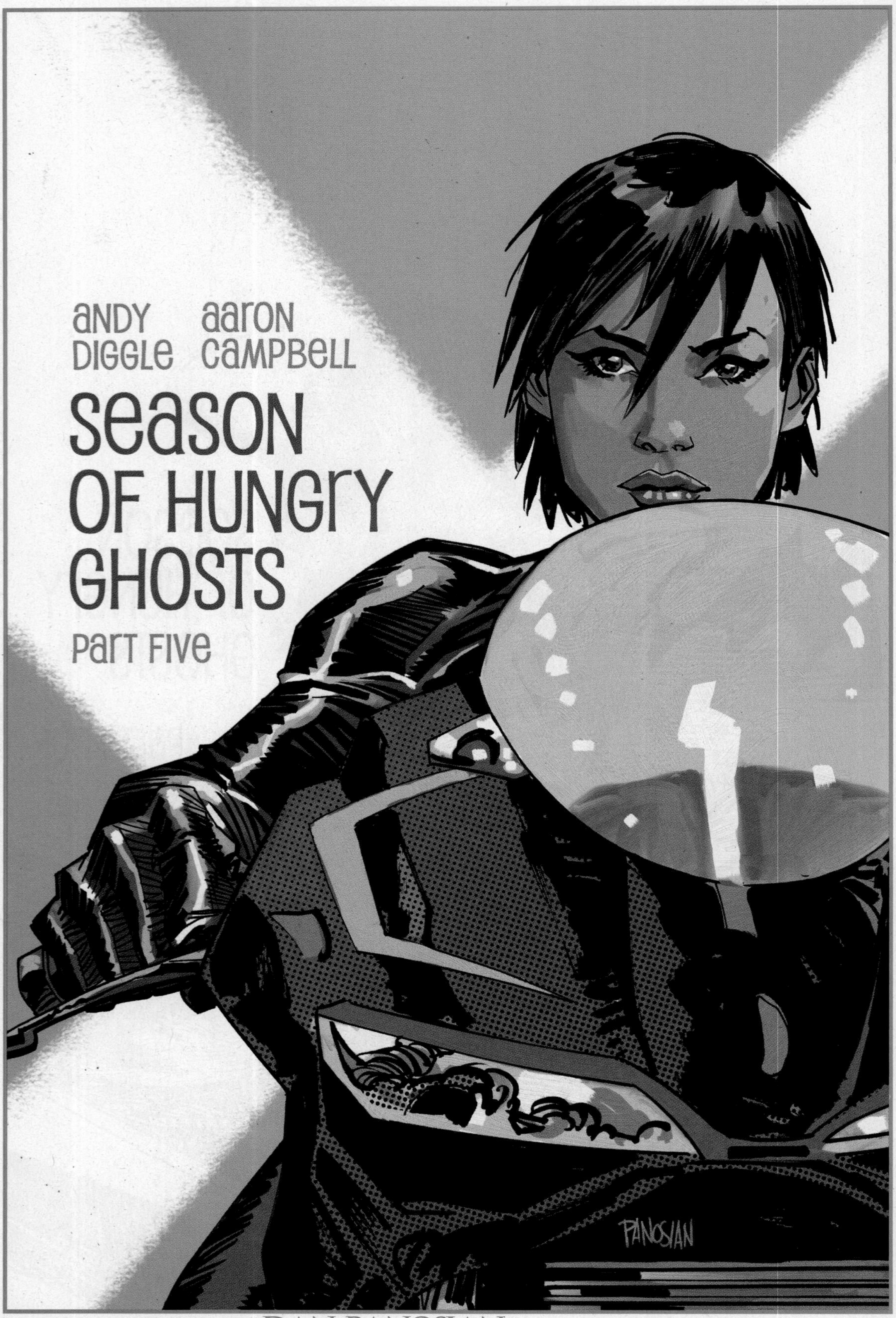
ANDY DIGGLE
AARON CAMPBELL
SEASON OF HUNGRY GHOSTS
PART FIVE
PANOSIAN

ISSUE FIVE COVER BY DAN PANOSIAN

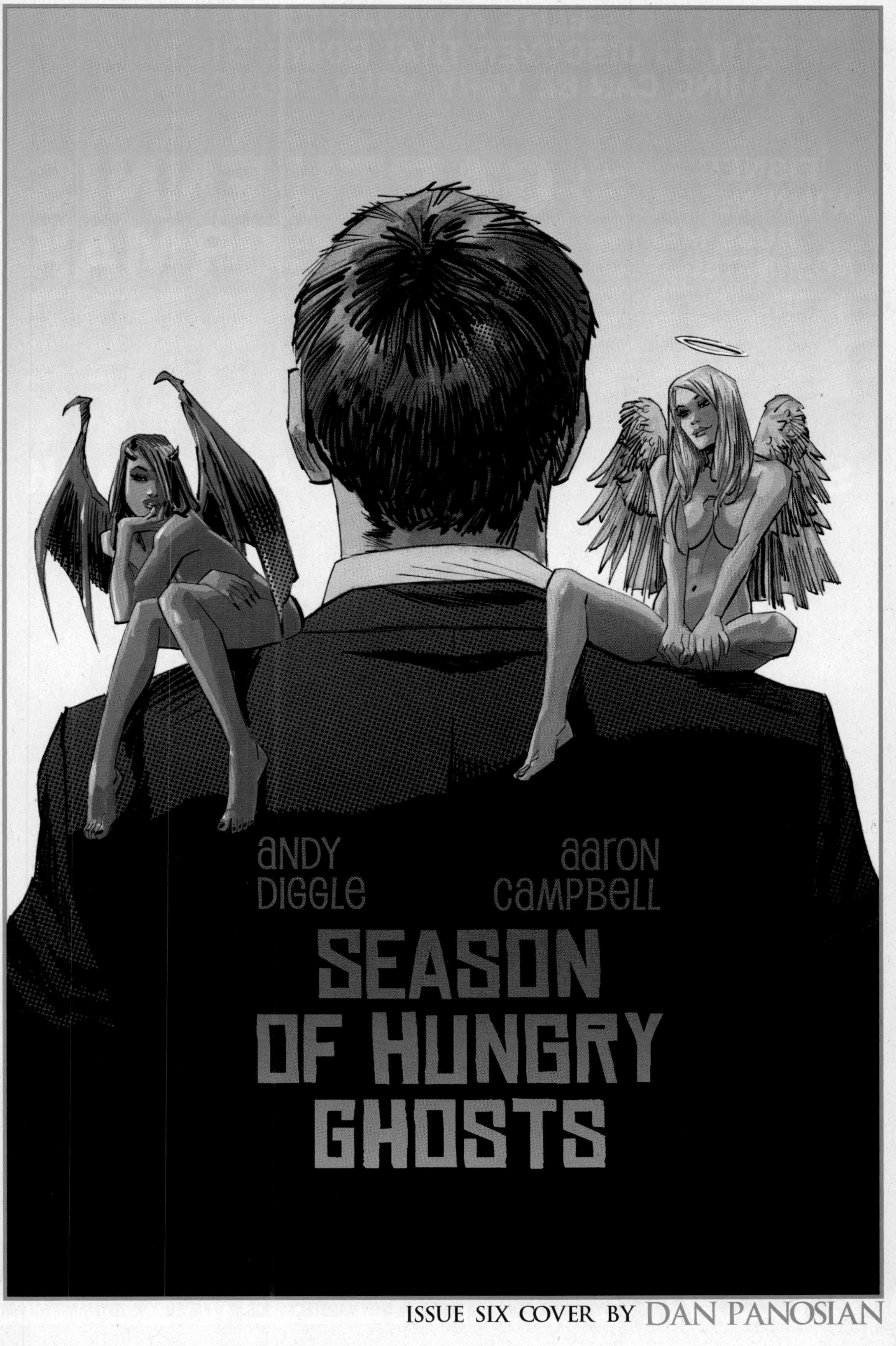
ANDY
DIGGLE
AARON
CAMPBELL
SEASON
OF HUNGRY
GHOSTS

ISSUE SIX COVER BY DAN PANOSIAN

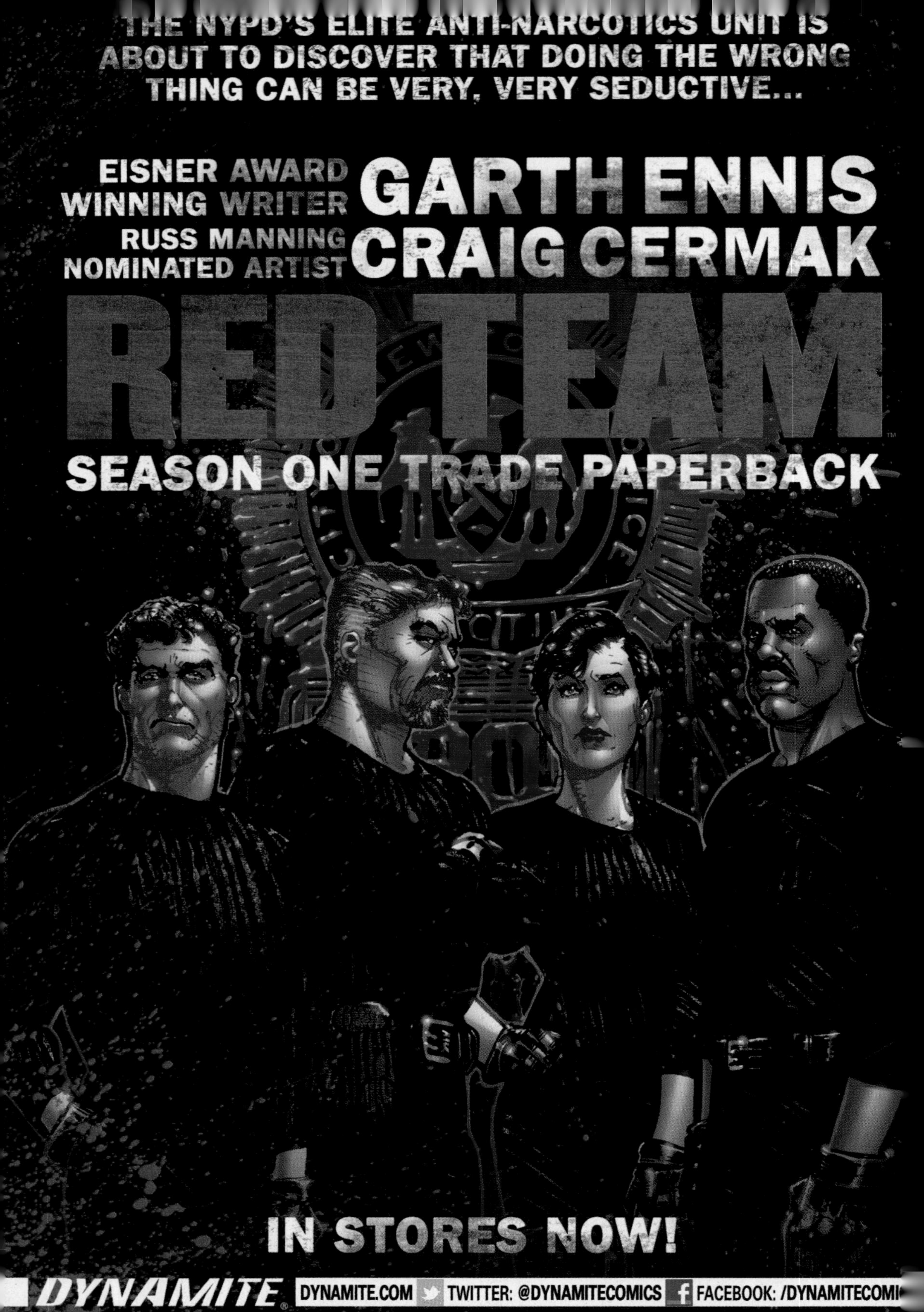

THE NYPD'S ELITE ANTI-NARCOTICS UNIT IS ABOUT TO DISCOVER THAT DOING THE WRONG THING CAN BE VERY, VERY SEDUCTIVE...
EISNER AWARD WINNING WRITER
GARTH ENNIS
RUSS MANNING NOMINATED ARTIST
CRAIG CERMAK
RED TEAM™
SEASON ONE TRADE PAPERBACK
IN STORES NOW!
DYNAMITE®
DYNAMITE.COM
TWITTER: @DYNAMITECOMICS
FACEBOOK: /DYNAMITECOMI

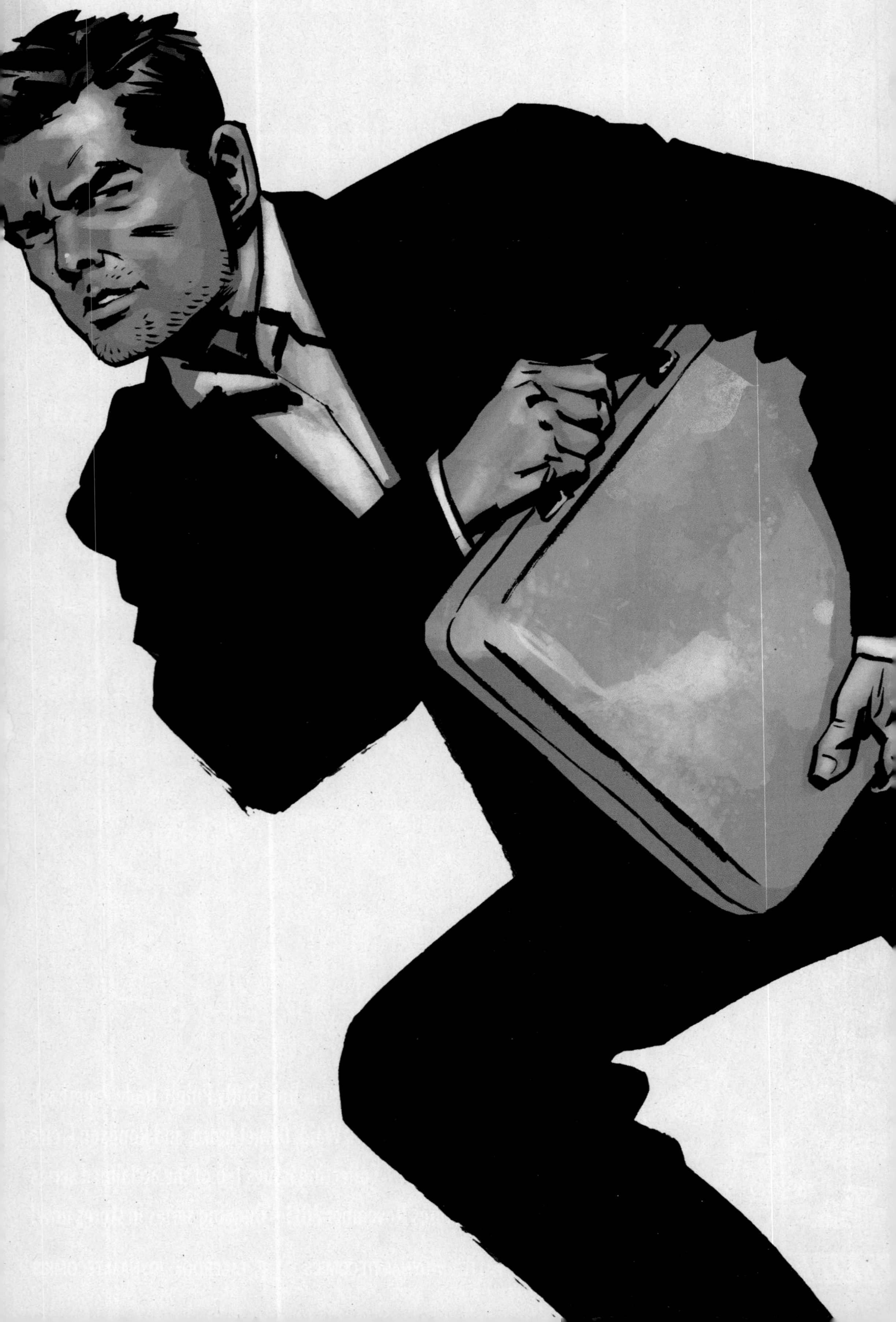